Personal Finance
For Canadians
FOR
DUMMIES®
5TH EDITION

by Eric Tyson, MBA and Tony Martin, B.Comm

John Wiley & Sons Canada, Ltd.

Personal Finance For Canadians For Dummies®, 5th Edition

Published by
John Wiley & Sons Canada, Ltd
6045 Freemont Boulevard
Mississauga, Ontario, L5R 4J3
`www.wiley.com`

For general information on John Wiley & Sons Canada, Ltd., including all books published by Wiley
Publishing, Inc., please call our warehouse, Tel 1-800-567-4797. For reseller information, including discounts and premium sales, please call our sales department, Tel 416-646-7992. For press review copies,
author interviews, or other publicity information, please contact our marketing department, Tel 416-646-
4584, Fax 416-236-4448.

For technical support, please visit `www.wiley.com/techsupport`.

Wiley also publishes its books in a variety of electronic formats. Some content that appears in print may
not be available in electronic books.

Library and Archives Canada Cataloguing in Publication Data

Tyson, Eric (Eric Kevin)

      Personal finance for Canadians for dummies / Eric Tyson, Tony Martin. — 5th ed.

Includes index.

First published in 1995 under title: Personal finance for dummies for Canadians.

ISBN 978-0-470-67988-3

      1. Finance, Personal — Canada. I. Martin, Tony (Tony M.) II. Title.
HG179.T97 2010   332.02400971   C2010-905963-8
ISBN 978-0-470-96481-1 (ebk); 978-0-470-96479-8 (ebk); 978-0-470-96480-4 (ebk)

Printed in the United States

1 2 3 4 5 RRD 15 14 13 12 11

WILEY

About the Authors

Eric Tyson first became interested in money more than three decades ago. After his father was laid off during the 1973 recession and received some retirement money from Philco-Ford, Eric worked with his dad to make investing decisions with the money. A couple years later, Eric won his high school's science fair with a project on what influences the stock market. Dr. Martin Zweig, who provided some guidance, awarded Eric a one-year subscription to the *Zweig Forecast,* a famous investment newsletter. Of course, Eric's mom and dad share some credit with Martin for Eric's victory.

Today, Eric is an internationally acclaimed and best-selling personal finance book author, syndicated columnist, and speaker. He has worked with and taught people from all financial situations, so he knows the financial concerns and questions of real folks just like you. Despite being handicapped by an MBA from the Stanford Graduate School of Business and a BS in Economics and Biology from Yale University, Eric remains a master of "keeping it simple."

Eric's work has been featured and quoted in hundreds of local and national publications, including *Newsweek, The Wall Street Journal, Los Angeles Times, Chicago Tribune, Forbes, Kiplinger's Personal Finance* magazine, *Parenting, Money, Family Money,* and *Bottom Line/Personal;* on NBC'S *Today Show,* ABC, CNBC, PBS *Nightly Business Report,* CNN, and FOX-TV; and on CBS national radio, NPR *Sound Money,* Bloomberg Business Radio, and Business Radio Network.

Eric's Web site is www.erictyson.com.

Tony Martin has always had an innate understanding of money. Instead of getting his (tiny) allowance paid out to him weekly in shiny coins like his brothers did, he asked him mom to keep track of how much he was owed.

After emerging from Queen's University business school with a B.Comm — despite a transcript that listed courses such as "Electronic Music" and "The Philosophy of Religion," Tony set off to see the world. On his return he joined CBC radio, and ever since has been helping people understand the world of money.

Tony is also the co-author with Eric of *Investing For Canadians For Dummies.* His widely read column "Me and My Money" appears in "Net Worth," *The Globe and Mail*'s weekend personal finance section. His work has been featured in many leading publications, including *ROB Magazine, Reader's Digest,* and *Canadian Business.* Tony is a frequent commentator and speaker on personal finance and investing and regularly appears on television and radio, including CBC Radio, CBC Television, Report on Business Television, and TVOntario.

He has also been instrumental in the design and development of many online resources, including a complete online investor training program using simulated stock market transactions.

Tony's Web site is www.tonymartintm.com.

Dedication

This book is hereby and irrevocably dedicated to our family and friends, as well as to our clients and customers, who ultimately have taught us everything we know about how to explain financial terms and strategies so that all of us may benefit.

Authors' Acknowledgements

Eric: Being an entrepreneur involves endless challenges, and without the support and input of my good friends and mentors Peter Mazonson, Jim Collins, and my best friend and wife, Judy, I couldn't have accomplished what I have.

I hold many people accountable for my perverse and maniacal interest in figuring out the financial services industry and money matters, but most of the blame falls on my loving parents, Charles and Paulina, who taught me most of what I know that's been of use in the real world.

I'd also like to thank Michael Bloom, Chris Dominguez, Maggie McCall, David Ish, Paul Kozak, Chris Treadway, Sally St. Lawrence, K.T. Rabin, Will Hearst III, Ray Brown, Susan Wolf, Rich Caramella, Lisa Baker, Renn Vera, Maureen Taylor, Jerry Jacob, Robert Crum, Duc Nguyen, Maria Carmicino, and all the good folks at King Features for believing in and supporting my writing and teaching.

Many thanks to all the people who provided insightful comments on this edition and previous editions of this book, especially Bill Urban, Barton Francis, Mike van den Akker, Gretchen Morgenson, Craig Litman, Gerri Detweiler, Mark White, Alan Bush, Nancy Coolidge, and Chris Jensen.

And thanks to all the wonderful people at my publisher on the front line and behind the scenes, especially Mike Baker and Chad Sievers.

Tony: The support, good humour, and advice of many are essential to my success. There is no such thing as succeeding on one's own.

I owe special thanks to my wife, Jane Howard, and to my good friend Geoff Rockburn, who have both been endlessly supportive and helpful over the years. I'm grateful as always to my parents, Ruth and John, for teaching me so much about what really matters.

Many people in the personal finance industry have kindly offered me their assistance in penetrating, understanding, and explaining money matters. Many thanks to everybody who has generously shared insights and expertise, including Peter Volpe, Gena Katz, Sandra McLeod, Anthony Layton, Paul Hickey, Jim Bullock, Alisa Dunbar, Alan Silverstein, and Janet Freedman. In addition, I'd like to thank Karen Benzing, David Chilton, Patricia Davies, Dorothy Engleman, Dave Pyette, Jack Fleischmann, Peggy Wente, and Richard Quinlan for their support and encouragement over the years.

Many thanks as well to all the people who have provided insightful comments on this book, especially tax and financial planner extraordinaire Barton Francis, financial planner par excellence Warren Baldwin, and Mike van den Akker, Gretchen Morgensen, Craig Litman, Gerri Detweiler, Mark White, Alan Bush, Nancy Coolidge, and Chris Jensen. Special thanks to Becky Wong for her detailed and extremely helpful technical review of this book. And a well-earned tip of the hat this time 'round to Robert Hickey for his steadying hand and ongoing guidance. Finally, thanks to the wonderful people on the front line and behind the scenes — Pamela Vokey and Kelli Howey — for putting this 5th edition together.

Publisher's Acknowledgements

We're proud of this book; please send us your comments at http://dummies.custhelp.com. For other comments, please contact our Customer Care Department within the U.S. at 877-762-2974, outside the U.S. at 317-572-3993, or fax 317-572-4002.

Some of the people who helped bring this book to market include the following:

Acquisitions, Editorial, and Media Development

Editor: Robert Hickey

Copy Editor: Kelli Howey

Production Editor: Pamela Vokey

Technical Editor: Becky Wong

Editorial Assistant: Katie Wolsley

Cover Photo: © iStockphoto.com

Cartoons: Rich Tennant
(www.the5thwave.com)

Composition Services

Project Coordinator, U.S.: Lynsey Stanford

Layout and Graphics: Carl Byers, Mark Pinto

Proofreaders: Melissa Cossell, Leeann Harney

Indexer: Claudia Bourbeau

John Wiley & Sons Canada, Ltd

   Deborah Barton, Vice President and Director of Operations

   Jennifer Smith, Publisher, Professional and Trade Division

   Alison Maclean, Managing Editor, Professional & Trade Division

   Karen Bryan, Vice-President, Publishing Services

Publishing and Editorial for Consumer Dummies

   Diane Graves Steele, Vice President and Publisher, Consumer Dummies

   Kristin Ferguson-Wagstaffe, Product Development Director, Consumer Dummies

   Ensley Eikenburg, Associate Publisher, Travel

   Kelly Regan, Editorial Director, Travel

Composition Services

   Debbie Stailey, Director of Composition Services

Contents at a Glance

Introduction 1

Part I: Assessing Your Fitness and Setting Goals 7
Chapter 1: Improving Your Financial Literacy 9
Chapter 2: Measuring Your Financial Health 23
Chapter 3: Determining Where Your Money Goes 43
Chapter 4: Establishing and Achieving Goals......................................55

Part II: Saving More, Spending Less 77
Chapter 5: Dealing with Debt..79
Chapter 6: Reducing Your Spending 99
Chapter 7: Trimming Your Taxes..131

Part III: Building Wealth with Wise Investing 157
Chapter 8: Considering Important Investment Concepts.....................159
Chapter 9: Understanding Your Investment Choices...........................187
Chapter 10: Investing in Funds...207
Chapter 11: Registered Retirement Savings Plans..............................225
Chapter 12: Investing in Retirement Plans...245
Chapter 13: Investing Outside Retirement Plans 259
Chapter 14: Investing for Educational Expenses 277
Chapter 15: Investing in Real Estate: Your Home and Beyond 291

Part IV: Insurance: Protecting What You Have 327
Chapter 16: Insurance: Getting What You Need at the Best Price.........329
Chapter 17: Insurance on You: Life, Disability, and Health..................347
Chapter 18: Covering Your Assets...365

Part V: Where to Go for More Help 379
Chapter 19: Working with Financial Planners 381
Chapter 20: Using a Computer to Manage Your Money.......................399
Chapter 21: On Air and in Print...411

Part VI: The Part of Tens 419
Chapter 22: Survival Guide for Ten Life Changes 421
Chapter 23: Ten Tactics to Thwart Identity Theft and Fraud 435

Index 441

Table of Contents

Introduction 1

About This Book 2
Conventions Used in This Book 3
What You're Not to Read 3
Foolish Assumptions 3
How This Book Is Organized 4
Part I: Assessing Your Fitness and Setting Goals 4
Part II: Saving More, Spending Less 4
Part III: Building Wealth with Wise Investing 4
Part IV: Insurance: Protecting What You Have 4
Part V: Where to Go for More Help 5
Part VI: The Part of Tens 5
Icons Used in This Book 5
Where to Go from Here 6

Part 1: Assessing Your Fitness and Setting Goals 7

Chapter 1: Improving Your Financial Literacy 9

Talking Money at Home 10
Identifying Unreliable Sources of Information 12
Understanding how investment "gurus" are created 12
Considering the creation of a Canadian guru 14
Recognizing fake financial gurus 15
Understanding how undeserving investment gurus become
popular 17
Pandering to advertisers 17
Jumping Over Real and Imaginary Hurdles to Financial Success 18
Discovering what (or who) is holding you back 19
Developing good financial habits 20

Chapter 2: Measuring Your Financial Health 23

Avoiding Common Money Mistakes 23
Determining Your Financial Net Worth 25
Adding up your financial assets 26
Subtracting your financial liabilities 26
Crunching your numbers 27
Interpreting your net worth results 28
Examining Your Credit Reports and Credit Score 29
Understanding what your credit data includes and means 29
Obtaining your credit reports and score 30
Improving your credit reports and score 31
Getting credit report errors corrected 32

Knowing the Difference between Bad Debt and Good Debt 34
   Consuming your way to bad debt...................................34
   Recognizing bad debt overload 35
   Assessing good debt: Can you get too much?................36
   Playing the credit card float..37
Analyzing Your Savings 37
Evaluating Your Investment Knowledge................................39
Assessing Your Insurance Savvy 40

Chapter 3: Determining Where Your Money Goes 43

Examining Overspending..44
   Having access to credit..44
   Misusing credit cards..44
   Taking out car loans 45
   Bending to outside influences and agendas 46
   Spending to feel good 47
Analyzing Your Spending..47
   Tracking spending the low-tech way.............................48
   Tracking your spending on the computer 53

Chapter 4: Establishing and Achieving Goals. 55

Creating Your Own Definition of "Wealth" 55
   Acknowledging what money can't buy 56
   Managing the balancing act...57
Prioritizing Your Savings Goals 59
   Knowing what's most important to you.........................60
   Valuing retirement plans 60
   Dealing with competing goals 61
Building Emergency Reserves..61
Saving to Buy a Home 62
Saving to Buy a Business 63
Funding Kids' Educational Expenses 64
Saving for Big Purchases 64
Preparing for Retirement..65
   Figuring what you need for retirement 66
   Understanding your retirement building blocks 68
   Crunching numbers for your retirement 72
   Making up for lost time 74

Part II: Saving More, Spending Less.............................. 77

Chapter 5: Dealing with Debt. 79

Using Savings to Reduce Your Consumer Debt....................80
   Understanding how you gain..80
   Discovering money to pay down consumer debts 81

Decreasing Debt When You Lack Savings 82
    Reducing your credit card's interest rate.............................. 82
    Understanding credit card terms and conditions 83
    Cutting up your credit cards 83
    Discovering debit cards: The best of both worlds 84
Getting Help from Not-for-Profit Credit Counselling Agencies 85
    Understanding debt management programs 86
    Avoiding debt management programs and asking questions........ 88
Filing Bankruptcy... 89
    Understanding bankruptcy benefits.................................... 90
    Coming to terms with bankruptcy drawbacks.......................... 92
    Seeking bankruptcy advice.. 93
Considering a Consumer Proposal: An Alternative to Bankruptcy........ 93
Stopping the Spending/Consumer Debt Cycle................................ 94
    Resisting the credit temptation 95
    Identifying and treating a compulsion 96

Chapter 6: Reducing Your Spending **99**
Finding the Keys to Successful Spending 99
    Living within your means.. 100
    Looking for the best values 100
    Eliminating the fat from your spending 104
    Turning your back on consumer credit 105
Budgeting to Boost Your Savings 105
Reducing Your Spending 106
    Managing food costs... 107
    Saving on shelter... 110
    Cutting transportation costs 112
    Lowering your energy costs 116
    Controlling clothing costs 117
    Repaying your debt 117
    Indulging responsibly in fun and recreation 119
    Lowering your phone bills.. 121
    Spending wisely on technology....................................... 123
    Curtailing personal care costs 123
    Paring down professional expenses................................... 125
    Managing medical expenses... 125
    Eliminating costly addictions.. 126
    Keeping an eye on insurance premiums................................ 127
    Trimming your taxes 128

Chapter 7: Trimming Your Taxes **131**
Understanding the Taxes You Pay 131
    Focusing on your total taxes 131
    Recognizing the importance of your marginal tax rate 132
    Defining taxable income.. 133
    Being mindful of the second tax system: Alternative
        minimum tax.. 134

Trimming Employment Income Taxes 134
    Contributing to RRSPs and retirement plans 135
    Shifting some income 136
Increasing Your Deductions 136
    Child care expenses.. 136
    Alimony and maintenance payments 137
    Child support... 137
    Annual union and professional fees 137
    Business losses 137
    Interest on investment loans.. 137
    Married versus common-law partners.............................. 138
    Moving expenses.. 138
Making the Most of Tax Credits.. 139
    Maximizing your tax credits 140
    Deducting self-employment expenses.............................. 144
Reducing Investment Income Taxes 146
    Fill up those retirement plans 146
    Consider other tax-sheltered vehicles 146
    Select tax-friendly investments 147
    Make your profits long-term... 148
Getting Help from Tax Resources.. 149
    Assistance from the Canada Revenue Agency 150
    Preparation and advice guides 150
    Software and Web sites... 151
    Professional hired help.. 151
Dealing with an Audit 153
    Getting your act together.. 154
    Surviving the day of reckoning 154

Part III: Building Wealth with Wise Investing 157

Chapter 8: Considering Important Investment Concepts........... 159
Establishing Your Goals... 159
Understanding the Primary Investments 160
    Looking at lending investments 160
    Exploring ownership investments 161
Shunning Gambling Instruments and Behaviours..................... 162
    Forsake futures, options, and other derivatives............... 163
    Ditch daytrading 164
Understanding Investment Returns 164
Sizing Investment Risks 165
    Comparing the risks of stocks and bonds 166
    Focusing on the risks you can control............................. 167
    Discovering low-risk, high-return investments 167
Diversifying Your Investments.. 168
    Spreading the wealth: Asset allocation............................ 170
    Allocating money for the long term.................................. 171

Sticking with your allocations: Don't trade 172
Investing lump sums via dollar-cost averaging 173
Acknowledging Differences among Investment Firms 176
Focusing on the best firms 176
Places to consider avoiding 177
Seeing through Experts Who Predict the Future 181
Investment newsletters 182
Investment gurus 182
Leaving You with Some Final Advice 184

Chapter 9: Understanding Your Investment Choices 187

Slow and Steady Investments 187
Transaction/chequing accounts 187
Savings accounts and money market funds 188
Bonds 189
Building Wealth with Ownership Vehicles 191
Socking your money away in stocks 191
Generating wealth with real estate 196
Investing in small business (and your career) 201
Off the Beaten Path: Investment Odds and Ends 204
Precious metals 204
Annuities 204
Collectibles 205

Chapter 10: Investing in Funds 207

Understanding the Benefits of Mutual Funds 207
Exploring Various Fund Types 209
Money market funds 210
Bond funds 210
Stock funds 211
Balancing bonds and stocks: Hybrid funds 212
Canadian, U.S., international, and global funds 212
Index funds 213
Specialty (sector) funds 214
Selecting the Best Mutual Funds 215
Reading prospectuses and annual reports 215
Keeping costs low 216
Evaluating historical performance 218
Assessing fund manager and fund family reputations 218
Rating tax friendliness 219
Determining your needs and goals 220
Deciphering Your Fund's Performance 220
Interest and dividends 221
Capital gains 221
Share price changes 222
Evaluating and Selling Your Funds 222

Chapter 11: Registered Retirement Savings Plans..............225

Understanding How RRSPs Work 225
    The benefits of tax-deductible contributions...............................226
    The payoff from tax-deferred compound growth 227
Maximizing Your RRSP's Growth..228
    The payoff from starting an RRSP early..228
    Increasing your returns...229
Examining the Contribution Rules 230
    Checking out the contribution limits 231
    How much can you contribute?..233
Types of RRSPs 235
    Guaranteed RRSPs 235
    Mutual fund RRSPs 235
    Self-directed and brokerage-house RRSPs...................................236
Taking Money Out of Your RRSP before Retirement 237
    Regular withdrawals before retirement 237
    Special circumstances..237
Closing Down Your RRSP 238
    Registered Retirement Income Funds (RRIFs) 239
    Annuities 242

Chapter 12: Investing in Retirement Plans.....................245

Allocating Your Money in Retirement Plans 245
    Understanding the difference between an RRSP and
        the investments inside your RRSP 246
    Prioritizing retirement contributions...246
    Allocating money when your employer selects
        the investment options 247
    Allocating money in RRSPs 250
Annuities: An Odd Investment..254
Transferring Retirement Plans..255
    Transferring accounts you control..255
    Moving money from an employer's plan 258

Chapter 13: Investing Outside Retirement Plans 259

Getting Started 260
    Paying off high-interest debt 260
    Taking advantage of tax breaks 261
Taking Advantage of Tax-Free Savings Accounts (TFSAs)....................261
    Understanding how much you can contribute 261
    Understanding your TFSA investment choices............................262
    Making withdrawals from a TFSA 263
Understanding Registered Disability Savings Plans (RDSPs) 263
    Determining whether you're eligible for an RDSP 264
    Earning disability grants for an RDSP 264
    Withdrawing funds from an RDSP...265
Understanding Taxes on Your Investments................................265

Fortifying Your Emergency Reserves..266
    Bank and credit union accounts 266
    High-interest savings accounts 267
    Money market mutual funds..268
Investing for the Longer Term (A Few Years or More)..........................270
    Defining your time horizons 271
    Bonds and bond funds..272
    Guaranteed investment certificates (GICs) 272
    Stocks and stock funds 274
    Annuities 275
    Real estate..275
    Small-business investments 275

Chapter 14: Investing for Educational Expenses **277**
Strategizing to Pay for Educational Expenses......................................277
    Estimating university or college costs 278
    Setting realistic savings goals 279
Strategies for Saving for Education Expenses......................................280
    Registered Education Savings Plans (RESPs)..................................280
    In-trust accounts 283
    Obtaining Loans, Grants, and Scholarships 285
    Government student loans program 285
    Canada Access Grants..287
    Tips for getting loans, grants, and scholarships 287
Investing Educational Funds 288
    Good investments: No-load mutual funds 288
    Bad investments..288
    Overlooked investments 289

Chapter 15: Investing in Real Estate: Your Home and Beyond. **291**
Deciding Whether to Buy or Rent..291
    Assessing your timeline 292
    Determining what you can afford 292
    Calculating how much you can borrow 293
    Comparing the costs of owning versus renting 294
    Considering the long-term costs of renting....................................296
    Recognizing advantages to renting..298
Financing Your Home..298
    Understanding mortgage essentials 299
    Examining the difference between fixed- and variable-rate
        mortgages..303
    Avoiding the down payment blues 304
    Checking out the RRSP Home Buyers' Plan....................................305
    Finding the best lender 308
    Increasing your approval chances 310

Finding the Right Property 312
    Determining the right type of property 312
    Casting a broad net..313
    Finding out actual sale prices 313
    Researching the area...313
Working with Real Estate Agents...314
    Recognizing conflicts of interest...314
    Looking for the right qualities in real estate agents.................315
Putting Your Deal Together 317
    Negotiating 101...317
    Inspecting before you buy..318
    Remembering title insurance 319
After You Buy...319
    Refinancing your mortgage...320
    Mortgage life insurance...321
    Is a reverse mortgage a good idea? 322
Selling Your House 323
    Selling through an agent 323
    Selling without a real estate agent..324
    Determining whether you should keep your home
        until prices go up 324
    Considering keeping your home as an investment property
        after you move..325

Part IV: Insurance: Protecting What You Have............ 327

Chapter 16: Insurance: Getting What You Need at the Best Price. . .329

Discovering Our Three Laws of Buying Insurance....................................330
    Law I: Insure for the big stuff; don't sweat the small stuff............330
    Law II: Buy broad coverage 335
    Law III: Shop around and buy direct 336
Dealing with Insurance Problems...339
    Knowing what to do if you're denied coverage 339
    Dealing with insurance company problems....................................340
    Enlisting support..343

Chapter 17: Insurance on You: Life, Disability, and Health 347

Providing for Your Loved Ones: Life Insurance...348
    Determining how much life insurance to buy 348
    Looking at the Canada Pension Plan's survivor benefits..............349
    Comparing term life insurance to cash-value life insurance........351
    Making your decision 353
    Buying term insurance 354
    Getting rid of cash-value life insurance..356
    Considering the purchase of cash-value life insurance 356

Preparing for the Unpredictable: Disability Insurance.................357
Deciding whether you need coverage................................357
Determining how much disability insurance you need..............358
Identifying other features you need in disability insurance........359
Deciding where to buy disability insurance.......................360
Getting Care for the Road: Travel Medical Insurance..................361
Determining what coverage you already have.....................361
Buying travel medical insurance................................362
Long-Term Care Insurance...362

Chapter 18: Covering Your Assets...........................365

Insuring Where You Live...365
Dwelling coverage: The cost to rebuild...........................366
Personal property coverage: For your things.....................367
Liability insurance: Coverage for when others are harmed........367
Flood and earthquake insurance: Protection from
    Mother Nature...368
Deductibles: Your cost with a claim.............................369
Special discounts..369
Buying homeowner's or renter's insurance.......................370
Auto Insurance 101...371
Bodily injury/property damage liability.........................371
Uninsured or underinsured motorist liability....................371
Deductibles...372
Special discounts..372
Little-stuff coverage to skip...................................373
Buying auto insurance..373
Protecting against Mega-Liability: Umbrella Insurance.................374
Planning Your Estate...374
Wills, living wills, and medical powers of attorney..............375
Avoiding probate through living trusts..........................376
Planning your estate to minimize taxes triggered
    by your death..377

Part V: Where to Go for More Help.............................. 379

Chapter 19: Working with Financial Planners...................381

Surveying Your Financial Management Options.........................381
Doing nothing...381
Doing it yourself..382
Hiring financial help..382
Deciding Whether to Hire a Financial Planner........................385
How a good financial adviser can help...........................385
Why advisers aren't for everyone...............................387
Recognizing conflicts of interest...............................387

Finding a Good Financial Planner..391
  Soliciting personal referrals 391
  Seeking advisers through associations...................................392
Interviewing Financial Advisers: Asking the Right Questions 393
  What percentage of your income comes from clients' fees
    versus commissions?..394
  What portion of fees paid by clients is for money management
    versus hourly planning? 394
  What is your hourly fee? 394
  Do you also perform tax or legal services? 395
  What work and educational experience qualifies you
    to be a financial planner? 395
  Have you ever sold limited partnerships? Options? Futures?
    Commodities? 395
  Do you carry liability (errors and omissions) insurance?...........396
  Can you provide references from clients with needs
    similar to mine? 396
  Will you provide specific strategies and product recommendations
    that I can implement on my own if I choose? 397
  How is implementation handled? 397
Learning from Others' Mistakes 397

Chapter 20: Using a Computer to Manage Your Money 399

Surveying Software and Web Sites 399
  Adding up financial software benefits..................................400
  Surfing hazards online...400
Accomplishing Money Tasks on Your Computer.............................403
  Paying your bills and tracking your money..........................404
  Planning for retirement...405
  Preparing your taxes 406
  Researching investments..406
  Trading online 407
  Reading and searching periodicals 408
  Buying life insurance 408
  Preparing legal documents 409

Chapter 21: On Air and in Print. 411

Observing the Mass Media...411
  Alarming or informing us? 411
  Teaching questionable values...412
  Worshipping prognosticating pundits 413
Rating Radio and Television Financial Programs 413
Finding the Best Web Sites...414
Navigating Newspapers and Magazines 415
Betting on Books...415
  Understanding the book publishing business.......................416
  Books at the head of their class...417

Part VI: The Part of Tens 419

Chapter 22: Survival Guide for Ten Life Changes 421

Starting Out: Your First Job..421
Changing Jobs or Careers..422
Getting Married...423
Buying a Home 425
Having Children 425
Starting a Small Business..428
Caring for Aging Parents...429
Divorcing 430
Receiving a Windfall 431
Retiring..432

Chapter 23: Ten Tactics to Thwart Identity Theft and Fraud 435

Save Phone Discussions for Friends Only 436
Never Respond to E-Mails Soliciting Information....................436
Review Your Monthly Financial Statements 437
Secure All Receipts..437
Close Unnecessary Credit Accounts 437
Regularly Review Your Credit Reports 438
Keep Personal Info Off Your Cheques.....................................438
Protect Your Computer and Files..439
Protect Your Mail 439
Clean Out Your Wallet 439

Index 441

Introduction

You're probably not a personal finance expert, for good reason. Personal Finance 101 isn't typically offered in our schools — not in high school, and not even in the best universities and graduate programs. It should be.

However, even if you've gotten some financial education and acquired some financial knowledge over the years, you're likely a busy person who doesn't have enough hours in the day to get things done. That means you want to know how to diagnose your financial situation efficiently (and painlessly) to determine what you should do next. Unfortunately, after figuring out which financial strategies make sense for you, choosing specific financial products in the marketplace can be a nightmare. You have literally thousands of investment, insurance, and loan options to choose from. Talk about information overload!

To complicate matters even more, you probably hear about most products through advertising that can be misleading, if not downright false. Of course, some ethical and outstanding firms advertise, but so do those that are more interested in converting your hard-earned income and savings into their profits. And they may not be here tomorrow when you need them.

Perhaps you've ventured online and been attracted to the promise of "free" advice. Unfortunately, discerning the expertise and background (and even identity) of those behind various Web sites is nearly impossible. And, as we discuss in this book, conflicts of interest (many of which aren't disclosed) abound online.

As unfair as it may seem, numerous pitfalls await you when you seek help for your financial problems. The world is filled with biased and bad financial advice. We both constantly see and hear about the consequences of poor advice.

All too often, financial advice ignores the big picture and focuses narrowly on investing. Because money is not an end in itself but a part of your whole life, this book helps connect your financial goals and challenges to the rest of your life. You need a broad understanding of personal finance that includes all areas of your financial life: spending, taxes, saving and investing, insurance, and planning for major goals like education, buying a home, and retirement.

Even if you understand the financial basics, thinking about your finances in a holistic way can be difficult. Sometimes you're too close to the situation to be objective. Like the organization of your desk or home (or disorganization, as the case may be), your finances may reflect the history of your life more than they reflect a comprehensive plan for your future.

You want to know the best places to go for your circumstances, so this book contains specific, tried-and-proven recommendations. We also suggest where to turn next if you need more information and help.

About This Book

The book you hold in your hands reflects more hard work and brings you the freshest material for addressing your personal financial quandaries. Here are some of the major updates you may notice as you peruse the pages of this book:

- ✔ Coverage of new and revised tax laws and how to best take advantage of them
- ✔ The latest information on what's going on with government assistance programs like the Canada Pension Plan and Old Age Security, and what it means in terms of how you should prepare for and live in retirement
- ✔ Updated investment recommendations — especially in the areas of mutual funds/other managed investments and real estate — throughout Part III
- ✔ Details on the recently introduced Tax-Free Savings Accounts (TFSAs) and how to use them to save on taxes and save for the future
- ✔ Updated coverage of the best ways to reduce, minimize the cost of, and eliminate consumer debt
- ✔ Additional coverage of smart ways to use credit and qualify for the best loan terms, as well as how to understand — and improve — your credit scores
- ✔ Revised recommendations for where to get the best insurance deals and expanded coverage on preparing for natural disasters
- ✔ Expanded and updated coverage of how to use and make sense of the news and financial resources (especially online resources)

Aside from being packed with updated information, another great feature of this book is that you can read it from cover to cover if you want, or you can read each chapter and part without having to read what comes before, which is useful if you have better things to do with your free time. Handy cross-references direct you to other places in the book for more details on a particular subject.

Conventions Used in This Book

To help you navigate the waters of this book, we've set up a few conventions:

- ✔ We use *italics* for emphasis and to highlight new words or terms that we define.
- ✔ We use **boldface** text to indicate the action part of numbered steps and to highlight key words or phrases in bulleted lists.
- ✔ We put all Web addresses in `monofont` for easy identification.

What You're Not to Read

We've written this book so you can find information easily and easily understand what you find. And although we'd like to believe that you want to pore over every last word between the two yellow and black covers, we actually make it easy for you to identify "skippable" material:

- ✔ **Text in sidebars:** The sidebars are the shaded boxes that appear here and there. They include helpful information and observations but aren't necessary reading.
- ✔ **Anything with a Technical Stuff icon attached:** This information is interesting but not critical to your understanding of the topic at hand.

Foolish Assumptions

In writing this book, we've made some assumptions about you, dear reader:

- ✔ You want expert advice about important financial topics — such as paying off and reducing the cost of debt, planning for major goals, or investing — and you want answers quickly.
- ✔ Or perhaps you want a crash course in personal finance and are looking for a book you can read cover-to-cover to help solidify major financial concepts and get you thinking about your finances in a more comprehensive way.
- ✔ Or maybe you're just tired of picking up scattered piles of bills, receipts, and junk mail every time the kids chase the cat around the den, so you plan to use this book as a paperweight.

Seriously, though, this book is basic enough to help a novice get his or her arms around thorny financial issues. But we think advanced readers will be challenged, as well, to think about their finances in a new way and identify areas for improvement.

How This Book Is Organized

This book is organized into six parts, with each covering an area of your personal finances. Here's a summary of what you can find in each part.

Part 1: Assessing Your Fitness and Setting Goals

This part explains how to diagnose your current financial health and explores common reasons for any missing links in your personal finance knowledge. We all have dreams and goals, so in this part, we also encourage you to think about your financial (and personal) aspirations and figure out how much you should be saving if you want to retire someday or accomplish other important goals.

Part II: Saving More, Spending Less

Most people don't have gobs of extra cash. Therefore, this part shows you how to figure out where all your dollars are going and tells you how to reduce your spending. Chapter 5 is devoted to helping you get out from under the burden of high-interest consumer debt (such as credit card debt). We also provide specifics for reducing your tax burden.

Part III: Building Wealth with Wise Investing

Earning and saving money are hard work, so you should be careful when it comes to investing what you've worked so hard to save. In this part, we assist you with picking investments wisely and help you understand investment risks, returns, and a whole lot more. We explain all the major, and best, investment options. We recommend specific strategies and investments to use both inside and outside of tax-sheltered retirement plans. We also discuss buying, selling, and investing in real estate, as well as other wealth-building investments.

Part IV: Insurance: Protecting What You Have

Insurance is an important part of your financial life. Unfortunately, for most people insurance is a thoroughly overwhelming and dreadfully boring topic.

But perhaps we can pique your interest in this esoteric topic by telling you that you're probably paying more than you should for insurance and that you probably don't have the right coverage for your situation. This part tells you all you ever wanted to know (okay, fine — all you *never* wanted to know but probably should know anyway) about how to buy the right insurance at the best price.

Part V: Where to Go for More Help

As you build your financial knowledge, more questions and issues may arise. In this part, we discuss where to go and what to avoid when you seek financial information and advice. We also discuss hiring a financial planner as well as investigating resources in print, on the air, and online.

Part VI: The Part of Tens

The chapters in this part can help you manage major life changes and protect yourself from the increasingly common problem of identity theft.

Icons Used in This Book

The icons in this book help you find particular kinds of information that may be of use to you:

This nerdy-looking guy appears beside discussions that aren't critical when you just want to understand basic concepts and get answers to your financial questions. You can safely ignore these sections, but reading them can help deepen and enhance your personal financial knowledge. This stuff can also come in handy if you're ever on a game show or if you find yourself stuck on an elevator with a financial geek.

This target flags strategy recommendations for making the most of your money (for example, paying off your credit card debt with your lottery winnings).

This icon highlights the best financial products in the areas of investments, insurance, and so on. These products can help you implement our strategy recommendations.

This icon points out information that you'll definitely want to remember.

This icon marks things to avoid and points out common mistakes people make when managing their finances.

This icon alerts you to scams and scoundrels who prey on the unsuspecting.

This icon tells you when you should consider doing some additional research. Don't worry — we explain what to look for and what to look out for.

Where to Go from Here

This book is organized so you can go where you need to for complete information. Want advice on investing strategies, for example? Go to Part III for that. You can check out the table of contents to find broad categories of information and a chapter-by-chapter rundown of what this book offers, or you can look up a specific topic in the index.

If you're not sure where you want to go, you may want to turn a few pages and start at the beginning with Part I. It gives you all the basic info you need to assess your financial situation and points to places where you can find more detailed information for improving it.

Part I
Assessing Your Fitness and Setting Goals

The 5th Wave   By Rich Tennant

"Clifford's in the den balancing his chequebook."

In this part . . .

We discuss the concepts that underlie sensible personal financial management. You find out why you didn't know all these concepts before now (and whom you can blame). Here, you undergo a (gentle) financial physical exam to diagnose your current fiscal health, and we show you how to identify where your hard-earned dollars are going. We also cover understanding and improving your credit report and scores and how to plan for and accomplish your financial goals.

Chapter 1

Improving Your Financial Literacy

. . . .

In This Chapter

▶ Looking at what your parents and others taught you about money

▶ Questioning reliability and objectivity

▶ Overcoming real and imagined financial hurdles

. . . .

You don't have to look very far to find what is at the root of Canadians' financial woes: Study after study shows that we get a failing grade when it comes to financial literacy. Quite simply, many people lack even the most basic math and personal finance skills necessary to make critical financial decisions and informed choices about how to best save and spend their money. Consider the following:

✔ Almost one-third of Canadians have not started saving for retirement.

✔ Half of adult Canadians have difficulty carrying out simple math calculations.

✔ Almost half of all Canadians think they can deduct the interest on a home mortgage (they can't!), and that they reduce their risk by putting their money into only Canadian investments (they don't!).

✔ One survey found that almost 80 percent of people feel that the lowest-risk investments make the most sense when saving for retirement (they don't — because most people need to make their money grow in order to be able to retire).

✔ Just one-third of Canadians made a contribution (or planned to contribute) to an RRSP for the 2009 tax year. And just one in four was planning to contribute the maximum allowed.

✔ Nearly 80 percent of consumers do not know how the grace period on a credit card works. An even greater percentage don't understand that interest starts accumulating immediately for new purchases on credit cards with outstanding balances. *Very Good*

✔ Fifty-three percent of people who took a multiple-choice investing quiz did not know that total return was the best measure of a mutual fund's performance.

✔ Forty-three percent didn't know that owning a single stock was more risky than owning a basket of stocks.

Unfortunately, most Canadians don't know how to manage their personal finances because they were never taught how to do so. Their parents may have avoided discussing money in front of them, and most high schools and universities lack sufficient courses that teach this vital, lifelong-needed skill.

 Some people are fortunate enough to learn the financial keys to success at home, from knowledgeable friends, and from the best expert-written books like this one. Others either never discover the keys to success, or they learn them the hard way — by making lots of costly mistakes. People who lack knowledge make more mistakes, and the more financial errors you commit, the more money passes through your hands and out of your life. In addition to the enormous financial costs, you experience the emotional toll of not feeling in control of your finances. Increased stress and anxiety go hand in hand with not mastering your money.

This chapter examines where people learn about finances and helps you decide whether your current knowledge is helping you or holding you back. You can find out how to improve your financial literacy and take responsibility for your finances, putting you in charge and reducing your anxiety about money. After all, you have more important things to worry about, like what's for dinner.

Talking Money at Home

We were both fortunate — our parents instilled in us the importance of personal financial management. Our moms and dads taught us a lot of things that have been invaluable throughout our lives, and among those things were sound principles for earning, spending, and saving money. Our parents had to know how to do these things, because they were raising large families on (usually) one modest income. They knew the importance of making the most of what you have and of passing that vital skill on to your kids.

 In many families money is a taboo subject — parents don't level with their kids about the limitations, realities, and details of their budgets. Some parents we talk with believe that dealing with money is an adult issue and that kids should be insulated from it so that they can enjoy being kids. In many families, kids may hear about money *only* when disagreements and financial crises bubble to the surface. Thus begins the harmful cycle of children having negative associations with money and financial management.

In other cases, parents with the best of intentions pass on their bad money-management habits. You may, for example, have learned from a parent to buy things to cheer yourself up. Or you may have witnessed a family member maniacally chasing get-rich-quick business and investment ideas. Now we're not saying that you shouldn't listen to your parents. But in the area of personal finance, as in any other area, poor family advice and modelling can be problematic.

Think about where your parents learned about money management, and then consider whether they had the time, energy, or inclination to research choices before making their decisions. For example, if they didn't do enough research or had faulty information, your parents may mistakenly think that banks are the best places for investing money or that buying stocks is like going to Las Vegas. (You can find the best places to invest your money in Part III of this book.)

Personal finance at school

In schools, the main problem with personal finance education is the lack of classes, not that kids already know the information or that the skills are too complex for children to understand.

Nancy Donovan teaches personal finance to her fifth-grade math class as a way to illustrate how math can be used in the real world. "Students choose a career, find jobs, and figure out what their taxes and take-home paycheques will be. They also have to rent apartments and figure out a monthly budget," says Donovan. "Students like it, and parents have commented to me how surprised they are by how much financial knowledge their kids can handle." Donovan also has her students invest $10,000 (play money) and then track the investments' performance.

Urging schools to teach the basics of personal finance is just common sense. Children should be taught how to manage a household budget, the importance of saving money for future goals, and the consequences of overspending. Unfortunately, few schools offer classes like Donovan's. In most cases, the financial basics aren't taught at all.

In the minority of schools that do offer a course remotely related to personal finance, the class is typically in economics (and an elective at that). "Archaic theory is being taught, and it doesn't do anything for the students as far as preparing them for the real world," says one high school principal we know. Having taken more than our fair share of economics courses in university, we understand the principal's concerns.

Some people argue that teaching children financial basics is the parents' job. However, this well-meant sentiment is what we're relying on now, and for all too many it isn't working. In some families, financial illiteracy is passed on from generation to generation.

Education takes place in the home, on the streets, and in the schools. Therefore, schools must bear some responsibility for teaching this skill. However, if you're raising children, remember that no one cares as much as you do or has as much ability to teach the important life skill of personal money management.

In still other cases, the parents have the right approach, but the kids go to the other extreme out of rebellion. For example, if your parents spent money carefully and thoughtfully and at times made you feel denied, you may tend to do the opposite, buying yourself gifts the moment any extra money comes your way.

Although you can't change what the educational system and your parents did or didn't teach you about personal finances, you now have the ability to find out what you need to know to manage your finances.

If you have children of your own, we're sure you agree that kids really are amazing. Don't underestimate their potential or send them out into the world without the skills they need to be productive and happy adults. Buy them some good financial books when they head off to university or begin their first job.

Identifying Unreliable Sources of Information

Most people are smart enough to realize that they're not financial geniuses. So they set out to take control of their money matters by reading about personal finance or consulting a financial adviser. Because the pitfalls are numerous and the challenges significant when choosing an adviser, we devote Chapter 19 to the financial planning business and tell you what you need to know to avoid being fooled.

Reading is good. Reading is fundamental. But reading to find out how to manage your money can be dangerous if you're a novice. Misinformation can come from popular and seemingly reliable information sources, as we explain in the following sections.

Understanding how investment "gurus" are created

Before you take financial advice from anyone, examine her background, including professional work experience and education credentials. This is true whether you're getting advice from an adviser, writer, talk show host, or TV financial reporter.

If you can't easily find such information, that's usually a red flag. People with something to hide or a lack of something redeeming to say about themselves usually don't promote their background.

Talking up the book

One of the more common breed of "experts" who appear on the air and in print are mutual fund managers or financial newsletter writers who "talk up their book." To talk up the book is to give a positive spin to the investments you hold — and may plan to sell soon.

Here's a little more detailed explanation of the meaning of the phrase "talk up the book" by a professional money manager of Tony's acquaintance — Mark Riedl, a portfolio manager with Adaly Investment Management in Toronto: "A pundit enthusiastically detailing the merits of a stock to person(s), with intention of increasing level of interest in that stock, which hopefully translates into more investors buying the stock, whereby moving the stock price up. And yes, that stock is already owned by the pundit."

Of course, just because someone seems to have a relatively impressive-sounding background doesn't mean that she has your best interests in mind, or that he has honestly presented his qualifications.

Ideally, any "expert" that the media turn to would first be spoken with, his or her background researched and assessed, and biases considered. When the decision is made to use anyone as a commentator, his or her views should be presented in that context.

Of course, the media like people who get attention, and that tends to mean people who like attention. However, that should only up the ante in terms of the screening process that such "personalities" are put through. And when the decision is made to use them, their experience, expertise, and perspective — or lack thereof — should be part of the context in which their commentary is presented.

The problem is, that's a lot of work. Not to mention the long-standing trend of journalists having to work under tighter deadlines and fewer resources, a trend that's only been accelerated by the Internet and all the "free" content online.

The result is predictable. Writers need a comment or quote quickly. TV producers need talking heads that they can put in a chair to fill airtime, often at very short notice. If you're available — and hopefully will work for little or, even better, for free — you're in!

And what's the fastest way to get a comment for a print story or to find a body to fill a guest's chair for TV or radio? Tap the same folks that your peers have recently used. After all, they're ready and willing. And the more the media use someone as a commentator, the more the public — and other journalists! — view that person as credible, and the more, in turn, the average person and even reporters and television hosts and producers with business "expertise" look to the commentator as an expert whose opinions and perspective are sought-after, followed, and often acted upon.

Considering the creation of a Canadian guru

To understand the media and the business of financial gurus, consider the rapid rise of the media profile of one Kevin O'Leary. In a few short years, he's gone from doing guest spots on ROBTV (now BNN) — a channel watched largely by active investors — to regular appearances on the CBC and recurring roles as the hard-hitting bottom-line guy on CBC's *Dragons' Den* (and, more recently, ABC's *Shark Tank*), where he and his fellow judges listen to the pitches of would-be entrepreneurs.

His rise underscores the simple fact that media exposure just breeds further exposure, and the media starts reaching for better accolades. An October 2009 *Winnipeg Free Press* story described O'Leary as a noted private equity investor, who made US$3.7 billion selling his tech company, The Learning Company, to Mattel Inc.

A January 2010 story in *The Globe and Mail* continued in the same vein, saying, "In 1999, O'Leary sold his software company to the Mattel Toy company for a staggering $3.7-billion (U.S.) — still one of the largest deals in consumer software history."

On one hand, this is all well and good. After all, he's a successful businessman and investor who's a billionaire! At least, that's how the media sometimes introduce him.

But those few journalists who do a little more due diligence have a somewhat different perspective. If his "billionaire status" is why folks should pay attention to Mr. O'Leary's opinions, then there's a problem. Here's what Mark McQueen, president and CEO of Wellington Financial, a privately held bridge financing and venture debt fund, wrote: "According to the financial disclosure of the day, [Kevin O'Leary] cleared about US$6 million (pre tax) from his sale of the shares he had in TLC, and received another US$5.2 million (pre tax) as a departure package. . . . Not chump change . . . [b]ut nothing that puts Canada's best known Dragon in the 'Billionaire' league."

But surely even if O'Leary didn't himself pocket a billion, there's lots of business smarts here, because not only did he grow the company, he oversaw an enormous buyout. Yet that's not a perspective shared by many Mattel shareholders. Within a year of purchasing The Learning Company, Mattel was happy to get rid of the money-losing company for a fraction of the $3.6 billion it had paid. (The division lost $200 million in the second half of 1999 alone!)

Ultimately, according to research done by *Canadian Business* writer Stephen Gandel, Mattel got rid of The Learning Company in 2001 by basically giving away most of the division to a private-equity firm for free. One observer described the company O'Leary sold as "an ugly mess" that had "an awful lot of mismanagement."

The deal even made it onto a list of disastrous takeovers and colossal merger failures in a book — titled, appropriately enough, *Deals from Hell* — written by Robert F. Bruner, professor of business administration at the Darden School of Business at the University of Virginia. The deal's inclusion in the book puts it in the company of other massive financial disasters such as Sony Corporation's acquisition of Columbia Pictures and the infamous merger of AOL and Time Warner.

But meanwhile, Mr. O'Leary was busy launching his own mutual fund company, O'Leary Mutual Funds, where he's still chairman. And in just a two-year period, O'Leary's heavily promoted funds raised some $1 billion. No doubt some of this was due to the media's cheerleading, and some due to the promotion Mr. O'Leary did himself, at length, including on *SqueezePlay,* the BNN show he co-hosted. But despite the heavy promotion the O'Leary funds have turned in decidedly lacklustre performances, largely failing to even keep up with the corresponding market indexes — returns that investors could get through low-cost index funds.

All the while, the O'Leary brand keeps on growing, in part due to his own enthusiastic efforts, and in part due to the fertile conditions willingly offered up by the media. At some point, the fund company will likely go public, and when it does Mr. O'Leary will cash in big time, thanks to all the investors who have piled his funds. The one certain winner in all of this is bound to be Mr. O'Leary himself, who quite happily declared in an interview with Stephen Gandel that he has a very simple objective in life: To go to bed richer than when he woke up.

Recognizing fake financial gurus

You can't always accept stated credentials and qualifications at face value, because some people lie (witness the billions lost to hedge fund Ponzi-scheme man Bernie Madoff, who was brought down in 2008). You can't sniff out liars by the way they look, their résumé, their gender, or their age. You can, however, increase your chances of being tipped off by being skeptical (and by regularly reading the "Guru Watch" section of Eric's Web site at www. erictyson.com).

You can see a number of hucksters for what they are by using common sense in reviewing some of their outrageous claims. Some sources of advice, such as investment seminars put on by Wade Cook, lure you in by promising outrageous returns. The stock market has generated average annual returns of about 10 percent over the long term. However, Cook, a former taxi driver, promoted his seminars as an "alive, hands-on, do the deals, two-day intense course in making huge returns in the stock market. If you aren't getting 20 percent per month, or 300-percent annualized returns on your investments, you need to be there." (No kidding, and so should every investment manager and individual investor we know!)

Cook's get-rich-quick seminars, which cost more than $6,000, were so successful at attracting people that his company went public in the late 1990s and generated annual revenues of more than $100 million.

Cook's "techniques" included trading in and out of stocks and options on stocks after short holding periods of weeks, days, or even hours. His trading "strategies" can best be described as techniques using *technical analysis* — that is, using a stock's past price movements and volume to make predictions about how it will perform in the future.

The perils of following an approach that advocates short-term trading with the allure of high profits are numerous:

✔ You'll rack up enormous brokerage commissions.

✔ You won't make big profits — quite the reverse. If you stick with this approach, you'll do what the great majority of short-term traders do: Underperform the market averages.

✔ You'll make yourself a nervous wreck. This type of trading is gambling, not investing. Get sucked up in it, and you'll lose more than money — you may also lose the love and respect of your family and friends.

Sometimes applying a bit of simple math can help highlight the sheer absurdness of the claims some gurus make. If Cook's followers were able to indeed earn the 300-percent annual returns his seminars claimed to help them achieve, any investor starting with just $10,000 would vault to the top of the list of the world's wealthiest people (ahead of Bill Gates and Warren Buffett) in just 11 years! And if everyone who took his seminars did become that wealthy, governments would have to fire up a small town's worth of mints just to print up the extra gazillions in currency.

Understanding how undeserving investment gurus become popular

You may be wondering how people like Wade Cook become so popular despite the obvious flaws in their advice. Cook is a great example of how this happens. (See the preceding section for the goods on Cook.) He promoted his seminars through infomercials and other advertising, including radio ads on respected news stations. The high stock market returns of the 1990s brought greed back into fashion. (Our experience has been that you see more of this greed near market tops than you do near market bottoms.)

In the U.S., the attorneys general of numerous states sued Cook's company and sought millions of dollars in consumer refunds. The suits alleged that the company lied about its investment track record (not a big surprise — remember that this company claimed you'd make 300 percent per year in stocks!).

Cook's company settled the blizzard of state and Federal Trade Commission (FTC) lawsuits against his firm by agreeing to accurately disclose its trading record in future promotions and give refunds to customers who were misled by past inflated return claims. (That didn't stop Cook, however, from getting into more legal hot water — he's currently serving a seven-year prison term for failing to pay millions in personal income taxes.)

According to a news report by *Bloomberg News,* Cook's firm disclosed that it lost a whopping 89 percent of its own money trading during 2000, a year in which the stock market fared well. As Deb Bortner, director of the Washington State Securities Division and president of the North American Securities Administrators Association, observed, "Either Wade is unable to follow his own system, which he claims is simple to follow, or the system doesn't work."

Don't assume that someone with something to sell, who is getting good press and running lots of ads, will take care of you. That "guru" may just be good at press relations and self-promotion. Certainly, talk shows and the media at large can and do provide useful information on a variety of topics, but bad eggs sometimes turn up. These bad eggs may not always smell bad upfront. In fact, they may hoodwink people for years before finally being exposed. Please review Part V for the details on resources you can trust and those that could cause you to go bust!

Pandering to advertisers

Thousands of publications and media outlets — newspapers, magazines, Web sites, radio, TV, and so on — dole out personal financial advice and perspectives. Although many of these "service providers" collect revenue from subscribers, virtually all are dependent — in some cases, fully dependent (especially the Internet, radio, and TV) — on advertising dollars. Although advertising is a necessary part of capitalism, advertisers can taint and, in some cases, dictate the content of what you read, listen to, and view.

Be sure to consider how dependent a publication or media outlet is on advertising. We find that publications, radio stations, and TV channels that derive all their revenue from advertising are, not too surprisingly, the ones that most often create conflicts of interest by pandering to advertisers.

A huge amount of what's on the Internet is also advertiser-driven. Many of the investing sites on the Internet offer advice about individual stocks. Interestingly, such sites derive much of their revenue from online brokerage firms seeking to recruit customers who are foolish enough to believe that selecting their own stocks is the best way to invest. (See Part III for more information about your investment options.)

As you read various publications, watch TV, or listen to the radio, note how consumer-oriented these media are. Do you get the feeling that they're looking out for your interests? For example, if lots of auto manufacturers advertise, does the media outlet ever tell you how to save money when shopping for a car or the importance of buying a car within your means? Or are they primarily creating an advertiser-friendly broadcast or publication?

Jumping Over Real and Imaginary Hurdles to Financial Success

Perhaps you know that you should live within your means, buy and hold sound investments for the long term, and secure proper insurance coverage; however, you can't bring yourself to do these things. Everyone knows how difficult it is to break habits they've practised for many years. The temptation to spend money lurks everywhere you turn. Ads show attractive and popular people enjoying the fruits of their labours — a new car, an exotic vacation, and a lavish home.

Maybe you felt deprived by your tightwad parents as a youngster, or maybe you're bored with life and you like the adventure of buying new things. If only you could hit it big on one or two investments, you think, you could get rich quick and do what you really want with your life. As for disasters and catastrophes, well, those things happen to other people, not to you. Besides, you'll probably have advance warning of pending problems, so you can prepare accordingly, right?

Your emotions and temptations can quickly get the better of you. Certainly, part of successfully managing your finances involves coming to terms with your shortcomings and the consequences of your behaviours. If you don't, you may end up enslaved to a dead-end job so you can keep feeding your spending addiction. Or you may spend more time with your investments than you do with your family and friends. Or unexpected events may leave you reeling financially; disasters and catastrophes can happen to anyone at any time.

Discovering what (or who) is holding you back

A variety of personal and emotional hurdles can get in the way of making the best financial moves. As we discuss earlier in this chapter, a lack of financial knowledge (which stems from a lack of personal financial education) can stand in the way of making good decisions.

But we've seen some people caught in the psychological trap of blaming something else for their financial problems. For example, some people believe that all adults' problems can be traced back to childhood and how they were raised. Behaviours ranging from substance abuse and credit card addiction to sexual infidelity are supposedly caused by their roots.

We don't want to disregard the negative impact particular backgrounds can have on some people's tendency to make the wrong choices during their lives. Exploring your personal history can certainly yield clues to what makes you tick. That said, adults make choices and engage in behaviours that affect themselves as well as others. Some people also tend to blame their financial shortcomings on not earning more income. Such people believe that if only they earned more, their financial (and personal) problems would melt away.

Our experience working and speaking with people from diverse economic backgrounds has taught us that achieving financial success — and more importantly, personal happiness — has virtually nothing to do with how much income a person makes but rather with what she makes of what she has. We know financially wealthy people who are emotionally poor even though they have all the material goods they want. Likewise, we know people who are quite happy, content, and emotionally wealthy even though they're struggling financially.

Most Canadians — even those who have not had an "easy" life — should be able to come up with numerous things to be happy about and grateful for: a family who loves them; friends who laugh at their stupid jokes; the freedom to catch a movie or play or to read a good book; a great singing voice, sense of humour, or a full head of hair.

Developing good financial habits

After you understand the basic concepts and know where to buy the best financial products when you need them, you'll soon see that managing personal finances well is not much more difficult than other things you do regularly, like tying your shoelaces and getting to work each day.

Regardless of your income, you can make your dollars stretch farther if you practise good financial habits and avoid mistakes. In fact, the lower your income, the more important it is that you make the most of your income and savings (because you don't have the luxury of falling back on your next fat paycheque to bail you out).

More and more industries are subject to global competition, so you need to be on your financial toes now more than ever. Job security is waning; layoffs and retraining for new jobs are increasing. Putting in 30 years for one company and retiring with the gold watch and lifetime pension are becoming as rare as never having problems with your computer.

Speaking of company pensions, odds are increasing that you work for an employer that has you save toward your own retirement instead of providing a pension for you. Not only do you need to save the money, you must also decide how to invest it. Chapter 12 can help you get a handle on investing in retirement plans.

Personal finance involves much more than managing and investing money. It also includes making all the pieces of your financial life fit together; it means lifting yourself out of financial illiteracy. Like planning a vacation, managing your personal finances means forming a plan for making the best use of your limited time and dollars.

Intelligent personal financial strategies have little to do with your gender, ethnicity, or marital status. All people need to manage their finances wisely. Some aspects of financial management become more or less important at different points in your life, but for the most part the principles remain the same for everyone.

Knowing the right answers isn't enough. You have to practise good financial habits just as you practise other good habits, such as brushing your teeth. Don't be overwhelmed. As you read this book, make a short list of your financial marching orders and then start working away. Throughout this book, we highlight ways you can overcome temptations and keep control of your money rather than let your emotions and money rule you. (We discuss common financial problems in Chapter 2.)

What you do with your money is a quite personal and confidential matter. In this book, we try to provide guidance that can keep you in sound financial health. You don't have to take it all — pick what works best for you and understand the pros and cons of your options. But from this day forward, please don't make the easily avoidable mistakes or overlook the sound strategies that we discuss throughout this book.

If you're young, congratulations for being so forward-thinking in realizing the immense value of investing in your personal financial education. You'll reap the rewards for decades to come. But even if you're not so young, you surely have many years to make the most of the money you currently have, the money you're going to earn, and even the money you may inherit!

Throughout your journey, we hope to challenge and even change the way you think about money and about making important personal financial decisions — and sometimes even about the meaning of life. No, we're not philosophers, but we do know that money — for better but more often for worse — is connected to many other parts of our lives.

Chapter 2

Measuring Your Financial Health

· ·

In This Chapter

▶ Determining assets, liabilities, and your (financial) net worth

▶ Requesting (and fixing) your credit reports

▶ Making sense of your credit score

▶ Understanding bad debt, good debt, and too much debt

▶ Calculating your rate of savings

▶ Assessing your investment and insurance know-how

· ·

*H*ow financially healthy are you? When was the last time you took stock of your overall financial situation, including reviewing your spending, savings, future goals, and insurance? If you're like most people, you've either never done this exercise or you did so a long time ago.

This chapter guides you through a *financial physical* to help you detect problems with your current financial health. But don't dwell on your "problems." View them for what they are — opportunities for improving your financial situation. In fact, the more areas for improvement you can identify, the greater the potential you may have to build real wealth and accomplish your financial and personal goals.

Avoiding Common Money Mistakes

Financial problems, like many medical problems, are best detected early (clean living doesn't hurt, either). Here are the common personal financial problems we've seen in our work:

> ✔ **Not planning:** Human beings were born to procrastinate. That's why we have deadlines — and deadline extensions. Unfortunately, you may have no explicit deadlines with your personal finances. You can allow your credit card debt to accumulate, or you can leave your savings sitting in lousy investments for years. You can pay higher taxes, leave gaps in your retirement and insurance coverage, and overpay for financial products. Of course, planning your finances isn't as much fun as planning a

vacation, but doing the former can help you take more of the latter. See Chapter 4 for details on setting financial goals.

✔ **Overspending:** Simple arithmetic helps you determine that savings is the difference between what you earn and what you spend (assuming that you're not spending more than you're earning!). To increase your savings, you either have to work more, increase your earning power through education or job advancement, get to know a wealthy family who wants to leave its fortune to you, or spend less. For most people, especially over the short term, the thrifty approach is the key to building savings and wealth. Check out Chapter 3 for a primer on figuring out where your money goes; Chapter 6 gives advice for reducing your spending.

✔ **Buying with consumer credit:** Even with the benefit of today's lower interest rates, carrying a balance month-to-month on your credit card or buying a car on credit means that even more of your future earnings are going to be earmarked for debt repayment. Buying on credit encourages you to spend more than you can really afford. Chapter 5 discusses debt and credit problems.

✔ **Delaying saving for retirement:** Most people say that they want to retire by their mid-60s or sooner. But in order to accomplish this goal, most people need to save a reasonable chunk (around 10 percent) of their income starting sooner rather than later. The longer you wait to start saving for retirement, the harder reaching your goal will be. And you'll pay much more in taxes to boot if you don't take advantage of the tax benefits of investing through retirement plans. For information on planning for retirement, see Chapters 4, 10, and 12.

✔ **Falling prey to financial sales pitches:** Great deals that can't wait for a little reflection or a second opinion are often disasters waiting to happen. A sucker may be born every minute, but a slick salesperson is pitching something every second! Steer clear of people who pressure you to make decisions, promise you high investment returns, and lack the proper training and experience to help you. For important investment concepts and what kinds of investments to avoid, turn to Chapter 8.

✔ **Not doing your homework:** To get the best deal, shop around, read reviews, and get advice from objective third parties. You also need to check references and track records so that you don't hire incompetent, self-serving, or fraudulent financial advisers. (For more on hiring financial planners, see Chapter 19.) But with all the different financial products available, making informed financial decisions has become an overwhelming task. We do a lot of the homework for you with the recommendations in this book. We also explain what additional research you need to do and how to do it.

✔ **Making decisions based on emotion:** You're most vulnerable to making the wrong moves financially after a major life change (a job loss or

divorce, for example) or when you feel pressure. Maybe your investments plunged in value. Or perhaps a recent divorce has you fearing
that you won't be able to afford to retire when you planned, so you
pour thousands of dollars into some newfangled financial product. Take
your time and keep your emotions out of the picture. In Chapter 21, we
discuss how to approach major life changes with an eye on determining
what changes you may need to make to your financial picture.

✔ **Not separating the wheat from the chaff:** In any field in which you're not
an expert, you run the danger of following the advice of someone you
think is an expert but really isn't. This book shows you how to separate
the financial fluff from the financial facts. (Flip to Chapter 20 for information on how to evaluate financial advice online and Chapter 21 for how to
evaluate financial coverage in the mass media.) You are the person who is
best able to manage your personal finances. Educate and trust yourself!

✔ **Exposing yourself to catastrophic risk:** You're vulnerable if you and
your family don't have insurance to pay for financially devastating losses.
People without a savings reserve and support network can end up homeless. Many people lack sufficient insurance coverage to replace their
income. Don't wait for a tragedy to strike to find out whether you have the
right insurance coverage. Check out Part IV for more on insurance.

✔ **Focusing too much on money:** Placing too much emphasis on making
and saving money can warp your perspective on what's important in life.
Money is not the first or even second priority in happy people's lives.
Your health, relationships with family and friends, career satisfaction,
and fulfilling interests should be more important.

Determining Your Financial Net Worth

Your financial net worth is an important barometer of your monetary health.
Your net worth indicates your capacity to accomplish major financial goals,
such as buying a home, retiring, and withstanding unexpected expenses or
loss of income.

Your financial net worth has absolutely, positively *no* relationship to your
worth as a human being. This is not a test. You don't have to compare your
number with your neighbour's. Financial net worth is not the scorecard of life.

Your *net worth* is your financial assets minus your financial liabilities:

```
Financial assets - Financial liabilities = Net worth
```

The following sections explain how to determine those numbers.

Adding up your financial assets

A *financial asset* is real money or an investment you can convert into your favourite currency that you can use to buy things now or in the future. Financial assets generally include the money you have in bank accounts, stocks, bonds, and mutual funds (see Part III, which deals with investments). Money that you have in retirement plans (including those with your employer) and the value of any businesses or real estate that you own are also counted.

We generally recommend that you exclude your personal residence when figuring your financial assets. Include your home only if you expect to someday sell it or otherwise live off the money you now have tied up in it (perhaps by taking out a reverse mortgage, which we discuss in Chapter 15). If you plan on eventually tapping in to the *equity* (the difference between the market value and any debt owed on the property), add that portion of the equity that you expect to use to your list of assets.

Assets can also include your future expected Canada Pension Plan (or Quebec Pension Plan) benefits and registered pension payments (if your employer has such a plan). These assets are usually quoted in dollars per month rather than in a lump-sum value. We explain in a moment how to account for these monthly benefits when tallying your financial assets.

Consumer items — such as your car, clothing, stereo, and so forth — do *not* count as financial assets. We know that adding these things to your assets makes your assets *look* larger (and some financial software packages and publications encourage you to list these items as assets), but you can't live off them unless you sell them.

Subtracting your financial liabilities

To arrive at your financial net worth, you must subtract your *financial liabilities* from your assets. Liabilities include loans and debts outstanding, such as credit card and auto loan debts. When figuring your liabilities, include money you borrowed from family and friends — unless you're not gonna pay it back!

Include mortgage debt on your home as a liability *only* if you include the value of your home in your asset list. Be sure to also include debt owed on other real estate — no matter what (because you count the value of investment real estate as an asset).

Crunching your numbers

Table 2-1 provides a place for you to figure your financial assets. Go ahead and write in the spaces provided, unless you plan to lend this book to someone and you don't want to put your money situation on display. *Note:* See Table 4-1 in Chapter 4 to estimate your Canada Pension Plan (CPP) or Quebec Pension Plan (QPP) benefits.

Table 2-1	**Your Financial Assets**
Account	*Value*
Savings and investment accounts (including retirement plans):	
Example: Bank savings account	$5,000
_____	$_____
_____	$_____
_____	$_____
_____	$_____
_____	$_____
_____	$_____
	Total = $_____
Benefits earned that pay a monthly retirement income:	
Employer's pensions	$_____ / month
CPP (or QPP)	$_____ / month
	$\times$ 240*
	Total = $_____
Total Financial Assets (add the two totals) = $_____	

* To convert benefits that will be paid to you monthly into a total dollar amount, and for purposes of simplification, assume that you will spend 20 years in retirement. (Ah, think of two decades of lolly-gagging around — vacationing, harassing the kids, spoiling the grandkids, starting another career, or maybe just living off the fat of the land.) As a shortcut, multiply the benefits that you'll collect monthly in retirement by 240 (12 months per year times 20 years). Inflation may reduce the value of your pension from your employer if it doesn't contain a cost-of-living increase each year in the same way that the CPP or QPP does. Don't sweat this now — you can take care of that concern in the section on retirement planning in Chapter 4.

Now comes the potentially depressing part — figuring out your debts and loans in Table 2-2.

Table 2-2	Your Financial Liabilities
Loan	**Balance**
Example: Gouge 'Em Bank credit card	$4,000
_____	$_____
_____	$_____
_____	$_____
_____	$_____
_____	$_____
_____	$_____
Total Financial Liabilities =	$_____

Now you can subtract your liabilities from your assets to figure your net worth in Table 2-3.

Table 2-3	Your Net Worth
Find	**Write It Here**
Total Financial Assets (from Table 2-1)	$_____
Total Financial Liabilities (from Table 2-2)	− $_____
Net Worth =	$_____

Interpreting your net worth results

Your net worth is important and useful only to you and your unique situation and goals. What seems like a lot of money to a person with a simple lifestyle may seem like a pittance to a person with high expectations and a desire for an opulent lifestyle.

In Chapter 4, you can crunch numbers to determine your financial status more precisely for goals such as retirement planning. We also discuss saving toward other important goals in that chapter. In the meantime, if your net worth (excluding expected monthly retirement benefits such as those from CPP/QPP and pensions) is negative or less than half your annual income, take notice. If you're in your 20s and you're just starting to work, a low net worth is less concerning.

Getting rid of your debts — the highest-interest ones first — is the most important thing. Then you need to build a safety reserve equal to three to six months of living expenses. You should definitely find out more about getting out of debt, reducing your spending, and developing tax-wise ways to save and invest your future earnings.

Examining Your Credit Reports and Credit Score

You may not know it (or care), but you probably have a personal credit report and a credit score. Lenders examine your credit report and score before granting you a loan or credit line. This section highlights what you need to know about your credit reports and score, including how to obtain them and how to improve them.

Understanding what your credit data includes and means

A *credit report* contains information such as

- ✔ **Personal identifying information:** Your name, address, social insurance number, and so on

- ✔ **Record of credit accounts:** Details when each account was opened, latest balance, payment history, and so on

- ✔ **Bankruptcy filings:** Indicates whether you've filed bankruptcy in recent years

- ✔ **Inquiries:** Lists who has pulled your credit report because you've applied for credit

- ✔ **Public records:** This includes such events as a bankruptcy or judgments from lawsuits

Your *credit score,* which is not the same as your credit report, is a three-digit score based on the report. Lenders use your credit score as a predictor of your likelihood of defaulting on repaying your borrowings. As such, your credit score has a major impact on whether a lender is willing to extend you a particular loan and at what interest rate.

FICO is the leading credit score in the industry and was developed by Fair Isaac and Company. FICO scores (also known as Beacon scores) range from a low of 300 to a high of 900. Most scores fall in the 600s and 700s. Higher scores are better. While many lenders still use FICO the most, some rating bureaus have developed their own credit scoring systems, including a FICO competitor called VantageScore, which was created by Equifax, Experian, and TransUnion.

Regardless of the specific formula used, the higher your credit score, the lower your predicted likelihood of defaulting on a loan (see Figure 2-1). The "rate of credit delinquency" refers to the percentage of consumers who will become 90 days late or later in repaying a creditor within the next two years. As you can see in the chart, consumers with low credit scores have dramatically higher rates of falling behind in their loans. Thus, low credit scorers are considered much riskier borrowers, and fewer lenders are willing to offer them a given loan; those who do charge relatively high rates.

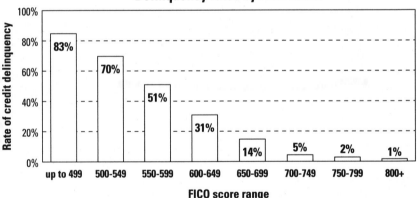

Delinquency rates by FICO score

Figure 2-1:
Lenders use credit scores to estimate how likely people are to default on a loan.

Source: Fair Isaac Corporation

Obtaining your credit reports and score

Given the importance of your personal credit report, you may be pleased to know that you're entitled to receive a free copy of your credit report annually from the two main credit bureaus in Canada (Equifax and TransUnion).

The Equifax and TransUnion Web sites promote their online services, encouraging you to pay for quick online access to your credit report. However, you can obtain a credit report for free by requesting it by mail. You need to submit a form (which you can print off online) along with photocopies of two government-issued pieces of identification.

✔ Equifax Canada National Consumer Relations
P.O. Box 190, Station Jean-Talon
Montreal, QC H1S 2Z2
1-800-465-7166
www.equifax.com

✔ TransUnion Consumer Relations Department
P.O. Box 338, LCD1
Hamilton, ON L8L 7W2
1-800-663-9980
www.transunion.ca

Residents of Quebec can use the following information to contact TransUnion:

Centre De Relations Aux Consommateurs TransUnion
1 Place Laval Ouest, Bureau 370
Laval, QC H7N 1A1
1-877-713-3393
www.transunion.ca

When you receive your reports, the best first step is to examine them for possible mistakes (more in a moment regarding fixing problems in your reports). You may be surprised to find that your credit reports do *not* include your credit score. The reason for this is quite simple: Although the credit agencies must provide a free credit report annually to those who request a copy, they aren't mandated to provide a credit score. Thus, if you want to obtain your credit score, it's going to cost you.

Finding the proper Web page to buy your credit score on a one-time basis without getting signed up for other far more costly ongoing services and monitoring can be a nightmare. If you do spring for your current credit score, be clear about what you're buying. You may not realize that you're agreeing to some sort of an ongoing credit monitoring service for, say, $50 to $100+ per year.

To help you avoid having to navigate the credit companies' sites — and avoid all their sales pitches — we strongly recommend calling a credit bureau's toll-free phone number to buy your credit report rather than visiting the credit bureau's Web site.

Improving your credit reports and score

Instead of simply throwing money into buying your credit scores or paying for some ongoing monitoring service to which you may not pay attention, take an interest in improving your credit standing and score. Working to boost your credit rating is especially worthwhile if you know that your credit report contains detrimental information.

The most important actions you can take to boost your attractiveness to lenders are the following:

- ✔ **Get both of your credit reports, and be sure they are accurate.** Correct errors (as we explain in the next section) and be especially sure to get accounts removed if they aren't yours and they show late payments or are in collection.

- ✔ **If your report includes late or missed payments more than seven years old, ask to have those removed.** Ditto for a bankruptcy more than ten years ago.

- ✔ **Pay all your bills on time.** To ensure on-time payments, sign up for automatic bill payment, which most companies (like phone and utility providers) enable you to use.

- ✔ **Be loyal if it doesn't cost you.** The older the loan accounts you have open, the better for your credit rating. Closing old accounts and opening a bunch of new ones generally lowers your credit score.

  But don't be loyal if it costs you! For example, when you're carrying credit card debt at a high interest rate and want to transfer that balance to a lower-rate card. If your current credit card provider refuses to match a lower rate you find elsewhere, move your balance and save yourself some money (see Chapter 5 for details).

- ✔ **Limit your debt and debt accounts.** The more loans, especially consumer loans, that you hold and the higher the balances, the lower your credit score will be.

- ✔ **Work to pay down consumer revolving debt (such as on credit cards).** Read Chapters 5 and 6 for suggestions.

Getting credit report errors corrected

If you obtain your credit report and find a blemish on it that you don't recognize as being your mistake or fault, do *not* assume that the information is correct. Credit reporting bureaus and the creditors who report information to these bureaus often make errors.

very true

You hope and expect that if a credit bureau has negative and incorrect information in your credit report and you bring the mistake to their attention they will graciously and expeditiously fix the error. If you believe that, you're the world's greatest optimist; perhaps you also think you won't have to wait in line to renew your passport or at the post office!

Odds are, you're going to have to fill out a form on a Web site, make some phone calls, or write a letter or two to fix the problems on your credit report. Here's how to correct most errors that aren't your fault:

- ✔ **If the credit problem is someone else's:** A surprising number of personal credit report glitches are the result of someone else's negative information getting on your credit report. If the bad information on your report is completely foreign-looking to you, tell the credit bureau and explain that you need more information because you don't recognize the creditor.

- ✔ **If the creditor made a mistake:** Creditors make mistakes, too. You need to write or call the creditor to get it to correct the erroneous information that it sent to the credit bureau. Phoning first usually works best. (The credit bureau should be able to tell you how to reach the creditor if you don't know how.) If necessary, follow up with a letter.

Whether you speak with a credit bureau or an actual lender, make notes of your conversations. If representatives say that they can fix the problem, get their names and extensions, and follow up with them if they don't deliver as promised. If you're ensnared in bureaucratic red tape, escalate the situation by speaking with a department manager.

Telling your side of the story

With a minor credit infraction, some lenders may simply ask for an explanation. Years ago, Eric had a credit report blemish that was the result of being away for several weeks and missing the payment due date for a couple small bills. When his proposed mortgage lender saw his late payments, the lender asked for a simple written explanation.

You and a creditor may not see eye to eye on a problem, and the creditor may refuse to budge. If that's the case, credit bureaus are generally required to allow you to add a 100-word explanation to your credit file.

Sidestepping "credit repair" firms

You may see ads online, and in newspapers and magazines, for credit repair companies that claim to fix your credit report problems. In the worst cases we've seen, these firms charge outrageous amounts of money and don't come close to fulfilling their marketing hype.

If you have legitimate glitches on your credit report, credit repair firms can't make the glitches disappear. Hope springs eternal, however — some people would like to believe that their credit problems can be fixed.

If your problems are fixable you can fix them yourself, and you don't need to pay a company big bucks to do it.

Very Good!?

Knowing the Difference between Bad Debt and Good Debt

Why do you borrow money? Usually, you borrow money because you don't have enough to buy something you want or need — like a university education. If you want to buy a four-year university education, you can easily spend $30,000, $50,000, or more. Not too many people have that kind of spare cash. So borrowing money to finance part of that cost enables you to buy the education.

How about a new car? A trip to your friendly local car dealer shows you that a new set of wheels will set you back at least $15,000. Although more people may have the money to pay for that than, say, the university education, what if you don't? Should you finance the car the way you finance the education?

The auto dealers and bankers who are eager to give you an auto loan say that you deserve and can afford to drive a nice, new car, and they tell you to borrow away (or lease, which we don't love either — please see Chapter 6). We just say, "No! No! No!" Why do we disagree with the auto dealers and lenders? For starters, we're not trying to sell you a car or loan from which we derive a profit! More importantly, there's a *big* difference between borrowing for something that represents a long-term investment and borrowing for short-term consumption.

If you spend, say, $1,500 on a vacation, the money is gone. Poof! You may have fond memories and photos, but you have no financial value to show for it. "But," you say, "vacations replenish my soul and make me more productive when I return. In fact, the vacation more than pays for itself!"

We're not saying that you shouldn't take a vacation. By all means, take one, two, three, or as many as you can afford yearly. But that's the point: *Take what you can afford.* If you have to borrow money in the form of an outstanding balance on your credit card for many months in order to take the vacation, you *can't afford* it.

Consuming your way to bad debt

We coined the term *bad debt* to refer to debt incurred for consumption, because such debt is harmful to your long-term financial health. (We used this term back in the early 1990s when the first edition of this book was published, and we're flattered that others have taken to using the phrase.)

You'll be able to take many more vacations during your lifetime if you save the cash in advance. If you get into the habit of borrowing and paying all that interest for vacations, cars, clothing, and other consumer items, you'll spend more of your future income paying back the debt and interest, leaving you with less money for your other goals.

The relatively high interest rates that banks and other lenders charge for bad (consumer) debt is one of the reasons you're less able to save money when using such debt. Money borrowed through credit cards, auto loans, and other types of consumer loans not only carries a relatively high interest rate, but also isn't tax-deductible.

We're not saying that you should never borrow money and that all debt is bad. Good debt, such as that used to buy real estate and small businesses, is generally available at lower interest rates than bad debt and may also be tax-deductible. If well managed, these investments may also increase in value. Borrowing to pay for educational expenses can also make sense. Education is generally a good long-term investment, because it can increase your earning potential.

Recognizing bad debt overload

Calculating how much debt you have relative to your annual income is a useful way to size up your debt load. Ignore, for now, good debt — the loans you may owe on real estate, a business, an education, and so on (we get to that in the next section). Right now, we're focusing on bad debt, the higher-interest debt used to buy items that depreciate in value.

To calculate your bad debt danger ratio, divide your bad debt by your annual income. For example, suppose you earn $40,000 per year. Between your credit cards and an auto loan, you have $20,000 of debt. In this case, your bad debt represents 50 percent of your annual income.

$$\frac{\text{bad debt}}{\text{annual income}} = \text{bad debt danger ratio}$$

The financially healthy amount of bad debt is zero. Not everyone agrees with us. One major credit card company says — in its "educational" materials, which it "donates" to schools to teach students about supposedly sound financial management — that carrying consumer debt amounting to 10 to 20 percent of your annual income is just fine.

When your bad debt danger ratio starts to push beyond 25 percent, it can spell real trouble. Such high levels of high-interest consumer debt on credit cards and auto loans grow like cancer. The growth of the debt can snowball and get out of control unless something significant intervenes. If you have consumer debt beyond 25 percent of your annual income, see Chapter 5 to find out how to get out of debt.

How much good debt is acceptable? The answer varies. The key question is: Are you able to save sufficiently to accomplish your goals? In the "Analyzing Your Savings" section later in this chapter we help you figure out how much you're actually saving, and in Chapter 4 we help you determine what you should save to accomplish your goals. (See Chapter 15 to find out how much mortgage debt is appropriate to take on when buying a home.)

Borrow money only for investments (good debt) — for purchasing things that retain and hopefully increase in value over the long term, such as an education, real estate, or your own business. Don't borrow money for consumption (bad debt) — for spending on things that decrease in value and eventually become financially worthless, such as cars, clothing, vacations, and so on.

Assessing good debt: Can you get too much?

As with good food, of course, you can get too much of a good thing, including good debt! When you incur debt for investment purposes — to buy real estate, for small business, even your education — you hope to see a positive return on your invested dollars.

But some real estate investments don't work out. Some small businesses crash and burn, and some educational degrees and programs don't have the intended outcome.

No magic formula can determine when you have too much "good debt." In extreme cases, we've seen entrepreneurs, for example, borrow up to their eyeballs to get a business off the ground. Sometimes this works and they end up financially rewarded, but in most cases it doesn't.

The lure of easy credit

We've both worked as management consultants and have done a lot of work with companies in the financial services industry, including some of the major credit card companies. Their game then, as it is now, was to push cards into the hands of as many people as possible who have a tendency and propensity to carry debt month to month at high interest rates. Their direct marketing campaigns are quite effective. Ditto for the auto manufacturers, who successfully entice many people who can't really afford to spend $20,000, $30,000, or more on a brand-new car to buy new autos financed with an auto loan or lease. And just as alcohol and cigarette makers target young people with their advertising, credit card companies are recruiting and grooming the next generation of overspenders on college and university campuses. Unbelievably, our highest institutions of learning receive large fees from credit card companies for being allowed to promote their cards on campus!

The result is that Canadians are now world leaders in personal debt. In 2010, one study found that our debt-to-income ratio puts us first among twenty advanced countries in the OECD. Worse, the recession in 2009 hardly put a damper on the willingness of households to take on more debt. It's no surprise that Canadians on average now save less than one percent of their disposable income, a huge drop from the savings rate of up to 20 percent that was common in the 1980s.

We offer two important questions to ponder and discuss with your loved ones about the seemingly "good debt" you're taking on:

- ✔ Are you and your loved ones able to sleep well at night and function well during the day, free from great worry about how you're going to meet next month's expenses?
- ✔ Are you and your loved ones financially able to save what you'd like to work toward your goals (see Chapter 4)?

See the debt-reduction strategies in Chapter 5 for more information.

Playing the credit card float

Given what we have to say about the vagaries of consumer debt, you may think that we're always against using credit cards. Besides the convenience credit cards offer — in not having to carry around extra cash and cheques, providing security deposits at hotels, and easing online purchases — you can receive another benefit from using a credit card: free use of the bank's money until the time the bill is due. (Some cards offer other benefits, such as frequent flyer miles, and we have those types of cards too. Also, purchases made on credit cards may be contested if the sellers of products or services don't stand behind what they sell.)

When you charge on a credit card that *does not have* an outstanding balance carried over from the prior month, you typically have several weeks (known as the *grace period*) from the date of the charge to the time when you must pay your bill. Making use of this grace period is called *playing the float*. Had you paid for this purchase by cash or cheque, you would have had to shell out the money sooner.

If you have difficulty saving money, and plastic tends to burn holes through your budget, forget the float game. You're better off not using credit cards. The same applies to those who pay their bills in full but spend more because it's so easy to do so with a piece of plastic. (For information on alternatives to using credit cards, see Chapter 5.)

Analyzing Your Savings

How much money have you actually saved in the past year? By that we mean the amount of new money you've added to your nest egg, stash, or whatever you like to call it.

Most people don't know or have only a vague idea of the rate at which they're saving money. The answer may sober, terrify, or pleasantly surprise you. In order to calculate your savings over the past year, you need to calculate your net worth as of today *and* as of one year ago.

The amount you actually saved over the past year is equal to the change in your net worth over the past year — in other words, your net worth today minus your net worth from one year ago. We know it may be a pain to find statements showing what your investments were worth a year ago, but bear with us: It's a useful exercise.

If you own your home, ignore this in the calculations. (However, you can consider the extra payments you make to pay off your mortgage principal faster as new savings.) And don't include personal property and consumer goods, such as your car, computer, clothing, and so on, with your assets.

When you have your net worth figures from both years, plug them into Step 1 of Table 2-4. If you're anticipating the exercise and are already subtracting your net worth of a year ago from what it is today in order to determine your rate of savings, your instincts are correct — but the exercise isn't quite that simple. You need to do a few more calculations in Step 2 of Table 2-4. Why? Well, counting the appreciation of the investments you've owned over the past year as savings wouldn't be fair. Suppose you bought 100 shares of a stock a year ago at $17 per share, and now the value is at $34 per share. Your investment increased in value by $1,700 during the past year. Although you'd be the envy of your friends at the next party if you casually mentioned your investments, the $1,700 of increased value is not really savings. Instead, it represents appreciation on your investments, so you must remove this appreciation from the calculations. (Just so you know, we're not unfairly penalizing you for your shrewd investments — you also get to add back the decline in value of your less-successful investments.)

Table 2-4		Your Savings Rate over the Past Year	
Step 1: Figuring your savings			
Today		*One Year Ago*	
Savings & investments	$_____	Savings & investments	$_____
– Loans & debts	$_____	– Loans & debts	$_____
= Net worth today	$_____	= Net worth 1 year ago	$_____
Step 2: Correcting for changes in value of investments you owned during the year			
Net worth today		$_____	
– Net worth 1 year ago		$_____	
– Appreciation of investments (over past year)		$_____	
+ Depreciation of investments (over past year)		$_____	
= Savings rate		$_____	

If all this calculating gives you a headache, you get stuck, or you just hate crunching numbers, try the intuitive, seat-of-the-pants approach: Save a regular portion of your monthly income. You can save it in a separate savings or retirement plan.

How much do you save in a typical month? Get out the statements for accounts you contribute to or save money in monthly. It doesn't matter if you're saving money in a retirement plan that you can't access — money is money.

Note: If you save, say, $200 per month for a few months, and then you spend it all on auto repairs, you're not really saving. If you contributed $5,000 to a Registered Retirement Savings Plan (RRSP), for example, but you depleted money that you had from long ago (in other words, it wasn't saved during the past year), don't count the $5,000 RRSP contribution as new savings.

You should be saving at least 5 to 10 percent of your annual income for longer-term financial goals such as retirement (Chapter 4 helps you to fine-tune your savings goals). If you're not, be sure to read Chapter 6 to find out how to reduce your spending and increase your savings.

Evaluating Your Investment Knowledge

Congratulations! If you've stuck with us from the beginning of this chapter, you've completed the hardest part of your financial physical. The physical is a whole lot easier from here on out!

Regardless of how much or how little money you have invested in banks, mutual funds, or other types of accounts, you want to invest your money in the wisest way possible. Knowing the rights and wrongs of investing is vital to your long-term financial well-being. Few people have so much extra money that they can afford major or frequent investing mistakes.

Answering yes or no to the following questions can help you determine how much time you need to spend with our Investing Crash Course in Part III, which focuses on investing. **Note:** The more "no" answers you reluctantly scribble, the more you need to find out about investing, and the faster you should turn to Part III.

_____ Do you understand the investments you currently hold?

_____ Is the money that you'd need to tap in the event of a short-term emergency in an investment where the principal does not fluctuate in value?

_____ Do you know what marginal income tax bracket you're in, and do you factor that in when choosing investments?

_____ For money outside of retirement plans, do you understand how these investments produce income and gains and whether these types of investments make the most sense from the standpoint of your tax situation?

_____ Do you have your money in different, diversified investments that aren't dependent on one or a few securities or one type of investment (that is, bonds, stocks, real estate, and so on)?

_____ Is the money that you're going to need for a major expenditure in the next few years invested in conservative investments rather than in riskier investments such as stocks?

_____ Is the money that you have earmarked for longer-term purposes (more than five years) invested to produce returns that are likely to stay ahead of inflation?

_____ If you currently invest in or plan to invest in individual stocks, do you understand how to evaluate a stock, including reviewing the company's balance sheet, income statement, competitive position, price–earnings ratio versus its peer group, and so on?

_____ If you work with a financial adviser, do you understand what that person is recommending that you do, are you comfortable with those actions and that adviser, and is that person compensated in a way that minimizes potential conflicts of interest in the strategies and investments he or she recommends?

Making and saving money are not guarantees of financial success; rather, they're prerequisites. If you don't know how to choose sound investments that meet your needs, you'll likely end up throwing money away, which leads to the same end result as never having earned and saved it in the first place. Worse still, you won't be able to derive any enjoyment from spending the lost money on things that you perhaps need or want. Turn to Part III to discover the best ways to invest; otherwise, you may wind up spinning your wheels working and saving.

Assessing Your Insurance Savvy

In this section, you have to deal with the prickly subject of protecting your assets and yourself with *insurance*. (The following questions help you get started.) If you're like most people, reviewing your insurance policies and coverages is about as much fun as a root canal. Open wide!

_____ Do you understand the individual coverages, protection types, and amounts of each insurance policy you have?

_____ Does your current insurance protection make sense given your current financial situation (as opposed to your situation when you bought the policies)?

_____ If you wouldn't be able to make it financially without your income, do you have adequate long-term disability insurance coverage?

_____ If you have family members who are dependent on your continued income, do you have adequate life insurance coverage to replace your income should you die?

_____ Do you know when it makes sense to buy insurance through discount brokers, fee-for-service advisers, and companies that sell directly to the public (bypassing agents) and when it doesn't?

_____ Do you carry enough liability insurance on your home, car (including umbrella/excess liability), and business to protect all your assets?

_____ Have you recently (in the last year or two) shopped around for the best price on your insurance policies?

_____ Do you know whether your insurance companies have good track records when it comes to paying claims and keeping customers satisfied?

That wasn't so bad, was it? If you answered no more than once or twice, don't feel bad — nine out of ten people make significant mistakes when buying insurance. Find your insurance salvation in Part IV. If you answered yes to all the preceding questions, you can spare yourself from reading Part IV, but bear in mind that many people need as much help in this area as they do in other aspects of personal finance.

Chapter 3

Determining Where Your Money Goes

In This Chapter

▶ Understanding why people overspend

▶ Assessing your spending

*O*ver the years, both of us have spoken in depth with hundreds of people about their finances: people who have small incomes, people who have six-figure and even seven-figure incomes, and all sorts of people in between. At every income level, people fall into one of the following three categories:

✔ People who spend more than they earn (accumulating debt)

✔ People who spend all that they earn (saving nothing)

✔ People who save 2, 5, 10, or even 20 percent (or more!)

We've seen $40,000 earners who save 20 percent of their income ($8,000), $80,000 earners who save just 5 percent ($4,000), and people earning well into six figures annually who save nothing or accumulate debt.

Suppose you currently earn $50,000 per year and spend all of it. You may wonder, "How can I save money?" Good question! Rather than knock yourself out at a second job or hustle for that next promotion, you may want to try living below your income — in other words, spending less than you earn. (We know spending less than you earn is hard to imagine, but you can do it.) Consider that for every discontented person earning and spending $50,000 per year, someone else is out there making do on $45,000.

A great many people live on less than you make. If you spend as they do, you can save and invest the difference. In this chapter, we examine why people overspend and help you look at your own spending habits. When you know where your money goes, you can find ways to spend less and save more (see Chapter 6) so that, someday, you too can live richly and achieve your life goals.

Examining Overspending

If you're like most people, you must live within your means in order to accomplish your financial goals. Doing so requires spending less than you earn and then investing your "savings" intelligently (unless you plan on winning the lottery or receiving a large inheritance). To put yourself in a position that allows you to start saving, take a close look at your spending habits.

Many folks earn just enough to make ends meet. And some can't even do that; they simply spend more than they make. The result of such spending habits is, of course, an accumulation of debt.

Most of the influences in society encourage you to spend. Think about it: More often than not, you're referred to as a *consumer* in the media and in the hallowed halls of the federal government. You're not referred to as a person, a citizen, or a human being. Here are some of the adversaries you're up against as you attempt to control your spending.

Having access to credit

As you probably already know, spending money is easy. Thanks to innovations like bank machines and credit cards, your money is always available, 24/7. Larger retailers pitch their own credit cards, and so does the gas station across the street.

Sometimes it may seem as though lenders are trying to give away money by making credit so easily available. But this free money is a dangerous illusion. Credit is most dangerous when you make consumption purchases you can't afford in the first place. When it comes to consumer debt (credit cards, auto loans, and the like), lenders aren't giving away anything except the opportunity for you to get in over your head, rack up high interest charges, and delay your progress toward your financial and personal goals.

Misusing credit cards

The modern-day bank credit card was invented by Bank of America near the end of the baby boom. The credit industry has been booming along with the boomers ever since.

If you pay your bill in full every month, credit cards offer a convenient way to buy things with an interest-free, short-term loan. But if you carry your debt over from month to month at high interest rates, credit cards encourage you to live beyond your means. Credit cards make it easy and tempting to spend money that you don't have.

You'll never pay off your credit card debt if you keep charging on your card and make only the minimum monthly payments. Interest continues to pile up on your outstanding debt. Paying only the minimum monthly payment can lead to your carrying high-interest debt on your card for decades (not just months or years)!

Some credit card companies are now trying to sell cardholders "insurance" at a cost of around 10 percent annually to pay the minimum payments due on credit card balances for those months when the debtor is unable to pay because of some life transition event (such as a job layoff). One such card normally charges a 13-percent annual interest rate on credit card balances, so with the insurance charges the annual interest rate is 23 percent!

If you have a knack for charging up a storm and spending more than you should with those little pieces of plastic, only one solution exists: Get rid of your credit cards. Put scissors to the plastic. Go cold turkey. You can function without them. (See Chapter 5 for details on how to live without credit cards.)

Taking out car loans

Walking onto a car lot and going home with a new car that you could never afford if you had to pay cash is easy. The dealer gets you thinking in terms of monthly payments that sound small when compared to what that four-wheeler is *really* gonna cost you. Auto loans are easy for just about anyone to get (except maybe a recently paroled felon).

Suppose you're tired of driving around in your old clunker. The car is battle-scarred and boring, and you don't like being seen in it. Plus, the car is likely to need more repairs in the months ahead. So off you go to your friendly local car dealer.

You start looking around at all the shiny, new cars, and then — like the feeling you experience when spotting a water fountain on a scorching hot day — there it is: your new car. It is sleek and clean, and has air conditioning, four-wheel drive, a GPS, and built-in video screens. Before you can read the fine print on the sticker page on the side window, the salesperson moseys on up next to you. He gets you talking about how nice the car is, the weather, or the hockey season — anything but the sticker price of that car.

"How," you begin to think to yourself, "can this guy afford to spend time with me without knowing if I can afford this thing?" After a test drive and more talk about the car, the weather, and your love life (or lack thereof) comes your moment of truth. The salesperson, it seems, doesn't care about how much money you have. Whether you have lots of money or very little doesn't matter. Anybody can afford it. The car is only $399 a month!

"That price isn't bad," you think. Heck, you were expecting to hear that the car would cost you at least 25 grand. Before you know it, the dealer runs a credit report on you and has you sign a few papers, and minutes later you're driving home with your new car.

The dealer wants you to think in terms of monthly payments because the cost *sounds* so cheap: $399 for a car. But, of course, that's $399 per month, every month, for many, many months. You're gonna be payin' for ages — after all, you just bought a car that cost a huge chunk (perhaps 100 percent or more) of your yearly take-home income!

But it gets worse. What does the total sticker price come to when interest charges are added in? (Even if interest charges are low, you may still be buying a car with a sticker price you can't afford.) And what about the cost of insurance, registration, and maintenance over the seven or so years that you'll own the car? Now you're probably up to more than a year's worth of your income. Ouch! (See Chapter 6 for information on how to spend what you can afford on a car.)

Bending to outside influences and agendas

You go out with some friends to dinner, a ballgame, or a show. Try to remember the last time one of you said, "Let's go someplace (or do something) cheaper. I can't afford to spend this much." On the one hand, you don't want to be a stick in the mud. But on the other hand, some of your friends have more money than you do — and the ones who don't may be running up debt fast.

Some people just have to see the latest hit movie, wear the latest designer clothes, or get the newest handheld personal digital assistant. They don't want to feel left out or behind the times.

When was the last time you heard someone say that she decided to forgo a purchase because she was saving for retirement or a home purchase? It doesn't happen often, does it? Just dealing with the here-and-now and forgetting your long-term needs and goals is tempting. This mindset leads people to toil away for too many years in jobs they dislike.

Living for today has its virtues: Tomorrow *may* not come. But odds are good that it will. Will you still feel the same way about today's spending decisions tomorrow? Or will you feel guilty that you once again failed to stick to your goals?

Your spending habits should be driven by your desires and plans, not those of others. If you haven't set any goals yet, you may not know how much you should be saving. Chapter 4 helps you kick-start the planning and saving process.

Spending to feel good

Life is full of stress, obligations, and demands. "I work hard," you say, "and darn it, I deserve to indulge!" Especially after your boss took the credit for your last great idea or blamed you for her last major screwup. So you buy something expensive or go to a fancy restaurant. Feel better? You won't when the bill arrives. And the more you spend, the less you save, and the longer you'll be stuck working for jerks like your boss!

Just as people can become addicted to alcohol, tobacco, television, and the Internet, some people also become addicted to the high they get from spending. Researchers can identify a number of psychological causes for spending addiction, with some relating to how your parents handled money and spending. (And you thought you'd identified all the problems you can blame on Mom and Dad!)

If your spending and debt problems are chronic, or even if you'd simply like to be a better consumer and saver, see Chapter 5 for more information.

Analyzing Your Spending

Brushing your teeth, eating a diverse diet including plenty of fruits and vegetables, and exercising regularly are good habits. Spending less than you earn and saving enough to meet your future financial objectives are the financial equivalents of these habits.

Despite relatively high incomes compared with the rest of the world, most Canadians have a hard time saving a good percentage of their incomes. Why? Because they spend too much — often far more than necessary.

The first step to saving more of the income that you work so hard for is to figure out where that income typically gets spent. The spending analysis in the next section helps you determine where your cash is flowing. You should do the spending analysis if any of the following apply to you:

- ✔ You aren't saving enough money to meet your financial goals. (If you're not sure whether this is the case, please see Chapter 4.)

- ✔ You feel as though your spending is out of control, or you don't really know where all your income goes.

- ✔ You're anticipating a significant life change (for example, marriage, leaving your job to start a business, having children, retiring, and so on).

If you're already a good saver, you may not need to complete the spending analysis. After you save enough to accomplish your goals, we don't see as much value in continually tracking your spending. You've already established the good habit — saving. Tracking exactly where you spend your money month after month is *not* the good habit. (You may still benefit from perusing our smarter spending recommendations in Chapter 6.)

The immediate goal of a spending analysis is to figure out where you typically spend your money. The long-range goal is to establish a good habit: Maintaining a regular, automatic savings routine.

Notice the first four letters in the word *analysis*. (You may never have noticed, but we feel the need to bring it to your attention.) Knowing where your money is going each month is useful, and making changes in your spending behaviour and cutting out the fat so you can save more money and meet your financial goals is terrific. However, you may make yourself and those around you miserable if you're anal-retentive about documenting precisely where you spend every single dollar and cent.

Saving what you need to achieve your goals is what matters most.

Tracking spending the low-tech way

Analyzing your spending is a little bit like being a detective. Your goal is to reconstruct the crime of spending. You probably have some major clues at your fingertips or piled somewhere on the desk or table where you pay bills.

Unless you keep meticulous records that detail every dollar you spend, you won't have perfect information. Don't sweat it! A number of sources should enable you to detail where you've been spending your money. To get started, get out/access your

- ✔ Recent pay stubs
- ✔ Tax returns
- ✔ Online banking/bill payment record
- ✔ Chequebook register or cancelled cheques (and monthly debit card transactions)
- ✔ Credit and charge card bills

Ideally, you want to assemble the documents needed to track one year of spending. But if your spending patterns don't fluctuate greatly from month to month (or if your dog ate some of the old bills), you can reduce your data gathering to one six-month period, or to every second or third month for the past year. If you take a major vacation or spend a large amount on gifts during certain months of the year, make sure you include these months in your analysis.

Purchases made with cash are the hardest to track because they don't leave a paper trail. Over the course of a week or perhaps even a month, you *could* keep a record of everything you buy with cash. Tracking cash can be an enlightening exercise, but it can also be a hassle. If you're lazy like we sometimes are or you lack the time and patience, try *estimating*. Think about a typical week or month — how often do you buy things with cash? For example, if you eat lunch out four days a week, paying around $7 per meal, that's about $120 a month. You may also want to try adding up all the cash withdrawals from your chequing account statement and then working backward to try to remember where you spent the cash.

Separate your expenditures into as many useful and detailed categories as possible. Table 3-1 gives you a suggested format; you can tailor it to fit your needs. Remember, if you lump too much of your spending into broad, meaningless categories like *Other,* you'll end up right back where you started — wondering where all the money went. (***Note:*** When completing the tax section in Table 3-1, report the total tax you paid for the year as tabulated on your annual income tax return — and take the total Canada Pension Plan (or Quebec Pension Plan) and Employment Insurance deductions paid from your end-of-year tax slips rather than the tax withheld or paid during the year.)

Table 3-1	Detailing Your Spending	
Category	*Monthly Average ($)*	*Percentage of Total Gross Income (%)*
Taxes, taxes, taxes (income)		_____
Federal	_____	
Provincial	_____	
CPP (or QPP)	_____	
Employment insurance premiums	_____	
The roof over your head		_____
Rent	_____	
Mortgage	_____	
Property taxes	_____	
Gas/electricity/oil	_____	
Water/garbage	_____	
Phones	_____	
Cable TV & Internet	_____	
Housekeeper/gardener	_____	
Furniture/appliances	_____	
Maintenance/repairs	_____	

(continued)

Table 3-1 *(continued)*

Category	Monthly Average ($)	Percentage of Total Gross Income (%)
Food, glorious food		_____
Supermarket	_____	
Restaurants and takeout	_____	
Getting around		_____
Gasoline	_____	
Maintenance/repairs	_____	
Provincial vehicle registration fees	_____	
Parking and tolls	_____	
Bus or subway fares/passes	_____	
Style		_____
Clothing	_____	
Shoes	_____	
Jewellery (watches, earrings)	_____	
Dry cleaning	_____	
Debt repayments (excluding mortgage)		_____
Credit/charge cards	_____	
Auto loans	_____	
Student loans	_____	
Other	_____	
Fun stuff		_____
Entertainment (movies, concerts)	_____	
Vacation and travel	_____	
Gifts	_____	
Hobbies	_____	
Subscriptions/memberships	_____	
Pets	_____	
Other	_____	
Personal care		_____
Haircuts	_____	
Health club or gym	_____	
Makeup	_____	
Other	_____	

Category	Monthly Average ($)	Percentage of Total Gross Income (%)
Personal business		_____
Accountant/lawyer/financial adviser	_____	
Other	_____	
Health care		_____
Physicians and hospitals	_____	
Drugs	_____	
Dental and vision	_____	
Therapy	_____	
Insurance		_____
Homeowner's/renter's	_____	
Auto	_____	
Health	_____	
Life	_____	
Disability	_____	
Umbrella liability	_____	
Educational expenses		_____
Tuition	_____	
Books	_____	
Supplies	_____	
Room and board	_____	
Living expenses	_____	
Children		_____
Day care	_____	
Toys	_____	
Activities	_____	
Child support	_____	
Charitable donations	_____	_____
Other		_____
_____	_____	
_____	_____	
_____	_____	
_____	_____	
_____	_____	

Don't waste time on financial administration

Tom is the model of financial organization. His financial documents are neatly organized into colour-coded folders. Every month, he enters all his spending information into his computer. He even carries a notebook to detail his cash spending so that every penny is accounted for.

Tom also balances his chequebook "to make sure that everything is in order." He can't remember the last time his bank made a mistake, but he knows someone who once found a $50 error.

If you spend seven hours per month balancing your chequebook and detailing all your spending (as Tom does), you may be wasting nearly two weeks' worth of time per year — the equivalent of two-thirds of your vacation time if you take three weeks annually.

Suppose that, every other year, you're "lucky" enough to find a $100 error the bank made in its favour. If you spend just three hours per month tracking your spending and balancing your chequebook to discover this glitch, you'll be spending 72 hours over two years to find a $100 mistake. Your hourly pay: a wafer-thin $1.39 per hour. You can make more flipping burgers at a burger joint. (Note: If you make significant-sized deposits or withdrawals, make sure that you capture them on your statement.)

To add insult to injury, you may not have the desire and energy to do the more important stuff after working a full week and doing all your financial and other chores. Your big personal financial picture — establishing goals, choosing wise investments, securing proper insurance coverage — may continue to be shoved to the back burner. As a result, you may lose thousands of dollars annually. Over the course of your adult life, this amount can translate into tens or even hundreds of thousands of lost dollars.

Tom, for example, didn't know how much he should be saving to meet his retirement goals. He didn't review his employer's benefit materials, so he didn't understand his insurance and retirement plan options. He knew that he paid a lot in taxes, but he wasn't sure how to reduce his taxes.

You want to make the most of your money. Unless you truly enjoy dealing with money, you need to prioritize the money activities you work on. Time is limited, and life is short. Working harder on financial administration doesn't earn you bonus points. The more time you spend dealing with your personal finances, the less time you have available to gab with friends, watch a good movie, read a good novel, and do other things you really enjoy.

Don't get us wrong — nothing is inherently wrong with balancing your chequebook. In fact, if you regularly bounce cheques because you don't know how low your balance is, the exercise may save you a lot in returned cheque (NSF) fees. However, if you keep enough money in your chequing account that you don't have to worry about the balance reaching $0, or if you have overdraft protection, balancing your chequebook is probably a waste of time even if your hourly wages aren't lofty.

If you're busy, consider ways to reduce the amount of time you spend on routine financial tasks like bill paying. Many companies, for example, allow you to pay your monthly bills electronically via your bank chequing account or your credit card. (Don't use this latter option unless you pay your credit card bill in full each month.) The fewer bills you have to pay, the fewer separate cheques and envelopes you must process each month. That translates into more free time — and fewer paper cuts!

Tracking your spending on the computer

Software programs and Web sites can assist you with paying bills and tracking your spending. The main advantage of using software or Web sites is that you can continually track your spending as long as you keep entering the information. Software packages and Web sites can even help speed up the cheque-writing process (after you figure out how to use them, which isn't always an easy thing to do).

But you don't need a computer and fancy software to pay your bills and figure out where you're spending money. Many people we know can't keep current with all the data-entry for more than a few months. If tracking your spending is what you're after, you need to enter information from the bills you pay by cheque and the expenses you pay by credit card, debit card, automatic withdrawals, and cash. Like home exercise equipment and exotic kitchen appliances, such software often ends up in the consumer graveyard.

Paper, pencil, and a calculator work just fine for tracking your spending. For those of you who want to try computerizing your bill payments and expense tracking, we recommend the best software packages and discuss Web sites in detail in Chapter 19.

Chapter 4

Establishing and Achieving Goals

In This Chapter

▶ Defining what matters most to you

▶ Setting and prioritizing your financial goals

▶ Saving for unexpected expenses, a real estate purchase, a small business, or educational needs

▶ Estimating what you need for retirement and making up for lost time

*I*n our work in the personal finance world, we regularly ask people what their short- and long-term personal and financial goals are. Many people report that reflecting on this question is incredibly valuable, because they haven't considered it for a long time — if ever.

In this chapter, we help you dream about what you want to get out of life. Although our expertise is in personal finance, we wouldn't be doing our job if we didn't get you to consider your non-financial goals and how money fits into the rest of your life's ambitions. So before we jump into how to establish and save toward common financial goals, we want to take a moment to discuss how you think about making and saving money, as well as how to best fit your financial goals into the rest of your life.

Creating Your Own Definition of "Wealth"

Peruse any major financial magazine, newspaper, or Web site and you'll quickly see our culture's obsession with financial wealth. The more money financial executives, movie stars, or professional athletes have, the more publicity and attention they seem to get. In fact, many publications go as far as ranking those people who earn the most or have amassed the greatest wealth!

We're frankly perplexed at why many of the most affluent and highest-income earners maintain workaholic schedules despite being married and having kids. From what we observe, our society seems to define *wealth* as fat paycheques; huge investment account balances; the ability to hire full-time employees to raise children; being too busy with a career to maintain friendships or take an interest in neighbours, community, or important social problems; and the freedom to be unfaithful and dump your spouse when you're no longer pleased with him or her.

Of course, you don't need to buy into any of these concepts. The following sections can help you gain some perspective.

Acknowledging what money can't buy

Recall the handful of best moments in your life. Odds are, these times don't include the time you bought a new car or found a designer sweater that you liked. The old saying is true: The most enjoyable and precious things of value in your life can't be bought.

The following statement should go without saying, but we must say it, because too many people act as if it isn't so: Money can't buy happiness. It's tempting to think that if you could only make 20 percent more, or twice as much, you'd be happier because you'd have more money to travel, eat out, and buy that shiny new giant high-definition TV technology you've been eyeing. Right? Not so. A great deal of thoughtful research suggests that little relationship exists between money and happiness. *Not true*

But try to live without it is impossible

"Wealth is like health: Although its absence can breed misery, having it is no guarantee of happiness," says psychology professor Dr. David G. Myers, who has written and researched happiness across cultures for decades. Despite the availability of the BlackBerry and myriad other technological gadgets and communication devices, cheap air travel, microwaves, personal computers, voice mail, and all the other stuff that's supposed to make life easier and more enjoyable, they haven't done much to make our lives happier. One survey by the University of Chicago's National Opinion Research Center found that people aren't any happier than they were four decades ago, even though incomes, after being adjusted for inflation, have more than doubled during that time.

What's your relationship with money?

Over the years in our work in the personal finance world, we've come to find that how a person relates to and feels about money has a great impact on how good he is at managing his money and making important financial decisions. For example, knowing that you have a net worth of negative $13,200 because of credit card debt is useful, but it's probably not enough information for you to do something constructive about your problem. A logical next step would be to examine your current spending and take steps to reduce your debt load.

Although we cover practical solutions to common financial quandaries later in this book, we also discuss the more touchy-feely side of money. For example, some people who continually rack up consumer debt have a spending addiction. Other people who jump in and out of investments and follow them like a hawk have psychological obstacles that prevent them from holding on to investments.

And then you have those somewhat philosophical and psychological issues relating to money and the meaning of life. Saving more money and increasing your net worth aren't always the best approaches. In our work, we've come across numerous people who attach too much significance to personal wealth accumulation and neglect important human relationships in their pursuit of more money. Some retirees have a hard time loosening the purse strings and actually spending some of the money they worked so hard to save for their golden years.

Balancing your financial goals with other important life goals is key to your happiness. What's the point, for example, of staying in a well-paying, admired profession if you don't care for the work and you're mainly doing it for the financial rewards? Life is too short and precious for you to squander away your days.

So as you read through the various chapters and sections of this book, please consider your higher life goals and purposes. What are your non-financial priorities (family, friends, causes), and how can you best accomplish your goals with the financial resources you do have?

Managing the balancing act

Believe it or not, some people save too much. In our work, we've seen plenty of people who fall into that category. If making and saving money are good things, then the more the better, right? Well, take the admittedly extreme case of Anne Scheiber, who, on a modest income, started saving at a young age, allowing her money to compound in wealth-building investments such as stocks over many years. As a result, she was able to amass $20 million before she passed away at the age of 101.

Scheiber lived in a cramped studio apartment and never used her investments. She didn't even use the interest or dividends — she lived solely on her Social Security benefits and the small pension from her employer. Scheiber was extreme in her frugality and obsessed with her savings. As reported by James Glassman in *The Washington Post,* "She had few friends . . . she was an unhappy person, totally consumed by her securities accounts and her money."

Most people, ourselves included, wouldn't choose to live and save the way that Scheiber did. She saved for the sake of saving: no goal, no plan, no reward for herself. Saving should be a means to an end, not something that makes you *mean* to the end.

Even those who are saving for an ultimate goal can become consumed by their saving habits. We see some people pursuing higher-paying jobs and pinching pennies in order to retire early. But sometimes they make too many personal sacrifices today while chasing after some vision of their lives tomorrow. Others get consumed by work and then don't notice or understand why their family and friends feel neglected.

Another problem with seeking to amass wealth is that tomorrow may not come. Even if all goes according to plan, will you know how to be happy when you're not working if you spend your entire life making money? More importantly, who will be around to share your leisure time? One of the costs of an intense career is time spent away from friends and family. You may realize your goal of retiring early, but you may be putting off too much living today in expectation of living tomorrow. As Charles D'Orleans said in 1465, "It's very well to be thrifty, but don't amass a hoard of regrets."

Of course, at the other extreme are spendthrifts who live only for today. A friend once said, "I'm not into delayed gratification." "Shop 'til you drop" seems to be the motto of this personality type. "Why save when I might not be here tomorrow?" reasons this type of person.

The danger of this approach is that tomorrow may come after all, and most people don't want to spend all their tomorrows working for a living. The earlier neglect of saving, however, may make it necessary for you to work when you're older. And if for some reason you can't work and you have little money to live on, much less live enjoyably, the situation can be tragic. The only difference between a person without any savings or access to credit and some homeless people is a few months of unemployment.

Making and saving money are like eating food. If you don't eat enough, you may suffer. If you eat too much, the overage may go to waste or make you overweight. The right amount, perhaps with some extra to spare, affords you a healthy, balanced, peaceful existence. Money should be treated with respect and acknowledged for what it is — a means to an end and a precious resource that shouldn't be thoughtlessly squandered and wasted.

As Dr. David Myers, whom we introduce earlier in this chapter, says: "Satisfaction isn't so much getting what you want as wanting what you have. There are two ways to be rich: one is to have great wealth, the other is to have few wants." Find ways to make the most of the money that does pass through your hands, and never lose sight of all that is far more important than money.

Prioritizing Your Savings Goals

Many people we know have financial goals. The rest of this chapter discusses the most common financial goals and how to work toward them. See whether any of the following reflect your ambitions:

- ✔ **Becoming part of the landed gentry:** Renting and dealing with landlords can be a financial and emotional drag, so most folks want to buy into the Canadian dream and own some real estate — the most basic of which is your own home. (Despite the slide in some property prices in the late 2000s, real estate has a pretty solid track record as a long-term investment.)

- ✔ **Making major purchases:** Most folks need to plan ahead for major purchases such as a car, living room furniture, vacation trips, and so on.

- ✔ **Retiring:** No, retiring doesn't imply sitting on a rocking chair watching the world go by while hoping that some long-lost friend, your son's or daughter's family, or the neighbourhood dog comes by to visit. Retiring is a catchall term for discontinuing full-time work or perhaps not even working for pay at all.

- ✔ **Educating the kids:** No, all those diaper changes, late-night feedings, and trips to the zoo aren't enough to get Junior out of your house and into the real world as a productive, self-sufficient adult. You may want to help your children get a post-secondary education. Unfortunately, that can cost a truckload of dough.

- ✔ **Owning your own business:** Many employees want to face the challenges and rewards that come with being the boss. The primary reason why most people continue just to dream is that they lack the money to leave their primary job. Although many businesses don't require gobs of start-up cash, almost all require that you withstand a substantial reduction in your income during the early years.

Because everyone is different, you can have goals (other than those in the previous list) that are unique to your own situation. Accomplishing such goals almost always requires saving money. As one of our favourite Chinese proverbs says, "Do not wait until you are thirsty to dig a well." In other words, don't wait to save money until you're ready to accomplish a personal or financial goal!

Knowing what's most important to you

Unless you earn really big bucks or have a large family inheritance to fall back on, your personal and financial desires will probably outstrip your resources. As a result, you have to prioritize your goals.

One of the biggest mistakes we see people make is rushing into financial decisions without considering what's really important to them. Because many people get caught up in the responsibilities of their daily lives, they often don't have time for reflection.

As a result of our experience teaching people — and talking with them — about personal financial management, we can tell you that the folks who accomplish their goals aren't necessarily smarter or higher-income earners than those who don't. People who identify their goals and then work toward them, which often requires changing some habits, are the ones who accomplish their goals.

Valuing retirement plans

Where possible, try to save and invest in plans that give you a tax advantage — precisely what retirement plans offer. These accounts, known by such enlightening acronyms and names as RRSP (Registered Retirement Savings Plan) and RPP (Registered Pension Plan), offer tax breaks to people of all economic means. Consider the following advantages to investing in retirement plans:

- ✔ **Contributions are usually tax-deductible.** By putting money in a retirement plan, not only do you plan wisely for your future, but you also get an immediate financial reward: lower taxes — and lower taxes means more money available for saving and investing. Contributions to retirement plans are generally not taxed at either the federal or provincial income tax level until withdrawal. If you're paying, say, 35 percent between federal and provincial taxes (see Chapter 7 to determine your tax bracket), a $5,000 contribution to a retirement plan lowers your taxes by $1,750.

- ✔ **In some company retirement plans, companies match a portion of your own contributions.** In addition to tax breaks, you get free extra money courtesy of your employer!

- ✔ **Returns on your investment compound over time without taxation.** After you put money into a registered retirement plan, any interest, dividends, and appreciation that money earns gets added to your account without being taxed. Of course, there's no such thing as a free lunch — these plans don't allow for complete tax avoidance. Yet you can get a really great lunch at a discount: You get to defer taxes on all the accumulating gains and profits until you withdraw the money down the road. Thus, more money is working for you over a longer period of time.

The tax rates on stock dividends and *capital gains* (the increase in the value of your stocks and mutual fund units) are lower than the tax rates on ordinary income such as that earned through working. This fact makes some people think that investing through registered retirement plans may not be worthwhile. The reasoning is that all the investment earnings on money inside these plans is taxed at the relatively high ordinary income tax rates — rather than the lower dividend and capital gains rates — when the money is withdrawn. By contrast, when you invest outside of registered retirement plans, you pay a lower rate of tax on stock dividends and on the sale of stocks and mutual fund units that have increased in value. We'll cut to the chase: The vast, vast majority of people are better off contributing to registered retirement plans (see Chapter 7 for more details).

Dealing with competing goals

Unless you enjoy paying higher taxes, why would you save money outside of registered retirement plans, which shelter your money from taxation? The reason is that some financial goals are not easily achieved by saving in registered retirement plans. Also, registered retirement plans have limits on the amount you can contribute annually.

If you're accumulating money for a down payment on a home or to start or buy a business, for example, you'll probably need to save money outside of a registered retirement plan. If you withdraw funds from a registered retirement plan, you have to include that money in your income and pay tax on it. (See the sidebar "Avoiding RRSP early-withdrawal penalties" for exceptions to this rule.) Because you're constrained by your financial resources, you need to prioritize your goals. Before funding your registered retirement plans and racking up those tax breaks, read on to consider your other goals.

Building Emergency Reserves

Because you don't know what the future holds, preparing for the unexpected is financially wise. Even if you're the lucky sort who finds loonies on every street corner, you can't control the sometimes chaotic world in which we live.

Conventional wisdom says that you should have approximately six months of living expenses put away for an emergency. This particular amount may or may not be right for you, because it depends, of course, on how expensive the emergency is. Why six months, anyway? And where should you put it?

How much of an emergency stash you need depends on your situation. We recommend saving the following emergency amounts under differing circumstances (in Chapter 12, we recommend preferred places to invest this money):

- **Three months' living expenses:** Choose this option if you have other accounts, such as an RRSP, or family members and close friends whom you can tap for a short-term loan. This minimalist approach makes sense when you're trying to maximize investments elsewhere (for example, in retirement plans) or you have stable sources of income (employment or otherwise).

- **Six months' living expenses:** This amount is appropriate if you don't have other places to turn for a loan or you have some instability in your employment situation or source of income.

- **Up to one year's living expenses:** Set aside this much if you don't have other places to turn for a loan and your income fluctuates wildly from year to year. This amount is also wise if your profession involves a high risk of job loss and finding another job could take a long time.

In the event that your only current source of emergency funds is a high-interest credit card, you should first save at least three months' worth of living expenses in an accessible account before funding a retirement plan or saving for other goals.

Saving to Buy a Home

When you're starting out financially, deciding whether to save money to buy a home or to put money into a retirement plan presents a dilemma. In the long run, owning your own home is a wise financial move. On the other hand, saving sooner for retirement makes achieving your goals easier.

Presuming both goals are important to you, you should be saving both toward buying a home *and* for retirement. If you're eager to own a home, you can throw all your savings toward achieving that goal and temporarily put your retirement savings on hold. Save for both purposes simultaneously if you're not in a rush.

If you're saving for a home, it can be a good idea to save at least some of that money inside an RRSP. Why? You can generally withdraw up to $25,000 from your RRSP to buy or build a home under the Home Buyers' Plan. Unlike regular RRSP withdrawals from an RRSP, money taken out under the Home Buyers' Plan isn't treated as income, and you don't have to pay tax on it. However, you do have to repay the money to your RRSP over the next 15 years. For more on the Home Buyers' Plan, see Chapter 15.

Saving to Buy a Business

When saving money for starting or buying a business, most people encounter the same dilemma they face when deciding to save to buy a house: If you fund your retirement plans to the exclusion of earmarking money for your small-business dreams, your entrepreneurial aspirations may never become a reality. Generally, we advocate hedging your bets by saving money in your tax-sheltered retirement plan as well as toward your business venture. As we discuss in Part III, an investment in your own small business can produce great rewards, so you may feel comfortable focusing your savings on your own business.

TIP

Avoiding penalties on RRSP withdrawals

Opportunities exist to avoid the tax bill you're usually hit with when you withdraw money early from your RRSP. You can withdraw up to $25,000 tax-free from an RRSP if you put the money toward buying or building a home and you meet all the requirements. One key condition is that you have to repay the money over the next 15 years. (See Chapter 15 for the details.) You can also take out up to $10,000 a year tax-free to pay for the cost of full-time training or postsecondary education for you or your spouse under the Lifelong Learning Plan. You can take out the money over a four-year period, and the overall maximum you can withdraw is $20,000. The money has to be repaid over the next ten years, starting the fifth year after the first withdrawal.

If you lose a job and your cash flow dries up, you may turn to your RRSP to make ends meet. If you do withdraw money from your RRSP, that money is counted as part of your annual income and is taxed at your regular tax rate.

If you're not working, or earning so little income that you need to raid your retirement plan, you will almost certainly be in a low tax bracket, and that money will be taxed at a very low rate. The lower amount of tax you will pay as compared to the taxes you would have paid on that money had you not sheltered it in a registered retirement plan in the first place should minimize the tax costs.

When you do make a withdrawal from your RRSP, the plan administrators are required by the government to hold back some of the money as a sort of tax down payment. The withholding tax rates (unless you live in Quebec) are 10 percent on the first $5,000, 20 percent for any amount between $5,000 and $15,000, and 30 percent on any amount beyond $15,000. In Quebec, the amount withheld is a combination of half the federal withholding rate plus a 16 percent Quebec withholding, regardless of the amount.

The withholding rates are calculated on each individual transaction. If you need to withdraw a large amount, consider breaking the amount you need into separate withdrawals of no more than $5,000 each. This will minimize the amount of tax held back, and maximize the amount of money you can get your hands on. However, don't forget that the withholding tax may not be sufficient to cover all the tax you'll owe, given that the withdrawals will be included in that year's annual income come tax time. Plan ahead.

Funding Kids' Educational Expenses

Wanting to provide for your children's future is perfectly natural, but doing so before you've saved adequately toward your own goals can be a major financial mistake. This concept may sound selfish, but you need to take care of *your* future first. You should generally first take advantage of saving through your tax-sheltered retirement plans before you set aside money in custodial savings accounts for your kids. This practice isn't selfish: Do you really want to have to leech off your kids when you're old and frail because you didn't save any money for yourself? (See Chapter 14 for a complete explanation of how to save for educational expenses, including the benefits of Registered Education Savings Plans, or RESPs.)

Saving for Big Purchases

If you want to buy a car, a canoe, or a plane ticket to Thailand, do not, we repeat, do not buy such things with *consumer credit* (that is, finance the purchase on a credit card or with an auto loan that has you paying month to month). As we explain in Chapter 5, cars, boats, vacations, and the like are consumer items, not wealth-building investments such as real estate or small businesses. A car begins to depreciate the moment you drive it off the sales lot. A plane ticket is worthless the moment you arrive back home. (We know your memories will be priceless, but they won't pay the bills.)

Don't deny yourself gratification; just learn how to delay it. Get into the habit of saving for your larger consumer purchases to avoid paying more for them over time with high-interest consumer credit. When saving up for a consumer purchase such as a car, a money market account, a Tax-Free Savings Account, or a high-interest savings account is a good place to store your short-term savings. (See Chapter 7 for more on Tax-Free Savings Accounts and Chapter 13 for more on saving for short-term goals.)

Paying for high-interest consumer debt can cripple your ability not only to save for long-term goals but also to make major purchases in the future. Interest on consumer debt is exorbitantly expensive — upward of 20 percent on many credit cards. When contemplating the purchase of a consumer item on credit, add up the total interest you'd end up paying on your debt and call it the price of instant gratification.

Preparing for Retirement

Many people toil away at work, dreaming about a future in which they can stop the daily commute and grind, get out from under that daily deluge of voice mails, e-mails, and other never-ending technological intrusions, and finally do what they want, when they want. People often assume that this magical day will arrive either on their next true day off or when they retire or win the lottery — whichever comes first.

We've never cared much for the term *retire*. The word seems to imply idleness or the end of usefulness to society. But if retirement means not having to work at a job (especially one you don't enjoy) and having financial flexibility and independence, then we're all for it.

Being able to retire sooner rather than later is part of the Canadian dream. But this idea has some obvious problems. First, you set yourself up for disappointment. If you want to retire by your mid-60s (when the Canada Pension Plan or Quebec Pension Plan kicks in), you need to save enough money to support yourself for 20 years, maybe longer. Two decades is a long time to live off your savings. You're going to need a good-sized chunk of money — more than most people realize.

The earlier you hope to retire, the more money you need to set aside, and the sooner you have to start saving — unless you plan to work part-time in retirement to earn more income! See Chapter 11 for more details about how to save for retirement.

Many of the people we speak to say that they do want to retire, and most say "the sooner, the better." Yet one recent survey found that just 36 percent of Canadians have planned or are planning for retirement. And 32 percent haven't even begun to save for retirement. When Eric asked one of his middle-aged counselling clients, who had saved little for retirement, when he would like to retire, he deadpanned, "Sometime before I die." If you're in this group (and even if you're not), determine where you stand financially regarding retirement. If you're like most working people, you need to increase your savings rate for retirement.

Don't neglect non-financial preparations for retirement

Investing your money is just one (and not even the most important) aspect of preparing for your retirement. In order to enjoy the lifestyle that your retirement savings will provide you, you need to invest energy into other areas of your life as well:

✔ Few things are more important than your health. Without your health, enjoying the good things in life can be hard. Unfortunately, many people aren't motivated to care about their health until *after* they discover problems. By then, it may be too late.

  Although exercising regularly, eating a balanced and nutritious diet, and avoiding substance abuse can't guarantee you a healthful future, these good habits go a long way toward preventing many of the most common causes of death and debilitating disease. Regular medical exams also are important in detecting problems early.

✔ In addition to your physical health, be sure to invest in your psychological health.

People live longer and have happier and healthier lives when they have a circle of family and friends around them for support.

Unfortunately, many people become more isolated and lose regular contact with business associates, friends, and family members as they grow older.

Happy retirees tend to stay active, getting involved in volunteer organizations and new social circles. They may travel to see old friends or younger relatives who may be too busy to visit them.

Treat retirement life like a bubbly, inviting hot tub set at 39 degrees Celsius. You want to ease yourself in nice and slow; jumping in hastily can take most of the pleasantness out of the experience. Abruptly leaving your job without a plan for spending all that free time is an invitation to boredom and depression. Everyone needs a sense of purpose and a sense of routine. Establishing hobbies, volunteer work, or a sideline business while gradually cutting back your regular work schedule can be a terrific way to ease into retirement.

Figuring what you need for retirement

If you hope to someday reduce the time you spend working or cease working altogether, you'll need sufficient savings to support yourself. Many people — particularly young people and those who don't work well with numbers — underestimate the amount of money needed to retire. To figure out how much you should save per month to achieve your retirement goals, you need to crunch a few numbers. (Don't worry — this number-crunching should be easier than doing your taxes.)

✛ Luckily for you, you don't have to start cold. Studies show how people typically spend money before and during retirement. Most people need about 70 to 80 percent of their pre-retirement income throughout retirement to maintain their standard of living. For example, if your household earns $50,000 per year before retirement, you're likely to need $35,000 to $40,000 (70 to 80 percent of $50,000) per year during retirement to live the way you're accustomed to living. The 70 to 80 percent is an average. Some people may need more simply because they have more time on their hands to spend their money. Others adjust their standard of living and live on less.

So how do you figure out what you're going to need? The following three profiles provide a rough estimate of the percentage of your pre-retirement income you're going to need during retirement. Pick the one that most accurately describes your situation. If you fall between two descriptions, pick a percentage in between those two.

To maintain your standard of living in retirement, you need

✔ **65 percent of your pre-retirement income if you**

- Save a large amount (15 percent or more) of your annual earnings

- Are a high-income earner

- Will own your home free of debt by the time you retire

- Do not anticipate leading a lifestyle in retirement that reflects your current high income

If you're an especially high-income earner who lives well beneath your means, you may be able to do just fine with even less than 65 percent. Pick an annual dollar amount or percentage of your current income that will allow the kind of retirement lifestyle you desire.

✔ **75 percent of your pre-retirement income if you**

- Save a reasonable amount (5 to 14 percent) of your annual earnings

- Will still have some mortgage debt or a modest rent to pay by the time you retire

- Anticipate having a standard of living in retirement that's comparable to what you have today

✔ **85 percent of your pre-retirement income if you**

- Save little or none of your annual earnings (less than 5 percent)

- Will have a relatively significant mortgage payment or sizeable rent to pay in retirement

- Anticipate wanting or needing to maintain your current lifestyle throughout retirement

Of course, you can use a more precise approach to figure out how much you need per year in retirement. Be forewarned, though, that this more personalized method is far more time-consuming, and because you're making projections into an uncertain future it may not be any more accurate than the simple method we just explained. If you're data-oriented, you may feel comfortable tackling this method: You need to figure out where you're spending your money today (worksheets are available in Chapter 3) and then work up some projections for your expected spending needs in retirement (the information in Chapter 19 may help you, as well).

Understanding your retirement building blocks

Did you play with Lego blocks or Tinkertoys when you were a child? You start by building a foundation on the ground, and then you build up. Before you know it, you're creating bridges, castles, and animal figures. Although preparing financially for retirement isn't exactly like playing with blocks, the concept is the same: You need a basic foundation so that your necessary retirement reserves can grow.

If you've been working steadily you may already have a good foundation, even if you haven't been actively saving toward retirement. In the pages ahead, we walk you through the probable components of your future retirement income and show you how to figure how much you should be saving to reach particular retirement goals.

Counting on government benefits

If you think that you can never retire because you don't have any money saved, we're happy to inform you that you're probably wrong. You likely have some CPP/QPP and Old Age Security benefits coming to you. Although they will likely be bare-bones, some form of various government programs should be around to provide you with some income when you retire, no matter how old you are today. The Canada Pension Plan is one of the sacred cow political programs. Imagine what would happen to the group of politicians that voted not to pay any more benefits!

But, as many people now acknowledge — one poll found that around two-thirds of Canadians believe that government programs won't provide them with a secure income in their retirement years — they generally won't be enough to live on comfortably.

The Canada Pension Plan (or Quebec Pension Plan) is only intended to provide you with a subsistence level of retirement income for the basic necessities: food, shelter, and clothing. It's not intended to be your sole source of income. The Canada Pension Plan (or QPP) is designed to replace about a quarter of your pre-retirement income — but only up to a certain limit. Few people could maintain their current lifestyles without supplementing their CPP/QPP with personal savings and company retirement plans.

Figuring out the size of pension payments you will get from CPP/QPP

Two factors determine the amount of retirement pension you'll receive from the Canada Pension Plan (or QPP):

- **The number of years you contribute to the plan:** The more years you contribute, the higher your payments will be.

- **How much you contribute to the plan over those years:** When you're working, you pay a percentage of your earnings above $3,500 up to a maximum, which in 2010 was $47,200. This ceiling — the *yearly maximum pensionable earnings* — is regularly adjusted for inflation.

  The amount you have to put in is determined by the contribution rate, which also is adjusted from time to time. In 2010, the contribution rate was 9.9 percent. If you earn a salary, you pay half of your required CPP/QPP contributions and your employer pays the other half. In 2010, this meant that you contribute 4.95 percent, and your employer also contributes 4.95 percent. If you're self-employed, you pay the full amount yourself. Given the ceiling on pensionable earnings, the maximum that could be contributed in your name in 2010 was $4,672.80.

You don't make CPP/QPP contributions when you are receiving disability or retirement payments from the CPP/QPP. Also, when you turn 70, you stop paying into the plan even if you are still working and haven't yet started receiving your CPP/QPP retirement benefits.

The average monthly benefit in 2010 (assuming you retired at age 65) was just over $502.57, and the maximum possible monthly payment was about $934.17. The payments are set for life, and are fully indexed to inflation. An adjustment is made to reflect the change in the cost of living once a year, in January.

If you qualify for CPP/QPP and are no longer able to work due to a disability, you may be eligible for a disability pension. The maximum is slightly higher than regular CPP/QPP benefits. In 2010, the average disability benefit was $809.70, while the maximum was $1,126.76.

If you make CPP/QPP contributions, you should receive a statement summarizing your contributions every few years. If you want to get an estimate of the size of Canada Pension Plan benefits you can expect, contact Service Canada. (If you live in Quebec, contact the Quebec Pension Plan.)

You can start collecting as early as age 60 or as late as age 70. The amount of your monthly benefits will be permanently reduced by half a percent for every month before age 65 that you start drawing your pension. This works out to 6 percent a year; the reduction continues for the rest of your life. On the other hand, if you choose to delay receiving your CPP/QPP, your benefits will be increased by the same 0.5 percent a month for each month beyond your 65th birthday to a maximum of 30 percent.

Determining how much of your CPP/QPP will go to your spouse or partner when you die

If you are a member of the CPP/QPP and die, your family will get a one-time lump-sum *death benefit*. This payment is six times what your CPP/QPP retirement pension was — or would have been — at age 65, but can't be higher than a set maximum, which in 2010 was $2,500.

The second death benefit is called the *survivor's pension,* and is paid to your surviving spouse or common-law partner. The amount of the payment is a percentage of the deceased's benefits. This is calculated using the survivor's age and other factors. For survivors under the age of 65, the average monthly survivor's benefit in 2010 was about $364.74, and the maximum was $516.57. For those 65 or over, the average survivor's benefit in 2010 was just over $297.09, with the maximum set at $560.50. However, if the surviving spouse is also eligible to receive retirement benefits from his or her own CPP/QPP contributions, the total will usually be less than the sum of the two benefits.

Examining how much CPP/QPP will pay to your children when you die

A third death-related CPP/QPP benefit is the *children's benefit.* This is paid to your natural or adopted children, or children in your care and control at the time you die, and continues until the children turn 18. The benefits may continue up to age 25 as long as your child is going to school full-time at a recognized institution. If the benefits are stopped and then your child goes back to school and is still between the ages of 18 and 25, the benefits can be reinstated. This benefit is a flat rate that is adjusted annually. The maximum in 2010 was $214.85.

To get a more precise handle on your CPP benefits, you can call Service Canada or visit their Web site (800-277-9914; www.servicecanada.gc.ca). Follow the links to the Canada Pension Plan Statement of Contributions, which you can then view and print off. This statement gives you the history of your earnings and contributions, as well as estimates for any benefits you may be eligible to receive. Check your earnings record, because occasional errors do arise — and (surprise!) they usually aren't in your favour.

Planning your personal savings/investment strategy

Money you're saving toward retirement can include money under the mattress as well as money in a retirement plan such as a Registered Retirement Savings Plan or *RRSP* (see Chapter 11). You may have also earmarked investments in non-retirement accounts for your retirement.

The *equity* (the difference between the market value less any mortgage balances owed) you've built up in rental real estate can be counted toward your retirement as well. Deciding whether to include the equity in your primary residence (your home) is trickier. If you don't want to count on using this money in retirement, don't include it when you tally your stash. You may want to count a portion of your home equity in your total assets for retirement. Many people sell their homes when they retire and move to a lower-cost area, move closer to family, or downsize to a more manageable size of home. And increasing numbers of older retirees are tapping their home's equity through reverse mortgages (see Chapter 15 for information on mortgages).

Making the most of pensions

Pension plans are a benefit offered by some employers — mostly larger organizations and government agencies. Even if your current employer doesn't offer a pension, you may have earned pension benefits through a previous job.

The plans we're referring to are known as *defined-benefit plans.* With these plans, you qualify for a monthly benefit amount to be paid to you in retirement based on your years of service for a specific employer.

Although each company's plan differs, all plans calculate and pay benefits based on a formula. A typical formula might credit you with 1.5 percent of your salary for each year of service (full-time employment). For example, if you work ten years, you earn a monthly retirement benefit worth 15 percent of your monthly salary.

Pension benefits can be quite valuable. In the better plans, employers put away the equivalent of 5 to 10 percent of your salary to pay your future pension. This money is in addition to your salary — you never see it in your paycheque, and it isn't taxed. The employer puts this money away in an account for your retirement.

To qualify for pension benefits, you don't have to stay with an employer long enough to receive the 25-year gold watch. Depending on your province, an employee must be fully *vested* (entitled to receive full benefits based on years of service upon reaching retirement age) after either two or five years of full-time service.

Defined-benefit pension plans are becoming rarer for two major reasons:

- ✔ They're costly for employers to maintain. Many employees don't understand how these plans work and why they're so valuable, so companies don't get mileage out of their pension expenditures — employees don't see the money, so they don't appreciate the company's generosity.

- ✔ Most of the new jobs being generated are with small companies that typically don't offer these types of plans.

More employers offer plans that, instead of specifying how much you'll receive when you retire, only lay out how much you can put into the plan in your name. Known as *defined-contribution plans,* these plans allow you to save toward your retirement at your own expense rather than at your employer's expense. (To encourage participation in defined-contribution plans, many employers "match" a portion of their employees' contributions.) More of the burden and responsibility of investing for retirement falls on your shoulders with these plans, so it's important to understand how they work. Most people are ill-equipped to know how much to save and, just as importantly, how to invest the money. The retirement planning worksheet in the next section should help you get started with figuring out the amount you need to save. (Part III shows you how to invest.)

Crunching numbers for your retirement

Now that you've toured the components of your future retirement income, take a shot at tallying where you stand in terms of retirement preparations. Don't be afraid to do this exercise — it's not difficult, and you may find that you're not in such bad shape. We even explain how to catch up if you find that you're behind in saving for retirement.

Note: The following worksheet (Table 4-1) and the growth multiplier (Table 4-2) assume that you're going to retire at age 66 and that your investments will produce an annual rate of return that is 4 percent higher than the rate of inflation. For example, if inflation averages 3 percent, this table assumes that you will earn 7 percent per year on your investments.

Table 4-1	Retirement Planning Worksheet
Retirement Income or Needs	*Amount*
1. Annual retirement income needed in today's dollars (see earlier in this chapter)	$ _____ / year
2. Annual government benefits	– $ _____ / year

Retirement Income or Needs	Amount
3. Annual pension benefits (ask your benefits department); multiply by 60% if your pension won't increase with inflation during retirement	– $ _____ / year
4. Annual retirement income needed from personal savings (subtract lines 2 and 3 from line 1)	= $ _____ / year
5. Savings needed to retire at age 66 (multiply line 4 by 15)	$ _____
6. Value of current retirement savings	$ _____
7. Value of current retirement savings at retirement (multiply line 6 by growth multiplier in Table 4-2)	$ _____
8. Amount you still need to save (line 5 minus line 7)	$ _____
9. Amount you need to save per month (multiply line 8 by savings factor in Table 4-2)	$ _____ / month

To get a more precise handle on where you stand in terms of retirement planning turn to Chapter 20, where we recommend retirement planning software and Web sites that can ease your number-crunching burdens.

Table 4-2	Growth Multiplier	
Your Current Age	Growth Multiplier	Savings Factor
26	4.8	0.001
28	4.4	0.001
30	4.1	0.001
32	3.8	0.001
34	3.5	0.001
36	3.2	0.001
38	3.0	0.002
40	2.8	0.002
42	2.6	0.002
44	2.4	0.002
46	2.2	0.003
48	2.0	0.003
50	1.9	0.004
52	1.7	0.005
54	1.6	0.006
56	1.5	0.007

(continued)

Table 4-2 *(continued)*		
58	1.4	0.009
60	1.3	0.013
62	1.2	0.020
64	1.1	0.041

Making up for lost time

If the amount you need to save per month to reach your retirement goals seems daunting, all is not lost. Remember: Winners never quit, and quitters never win. Here are our top recommendations for making up for lost time:

- ✔ **Question your spending.** You have two ways to boost your savings: Earn more money or cut your spending (or do both!). Most people don't spend their money nearly as thoughtfully as they earn it. See Chapter 6 for suggestions and strategies for reducing your spending.

- ✔ **Be more realistic about your retirement age.** If you extend the age at which you plan to retire, you get a double benefit: You're earning and saving money for more years, and you're spending your nest egg over fewer years. Of course, if your job is making you crazy, this option may not be too appealing. Try to find work that makes you happy, and consider working, at least part-time, during your "early" retirement years.

- ✔ **Use your home equity.** The prospect of tapping the cash in your home can be troubling. After getting together the down payment, you probably worked for many years to pay off that sucker. You're delighted not to have to submit a mortgage payment to the bank anymore. But what's the use of owning a house free of mortgage debt when you lack sufficient retirement reserves? All the money that's tied up in the house can be used to help increase your standard of living in retirement.

  You have a number of ways to tap your home's equity. You can sell your home and either move to a lower-cost property or rent an apartment. In general, any money you make when you sell your home is not taxed. (The home must qualify as what the tax authorities call your principal residence. This essentially means it must be the place you call home. A rental property, for instance, doesn't qualify.) Another option is a *reverse mortgage,* in which you get a monthly income cheque as you build a loan balance against the value of your home. The loan is paid when your home is finally sold. (See Chapter 15 for more information about reverse mortgages.)

✔ **Get your investments growing.** The faster the rate at which your money grows and compounds, the less you need to save each year to reach your goals. (Make sure, however, that you're not reckless; don't take huge risks in the hopes of big returns.) Earning just a few extra percentage points per year on your investments can dramatically slash the amount you need to save. The younger you are, the more powerful the effect of compounding interest. For example, if you're in your mid-30s and your investments appreciate 6 percent per year (rather than 4 percent) faster than the rate of inflation, the amount you need to save each month to reach your retirement goals drops by about 40 percent! (See Part III, on investing.)

✔ **Turn a hobby into supplemental retirement income.** Even if you've earned a living in the same career over many decades, you have skills that are portable and can be put to profitable use. Pick something you enjoy and are good at, develop a business plan, and get smart about how to market your services and wares (check out the latest edition of the *Canadian Small Business Kit For Dummies* from Wiley, by Margaret Kerr and JoAnn Kurtz). Remember, as people get busier, more specialized services are created to support their hectic lives. A demand for quality, homemade goods of all varieties also exists. Be creative! You never know — you may wind up profiled in a business publication!

✔ **Invest to gain tax-free and other free money.** By investing in a tax-wise fashion, you can boost the effective rate of return on your investments without taking on additional risk.

In addition to the tax benefits you gain from funding most types of retirement plans in this chapter (see the earlier section, "Valuing retirement plans"), some employers offer free matching money. Also, you can invest money in a Tax-Free Savings Account (TFSA). Unlike an RRSP, your contributions have to be made with after-tax dollars, but when it's inside the money can grow tax-free, and you also don't pay any tax when you withdraw money from these accounts. See Chapter 7 for more on TFSAs.

As for money outside of tax-sheltered retirement plans and accounts, if you're in a relatively high tax bracket you may earn more by investing in low-tax investments and vehicles that minimize highly taxed distributions.

✔ **Think about inheritances.** Although you should never count on an inheritance to support your retirement, you may inherit money someday. If you want to see what impact an inheritance has on your retirement calculations, add a conservative estimate of the amount you expect to inherit to your current total savings in Table 4-1.

Part II
Saving More, Spending Less

The 5th Wave   By Rich Tennant

"No, Mrs. Moskowitz. There's just no way we can list the unpaid debt of gratitude your son owes you on his credit history."

In this part . . .

We detail numerous ways to make your dollars go toward building up your savings rather than toward wasteful spending. Are you buried in debt with little to show for it? Well, it's never too late to start digging out. Here you find out how to reduce your debt burden. We also devote an entire chapter to discussing taxes and how to legally minimize them.

Chapter 5

Dealing with Debt

. . . .

In This Chapter

▶ Lowering your debt with savings

▶ Getting out of debt when you don't have savings

▶ Contacting credit counselling agencies

▶ Understanding the pros and cons of filing bankruptcy

▶ Exploring an alternative to filing bankruptcy

▶ Halting your spending and staying out of debt

. . . .

*A*ccumulating *bad debt* (consumer debt) by buying things like new living room furniture or a new car that you really can't afford is like living on a diet of sugar and caffeine: a quick fix with little nutritional value. Borrowing on your credit card to afford an extravagantly expensive vacation is detrimental to your long-term financial health.

When debt is used for investing in your future, we call it *good debt* (see Chapter 2). Borrowing money to pay for an education, to buy real estate, or to invest in a small business is like eating fruits and vegetables for their vitamins. That's not to say that you can't get yourself into trouble when using good debt. Just as you can gorge yourself on too much "good food," you can absolutely develop financial indigestion from too much good debt.

In this chapter, we mainly help you battle the pervasive problem of consumer debt. Getting rid of your bad debts may be even more difficult than giving up the junk foods you love. But in the long run, you'll be glad you did; you'll be financially healthier and emotionally happier. And after you get rid of your high-cost consumer debt, make sure you practise the best way to avoid future credit problems: *Don't borrow with bad debt.*

Before you decide which debt reduction strategies make sense for you, you must first consider your overall financial situation (see Chapter 2) and assess your alternatives. (We discuss strategies for reducing your current spending — which help you free up more cash to pay down your debts — in Chapter 6.)

Using Savings to Reduce Your Consumer Debt

Many people build a mental brick wall between their savings and investment accounts and their consumer debt accounts. By failing to view their finances holistically, they simply fall into the habit of looking at these accounts individually. The thought of putting a door in that big brick wall doesn't occur to them. This section helps you see how your savings can be used to lower your consumer debt.

Understanding how you gain

If you have the savings to pay off consumer debt, like high-interest credit card and auto loans, consider doing so. (Make sure you pay off the loans with the highest interest rates first.) Sure, you diminish your savings, but you also reduce your debts. Although your savings and investments may be earning decent returns, the interest you're paying on your consumer debts is likely higher.

Paying off consumer loans on a credit card at, say, 12 percent is like finding an investment with a guaranteed return of 12 percent — *tax-free*. You would actually need to find an investment that yielded even more — anywhere from 16 to 24 percent, depending on your marginal tax rate — to net 12 percent after paying taxes in order to justify not paying off your 12-percent loans. The higher your tax bracket (see Chapter 7), the higher the return you need on your investments to justify keeping high-interest consumer debt.

Even if you think that you're an investing genius and you can earn more on your investments, swallow your ego and pay down your consumer debts anyway. In order to chase that higher potential return from investments, you need to take substantial risk. You *may* earn more investing in that hot stock tip or that bargain real estate, but more than likely, you won't.

If you use your savings to pay down consumer debts, be careful to leave yourself enough of an emergency cushion. (In Chapter 4, we tell you how to determine how large of an emergency reserve you should have.) You want to be in a position to withstand an unexpected large expense or temporary loss of income. On the other hand, if you use savings to pay down credit card debt, you can run your credit card balances back up in a financial pinch (unless your card gets cancelled), or you can turn to a family member or wealthy friend for a low-interest loan.

Discovering money to pay down consumer debts

Have you ever reached into the pocket of an old winter parka and found a rolled-up $20 bill you forgot you had? Stumbling across some forgotten funds is always a pleasant experience. But before you root through all your closets in search of stray cash to help you pay down that nagging credit card debt, check out some of these financial jacket pockets you may have overlooked:

- ✔ **Borrow against your cash-value life insurance policy.** If you were approached by a life insurance agent, she probably sold you a cash-value policy because it pays high commissions to insurance agents. Or perhaps your parents bought one of these policies for you when you were a child. Borrow against the cash value to pay down your debts. (*Note:* You may want to consider discontinuing your cash-value policy altogether and simply withdraw the cash balance — see Chapter 17 for details.)

- ✔ **Sell investments held outside of registered retirement plans.** Maybe you have some shares of stock or a Canada Savings Bond gathering dust in your safety deposit box. Consider cashing in these investments to pay down your consumer loans. Just be sure to consider the tax consequences of selling these investments. If possible, sell only those investments that won't generate a big tax bill.

- ✔ **Borrow against the equity in your home.** If you're a homeowner, you may be able to tap in to your home's *equity,* which is the difference between the property's market value and outstanding loan balance. You can generally borrow against real estate at a lower interest rate. Take care to ensure you don't overborrow on your home and risk losing it to your lender.

- ✔ **Borrow from friends and family.** They know you, love you, realize your shortcomings, and probably won't be as cold-hearted as some bankers. Money borrowed from family members can have strings attached, of course. Treating the obligation seriously is important. To avoid misunderstandings, write up a simple agreement listing the terms and conditions of the loan. Unless your family members are like the worst bankers we know, you'll probably get a fair interest rate, and your family will have the satisfaction of helping you out — just don't forget to pay them back.

Decreasing Debt When You Lack Savings

If you lack savings to throw at your consumer debts, not surprisingly, you have some work to do. If you're currently spending all your income (and more!), you need to figure out how you can decrease your spending (see Chapter 6 for lots of great ideas) or increase your income. In the meantime, you need to slow the growth of your debt.

Reducing your credit card's interest rate

Different credit cards charge different interest rates. So why pay 14, 16, or 18 percent (or more) when you can pay less? The credit card business is highly competitive. Until you get your debt paid off, slow the growth of your debt by reducing the interest rate you're paying. Here are sound ways to do that:

✔ **Apply for a lower-rate credit card.** If you're earning a decent income, you're not too burdened with debt, and you have a clean credit record, qualifying for lower-rate cards is relatively painless. Some persistence (and cleanup work) may be required if you have income and debt problems or nicks in your credit report. After you're approved for a new, lower-interest-rate card, you can simply transfer your outstanding balance from your higher-rate card.

Smaller financial institutions are often among the institutions with consistently low-interest-rate credit cards. Worth looking at are the low-rate cards offered by Alterna, Desjardins, and Laurentian Bank, as well as National Bank. Credit unions, including Vancity and Meridian Credit Union, also tend to have good low-rate cards. Most of the big banks now are offering low-rate cards as well. (As we point out in the section "Understanding credit card terms and conditions," when assessing low-rate cards make sure you consider the regular interest rate, not just the rate offered during the "introductory" period.)

✔ **Call the bank(s) that issued your current high-interest-rate credit card(s) and say that you want to cancel your card(s) because you found a competitor that offers no annual fee and a lower interest rate.** Your bank may choose to match the terms of the "competitor" rather than lose you as a customer. But be careful with this strategy, and consider just paying off or transferring the balance. Cancelling the credit card, especially if it's one you've had for a number of years, may lower your credit score.

✔ **While you're paying down your credit card balance(s), stop making new charges on cards that have outstanding balances.** Many people don't realize that interest starts to accumulate *immediately* when they carry a balance. You have no *grace period* — the 20 or so days you normally have to pay your balance in full without incurring interest charges — if you carry a credit card balance month to month.

Understanding credit card terms and conditions

Avoid getting lured into applying for a credit card that hypes an extremely low interest rate. One such card advertised a 1.9-percent rate, but you had to dig in to the fine print for the rest of the story.

First, any card that offers such a low interest rate will almost always honour that rate only for a short period of time — in this case, six months. After six months, the interest rate skyrocketed to nearly 15 percent.

But wait, there's more: Make just one late payment or exceed your credit limit, and the company raises your interest rate to 19.8 percent (or even 24 percent, 29 percent, or more) and slaps you with a $29 fee for each such infraction (some banks charge $39). If you want a cash advance on your card, you get socked with a fee equal to 3 percent of the amount advanced. (During the economic slowdown in the early 2000s, some banks were even advertising 0-percent interest rates — although that rate generally applied only to balances transferred from another card, and such cards were subject to all of the other vagaries discussed in this section.)

Now, we're not saying that everyone should avoid this type of card. Such a card may make sense for you if you want to transfer an outstanding balance and then pay off that balance within a matter of months, cancel the card, and avoid getting socked with the high fees on the card.

If you hunt around for a low-interest-rate credit card, be sure to check out all the terms and conditions. Start by reviewing the uniform rates and terms disclosure, which details the myriad fees and conditions (especially how much your interest rate can increase for missed or late payments). Also, be sure that you understand how the future interest rate is determined on cards that charge variable interest rates.

Cutting up your credit cards

If you have a pattern of living beyond your means by buying on credit, get rid of the culprit — the credit card. To kick the habit, a smoker needs to toss *all* the cigarettes, and an alcoholic needs to get rid of *all* the booze. Cut up *all* your credit cards and call the card issuers to cancel your accounts. And when you buy consumer items such as cars and furniture, do not apply for E-Z credit.

The world worked fine back in the years B.C. (Before Credit). Think about it: Just a couple generations ago, credit cards didn't even exist. People paid with cash and cheques — imagine that! You *can* function without buying anything on a credit card. In certain cases, you may need a card as collateral — such as when renting a car. When you bring back the rental car, however, you can pay with cash or a cheque. Leave the card at home in the back of your sock drawer or freezer, and pull (or thaw) it out only for the occasional car rental.

If you can trust yourself, keep a separate credit card *only* for new purchases that you know you can absolutely pay in full each month. No one needs three, five, or ten credit cards! You can live with one (and actually none), given the wide acceptance of most cards. Count 'em up, including retail store and gas cards, and get rid of 'em. Retailers such as department stores and gas stations just love to issue cards. Not only do these cards charge outrageously high interest rates, but they also are not widely accepted like Visa and MasterCard. Virtually all retailers accept Visa and MasterCard. More credit lines mean more temptation to spend what you can't afford.

If you decide to keep one widely accepted credit card instead of getting rid of them all, be careful. You may be tempted to let debt accumulate and roll over for a month or two, starting up the whole horrible process of running up your consumer debt again. Rather than keeping one credit card, consider exclusively using a debit card.

Discovering debit cards: The best of both worlds

Credit cards are the main reason today's consumers are buying more than they can afford. So logic says that one way you can keep your spending in check is to stop using your credit cards. But in a society that's used to the widely accepted Visa and MasterCard plastic for purchases, changing habits is hard. And you may be legitimately concerned that carrying your chequebook or cash can be a hassle or can be costly if you're mugged.

Debit cards truly offer the best of both worlds. The beauty of the debit card is that it offers you the convenience of making purchases with a piece of plastic without the temptation or ability to run up credit card debt. Debit cards keep you from spending money you don't have and help you live within your means. The big difference between debit cards and credit cards is that debit card purchase amounts are deducted electronically from your account the moment your purchase is approved.

If you switch to a debit card and you keep your account balance low and don't ordinarily balance your chequebook, you may need to start balancing it. Otherwise, you may face unnecessary bounced cheque charges.

Here are some other differences between debit and credit cards:

✔ **If you pay your credit card bill in full and on time each month, your credit card gives you free use of the money you owe until it's time to pay the bill.** Debit cards take the money out of your account almost immediately.

✔ **Credit cards make it easier for you to dispute charges for problematic merchandise through the issuing bank.** Most banks allow you to dispute charges for up to 60 days after purchase and will credit the disputed amount to your account pending resolution. Most debit cards offer a much shorter window, typically less than one week, for making disputes.

Getting Help from Not-for-Profit Credit Counselling Agencies

If your debt load is troubling you, consider contacting a not-for-profit credit counselling agency. Two umbrella organizations can help you find an approved agency in your area:

✔ Canadian Association of Credit Counselling Services
P.O. Box 189
Grimsby, ON L3M 4G3
800-263-0260
www.caccs.ca
info@ccacs.cas

✔ Credit Counselling Canada
720 Spadina Ave., Suite 202
Toronto, ON M5S 2T9
866-398-5999
www.creditcounsellingcanada.ca contact@ CreditCounsellingCanada.ca

Some credit counselling agencies are licensed by government departments, some are attached to Family Services departments, and some are independent. Their funding comes from a variety of different sources, including provincial governments, the United Way, local government, and creditors. Different offices have different funding arrangements.

The goal of non-profit credit counselling agencies is to offer no-cost (or low-cost) credit counselling. Depending on your situation, you may simply be given some ideas for free about how to manage your savings better, and assistance in budgeting. The agencies also put a strong emphasis on education to assist people in not continuing with debt-happy habits. A member organization can also contact creditors for you, set you up with a third-party mediator, or assist you in obtaining a consolidation loan.

Understanding debt management programs

If your situation warrants, credit counselling agencies can help work out a debt management program. (Typically, only about 10 percent of clients go this route.)

This would typically be recommended only if you were so deeply in debt you were unable to meet your minimum monthly payments and the interest was ballooning your outstanding debt.

In such cases, the counselling agency would work out your monthly living costs, which would include your mortgage, and determine what was left over. The agency would then negotiate with creditors to see if it can get them to stop any further interest charges or perhaps even reduce your debt.

You then make one monthly payment to the agency, which distributes the money to your various creditors. Depending on your situation, you may also be asked to pay a fee (which can range up to 10 percent of your payments) to the agency for its services in this case. Although enrolling in a debt-management program will affect your credit rating, your history is wiped clean two years after it is completed. By contrast, bankruptcy remains on your credit rating for seven years.

The usual maximum length of time you can take to repay your debts under such an arrangement is four years. If that isn't possible, bankruptcy may be a better choice.

If you have the resources to avoid a debt repayment plan, a credit counsellor should steer you away from this option because of the damage it does to your credit rating. On the other hand, if your situation is dire, counsellors should help you assess the very real benefits of bankruptcy.

If you're considering bankruptcy, first be sure to read the rest of this chapter. Second, interview any counselling agency you may be considering working with. Remember that you're the customer and you should do your homework first and be in control. Don't allow anyone or any agency to make you feel that they're in a position of power simply because of your financial troubles.

Beware potentially biased advice at credit counselling agencies

Leona Davis, whose family racked up significant debt due largely to unexpected medical expenses and a reduction in her income, found herself in trouble with too much debt. So she turned to one of the large, nationally promoted credit counselling services, which she heard about through its advertising and marketing materials.

The credit counselling agency Davis went to markets itself as a "non-profit community service." Davis, like many others we know, found that the "service" was not objective. After her experience, Davis feels that a more appropriate name for the organization she worked with would be the Credit Card Collection Agency. *We are in canada*

Unbeknownst to Davis — and many others — credit counselling agencies in the U.S. or based in the U.S. tend to get the vast majority of their funding from the fees that creditors pay them. These credit counselling agencies collect fees on a commission basis — just as collection agencies do! Their strategy is to place those who come in for help on their "debt management program." Under this program, counsellees like Davis agree to pay a certain amount per month to the agency, which in turn parcels out the money to the various creditors.

Because of Davis's tremendous outstanding consumer debt (it exceeded her annual income), her repayment plan was doomed to failure. Davis managed to make 10 months' worth of payments, largely because she raided a registered retirement account for $28,000. Had Davis filed bankruptcy (which she ultimately needed to do), she would've been able to keep her retirement money. But Davis's counsellor never discussed the bankruptcy option. "I received no counselling," says Davis. "Real counsellors take the time to understand your situation and offer options. I was offered one solution: a forced payment plan."

Others who have consulted similar agencies, including one of Eric's research assistants who, undercover, visited an office to seek advice, confirm that these types of agencies use a cookie-cutter approach to dealing with debt. Such agencies typically recommend that debtors go on a repayment plan that has the consumer pay, say, 3 percent of each outstanding loan balance to the agency, which in turn pays the money to creditors.

Unable to keep up with the enormous monthly payments, Davis finally turned to a lawyer and filed for bankruptcy — but not before she had unnecessarily lost thousands of dollars because of the biased recommendations.

Although their materials and counsellors aren't shy about highlighting the drawbacks to bankruptcy, their counsellors are reluctant to discuss the negative impact of signing up for a debt payment plan. Davis's counsellor never told her that restructuring her credit card payments would tarnish her credit reports and scores. The counsellor Eric's researcher met with also neglected to mention this important fact. When asked, the counsellor was evasive about the debt "management" program's impact on his credit report.

Avoiding debt management programs and asking questions

Probably the most important question to ask a counselling agency is whether it offers debt management programs (DMPs), where it puts you on a repayment plan with your creditors and gets paid a monthly fee for handling the payments. You do *not* want to work with an agency offering DMPs because of conflicts of interest. An agency can't offer objective advice about all your options for dealing with debt, including bankruptcy, if it has a financial incentive to put you on a DMP.

Here are some additional questions you should ask prospective counselling agencies you may hire:

- **What are your fees? Are there setup and/or monthly fees?** Get a specific price quote in writing.

- **What if I can't afford to pay your fees or make contributions?** If an organization won't help you because you truly can't afford to pay, the fees should be waived.

- **Do I have to sign a formal written agreement or contract with you?** Don't sign anything without reading it first. Make sure all verbal promises are in writing.

- **What kind of ongoing education do you provide?** If you're in financial difficulty it won't be solved overnight. You'll need to have ongoing education and counselling to be sure you'll be able to be financially stable over the long run.

- **Are you provincially licensed and accredited by Credit Counselling Canada or the Canadian Association of Credit Counselling Services?** Work only with a licensed and accredited agency.

- **How long have you been operating in the community?** Long-standing agencies have proven themselves to their clients, as without credibility they typically don't survive.

- **What are the qualifications of your counsellors? Are they certified by an outside organization? If so, by whom? If not, how are they trained?** Try to use an organization whose counsellors are trained by the Canadian Association of Credit Counselling Services.

- **What assurances can you give me that information about me (including my address, phone number, and financial information) will be kept confidential and secure?** Any reputable agency will provide you with a clearly written privacy policy.

> ✔ **How are your employees compensated? Are they paid more if I pay a fee, make a contribution, or sign up for certain services?** Employees who are paid depending on which options you choose are less likely to have your best interests in mind than those who earn a straight salary that isn't influenced by your choices.

Filing Bankruptcy

For consumers in over their heads, the realization that their monthly income is increasingly exceeded by their bill payments is usually a traumatic one. In many cases, years can pass before people consider drastic measures like filing bankruptcy. Both financial and emotional issues come into play in one of the most difficult and painful, yet potentially beneficial, decisions.

When Helen, a mother of two and a sales representative, contacted a lawyer, her total credit card debt equalled her annual gross income. As a result of her crushing debt load, she couldn't meet her minimum monthly credit card payments. Rent and food gobbled up most of her earnings. What little was left over went to the squeakiest wheel.

Creditors were breathing down Helen's back. "I started getting calls from collection departments at home and work — it was embarrassing," relates Helen. Helen's case is typical in that credit card debt was the prime cause of her bankruptcy.

As the debt load grew (partly exacerbated by the high interest rates on the cards), more and more purchases got charged — from the kids' clothing to repairs for the car. Finally, after running out of cash, she had to take a large cash advance on her credit cards to pay for rent and food.

Despite trying to work out lower monthly payments to keep everyone happy, most of the banks to which Helen owed money were inflexible. "When I asked one bank's Visa department if it preferred that I declare bankruptcy because it was unwilling to lower my monthly payment, the representative said yes," Helen says. After running out of options, Helen filed personal bankruptcy.

Eliminating your debt also allows you to start working toward your financial goals. Depending on the amount of debt you have outstanding relative to your income, you may need a decade or more to pay it all off. In Helen's case, at the age of 48 she had no money saved for retirement, and she was increasingly unable to spend money on her children.

[Handwritten margin note: Wrong. She was deceive + inthinking that out. was the only way out. Govement deception. When the third party. paid For it.]

Filing bankruptcy offers not only financial benefits but emotional benefits, as well. "I was horrified at filing, but it is good to be rid of the debts and collection calls — I should have filed six months earlier. I was constantly worried. When I saw homeless families come to the soup kitchen where I sometimes volunteer, I thought that someday that could be me and my kids," says Helen.

Understanding bankruptcy benefits

The point of bankruptcy is to give someone who is buried in debt a fresh start. When you declare bankruptcy, you assign (surrender) everything you own to someone who is licensed by the Superintendent of Bankruptcy to administer proposals and bankruptcies and to manage assets held in trust (called a *trustee in bankruptcy)* in exchange for the elimination of your debts. Annually, about 50,000 Canadian households (that's about 1 in every 200 households) file for personal bankruptcy.

With bankruptcy, certain types of debts can be completely eliminated, or *discharged.* Debts that typically can be discharged include credit card, medical, auto, utilities, and rent.

Debts that may *not* be cancelled generally include child support, alimony, taxes, and court-ordered damages. Helen was an ideal candidate for bankruptcy because her debts (credit cards) were dischargeable.

Also, because bankruptcy is a legal process, a *stay of proceedings* can prevent anybody from garnisheeing your income, and stops your creditors from calling.

Student loans

Student loans are generally not cancelled if bankruptcy is filed within seven years of completing your studies. (Prior to July 7, 2008, the limit was ten years.) You can, however, apply to be released from your student loans on the basis of financial hardship five years after you cease being a full- or part-time student. The court will likely discharge your student loans at that point if it is satisfied that you acted in good faith with respect to your student loan obligation, and that financial difficulty prevents you from repaying these debts. The court will also look at other factors including how you used your student loans, and your efforts to complete your studies.

Income tax debt

If you have more than $200,000 in personal income tax debt, and this is 75 percent or more of your total unsecured debts, you aren't eligible for an automatic discharge. (This new regulation came into effect September 18, 2009.) Instead, you have to request a court order to have your debts discharged.

Secured loans

Declaring personal bankruptcy deals only with unsecured creditors. A secured loan is money you've borrowed using an asset — a car or a house, for example — as a type of guarantee. If you don't repay the money you've borrowed, the lender can take possession of the asset. If you have a secured loan, the lender can simply repossess the asset.

In the case of car loans, the person going bankrupt can generally claim a provincial exemption and keep the vehicle. However, this requires continuing to make payments on the loan.

The roof over your head may also not be as secure as it first seems. Utilities are prevented from shutting your service off typically only during the winter months, and you may be required to pay a security deposit before they turn things back on. If you are a renter, bankruptcy can eliminate owed rent, but it doesn't prevent your landlord from proceeding to evict you. *land Lord*

One significant change brought in with the 2009 bankruptcy laws is that a secured lender can't terminate a contract simply because you've filed bankruptcy. If you have a car loan, for example, and your payments are up to date, you can generally keep the car and continue to make your loan payments. *JC*

TIP

They dont anything in Alberta

What you can keep when you file bankruptcy

You can retain certain property and assets even though you're filing for bankruptcy. In most provinces, you're allowed to keep a few thousand dollars' worth of personal effects. This generally includes clothing, jewellery, sports equipment, and so on. You can also hang on to furniture worth up to a total of $10,000 or so. You likely will also be able to keep a few thousand dollars' worth of the tools of your trade if such items are necessary for you to earn a living.

In addition, depending on the province that you live in, you may also be able to hang on to a vehicle worth no more than $5,000 or $6,000, assuming that you do not owe any money on

a car loan and you own the vehicle outright. You may also possibly retain a small amount of equity in your home. (One major exception is Alberta, which allows you to keep $40,000 worth of equity in your home.)

Thanks to the new bankruptcy rules, all Registered Retirement Savings Plans are protected and can't be seized (as of July 7, 2008). In addition to RRSPs, this includes Registered Retirement Income Funds (RRIFs) and Deferred Profit-Sharing Plans (DPSPs). However, any contributions made to an RRSP in the 12 months leading up to bankruptcy are not exempt.

Coming to terms with bankruptcy drawbacks

Filing bankruptcy, needless to say, has a number of drawbacks. First, bankruptcy appears on your credit report for anywhere from six to ten years, so you'll have difficulty obtaining credit, especially in the years immediately following your filing. However, if you already have problems on your credit report (because of late payments or a failure to pay previous debts), the damage has already been done. And without savings, you're probably not going to be making major purchases (such as a home) in the next several years anyway.

If you do file bankruptcy, getting credit in the future is still possible. You may be able to obtain a *secured credit card,* which requires you to deposit money in a bank account equal to the credit limit on your credit card. Of course, you'll be better off without the temptation of any credit cards and better served with a debit card. Also, know that if you can hold down a stable job, most creditors will be willing to give you loans within a few years of your filing bankruptcy. Almost all lenders ignore bankruptcy after five to seven years.

Another drawback of bankruptcy is that it costs money. We know this expense seems terribly unfair. You're already in financial trouble — that's why you're filing bankruptcy! Bankruptcy trustees are federally licensed, and their fees are regulated. Filing bankruptcy may set you back anywhere from several hundred dollars to $1,000 in court filing and legal fees. And, finally, most people find that filing bankruptcy causes emotional stress. Admitting that your personal income can't keep pace with your debt obligations is a painful thing to do. Although filing bankruptcy clears the decks of debt and gives you a fresh financial start, feeling a profound sense of failure (and sometimes shame) is common. Despite the increasing incidence of bankruptcy, bankruptcy filers are reluctant to talk about it with others, including family and friends.

Another part of the emotional side of filing bankruptcy is that you must open your personal financial affairs to court scrutiny and court control during the several months it takes to administer a bankruptcy. A court-appointed bankruptcy trustee oversees your case and tries to recover as much of your property as possible to satisfy the *creditors* — those to whom you owe money. Your assets can be sold, and the proceeds distributed to your creditors. In practice, though, the trustee will often make arrangements with you so that you can buy your assets back from your estate.

In addition, a portion of your income goes to your creditors, month in and month out. And if you happen to come into a lot of money before your bankruptcy is discharged, that too goes to the trustee to pay off your creditors.

[handwritten: 24 month the First time]
[handwritten: 36 month 2nd time]
[handwritten: New law]

After the paperwork is filed, you're officially "bankrupt" for nine months. Starting in September 2009, however, this period may be longer depending on your income. If your monthly net income is $200 or more over the allowable threshold, the bankruptcy period is extended by 12 months, to 21 months. Some people also feel that they're shirking responsibility by filing for bankruptcy. One client Eric worked with should have filed, but she couldn't bring herself to do it. She said, "I spent that money, and it's my responsibility to pay it back."

✦ Most banks make gobs and gobs of money from their credit card businesses. We can tell you that credit cards are one of the most profitable lines of business for banks. (Now you know why your mailbox is always filled with solicitations for more cards.) So if you file for bankruptcy, don't feel *too* bad about not paying back the bank. The nice merchants from whom you bought the merchandise have already been paid. *Charge-offs* — the banker's term for taking the loss on debt that you discharge through bankruptcy — are the banker's cost, which is another reason why the interest rate is so high on credit cards — and why you shouldn't borrow on credit cards.

Seeking bankruptcy advice

Be careful where you get advice about whether to file for bankruptcy. Trustees in bankruptcy who earn a fee from doing bankruptcy filings, for example, have a conflict of interest. All things being equal, their bias is to — you guessed it — *recommend bankruptcy,* which generates their fees.

If you want to learn more about the pros, cons, and details of filing for bankruptcy, pick up a copy of the *Bankruptcy Guide* by Earl Sands, published by Self-Counsel Press. Another good source of information is the Web site of the Office of the Superintendent of Bankruptcy at http://www.ic.gc.ca/eic/site/bsf-osb.nsf/Intro. The site includes a directory of trustees, as well as a helpful section called Alternatives to Bankruptcy.

Considering a Consumer Proposal: An Alternative to Bankruptcy

If your debts total $250,000 or less, a *consumer proposal* can be a good alternative to filing bankruptcy. With a consumer proposal, you can negotiate to repay only a portion of the money you owe. At the time you file your proposal, the debts covered by the proposal are frozen, and no more interest can be charged on them from that point on. In addition, your creditors are restricted from taking further legal action against you, and any garnishing of your wages is stopped (except for support and alimony payments).

A consumer proposal is similar to a debt repayment plan that a credit counselling agency might work out for you. It's an option when you have money coming in that will allow you to pay off a good portion of your debts but need more time to do so. Typically, a trustee assists you in assessing your assets and income, organizes a budget for you, and provides a few counselling sessions. Your trustee will present a detailed plan to your creditors detailing how much and when you'll pay them, to which the creditors have 45 days to respond. If a majority of your creditors accept the proposal, it is deemed to have been accepted by all of them. The agreement is legally binding.

A consumer proposal covers common unsecured debts, such as credit cards, lines of credit, and personal loans, as well as income taxes. In general, secured debt isn't covered under a consumer proposal. (*Secured debt* is money borrowed with an agreement that the lender can take possession of some of your property and sell it to recover their money if you fail to repay the loan.) In addition, alimony, child support, and legal fines aren't covered by the proposal. They remain payable in full.

Not in AI

A consumer proposal is often a sensible route to take, especially if you have a lot of assets and a regular income. In a regular bankruptcy, almost all your assets are sold. Under a consumer proposal, that may not be necessary if your creditors are willing to settle for a piece of your paycheque.

A consumer proposal is likely to be accepted only if your unsecured lenders foresee getting paid more than they would if you file bankruptcy. Also, some lenders may prefer you to file bankruptcy as it is a much more short-term, finite process for them. In contrast, under a consumer proposal you can arrange to spread your payments out over as much as five years. After you have completed your payments under the proposal, a record of the agreement remains in your credit history for two years.

Stopping the Spending/Consumer Debt Cycle

Regardless of how you deal with paying off your debt, you're in real danger of falling back into old habits. Backsliding happens not only to people who file bankruptcy but also to those who use savings or home equity to eliminate their debt. This section speaks to that risk and tells you what to do about it.

Resisting the credit temptation

Getting out of debt can be challenging, but we have confidence that you can do it with this book by your side. In addition to the ideas we discuss earlier in this chapter (such as eliminating all your credit cards and getting a debit card), the following list provides some additional tactics you can use to limit the influence credit cards hold over your life. (If you're concerned about the impact that any of these tactics may have on your credit rating, please see Chapter 2.)

- ✔ **Reduce your credit limit.** If you're not going to take the advice we give you earlier in this chapter and get rid of all your credit cards or switch to a debit card, be sure to keep a lid on your credit card's credit limit (the maximum balance allowed on your card). You don't have to accept the increase just because your bank keeps raising your credit limit to reward you for being such a profitable customer. Call your credit card service's toll-free phone number and lower your credit limit to a level you're comfortable with.

- ✔ **Replace your credit card with a debit card.** With a debit card, you can't make a purchase unless the money is in your account. You have no credit line or interest charges.

- ✔ **Never buy anything on credit that depreciates in value.** Meals out, cars, clothing, and shoes all depreciate in value. Don't buy these things on credit. Borrow money only for sound investments — education, real estate, or your own business, for example.

- ✔ **Think in terms of total cost.** Everything sounds cheaper in terms of monthly payments — that's how salespeople entice you into buying things you can't afford. Take a calculator along, if necessary, to tally up the sticker price, interest charges, and upkeep. The total cost will scare you. *It should.*

- ✔ **Stop the junk mail avalanche.** Look at your daily mail — we bet half of it is solicitations and mail-order catalogues. You can save some trees and time sorting junk mail by removing yourself from most mailing lists.

To remove your name from mailing lists, contact the Canadian Marketing Association and register with their Do Not Contact service. You can write them at 1 Concord Gate, Suite 607, Don Mills, ON M3C 3N6, or reach them by phone at 416-391-2362. You can also register through the association's Web site at www.the-cma.org.

To reduce unwanted telemarketing calls, register your phone number with the National Do Not Call List (DNCL) operated by the Canadian government. For more information, visit www.lnnte-dncl.gc.ca or call 866-580-DNCL (3625).

To remove your name from the major credit reporting agency lists that are used by credit card solicitation companies, call 888-567-8688.

Also, tell any credit card companies you keep cards with that you want your account marked to indicate that you don't want any of your personal information shared with telemarketing firms.

✔ **Limit what you can spend.** Go shopping with a small amount of cash and no plastic or cheques. That way, you can spend only what little cash you have with you!

Identifying and treating a compulsion

No matter how hard they try to break the habit, some people become addicted to spending and accumulating debt. It becomes a chronic problem that starts to interfere with other aspects of their lives and can lead to problems at work and with family and friends.

Debtors Anonymous (DA) is a non-profit organization that provides support (primarily through group meetings) to people trying to break their debt accumulation and spending habits. DA is modelled after the 12-step Alcoholics Anonymous (AA) program.

Like AA, Debtors Anonymous works with people from all walks of life and socioeconomic backgrounds. You can find people who are financially on the edge, $100,000-plus income earners, and everybody in between at DA meetings. Even former millionaires join the program.

DA has a simple questionnaire that helps determine whether you're a problem debtor. If you answer "yes" to at least 8 of the following 15 questions, you may be developing or already have a compulsive spending and debt accumulation habit:

✔ Are your debts making your home life unhappy?

✔ Does the pressure of your debts distract you from your daily work?

✔ Are your debts affecting your reputation?

✔ Do your debts cause you to think less of yourself?

✔ Have you ever given false information in order to obtain credit?

✔ Have you ever made unrealistic promises to your creditors?

✔ Does the pressure of your debts make you careless when it comes to the welfare of your family?

✔ Do you ever fear that your employer, family, or friends will learn the extent of your total indebtedness?

✔ When faced with a difficult financial situation, does the prospect of borrowing give you an inordinate feeling of relief?

✔ Does the pressure of your debts cause you to have difficulty sleeping?

✔ Has the pressure of your debts ever caused you to consider getting drunk?

✔ Have you ever borrowed money without giving adequate consideration to the rate of interest you're required to pay?

✔ Do you usually expect a negative response when you're subject to a credit investigation?

✔ Have you ever developed a strict regimen for paying off your debts, only to break it under pressure?

✔ Do you justify your debts by telling yourself that you are superior to the "other" people, and when you get your "break," you'll be out of debt?

To find a Debtors Anonymous (DA) support group in your area, check your local phone directory (in the "Business" section), or visit the DA Web site at www.debtorsanonymous.org. You can write to DA's headquarters for meeting locations in your area and a literature order form at the following address: Debtors Anonymous General Service Office, P.O. Box 920888, Needham, MA 02492-0009. You can also contact the DA's national headquarters by phone at 781-453-2743. If you live outside an area that has meetings, you can still benefit from the group by participating in telephone meetings and online chats. Details are provided on the DA Web site.

Chapter 6

Reducing Your Spending

. . . .

In This Chapter

▶ Getting the most for your money

▶ Increasing your savings

▶ Controlling and cutting costs

. . . .

*T*elling people how and where to spend their money is a risky undertaking, because most people like to spend money and hate to be told what to do. You'll be glad to hear that we don't tell you exactly where you must cut your spending in order to save more and accomplish your personal and financial goals. Instead, we detail numerous strategies that we have seen work for other people. The final decision for what to cut rests solely on you. Only you can decide what's important to you and what's dispensable.

We assume throughout these recommendations that you value your time. Therefore, we don't tell you to scrimp and save by doing things like cutting open a tube of toothpaste so that you can use every last bit of it. And we don't tell you to have your spouse do your ironing to reduce your dry-cleaning bills — no point in having extra money in the bank if your significant other walks out on you!

The fact that you're busy all the time may be part of the reason you spend money as you do. Therefore, the recommendations in this chapter focus on methods that produce significant savings but don't involve a lot of time. In other words, these strategies provide bang for the buck.

Finding the Keys to Successful Spending

For most people, spending money is a whole lot easier and more fun than earning it. Far be it from us to tell you to stop having fun and turn into a penny-pinching, stay-at-home miser. Of course you can spend money. But there's a world of difference between spending money carelessly and spending money *wisely*.

If you spend too much and spend unwisely, you put pressure on your income and your future need to continue working. Savings dwindle, debts may accumulate, and you can't achieve your financial goals.

If you dive in to details too quickly, you may miss the big picture. So before we jump into the specific areas where you can trim your budget, we give you our four overall keys to successful spending. These four principles run through our recommendations in this chapter.

Living within your means

Spending too much is a *relative* problem. Two people can each spend $40,000 per year yet still have drastically different financial circumstances. How? Suppose that one of them earns $50,000 annually, while the other makes $35,000. The $50,000 income earner saves $10,000 each year. The $35,000 wage earner, on the other hand, accumulates $5,000 of new debt (or spends that amount from prior savings). So, spend within your means.

Certain people — and you know who they are — bring out the big spender in you. Do something else with them besides shopping and spending. If you can't find any other activity to share with them, try shopping with limited cash and no credit cards. That way, you can't overspend on impulse.

How much you can safely spend while working toward your financial goals depends on what your goals are and where you are financially. Chapter 4 assists you with figuring how much you should be saving and what you can afford to spend while still accomplishing your financial goals.

Looking for the best values

You can find high quality and low cost in the same product. Conversely, paying a high price is no guarantee that you're getting high quality. Cars are a good example. Whether you're buying a subcompact, a sports car, or a luxury four-door sedan, some cars are more fuel-efficient and cheaper to maintain than rivals that carry the same sticker price.

When you evaluate the cost of a product or service, think in terms of total, long-term costs. Suppose you're comparing the purchase of two used cars: the Solid Sedan, which costs $21,995, and the Clunker Convertible, which weighs in at $18,995. On the surface, the convertible appears to be cheaper. However, the price that you pay for a car is but a small portion of what that car ultimately costs you. If the convertible is costly to operate, maintain, and insure over the years, it could end up costing you much more than the sedan would. Sometimes, paying more upfront for a higher-quality product or service ends up saving you money in the long run.

People who sell particular products and services may initially appear to have your best interests at heart when they steer you toward something that isn't costly. However, you may be in for a rude awakening when you discover the ongoing service, maintenance, and other fees you face in the years ahead. Salespeople are generally trained to pitch you a lower-cost product if you indicate that's what you're after.

Don't waste money on brand names

You don't want to compromise on quality, especially in the areas where quality is important to you. But you also don't want to be duped into believing that brand-name products are better or worth a substantially higher price. Be suspicious of companies that spend gobs on image-oriented advertising. Why? Because heavy advertising costs many dollars, and as a consumer of those companies' products and services, you pay for all that advertising.

All successful companies advertise their products. Advertising is cost-effective and good business if it brings in enough new business. But you need to consider the products and services and the claims that companies make.

Branding is used in many fields to sell overpriced, mediocre products and services to consumers. Does a cola beverage really taste better if it's "the real thing" or "the choice of a new generation"? Consider all the silly labels and fluffy marketing of beers. When it comes to mainstream beers, blind taste testing demonstrates little if any difference between the more expensive brand-name products and the cheaper, less heavily advertised ones. And yes, that means we believe the notion of value extends to drinking one good microbrewery pale ale rather than two bubbly near-water marketing juggernauts.

Take the lowly can of paint. When you can buy high-quality paints for about $20 to $30 a gallon, do you really think that a $50 — or $100! — can of paint blessed with the name of Martha Stewart or Ralph Lauren is that much better? D/L Laboratories, a testing firm, compared these expensive snooty paints to $20-per-gallon high-quality alternatives and found no difference that was worth paying for. In fact, one of the "gourmet" paints splattered more, had a less uniform sheen, didn't cover the surface as well, was more prone to run when applied, and emitted a high level of volatile compounds! Some other high-brow brands didn't fare much better. As people in the trade can tell you, if you find a particular colour of paint you like in a pricey brand-name line, thanks to computer-based matching you can match it at a far lower cost.

Now, if you can't live without your Coca-Cola or Coors Light, and you think that these products are head and shoulders above the rest, drink them to your heart's content. But question the importance of the name and image of the products you buy. Companies spend a lot of money creating and cultivating an image, which has zero impact on how their products taste or perform.

Get your money back

Take a look around your home for items you never use. Odds are you have some (maybe even many). Returning such items to where you bought them can be cathartic; it also reduces your home's clutter and puts more money in your pocket.

Also, think about the last several times you bought a product or service and didn't get what was promised. What did you do about it? Most people do nothing and let the derelict company off the hook. Why? Here are some common explanations for this type of behaviour:

- ✔ **Low standards:** Consumers have come to expect shoddy service and merchandise because of the common lousy experiences they've had.

- ✔ **Conflict avoidance:** Most people shun confrontation. It makes them tense and anxious, and it churns their stomachs.

- ✔ **Hassle aversion:** Most companies don't make it easy for complainers to get their money back or obtain satisfaction. To get restitution from some companies, you need the tenacity and determination of a pit bull.

You can increase your odds of getting what you expect for your money by doing business with companies that:

- ✔ **Have fair return policies:** Don't purchase any product or service until you understand the company's return policy. Be especially wary of buying from companies that charge hefty "restocking" fees for returned merchandise or simply don't allow returns at all. Reputable companies offer full refunds and don't make you take store credit (although taking credit is fine if you're sure that you'll use it soon and that the company will still be around).

- ✔ **Can provide good references:** Suppose you're going to install a fence on your property, and, as a result, you're going to be speaking with fencing contractors for the first time. You can sift out many inferior firms by asking each contractor that you interview for at least three references from people in your local area who have had a fence installed in the past year or two.

- ✔ **Are committed to the type of product or service they provide:** Suppose your chosen fencing contractor does a great job, and now that you're in the market for new gutters on your home, the contractor says that he does gutters, too. Although the path of least resistance would be to simply hire the same contractor for your gutters, you should inquire about how many gutters the contractor has installed and also interview some other firms that specialize in such work. Because your fencing contractor may have done only a handful of gutter jobs, he may not know as much about such work.

Following these guidelines can greatly diminish your chances of having unhappy outcomes with products or services you buy. And here's another important tip: Whenever possible, pay with a credit card if your credit's in good standing. Doing so enables you to dispute a charge within 60 days and gives you leverage for getting your money back.

Recognizing the Better Business Bureau's conflicts of interest

The Better Business Bureau (BBB) states that its mission is "to promote and foster the highest ethical relationship between businesses and the public." The reality of the typical consumer's experience of dealing with the BBB doesn't live up to the BBB's marketing. BBBs are non-profits and are not agencies of any governmental body.

"They don't go after local established businesses — they are funded by these same businesses. The BBB certainly has a good public relations image, better than what is warranted. They don't do all that much for consumers," says veteran consumer advocate Ralph Nader.

"It's a business trade organization, and each local BBB is basically independent like a franchise," says John Bear, an author of consumer advocacy books including *Send This Jerk the Bedbug Letter: How Companies, Politicians, and the Mass Media Handle Complaints & How to Be a More Effective Complainer* (Ten Speed Press). "By and large, when somebody has a problem with a company and they fill out a complaint form with the BBB, if the company is a member of the BBB, there's ample evidence that consumers often end up not being satisfied. The BBB protects their members."

Particularly problematic among the BBB's pro-business practices are the company reports the BBB keeps on file. The BBB often considers a legitimate complaint satisfactorily resolved even when you're quite unhappy and the company is clearly not working to satisfy the problems for which it's responsible.

Bear also cites examples of some truly troubling BBB episodes. In one case, he says that a diploma mill (a company that sells degrees but provides little, if any, education) in Louisiana was a member of the local BBB. "When complaints started coming in," says Bear, "the BBB's response was always that the company met their standards and that the complaints were resolved. The reality was that the complaints weren't satisfactorily resolved, and it took about two years until complaints reached into the hundreds for the BBB to finally cancel the diploma mill's membership and give out a bland statement about complaints. Two months later, the FBI raided the company. Millions of consumers' dollars were lost because the BBB didn't do its job."

The Toronto office of the BBB also has had its share of troubles. In the late nineties, the branch was engulfed in a spending scandal, including the finding of a forensic audit that the then-president had been given a $1 million "termination" package and immediately rehired. In 2000, a former director and chair of the Toronto BBB was found guilty of securities violations. The office had its licence revoked by the governing body in 2001. The truth about some BBBs is unfortunate, because as consumer protection agencies are being hit by cutbacks, and dissatisfied consumers are being shunted to the BBB, more people are in for unsatisfactory experiences with an organization that does not go to bat for them.

If you find that you're unable to make progress when trying to get compensation for a lousy product or service, here's what we recommend you do:

- ✔ **Document:** Taking notes whenever you talk to someone at a company can help you validate your case down the road, should problems develop. Obviously, the bigger the purchase and the more you have at stake, the more carefully you should document what you've been promised. In many cases, though, you probably won't start carefully noting each conversation until a conflict develops. Keep copies of companies' marketing literature, because such documents often make promises or claims that companies fail to live up to in practice.

- ✔ **Escalate:** Some frontline employees either aren't capable of resolving disputes or lack the authority to do so. No matter what the cause, speak with a department supervisor and continue escalating from there. For every conversation you have along the way, record the name and the position of the person, the points you raised, and any advice, direction, or promises made by the company representative. If you're still not making progress, lodge a complaint to whatever regulatory agency (if any) oversees such companies. Also, be sure to tell your friends and colleagues not to do business with the company (and let the company know that you're doing this until your complaint is resolved to your satisfaction). And consider contacting a consumer help group — these groups are typically sponsored by broadcast or print media in metropolitan areas. They can be helpful in resolving disputes or shining adverse publicity on disreputable companies or products.

- ✔ **Litigate:** If all else fails, consider taking the matter to small claims court if the company continues to be unresponsive. (Depending on the amount of money at stake, this tactic may be worth your time.) The maximum dollar limit that you may recover in most provinces is $25,000. For larger amounts than those allowed in small claims court in your province, you can, of course, hire a lawyer and pursue the traditional legal channels — although you may end up throwing away more of your time and money. Mediation and arbitration are generally a better option than following through on a lawsuit.

Eliminating the fat from your spending

If you want to reduce your overall spending by, say, 10 percent, you can just cut all of your current expenditures by 10 percent. Or you can reach your 10-percent goal by cutting some categories a lot and others not at all. You need to set priorities and make choices about where you want and don't want to spend your money.

What you spend your money on is sometimes a matter of habit rather than what you really want or value. For example, some people shop at whatever stores are close to them.

Eliminating fat doesn't necessarily mean cutting back on your purchases: You can save money by buying in bulk. Some stores specialize in selling larger packages or quantities of a product at a lower price because they save money on the packaging and handling. If you're single, shop with a friend and split the bulk purchases.

Turning your back on consumer credit

As we discuss in Chapters 3 and 5, buying items that depreciate — such as cars, clothing, and vacations — on credit is hazardous to your long-term financial health. Buy only what you can afford today. If you'll be forced to carry a debt for months or years on end, you can't really afford what you're buying on credit today.

Without a doubt, *renting to own* is the most expensive way to buy. Here's how it works: You see a huge ad blaring "$12.95 for a Blu-ray player!" Well, the ad has a big hitch: That's $12.95 per week, for many weeks. When all is said and done (and paid), buying a $100 Blu-ray player through a rent-to-own store costs a typical buyer more than $375!

Welcome to the world of rent-to-own stores, which offer cash-poor consumers the ability to lease consumer items and, at the end of the lease, an option to buy.

If you think that paying a 20-percent interest rate on a credit card is expensive, consider this: The effective interest rate charged on many rent-to-own purchases exceeds 100 percent; in some cases, it may be 200 percent or more! Renting to own makes buying on a credit card look like a great deal.

We're not sharing this information to encourage you to buy on credit cards, but to point out what a ripoff renting to own is. Such stores prey on cashless consumers who either can't get credit cards or don't understand how expensive renting to own really is. Forget the instant gratification, and save a set amount each week until you can afford what you want.

Budgeting to Boost Your Savings

When most people hear the word *budgeting,* they think unpleasant thoughts — like those the word *dieting* brings to mind — and rightfully so. But budgeting can help you move from knowing how much you spend on various things to successfully reducing your spending.

The first step in the process of *budgeting,* or planning your future spending, is to analyze where your current spending is going (refer to Chapter 3). After you do that, calculate how much more you'd like to save each month. Then comes the hard part: deciding where to make cuts in your spending.

Suppose you're currently not saving any of your monthly income and you want to save 10 percent for retirement. If you can save and invest through a tax-sheltered retirement savings plan, you don't actually need to cut your spending by 10 percent to reach a savings goal of 10 percent (of your gross income).

When you contribute money to a Registered Retirement Savings Plan (RRSP), you reduce your federal and provincial taxes. If you're a moderate-income-earner paying, say, 35 percent in taxes on your marginal income, you actually need to reduce your spending by only 6.54 percent to save 10 percent. The "other" 3.5 percent of the savings comes from the lowering of your taxes. (The higher your tax bracket, the less you need to cut your spending to reach a particular savings goal.)

So to boost your savings rate to 10 percent, go through your current spending category by category until you come up with enough proposed cuts to reduce your spending by 6 or 7 percent. Make your cuts in the areas that will be the least painful and where you're getting the least value from your current level of spending. Another method of budgeting involves starting completely from scratch rather than examining your current expenses and making cuts from that starting point. Ask yourself how much you'd like to spend on different categories. The advantage of this approach is that it doesn't allow your current spending levels to constrain your thinking. You'll likely be amazed at the discrepancies between what you think you should be spending and what you actually are spending in certain categories.

Reducing Your Spending

As you read through the following strategies for reducing your spending, please keep in mind that some of these strategies will make sense for you and some of them won't. Start your spending reduction plan with the strategies that come easily. Work your way through them. Keep a list of the options that are more challenging for you — ones that may require more of a sacrifice but be workable if necessary to achieve your spending and savings goals.

No matter which of the ideas in this chapter you choose, rest assured that keeping your budget lean and mean pays enormous dividends. After you implement a spending reduction strategy, you'll reap the benefits for years to come. Take a look at Figure 6-1: For every $1,000 that you shave from your annual spending (that's just $83 per month), check out how much more money you'll have down the road. (This chart assumes that you invest your newfound savings in an RRSP, you average 10-percent-per-year returns on your investments, and you're in a moderate combined federal and provincial tax bracket of 35 percent — see Chapter 7 for information on tax brackets.)

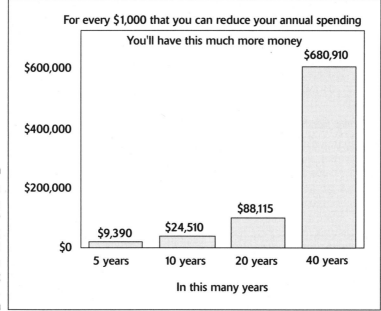

For every $1,000 that you can reduce your annual spending

You'll have this much more money

$680,910

$600,000

$400,000

$200,000

$88,115

$24,510

$9,390

$0

5 years | 10 years | 20 years | 40 years

In this many years

Figure 6-1:
Reducing
your
spending
can yield
large
investment
sums.

Managing food costs

Not eating is one way to reduce food expenditures; however, this method tends to make you weak and dizzy, so it's probably not a viable long-term strategy. The following culinary strategies can keep you on your feet — perhaps even improve your health — and help you save money.

Eating out frugally

Eating meals out and getting takeout can be timesavers, but they rack up big bills if done too often and too lavishly. Eating out is a luxury — think of it as hiring someone to shop, cook, and clean up for you. Of course, some people either hate to cook or don't have the time, space, or energy to do much in the kitchen. If this sounds like you, choose restaurants carefully and order from the menu selectively.

Consider the following tips for eating out:

- ✔ **Avoid beverages, especially alcohol.** Most restaurants make huge profits on beverages. Drink water instead. (Water is healthy, and it reduces the likelihood that you'll want a nap after a big meal.)

- ✔ **Order vegetarian.** Vegetarian dishes generally cost less than meat-based entrees (and they're generally better for you).

We're not trying to be killjoys here. We're not saying you should live on bread and water. You can have dessert — heck, have some wine, too, for special occasions! Just try not to eat dessert with every meal. Try eating appetizers and dessert at home, where they're a lot less expensive.

Also, consider finding out more about how to cook. Folks who eat out a lot do so in part because they don't really know how to cook.

Eating healthy at home without spending a fortune

As evidenced by the preponderance of diet and weight loss books on the bestseller lists — and the growth of natural and organic departments in grocery stores — Canadians are trying to eat healthier. Concerned about all the pesticides, antibiotics, and hormones that end up in the food supply, Canadians are increasing their organic food purchases at a fast rate.

Problem is, financially speaking, better quality food, especially organic food, can cost more — sometimes much more, but not always. A number of studies we've seen demonstrate that highly processed foods, which are less nutritious and worse for your health, can be as costly or even more expensive than fresh, so-called whole foods. The key to not overspending on fresher, healthier, and organic foods is to be flexible when you're at the grocery store. Buy more of what is currently less expensive, and stock up on sale items that aren't perishable.

According to various studies, spending the money to buy organic makes the most sense and offers you the best health benefits when buying the following foods:

- ✔ **Produce:** Apples, bell peppers, celery, cherries, hot peppers, imported grapes, nectarines, peaches, pears, potatoes, red raspberries, spinach, and strawberries have historically been found to carry the greatest amount of pesticides, even after washing.

- ✔ **Meat, poultry, eggs, and dairy:** By going organic, you avoid supplemental hormones and antibiotics. You also greatly reduce the risk of exposure to the agent believed to cause mad cow disease and minimize exposure to other potential toxins in non-organic feed.

- ✔ **Baby food:** Baby food is typically loaded with condensed fruits and vegetables, thus concentrating pesticide residues. Also, children's small and developing bodies are especially vulnerable to toxins.

One area where many folks are wasting money is in buying bottled water. Although tap water often does leave something to be desired, bottled water is typically not as pure as some folks think. You can save hundreds of dollars annually and drink cleaner water by installing a water filtration system at home and improving your tap (or well) water.

Joining a wholesale superstore

Superstores such as Costco enable you to buy groceries in bulk at wholesale prices. And contrary to popular perception, you don't have to buy 1,000 rolls of toilet paper at once — just 24.

We've performed price comparisons between wholesale superstores and retail grocery stores and found that wholesalers charge about 30 percent less for the exact same stuff — all without the hassle of clipping coupons or hunting for which store has the best price on paper towels this month! And despite being cheaper, the quality and freshness in these stores is often far superior to that found in regular grocery chains. (At these discount prices, you only need to buy about $150 per year to recoup the membership fees to stores like Costco, which start at around $50.)

In addition to saving you lots of money, buying in bulk requires fewer shopping trips. You'll have more supplies around your humble abode — so you'll have less need to eat out (which is costly) or make trips (which wastes time and gasoline) to the local grocer, who may be really nice but charges the most.

Perishables run the risk of living up to their name, so buy only what you can reasonably use. Repackage bulk packs into smaller quantities and store them in the freezer if possible. If you're single, shop with a friend and split the order. Also, be careful when you shop at the warehouse clubs — you may be tempted to buy things you don't really need. These stores carry all sorts of items, including the newest high-definition TVs, computers, furniture, clothing, complete sets of baseball cards, and giant canisters of biscotti — so wallet and waistline beware! Try not to make impulse purchases, and be especially careful when you have kids in tow.

To find a superstore near you, check your local phone directory. You can also find a Costco store near you by visiting the Costco Web site at www. costco.ca or calling 800-463-3783.

One of the biggest problems with superstores like Costco is they are tremendously car-dependent. It's hard to stuff a bargain-priced bag of 24 rolls of toilet paper into a knapsack to carry it home! And because superstores tend to be located in outlying areas, they are often difficult if not impossible to get to by transit. Don't forget to factor in the extra transportation costs — and the wear-and-tear on the planet — when assessing the value of shopping at such superstores.

Saving on shelter

Housing and all the costs associated with it (utilities, furniture, appliances, and, if you're a homeowner, maintenance and repairs) can gobble a large chunk of your monthly income. We're not suggesting that you live in a tent or a tree fort (though they would be less costly), but like many people you may be overlooking opportunities to save money in this category.

Reducing rental costs

Rent can take up a sizeable chunk of your monthly take-home pay. Many people consider rent to be a fixed and inflexible part of their expenses, but it's not. If you're renting, here's what you can do to cut down your costs:

- ✔ **Move to a lower-cost rental.** Of course, a lower-cost rental may not be as nice — it may be smaller, lack a private parking spot, or be located in a less popular area. Remember that the less you spend renting, the more you can save toward buying your own place. Just be sure to factor in all the costs of a new location, including the possible higher commuting costs.

- ✔ **Share a rental.** Living alone has some benefits, but financially speaking, it's a luxury. If you rent a larger place with roommates, your rental costs will go way down, and you'll get more home for your rental dollars. You have to be in a sharing mood, though. Roommates can be a hassle at times, but they can also be a plus — you get to meet all sorts of new people, and you have someone else to blame when the kitchen's a mess.

- ✔ **Negotiate your rental increases.** Every year, like clockwork, your landlord bumps up your rent by a certain percentage. If your local rental market is soft or your living quarters are deteriorating, stand up for yourself! You have more leverage and power than you probably realize. A smart landlord doesn't want to lose good tenants who pay rent on time. Filling vacancies takes time and money. State your case: You've been a responsible tenant, and your research shows comparable rentals going for less. Crying "poor" may help, too. At the very least, if you can't stave off the rent increase, maybe you can wrangle some improvements to the place.

- ✔ **Buy rather than rent.** Purchasing your own place may seem costly, but in the long run owning should be cheaper than renting, and you'll have something to show for it in the end. If you purchase real estate with a 25-year fixed-rate mortgage, your mortgage payment (which is your biggest ownership expense) will bounce around somewhat as overall interest rates rise and fall. Only your property taxes, maintenance, and insurance costs will generally steadily rise, because they are exposed to the vagaries of inflation.

   As a renter, however, your entire monthly housing cost can rise with increases in the cost of living (unless you're the beneficiary of a rent-controlled apartment). See Chapter 14 to find out the smart way to buy real estate.

Reducing homeowner expenses

As every homeowner knows, houses suck up money. Be especially careful to watch your money in this area of your budget.

- **Know what you can afford.** Don't make the mistake of overspending when buying a home. Whether you're on the verge of buying your first home or trading up to a more costly property, crunch some realistic numbers before you commit. If too little money is left over for your other needs and wants — such as taking trips, eating out, enjoying hobbies, or saving for retirement — your new dream house may become a financial prison.

  Calculate how much you can afford to spend monthly on a home. Do the exercises in Chapter 3, on where you're spending your money, and Chapter 4, on saving for retirement, to help you calculate the amount you can afford.

  Although real estate can be a good long-term investment, you can end up pouring a large portion of your discretionary dollars into your home. In addition to decorating and remodelling, some people feel the need to trade up to a bigger home every few years. Of course, after they're in their new home, the remodelling and renovation cycle simply begins again, which costs even more money. Most home renovations or remodels will never recoup anything close to what they cost. In addition, a major remodel may result in higher property taxes, as well as higher homeowner's insurance costs. Appreciate what you have, and remember that homes are for living in, not museums for display. If you have children, why waste a lot of money on expensive furnishings that take up valuable space and require you to constantly nag your kids to tread carefully? And don't covet — the world will always have people with bigger houses and more toys than you.

- **Rent out a room.** Because selling your home to buy a less expensive place can be a big hassle, consider taking in a tenant (or charge those adult "children" still living at home!) to reduce your housing expenses. Check out the renter thoroughly: Get references, run a credit report, and talk about ground rules and expectations before sharing your space. Don't forget to check with your insurance company to see whether your homeowner's policy needs adjustments to cover potential liability from renting.

- **Appeal your property-tax assessment.** If you bought your property when housing prices were higher in your area than they are now, you may be able to save money by appealing your assessment. If you live in an area where your assessment is based on how the local assessor valued the property (rather than what you paid for your home), your home may be overassessed.

  Check with your local assessor's office for the appeals procedure you need to follow. An appraiser's recent evaluation of your property may help. Review how the assessor valued your property compared with similar ones nearby — mistakes happen.

✔ **Reduce utility costs.** Sometimes you have to spend money to save money. Old refrigerators, for example, can waste a lot of electricity. Insulate to save on heating and air-conditioning bills. Install water flow regulators in shower heads. When planting your yard, don't select water-guzzling plants, and keep your lawn area reasonable. Even if you don't live in an area susceptible to droughts, why waste water (which isn't free) unnecessarily? Recycle — recycling means less garbage, which translates into lower trash bills (because you won't be charged for using larger garbage containers) and benefits the environment by reducing landfill. (Of course, reducing the use of plastics and other recyclables in the first place is best for the environment.)

Cutting transportation costs

Canada remains a car-driven — and car-centric — society. In most other countries, cars are a luxury. If more people in Canada (and the U.S.) thought of cars as a luxury, we might have far fewer financial problems (and accidents). Not only do cars pollute the air and clog the highways, but they also cost you a bundle.

Purchasing a quality car and using it wisely can save you money. Using other transportation alternatives can also help you save.

Contrary to advertising slogans, cars aren't built to last; manufacturers don't want you to stick with the same car year after year. New models are constantly introduced with new features and styling changes. Getting a new set of wheels every few years is an expensive luxury. Don't try to keep up with the Joneses as they show off their new cars every year — for all you know, they're running themselves into financial ruin trying to impress others. Let your neighbours admire you for your thriftiness and wisdom instead.

Research before you buy a car

When you buy a car, you don't just pay the initial sticker price: You also have to pay for gas, insurance, registration fees, maintenance, and repairs. You may also have to pay sales tax and GST/HST. Don't compare simple sticker prices; think about the total, long-term costs of car ownership.

Speaking of total costs, remember that you're also trusting your life to the car. With about 3,500 Canadians killed in auto accidents annually (about one-third of drivers killed are legally impaired), safety should be an important consideration as well. Air bags, for example, may save your life.

Consumer Reports publishes a number of useful buying guides for new and used cars. You can find *Consumer Reports* on the Internet at `www.consumer reports.org`. Check out the annual *Lemon-Aid* books put out by Phil Edmonston for a detailed assessment of defects, repair costs, and safety ratings. He has different titles dealing with new cars, used cars, new trucks and vans, and used trucks and vans (including minivans). The books also detail average resale prices by model and year. For you data jocks, IntelliChoice (`www.intellichoice.com`) provides information about all categories of ownership costs, warranties, and dealer costs for new cars, which are rated based on total ownership costs. Edmunds (`www.edmunds.com`) provides more general information about different makes and models of both new and used cars. Please be aware that these latter two sites have advertising and may receive referral fees if you buy a car through a dealer their Web site refers you to.

Don't lease, don't borrow: Buy your car with cash

The main reason people end up spending more than they can afford on a car is that they finance the purchase. As we discuss in Part I, you should avoid borrowing money for consumption purchases, especially for items that depreciate in value (like cars). A car is most definitely *not* an investment.

Leasing is generally more expensive than borrowing money to buy a car. Leasing is like a long-term car rental. Everyone knows how well rental cars get treated — leased cars are treated just as well, which is one of the reasons leasing is so costly.

Unfortunately, the practice of leasing cars or buying them on credit is increasingly becoming the norm in our society. This approach is certainly attributable to a lot of the misinformation that's spread by car dealers and, in some cases, the media. Consider the magazine article titled "Rewards of Car Leasing." The article claims that leasing is a great deal when compared to buying. Ads for auto dealers advertising auto leasing are placed next to the article. The magazine, by the way, is free to subscribers — which means that 100 percent of its revenue comes from advertisers such as auto dealers. Also be aware that because of the influence of advertising (and ignorance), leasing is widely endorsed on Web sites that purport to provide information on cars.

"But I can't buy a new car with cash," you may be thinking. Some people feel that it's unreasonable of us to expect them to use cash to buy a new car, but we're trying to look out for your best long-term financial interests. Please consider the following:

✔ If you lack sufficient cash to buy a new car, we say, don't buy a new car! Most of the world's population can't even afford a car, let alone a new one! Buy a car that you can afford — which for most people is a used one.

✔ Don't fall for the rationale that says buying a used car means lots of maintenance, repair expenses, and problems. Do your homework and buy a good quality used car (see the preceding section, "Research before you buy a car"). That way, you can have the best of both worlds. A good used car costs less to buy and, thanks to lower insurance costs, less to operate.

✔ You don't need a fancy car to impress people for business purposes. Some people we know say that they absolutely must drive a nice, brand-spanking-new car to set the right impression for business purposes. We're not going to tell you how to manage your career, but we will ask you to consider that if clients and others see you driving an expensive new car, they may think that you spend money wastefully or you're getting rich off of them!

Replace high-cost cars

Maybe you realize by now that your car is too expensive to operate because of insurance, gas, and maintenance costs. Or maybe you bought too much car — people who lease or borrow money for a car frequently buy a far more expensive car than they can realistically afford.

Sell your expensive car and get something more financially manageable. The sooner you switch, the more money you'll save. Getting rid of a car on a lease is a challenge, but it can be done. We know of one person who, when he lost his job and needed to slash expenses, convinced the dealer (by writing a letter to the owner) to take the leased car back.

Use regular unleaded gas

A number of studies have shown that "super-duper-ultrapremium" gasoline isn't worth the extra expense. Make sure you buy gasoline that has the minimum octane rating recommended for your vehicle (consult your owner's manual), but paying more for the higher octane "premium" gasoline just wastes money. Your car doesn't run better; you just pay more for gas. Also, don't use credit cards to buy your gas if you have to pay a higher price to do so.

Service your car regularly

Sure, servicing your car (for example, changing the oil every 5,000 or 10,000 kilometres) costs money, but it saves you dough in the long run by extending the operating life of your car. Servicing your car also reduces the chance that your car will conk out in the middle of nowhere, which requires a humongous towing charge to a service station. Stalling on the highway during peak rush hour and having thousands of angry commuters stuck behind you is even worse.

Keep cars to a minimum

We've seen households that have one car per person — four people, four cars! Some people have a "weekend" car that they use only on days off! For most households, maintaining two or more cars is an expensive extravagance. Try to find ways to make do with fewer cars.

You can move beyond the confines of owning a car by either carpooling or riding buses or trains to work. Some employers give incentives for taking public transit to work, and some cities and municipalities offer assistance for setting up vanpools or carpools along popular routes. By leaving the driving to someone else, you can catch up on reading or just relax on the way to and from work. You also help reduce pollution.

When you're considering the cost of living in different areas, don't forget to factor in commuting costs. One advantage of living close to work, or at least close to public transit systems, is that you may be able to make do with fewer cars (or no car at all) in your household.

Use a car-sharing service

If you need a car — or access to a second car — only occasionally, consider signing up for a car-sharing service. For a small monthly or yearly membership fee, you get access to the service's fleet. You can book cars over the phone or online. Rather than having a lot of vehicles in a few major locations, car-sharing services try to make it easy for you by having a few vehicles in a whole lot of locations. If you're lucky, there may be a location just a few blocks' walk away.

One of the bigger players is Zipcar (www.zipcar.com), but many smaller regional companies exist. In British Columbia, look for the Co-operative Auto Network (www.cooperativeauto.net), and in Quebec, CommunAuto (www.communauto.com). Some car-sharing services focus on a single urban centre, like Toronto's AutoShare (www.autoshare.com).

Check out www.carsharing.ca, which maintains a list of car-sharing services across the country.

Buy commuter passes

In many areas, you can purchase train, bus, or subway passes to help reduce the cost of commuting. Many toll bridges also have booklets of tickets or passes that you can buy at a discount. Electronic passes help you keep moving, and eliminate sitting in toll collection lines that waste your time and gas. There is also a federal tax credit for money spent on weekly or monthly transit passes and electronic payment cards. The tax credit will cut the cost of transit passes and cards by around 15 percent.

Go by bike

Biking is a great way to get around. You don't spend on gas, you don't pollute, and you get some exercise! And, especially at rush hour, gently pedalling home and taking in the sights from your saddle is no doubt less stressful than fighting bumper-to-bumper traffic. Many Canadian cities have finally come around to the fact that if they build bike paths, people will bike more. Go online or contact your area's biking association to find the most hassle-free bikes routes to follow. Spend a little on comfortable, warm biking clothes, and you'll find it's often possible to bike the whole year 'round, except for those days when a big rain or snowstorm strikes. Pressure local politicians to support more and better-protected bike lanes. The more people bicycling in a city, the safer everybody is.

Lowering your energy costs

Escalating energy prices remind us all how much we depend upon and use oil, electricity, and natural gas in our daily lives. A number of terrific Web sites are packed with suggestions and tips for how to lower your energy costs. Before we present those to you, however, here are the basics:

- **Drive fuel-efficient cars.** If you're safety minded, you know how dangerous driving can be, and may avoid the gas-sipping pint-size vehicles. But you can drive safe — and often small — cars that are fuel-efficient (see the section "Research before you buy a car").

- **Be thrifty at home.** Get all family members on the same page, without driving them crazy, to turn off lights they don't need. Turn down the heat at night, which saves money and helps you sleep better, and turn it down when no one is home. *Hint:* If people are walking around your home during the winter with shorts on instead of wearing sweaters, turn the heat down!

- **Service and maintain what you have.** Anything that uses energy — from your cars to your furnace — should be regularly serviced. For instance, make sure you clean your filters.

- **Investigate energy efficiency before you buy.** This advice applies not only to appliances but also to an entire home. Some builders are building energy efficiency into their new homes.

The following are our favourite Web sites for energy information and tips:

- Natural Resources Canada's Office of Energy Efficiency (`http://oee.nrcan-rncan.gc.ca`)

- The U.S. Department of Energy's Energy Efficiency & Renewable Energy (`www.energysavers.gov`)

Controlling clothing costs

Given the amount of money that some people spend on clothing and related accessories, we've come to believe that people in nudist colonies must be great savers! But you probably live among the clothed mainstream of society, so here's a short list of economical ideas:

- ✔ **Avoid clothing that requires dry cleaning.** When you buy clothing, try to stick with cottons and machine-washable synthetics rather than wools or silks that require dry cleaning. Check labels before you buy clothing.

- ✔ **Don't chase the latest fashions.** Fashion designers and retailers are constantly working to tempt you to buy more. Don't do it. Ignore publications that pronounce this season's look. In most cases, you simply don't need to buy racks of new clothes or an entire new wardrobe every year. If your clothes aren't lasting at least ten years, you're probably tossing them before their time or buying clothing that isn't very durable.

  True fashion, as defined by what people wear, changes quite slowly. In fact, the classics never go out of style. If you want the effect of a new wardrobe every year, store last year's purchases away next year and then bring them out the year after. Or rotate your clothing inventory every third year. Set your own fashion standards. Buy basic, and buy classic — if you let fashion gurus be your guide, you'll end up with the biggest wardrobe in the poorhouse!

- ✔ **Minimize accessories.** Shoes, jewellery, handbags, and the like can gobble large amounts of money. Again, how many of these accessory items do you really need? The answer is probably very few, because each one should last many years.

Go to your closet or jewellery box and tally up the loot. What else could you have done with all that cash? Do you see things you regret buying or forgot you even had? Don't make the same mistake again. Have a garage sale if you have a lot of stuff that you don't want. Return recent unused purchases to stores.

Repaying your debt

In Chapter 5, we discuss strategies for reducing the cost of carrying consumer debt. The _best_ way to reduce the costs of such debt is to avoid it in the first place when you're making consumption purchases.

You can avoid consumer debt by eliminating your access to credit or by limiting your purchase of consumer items to what you can pay off each month. Borrow only for long-term investments (see Chapter 2 for more information).

Don't keep a credit card that charges you an annual fee, especially if you pay your balance in full each month. Many no-fee credit cards exist — and some even offer you a benefit for using them.

A number of cards offer a straight 1 percent cash rebate on all your spending, including Citi Enrich MasterCard and MBNA Premier Rewards Platinum Plus MasterCard. But read the fine print, as some pay out the full 1 percent only after your spending in the year passes a certain level. The CIBC 1% Dividend Visa, for example, pays only 0.25 percent on the first $1,500 of spending and 0.50 percent on the next $1,500. The 1 percent rebate applies on your spending only when you've passed the $3,000 mark. Some other cards to consider are:

- ✔ **Canadian Tire Cash Advantage MasterCard (800-347-2683).** Like the CIBC card mentioned above, this card has a stepped reward system. You'll earn 0.25 percent on the first $1,500 in purchases, 0.5 percent on purchases above $1,500 and up to $3,000, 1 percent on purchases above $3,000, and 1.5 percent on purchases above $24,000. You earn double those reward levels on purchases at Canadian Tire stores and gas bars, as well as Mark's Work Wearhouse.

- ✔ **Costco TrueEarnings American Express (800-463-3783).** On regular purchases, the rebate is 0.25 percent for the first $1,000 a year, 0.50 percent on the next $2,000, and 1 percent for purchases over $3,000. You also get a 2 percent rebate on your first $3,000 of eligible gas purchases in a year, and 1 percent on any further gas charges. A 3 percent rebate on eligible restaurant purchases is also available.

- ✔ **President's Choice Financial MasterCard (888-872-4724).** For each dollar you spend you get 10 PC points. When you have 20,000 points, you can redeem the points for groceries. The rebate works out to 1 percent.

Consider the cards in the preceding list only if you pay your balance in full each month, because no-fee cards typically don't offer the lowest interest rates for balances carried month-to-month. The small rewards that you earn really won't do you much good if they're more than wiped out by interest charges.

If you have a credit card that charges an annual fee, try calling the company and saying you want to cancel the card because you can get a competitor's card without an annual fee. Many banks will agree to waive the fee on the spot. Some require you to call back yearly to cancel the fee — a hassle that can be avoided by getting a true no-fee card.

Some cards that charge an annual fee and offer credits toward the purchase of a specific item, such as a car or airline ticket, may be worth your while if you pay your bill in full each month and charge $10,000 or more annually. *Note:* Be careful — you may be tempted to charge more on a card that rewards you for more purchases. Spending more in order to rack up bonuses defeats the purpose of the credits.

Indulging responsibly in fun and recreation

Having fun and taking time out for R and R can be money well spent. But when it comes to fun and recreation, financial extravagance can wreck an otherwise good budget.

Entertainment

If you adjust your expectations, entertainment doesn't have to cost a great deal of money. Many movies, theatres, museums, and restaurants offer discount prices on certain days and times.

Cultivate some interests and hobbies that are free or low-cost. Visiting with friends, hiking, reading, and playing sports can be good for your finances as well as your health.

Vacations

For many people, vacations are a luxury. For others, regular vacations are essential parts of their routine. Regardless of how you recharge your batteries, remember that vacations aren't investments, so you shouldn't borrow through credit cards to finance your travels. After all, how relaxed will you feel when you have to pay all those bills?

Try taking shorter vacations that are closer to home. Have you been to a provincial or national park recently? Take a vacation at home, visiting the sites in your local area. Great places that you've always wanted to see but haven't visited for one reason or another are probably located within 300 kilometres of you. Or you may want to just block out some time and do what family pets do: Relax around your home and enjoy some naps.

If you do travel a long way to a popular destination, travel during the off-season for the best deals on airfares and hotels. Keep an eye out for discounts and "bought-but-unable-to-use" tickets advertised in your local paper.

Numerous Web sites can help you find low-cost travel options as well. Some of the sites we suggest are:

- ✔ www.belairtravel.com
- ✔ www.cheapflights.ca
- ✔ www.expedia.ca
- ✔ www.flightcentre.ca
- ✔ www.itravel2000.com
- ✔ www.selloffvacations.com
- ✔ www.travelocity.ca

Also, be sure to shop around, even when working with a travel agent. Travel agents work on commission, so they may not try hard to find you the best deals. Tour packages, when they meet your interests and needs, can also save you money. If you have flexible travel plans, courier services can cut your travel costs significantly (but make sure that the company is reputable).

Gifts

Think about how you approach buying gifts throughout the year — especially during the holidays. We know people who spend so much on their credit cards during the year-end holidays that it takes them until late spring or summer to pay their debts off!

Although we don't want to deny your loved ones gifts from the heart — or deny you the pleasure of giving them — spend wisely. Homemade gifts are less costly to the giver and may be dearer to recipients. Many children actually love durable, classic, basic toys. If the TV commercials dictate your kids' desires, it may be time to toss the TV or set better rules for what the kids are allowed to watch. Use services that let you record desired shows so you can zap through the ubiquitous commercials.

Some people forget their thrifty shopping habits when gift-buying, perhaps because they don't like to feel cheap when buying a gift. As with other purchases you make, paying careful attention to where and what you buy can save you significant dollars. Don't make the mistake of equating the value of a gift with its dollar cost.

And here's a good suggestion for getting rid of those old, unwanted gifts: Hold a holiday party, and have a *white elephant* gift exchange: Everyone brings a wrapped, unwanted gift from the past and exchanges it with someone else. After the gifts are opened, trading is allowed. (Just be sure not to bring a gift that was given to you by any of the exchange participants!)

Lowering your phone bills

Because of improved technology and increased competition, telephoning costs continue to fall. However, Canadians still face some of the highest bills in the world thanks to our longstanding tradition of limiting new players and allowing ruses like the recently abandoned "system access fee," which phone companies positioned as a required regulatory fee. It actually was nothing of the kind (despite the strange fact that many different phone companies charged their customers exactly the same amount each month!), and when consumer pressure grew to be too much the fictitious "fee" was quietly abandoned.

Making calls over the Internet (VoIP), using services such as Skype, is also quickly becoming a viable low-cost choice. While VoIP doesn't yet match the quality or reliability of landlines or cell service, it's still a great option if you regularly make long-distance calls, particularly to family and friends in another country or on another continent.

If you haven't looked for lower rates in recent years, you're probably paying more than you need to for quality phone service. Unfortunately, shopping among the many service providers is difficult. Plans come with different restrictions, minimums, and bells and whistles. To save on your phone bills, begin by looking at your phone company's other calling plans. You may have to switch companies to reduce your bill, but we find that many people can save significantly with their current phone company simply by getting on a better calling plan. So before you spend hours shopping around, contact your current local and long distance providers and ask them which of their calling plans offer the lowest cost for you based on the patterns of your calls. Cellphones are ubiquitous. And although being able to make calls from wherever you are can be enormously convenient, you can spend a lot of money for service given the myriad extra charges. On the other hand, if you're able to take advantage of the free minutes many plans offer (on weekends, for example), a good cellphone service can save you money.

In addition to downloads, text messaging, Web surfing, and other services, kids (and adults) can find all sorts of entertaining ways to run up huge cellphone bills each month. Also, we hear a lot of complaints from parents about kids talking too much and going over their minute allowances and racking up large extra-usage charges.

The primary reason why some parents elect to provide a cellphone to their teenage children is for safety — the ability to call home for a ride, and so on. Thus, you don't need all of the costly bells and whistles. A cellphone need only be set up to place and receive calls.

To avoid the extra costs of exceeding the minutes allowed under a plan, you have a few options:

✔ **Examine family plan options that don't limit minutes so strictly.** Shop around and make sure you sign up with the best calling plan and carrier given your typical usage. Reputable carriers let you test out their services. They also offer full refunds if you're not satisfied after a week or two of service.

✔ **Set and enforce limits.** If you provide a cellphone to a child, keep in mind that kids don't need to talk for hours.

✔ **Check out prepaid plans that have no contract obligation.** Costs start as low as 10 cents per minute for calls, and you pay only for what you use. If you typically use a few hundred minutes per month or less, you should save money with one of these plans. Look at companies like TracFone or Virgin Mobile.

Here are some sites that can help you assess and compare different plans:

✔ www.cellphone.ca

✔ www.cellphoneratecalculator.com

✔ www.comparecellular.com

✔ www.telecomparisons.com

A thoughtful letter is usually cheaper, more appreciated, and longer lasting than a phone call. Just block out an hour, grab a pen and paper, and rediscover the lost art form of letter writing. Formulating your thoughts on paper can be clarifying and therapeutic. Computer users may find that they can also save money by sending e-mail.

Spending wisely on technology

We've got e-mail, cellphones, smart phones, voice mail, satellite TV, the Internet, and too many other ways to stay in touch and entertained 24/7. Visit a store that sells electronics, and you'll find no end to new gadgets.

Although we enjoy choices and convenience as much as the next person, we also see the detrimental impact these technologies have on people's lives. As it is, most families struggle to find quality time together given their work obligations, long school days, and various other activities. At home, all these technology choices and options compete for attention and often pull families apart. The cost for all these services and gadgets adds up, leading to continued enslavement to your career. Err on the side of keeping your life simple. Doing so costs less, reduces stress, and allows more time for the things that really do matter in life.

Especially when it comes to new technology and gadgets, don't be among the first to get something. HDTV is a good example why — in the early years, these new television sets were extremely costly and more prone to problems. Now, prices are down substantially, and sets are more reliable.

The worst way to shop for electronics and technology-based products is to wander around stores that sell lots of these goods and having a salesperson pitch you things. These folks are trained in what buttons to push to get you to whip out your Visa card and be on your way with things you don't know how you ever could've lived without. Educate yourself and determine what you really need instead of going to a store and being seduced by a salesperson.

Read articles — *Consumer Reports* is a helpful publication. CNET (www.cnet.com) is also a useful source.

Curtailing personal care costs

You have to take care of yourself, but as with anything else, you can find ways to do it that are expensive, and you can find ways that save you money. Try this money-saving advice:

✔ **Hair care:** Going bald is one way to save money in this category. Eric is working on this one himself. In the meantime, if you have hair to be trimmed, a number of no-frills, low-cost hair-cutting joints can do the job. Supercuts is one of the larger hair-care chains. You may insist that your stylist is the only one who can manage your hair the way you like it. At the prices charged by some of the trendy hair places, you have to really adore what they do to justify the cost. Consider going periodically to a no-frills stylist for maintenance after getting a fabulous cut at a more expensive place. If you're daring, you can try getting your hair cut at a local training school.

For parents of young children, buying a simple-to-use home haircutting electric shaver (such as Wahl's) can be a great time- and money-saver — no more agonizing trips with little ones to have their hair cut by a "stranger." The kit pays for itself after just two haircuts!

✔ **Other personal-care services:** As long as we're on the subject of outward beauty, we have to say that, in our personal opinion, the billions spent annually on cosmetics are largely a waste of money (not to mention all the wasted time spent applying and removing them). Women look fine without makeup. (In most cases, they look better.) And having regular facials, pedicures, and manicures can add up quickly.

✔ **Health club expenses:** Money spent on exercise is almost always money well spent. But you don't have to belong to a trendy club to receive the benefits of exercise. If you belong to a gym or club for the social scene (whether for dating or business purposes), you have to judge whether it's worth the cost.

Local schools, colleges, and universities often have tennis courts, running tracks, swimming pools, basketball courts, and exercise rooms, and they may provide instruction as well. Community centres offer fitness programs and classes, too. Metropolitan areas that have lots of health clubs undoubtedly have the widest range of options and prices. *Note:* When figuring the cost of membership, be sure to factor in the cost of travel to and from the club, as well as any parking costs (and the realistic likelihood of going there regularly to work out).

Don't forget that healthy exercise can be done indoors or out, free of charge. Isn't hiking in the park at sunset more fun than pedalling away on a stationary bike, anyway? You may want to buy some basic gym equipment for use at home. Be careful, though: Lots of rowing machines and weights languish in a closet after their first week at home.

Paring down professional expenses

Accountants, lawyers, and financial advisers can be worth their expense if they're good. But be wary of professionals who create or perpetuate work and have conflicts of interest in their recommendations.

Make sure you get organized before meeting with professionals for tax, legal, or financial advice. Do some background research to evaluate their strengths and biases. Set goals and estimate fees in advance so you know what you're getting yourself into.

Computer and printed resources (see Chapters 20 and 21) can be useful, low-cost alternatives and supplements to hiring professionals.

Managing medical expenses

Healthcare is a big topic nowadays. The cost of healthcare is going up fast, and more and more basic services that were once covered by provincial plans now need to be paid out of your own pocket. If you are eligible for your province's health insurance plan, it will generally cover most of your basic healthcare needs. But you typically have to pay many costs yourself, including dental, vision, and chiropractic. (Chapter 17 explains how to shop for health insurance.)

Medical care and supplies are like any other services and products — prices and quality vary. And medicine in Canada, like any other profession, is a business. A conflict of interest exists whenever the person recommending treatment benefits financially from providing that treatment. Many studies have documented some of the unnecessary surgeries and medical procedures that have resulted from this conflict of interest. And remember, even if a particular service is covered by your provincial healthcare plan, you are still paying for it through your taxes.

Therapy can be useful and even lifesaving. Have a frank talk with your therapist about how much total time and money you can expect to spend and what kind of results you can expect to receive. As with any professional service, a competent therapist gives you a straight answer if he is looking out for your psychological and financial well-being.

Alternative medicine (holistic, for example) is gaining attention because of its focus on preventive care and the treatment of the whole body or person. Although alternative medicine can be dangerous if you're in critical condition, alternative treatment for many forms of chronic pain or disease may be worth investigating. Alternative medicine may lead to better *and* lower-cost healthcare.

If you have to take certain drugs on an ongoing basis and pay for them out-of-pocket, ordering through a mail-order company can bring down your costs and help make refilling your prescriptions more convenient. If you have a supplemental healthcare plan, the administrators should be able to provide more information about this option.

Examine your employer's benefit plans. Make sure you pay close attention to the "use it or lose it" provisions of each plan.

Eliminating costly addictions

Human beings are creatures of habit. Everybody has habits they wish they didn't have, and breaking those habits can be very difficult. Costly habits are the worst. The following tidbits may nudge you in the right direction toward breaking your own financially draining habits.

✔ **Kick the smoking habit.** Despite the decline in smoking over the past few decades, almost one in five Canadians still smokes. The smokeless tobacco habit, which also causes long-term health problems, is on the increase. Canadians spend about $6 billion annually on tobacco products. Someone who smokes a pack a day will spend over $3,600 a year on cigarettes. The increased medical costs and the costs of lost work time are even greater, estimated at anywhere from $3 billion to $7 billion a year. (Of course, if you continue to smoke, you may eliminate the need to save for retirement.)

Check with local hospitals for smoking-cessation programs. If you want to quit, the Canadian Cancer Society (888-939-3333; www.cancer.ca) offers a self-help program, along with a hotline. The Society can also refer you to local programs. The Canadian Lung Association (888-566-5864; www.lung.ca) offers tips on how to quit and can refer you to provincial associations, many of which offer programs to help you stop smoking.

✔ **Stop abusing alcohol and other drugs.** Thousands of Canadians seek treatment annually for alcoholism or drug abuse. These addictive behaviours, like spending, transcend all educational and socioeconomic lines in our society. Even so, studies have demonstrated that only one in seven alcohol or drug abusers seek help. Three of the ten leading causes of death — cirrhosis of the liver, accidents, and suicides — are associated with excessive alcohol consumption.

To find a local Alcoholics Anonymous chapter, look in the telephone book or visit `www.alcoholics-anonymous.org`. For drug addiction, start by contacting your provincial ministry of health. You can also dig up lists of sources for help online. One good example is Ontario's Drug and Alcohol Registry of Treatment (`www.dart.on.ca`). Another starting point is the Centre for Addiction and Mental Health (`www.camh.net`).

✔ **Don't gamble.** The house *always* comes out ahead in the long run. Why do you think so many governments run lotteries? Because governments make money on people who gamble, that's why.

Casinos, horse and dog racetracks, and other gambling establishments are sure long-term losers for you. So, too, is the short-term trading of stocks, which isn't investing but gambling. Getting hooked on the dream of winning is easy. And sure, occasionally you win a little bit (just enough to keep you coming back). Every now and then, a few folks win a lot. But your hard-earned capital mostly winds up in the pockets of the casino owners.

If you gamble just for the entertainment, take only what you can afford to lose. Gamblers Anonymous (213-386-8789; `www.gamblersanonymous.org`) helps those for whom gambling has become an addiction. The Web site also provides listings of meeting times and locations across the country.

Keeping an eye on insurance premiums

Insurance is a vast minefield. In Part IV, we explain the different types of coverage, suggest what to buy and avoid, and detail how to save on policies. The following list explains the most common ways people waste money on insurance:

✔ **Keeping low deductibles.** The *deductible* is the amount of a loss that must come out of your pocket. For example, if you have an auto insurance policy with a $100 collision deductible and you get into an accident, you pay for the first $100 of damage, and your insurance company picks up the rest. Low deductibles, however, translate into much higher premiums for you. In the long run, you save money with a higher deductible, even when factoring in the potential for greater out-of-pocket costs to you when you do have a claim. Insurance should protect you from economic disaster. Don't get carried away with a really high deductible, which can cause financial hardship if you have a claim and lack savings.

If you have a lot of claims, you won't come out ahead with lower deductibles, because your insurance premiums will escalate. Plus, low deductibles mean more claim forms to file for small losses (creating more hassle). Filing an insurance claim usually isn't an enjoyable or quick experience.

✔ **Covering small potential losses or unnecessary needs.** You shouldn't buy insurance for anything that won't be a financial catastrophe if you have to pay for it out of your own pocket. Although the postal service isn't perfect, insuring inexpensive gifts sent in the mail isn't worth the price. And if no one's dependent on your income, you don't need life insurance either. (Who'll be around to collect when you're gone?)

✔ **Failing to shop around.** Rates vary *tremendously* from insurer to insurer. In Part IV, we recommend the best companies to call for quotes and other cost-saving strategies.

Trimming your taxes

Taxes are probably one of your largest — if not *the* largest — expenditures. (So why is it last here? Read on to find out.)

Retirement savings plans are one of the best and simplest ways to reduce your tax burden. (We explain more about retirement savings plans in Chapter 12.) Unfortunately, most people can't take full advantage of these plans because they spend everything they make. So not only do they have less savings, but they also pay higher income taxes — a double whammy.

We've attended many presentations where a fast-talking investment guy in an expensive suit lectures about the importance of saving for retirement and explains how to invest your savings. Yet details and tips about finding the money to save (the hard part for most people) are left to the imagination.

In order to take advantage of the tax savings that come through retirement savings plans, you must first spend less than you earn. Only then can you afford to contribute to these plans. That's why the majority of this chapter is about strategies to reduce your spending.

Reduced sales tax is another benefit of spending less and saving more. When you buy most consumer products, you either pay a provincial sales tax and the GST or a combined tax, the Harmonized Sales Tax (HST). Therefore, when you spend less money and save more in retirement plans, you reduce your income and your sales taxes. (See Chapter 7 for detailed tax-reduction strategies.)

Cellphones and kids can be a dangerous mix

Everywhere you look these days it seems as if every teen (and just as often, every adult) has a cellphone. Cellphones are a great way for parents to keep in contact with their children, especially in emergencies. Along with cellphones come important safety issues when teens get caught up in using cellphones. Keep the following in mind:

✔ A number of studies have raised concerns about the impact of repeated cellphone usage on the brain and the possible linkage between brain tumours and usage of cellphones held near the side of one's head. Getting teens who talk on the phone a lot to use earpieces connected to the cellphone is easier said than done.

✔ A second health concern with cellphone usage is the common occurrence of older teens doing things with their phones while driving. Horrible accidents have happened not only with teens fiddling with their phones while placing and receiving calls but also while typing out text messages and doing other things on the phone. Although increasing numbers of provinces have implemented laws requiring cellphone users to have hands-free devices, few have any laws dealing with texting and other similar driving distractions.

Chapter 7

Trimming Your Taxes

. . . .

In This Chapter

▶ Understanding the importance of marginal tax rates

▶ Reducing employment income taxes and increasing your deductions and credits

▶ Lowering investment income taxes

▶ Getting help from tax resources and handling an audit notice

. . . .

*Y*ou pay a lot of money in taxes — probably more than you realize. Few people know just how much they pay in taxes each year. Most people remember whether they received a refund or owed money on their return. But when you file your tax return, all you're doing is settling up with tax authorities over the amount of taxes you paid during the year versus the total tax that you owe based on your income and deductions.

Understanding the Taxes You Pay

Some people feel lucky when they get a refund, but all a refund really indicates is that you overpaid in taxes during the year. You should have had this money in your own account all along. If you're consistently getting big refunds, you need to pay less tax throughout the year.

Instead of focusing on whether you're going to get a refund when you complete your annual tax return, you should concentrate on the total taxes you pay, which we discuss in the following section.

Focusing on your total taxes

To find out the *total* taxes you pay, get out your tax return. On the federal T1 General form, there will be a line called "Total payable." On recent returns, this is line 435. Next, subtract any credits — including your provincial tax credits — deducted from your total tax payable, except for tax that you've already had deducted (line 437) or tax you paid in instalments (line 476). The resulting number you'll see is probably one of your largest expenses.

The goal of this chapter is to help you legally and permanently reduce your total taxes. Understanding the tax system is the key to reducing your tax burden — if you don't, you'll surely pay more taxes than necessary. Your tax ignorance can lead to mistakes, which can be costly if the CRA catches your underpayment errors. With the proliferation of computerized information and data tracking, discovering mistakes has never been easier.

The tax system, like other public policy, is built around incentives to encourage desirable behaviour and activity. For example, saving for retirement is considered desirable because it encourages people to prepare for a time in their lives when they may be less able or interested in working so much and when they may have additional expenses for needed healthcare. Therefore, the government offers all sorts of tax perks, which we discuss later in this chapter, to encourage people to save in retirement plans.

Not all people follow the path the government encourages — after all, it's a free country. However, the *fewer* desirable activities you engage in, the more you pay in taxes. If you understand the options, you can choose the ones that meet your needs as you approach different stages of your financial life.

Recognizing the importance of your marginal tax rate

When it comes to taxes, *not all income is treated equally.* This fact is far from self-evident. If you work for an employer and earn a constant salary during the course of a year, a steady and equal amount of taxes is deducted from each paycheque. Thus, it appears as though all that earned income is being taxed equally.

In reality, however, you pay less tax on your first dollars of earnings and more tax on your *last* dollars of earnings. For example, if you're single and your taxable income (a term we define in the next section) totalled $45,000 during 2009, you would not pay any tax on the first $10,319 because of a tax credit that offsets the tax on that income. Your combined federal and provincial tax rate would be approximately 24 percent on income from $10,320 to $40,726. Your tax rate would be 36 percent on income between $40,727 and $81,452, 42 percent on income from $81,453 to $126,264, and 46 percent on income over $126,264.

Table 7-1 gives the approximate combined federal and provincial tax rates. (Your actual marginal bracket may be somewhat higher or lower, depending on the tax rate in your province.)

Table 7-1	Approximate 2009 Combined Federal and Provincial Income Tax Brackets and Rates
Taxable Income	**Tax Rate (Bracket)**
$0–$10,319	0% (Due to tax credit)
$10,320–$40,726	24%
$40,727–$81,452	36%
$81,453–$126,264	42%
Over $126,264	46%

Your *marginal tax rate* is the rate of tax you pay on your *last,* or so-called *highest,* dollars of income. In the example of a single person with taxable income of $45,000, that person's marginal tax rate is 36 percent. In other words, she effectively pays 36 percent tax on her last dollars of income — those dollars in excess of $40,726.

Marginal tax rates are a powerful concept. Your marginal tax rate allows you to quickly calculate the additional taxes you'd have to pay on additional income. Conversely, you can delight in quantifying the amount of taxes you save by reducing your taxable income, either by decreasing your income or by increasing your deductions.

Defining taxable income

Taxable income is the amount of income on which you actually pay income taxes. (In the sections that follow, we explain strategies for reducing your taxable income.) The following reasons explain why you don't pay taxes on your total income:

- ✔ **Not all income is taxable.** For example, any profit you make when you sell the home you live in — your principal residence — generally isn't taxable. Neither is the profit you earn on money invested inside tax-favoured plans such as RRSPs and Tax-Free Savings Accounts. (If you earn interest on money outside such accounts, it's taxed at the same rate as your regular employment income. Other income, such as that from stock dividends and long-term capital gains, is taxed at lower rates.)

- ✔ **You get to subtract deductions from your income.** Some deductions are available to you just for being a living, breathing human being. In 2009, every taxpayer resident in Canada got a federal exemption — known as the basic personal amount — on their first $10,320 of income. When you contribute to qualified retirement plans such as an RRSP, you also effectively get a deduction.

Being mindful of the second tax system: Alternative minimum tax

You may find this hard to believe, but a second tax system actually exists (as if the first tax system weren't already complicated enough). This second system may raise your taxes even higher than they would normally be.

Over the years, as the government grew hungry for more revenue, taxpayers who slashed their taxes by claiming lots of deductions or exclusions from taxable income came under greater scrutiny. So the government created a second tax system — the alternative minimum tax (AMT) — to ensure that those with high deductions or exclusions pay at least a certain percentage of taxes on their incomes.

If you have a lot of deductions or exclusions from income taxes, you may fall prey to AMT. Even if you're not claiming a lot of deductions or using tax-sheltered investments such as limited partnerships, you may also get tripped up by AMT. For instance, someone who receives a substantial capital gain — say, a farmer who sells off a large plot of land — may find that the AMT kicks in.

AMT restricts you from claiming certain deductions and requires you to add back in some capital gains that are normally not taxed. You then take a $40,000 exemption, and calculate your federal tax at 15 percent (for 2009). You can use most personal tax credits, except for the dividend tax and the investment tax credits, just as you would when calculating your regular tax.

You're not done yet. You need to carry out a similar calculation for your provincial taxes. The minimum tax rate will range from around 34 percent to 57 percent of the federal minimum tax with adjustments for provincial credits and surtaxes. (If you live in Quebec you follow different rules; contact the provincial tax authorities for more information.)

You have to figure your tax under the AMT system and under the other system, and then pay whichever amount is higher.

Trimming Employment Income Taxes

You're supposed to pay taxes on income you earn from work. Countless illegal ways are available to reduce your employment income — for example, not reporting it — but if you use them, you can very well end up paying a heap of penalties and extra interest charges on top of the taxes you owe. And you may even get tossed in jail. Because we don't want you to serve jail time or lose even more money by paying unnecessary penalties and interest, this section focuses on the *legal* ways to reduce your taxes.

The CRA can authorize your employer to reduce the amount of income tax withheld on your employment income if you request that it take into account tax deductions such as child care expenses and RRSP contributions. Send a completed CRA Form T1213, "Request to Reduce Tax Deductions at Source," with all supporting documents to the Client Services Division of your local tax services office. You can obtain the form through your employer's payroll department, by calling the CRA at 800-959-2221, or by visiting the CRA Web site at www.cra-arc.gc.ca.

Contributing to RRSPs and retirement plans

An RRSP or employer's pension plan is one of the few painless and authorized ways to reduce your taxable employment income. Besides reducing your taxes, retirement plans help you build up a nest egg so that you don't have to work for the rest of your life.

You can exclude money from your taxable income by tucking it away in an RRSP or employer-based retirement plan. If your marginal tax rate is 36 percent, and you contribute $1,000 to one of these plans, you reduce your taxes by $360. Do you like the sound of that? How about this: Contribute another $1,000, and your taxes drop another $360 (as long as you're still in the same marginal tax rate). And when it's inside a retirement plan, your money can compound and grow without taxation.

Many people miss this great opportunity for reducing their taxes because they *spend* all (or too much) of their current employment income and, therefore, have nothing (or little) left to put into an RRSP or retirement plan. If you're in this predicament, you need to reduce your spending before you can contribute money to a retirement plan. (Chapter 6 explains how to decrease your spending.)

If your employer doesn't offer the option of saving money through a retirement plan, see whether you can drum up support for it. Lobby the benefits and human resources departments. If they resist, you may want to add this to your list of reasons for considering another employer. Many employers offer this valuable benefit, but some don't. Some company decision-makers either don't understand the value of these plans or feel that they're too costly to set up and administer.

If your employer doesn't offer a retirement or pension plan, an RRSP is your best bet. (You may also be able to contribute to an RRSP after contributing the maximum to your employer's pension plan.) Chapter 11 can help you determine whether you should contribute to an RRSP and how to make the most of registered retirement plans.

Shifting some income

Income shifting, which has nothing to do with money laundering, is a more esoteric tax-reduction technique that's an option only to those who can control *when* they receive their income.

For example, suppose your employer tells you in late December that you're eligible for a bonus. You're offered the option to receive your bonus in either December or January. If you're pretty certain that you'll be in a higher tax bracket next year, you should choose to receive your bonus in December.

Or suppose you run your own business and you think that you'll be in a lower tax bracket next year. Perhaps you plan to take time off to be with a newborn or take an extended trip. You may be able to push a big contract off until January, so the income is earned and taxed in the next tax year.

Increasing Your Deductions

Deductions are amounts you subtract from your gross income before calculating the tax you owe. To determine just what a deduction is worth, multiply it by your marginal tax rate.

In the following sections, we detail some of the more common deductions you may be able to take advantage of. The dollar figures we use are for 2009 — many will likely have been revised for subsequent years.

Child care expenses

Many of the costs of having others take care of your children can be deducted from your income. Babysitters, day nurseries, daycare, day camps, and boarding school expenses all qualify. However, the expenses must be incurred to enable you either to work or to take an occupational training course.

You can deduct up to $7,000 of expenses for each child who is under age 7 at the end of the year, and up to $4,000 for each child ages 7 to 16. Your total deduction can't be greater than two-thirds of the salary or net business income (technically, *earned income*) of the lower-earning spouse. Note that for Quebec residents, child care expenses give you a refundable credit, not a deduction, and different limits apply.

Alimony and maintenance payments

Alimony or maintenance payments you make to an ex-spouse can be deducted as long as they are made following a decree, order, judgment, or written agreement. To be deductible, they must be an allowance that is paid out in regular, predetermined payments. You can't deduct any transfers of property or one-time payments you make as part of a settlement.

Child support

Child support payments that are made according to an agreement that was reached before May 1, 1997, and that are established in advance as an allowance that involves recurring payments are generally deductible. Like alimony payments, the amounts must be predetermined, paid under a written agreement or under a decree, order, or judgment of a competent tribunal, and paid on a periodic basis. You also must be living apart from your spouse or ex-spouse because of a marriage breakdown at the time the payment is made.

Annual union and professional fees

Regular annual dues (often deducted from your paycheque) are deductible, but you can't claim initial fees or special assessments. Fees paid to professional organizations are deductible only if they must be paid to maintain a professional standing recognizable by law, such as a registered nurse. You can generally deduct dues you pay to voluntarily belong to work-related organizations if you are self-employed.

Business losses

You can use losses from an unincorporated business or professional practice to reduce your employment or professional income. Say that you have a salaried job in a car plant, and you start up a contracting business. If your business expenses are greater than the income it brings in, you can subtract your losses from your other income.

Interest on investment loans

If you borrow money to buy investments or to earn income from a business, the interest can be deducted. (This rule doesn't apply to money borrowed to make an RRSP contribution.) You'll need to keep a record of any money you borrow and use to invest and the interest you pay during the year.

Married versus common-law partners

Although your mother likely wouldn't agree, you're as good as married in the eyes of the tax authorities if you have been living in a common-law relationship for more than a year. If so, you are subject to the same tax rules that apply to legally married couples.

You are considered to be common-law spouses if you and your partner "cohabit in a conjugal relationship," and either have had a child together or have been living together continuously for at least 12 months. You are deemed to have "separated" — or lost your common-law status — only if you are separated for more than 90 days due to the relationship breaking down.

If you are living common-law, you can't claim the "equivalent-to-married" credit for a child. On the other hand, you can take advantage of planning opportunities including setting up a spousal RRSP and pooling some expenses to take the most advantage of various credits.

Since 2001, same-sex couples who have lived together for at least one year have been treated by the tax authorities in the same way as opposite-sex common-law couples.

Moving expenses

Eligible moving expenses can be a very valuable deduction. If you start a business or start working at a new location and move to a home that is at least 40 kilometres closer by road to your new business or job location than your old home, the associated costs can be claimed as a deduction. Moving to Canada from another country — or moving from Canada *to* another country — doesn't qualify.

Eligible expenses include the travelling costs to move you and your family (including food and lodging along the way) and your household belongings, as well as any related storage costs. In addition, you can deduct the cost of selling your old home, including the real estate commissions, and the legal bills on purchasing your new home.

Expenses can be deducted only against income that is earned in the new location. If you are unable to deduct all the expenses in the year of the move, the remainder can be deducted in future years. So don't forget to carry that deduction forward.

Students who move so they can attend university or another postsecondary institution full time can also deduct moving expenses. The expenses must be deducted against taxable scholarships, bursaries, research grants, or fellowships. Students can also claim moving expenses if the move is in order to take a job — including a summer job — or to start a business.

Getting organized

Locating your tax slips and all the other scraps of paper you need when you're completing your tax return can be a hassle. Setting up a filing system can be a big timesaver:

✔ **One receptacle:** If you have limited patience for setting up neat file folders, and you lead an uncomplicated financial life (that is, you haven't saved receipts throughout the year), you can confine your filing to January and February. During those months, you should receive tax summary statements on wages paid by your employer (T4), taxable dividend income from Canadian corporations (T5), income from profit-sharing plans (T4PS), and interest income (T5 for bank account and regular interest Canada Savings Bond "R" bonds; T5008 for T-bills). If you're older, you may also get a slip for Old Age Security income (T4AOAS) and the Canada Pension Plan or Quebec Pension Plan (T4A(P)). Set up a folder that's labelled with something

easy to remember ("2010 Taxes" is a brilliant choice), and dump these papers as well as your tax booklet into it. When you're ready to crunch numbers, you should have everything you need to complete the form.

✔ **Accordion-type file:** Organizing the bills you pay into individual folders during the entire year is a more thorough approach. This method is essential if you own your own business and need to tabulate your expenditures for office supplies each year. No one is going to send you a form totalling your annual office expenditures — you're on your own.

✔ **Software as a receptacle:** Software programs can help organize your tax information during the year and save you time and accounting fees come tax-preparation time. See Chapter 20 for more information about tax and financial software.

Making the Most of Tax Credits

Tax credits are different from deductions in one fundamental way. Deductions are subtracted from your income before your tax bill is calculated. After your tax bill has been calculated from your taxable income, credits are applied against your tax bill as though you've already paid that amount in taxes. As a result, your taxes are reduced by the full amount of the credit. A $500 credit is worth the same amount to everybody — it reduces the tax you have to pay by $500.

Most credits are *non-refundable*, which means that they can't be used to make your tax liability less than zero. If you have $1,500 in credits left over after wiping out your federal tax payable, that's as good as it gets. The government won't send you a cheque for $1,500.

All the provinces (except Quebec) calculate their piece of your tax bill by applying their marginal rates directly to your taxable income. This is known as the *tax-on-income,* or TONI, method.

Previously, provincial taxes were calculated as a percentage of your basic federal tax bill; this was known as the *tax-on-tax* method. Credits were generally deducted from your federal tax bill before your provincial taxes and surtaxes were calculated. With the TONI method, both the federal and provincial governments calculate your tax by multiplying your income by their respective tax rate. You then separately deduct your federal and provincial tax credits from the corresponding gross tax payable to arrive at what's called your basic federal and basic provincial tax.

With the old tax-on-tax system, tax credits were worth from 50 to 70 percent more than the straight federal credit. By cutting your federal taxes you also reduced your provincial taxes and surtaxes. When they moved to the TONI method, the provinces were required to maintain the basic credits that are offered at the federal level. The value of a federal credit will be about 40 to 70 percent more when the provincial tax credit is factored in.

Maximizing your tax credits

In the following sections are some common credits that may be available to you and your family, and some tips on how to maximize them. *Note:* Most of the dollar figures are from the 2009 tax year. Check your tax guide for the specific amounts for the year you're filing for.

Basic personal tax credit

Everyone gets a basic federal credit, which for the 2009 tax year was $1,548. (Going through the form, you claim a "basic personal amount" — $10,320 for 2009 — which is then multiplied by 15 percent.)

Spousal credit

You can claim a federal spousal credit of $1,548 if your spouse (including a common-law spouse) earned less than $10,320. If the spouse makes more than the cut-off amount, the lower-earning partner may be able to get under the threshold by making an RRSP contribution.

Wholly dependent person credit

You can claim this credit if you're single, separated, divorced, or widowed and you support a relative who lives with you. (This used to be known as the *equivalent-to-married* credit.) The most common example of this is a single mother. However, whether you're a man or a woman, you can claim this credit if you're financially responsible for supporting a child, parent, or other relative. The only conditions are that the dependant must be related to you, completely financially dependent on you, living in Canada, and, except in the case of a parent or grandparent, under 18 years old at some point in the tax year. (The age limit doesn't apply if the person is dependent on you because of a mental or physical disability.) You can't claim this credit if you have a common-law or same-sex spouse. The amounts are the same as the spousal credit.

Charitable donations credit

As long as you get an official tax receipt, you can earn credits from most contributions made to charities. In addition to cash contributions, you can often gain tax credits when you donate items of significant value, such as a used computer. The amount of the receipt must reflect the item's fair market value. However, you can't get a receipt for your time or the expenses you ring up while doing charitable work.

The first $200 you donate earns you a 15 percent federal tax credit, which works out to about 24 percent after your savings on provincial taxes are accounted for. For donations beyond the $200 level, though, your donations give you a 29 percent federal tax credit, worth about 45 percent after the savings on provincial taxes are counted. (This makes your donations above $200 worth about as much as a deduction if you're in the top tax bracket.)

If you donate only small amounts each year, pool several years' contributions to put you over the $200 donation level. You can also combine your spouse's and your own contributions on one return. This avoids both of you having to get the lower credit on the first $200. You don't have to claim a charitable deduction in the year that it's made. Unclaimed contributions can be carried forward and claimed on your return in any of the five years after the year in which you make the charitable contribution.

Education tax credits

A couple of credits are available to students and their families:

- ✔ **Tuition tax credit:** Students receive a credit worth 15 percent of tuition fees (as long as they total more than $100 per institution) paid to a Canadian university, college, or other postsecondary institution during the year. Fees paid to an institution certified by Employment and Immigration Canada are also eligible. Tuition paid to universities outside Canada may be eligible as well, but fees paid to private elementary schools or high schools don't earn you a tax credit.

  A lot more than just the standard admission charges or tuition can be included here. You can also claim library and lab costs, exam fees, and mandatory computer service fees. As well, you can include mandatory associated fees such as those for health services and athletics.

✔ **Federal education tax credit:** If you study full-time at a postsecondary institution, you also get a federal education tax credit, which in 2009 was $62 per month. Students with qualifying disabilities can generally claim this amount even if they are studying only part-time.

If you are studying part-time, for every month in which you attended an eligible program for at least three consecutive weeks, and which involved at least 12 hours of course work per month, the education amount is around $18. You can also claim the education tax credit for postsecondary education that's related to your job, as long as your employer doesn't reimburse you for any of the costs.

If the student in your family doesn't need to use all — or any — of the tuition fee tax credit or the education credit to bring her federal tax bill to zero, the credits don't go to waste. Up to $750 of the unused portion of either — or both — credits generally can be transferred to a parent, grandparent, or spouse. Unused tuition and education amounts can also be carried forward and claimed against your income in future years.

Medical expenses credit

A surprisingly wide range of medical costs and health-related expenditures are eligible for a credit, but you generally have to submit all your receipts.

After totalling your expenses, you can claim only the amount that exceeds 3 percent of your net income. In 2009, the federal credit was 15 percent of this amount.

To maximize the benefit of this credit, one spouse can and should claim the entire family's medical expenses. The spouse with the lowest income generally should make the claim, to get over the 3 percent floor as quickly as possible. Further, in any tax year you can claim your expenses for any 12 months ending in that particular year. If you have a lot of bills in the fall and spring, for example, it may pay to make your claim run from August 1 to July 31.

You can include a broad range of medical costs in calculating this credit. Add up any payments to doctors, nurses, dentists, and public or licensed private hospitals for medical or dental care. In addition, you can include payments for any prescription drugs and medications, eyeglasses, and therapy for speech or hearing problems. You can also include any premiums for private health insurance plans. (That includes the cost of travel insurance for your vacations out of the country; see Chapter 17 for more information.) You can't claim any expenses that you are reimbursed for from, say, a company dental plan, but any deductibles you pay do qualify.

Low-income earners who have high medical bills may also be able to take advantage of the medical expense supplement. For 2009, the supplement was the lesser of 25 percent of both medical expenses and disability supports expenses or $1,067. This is further reduced by 5 percent of combined net income (taxpayer and spouse) in excess of a ceiling amount, which in 2009 was $23,633. It is eliminated when combined net income reaches a set maximum, which for 2009 was $44,973.

Pension income credit

You can claim a credit for a small amount of certain types of pension income, called *qualifying* pension income. This generally means payments that are received from a private pension. If you are 65 or older, or are receiving benefits due to your spouse's death, payments from a Registered Retirement Income Fund, the income portion of a regular annuity, and payments from annuities from an RRSP or deferred profit-sharing plan also qualify. Canada Pension Plan, Old Age Security, or Guaranteed Income Supplement payments do not qualify. For the 2009 tax year, the federal tax credit was 15 percent on the first $2,000 of *qualifying* pension income. If you're unable to use the credit, it may be transferred to your spouse.

Age 65 or older

If you are 65 or older by the end of the year, you can claim a federal tax credit — the *age credit*. In 2009, the credit went up to $6,048, making it worth $961. However, this credit is reduced if your net income is more than a certain amount (in 2009 this was $33,312), and is completely eliminated if your income exceeds a set level, which in 2009 was $72,632.

Disability credit

You are eligible for a federal credit if you have a severe and prolonged mental or physical impairment. In 2009, the federal credit was $1,079. Depending on the type of disability, it must be certified by the relevant professional (medical doctor, optometrist, audiologist, occupational therapist, or psychologist).

Families that care for children with severe disabilities can also receive a supplementary credit of up to $630 (in 2009). This is usually reduced by child care expenses and attendant care expenses in excess of a few thousand dollars.

If a dependent relative doesn't earn enough income to use all of his or her disability credit, a supporting relative can use any unused amount. The eligible dependant can be a spouse, child, grandchild, parent, grandparent, sibling, aunt, uncle, niece, or nephew. In addition, lower-income families caring for a child eligible for the disability tax credit may also qualify for Child Disability Benefit payments.

If a parent supports a disabled child who is over 18 years old, the parent is allowed an additional federal credit. This credit was $630 for the 2009 tax year. However, the credit is reduced if the infirm dependant earns more than $5,956, and is zero if the dependant's income exceeds $10,154.

A *caregiver's credit* is also available to caregivers who provide in-home care for elderly or infirm relatives living in the same house. In 2009, the maximum credit was $630. This credit is reduced if the infirm relative has an income of between $14,321 and $18,507, and eliminated if it exceeds that amount. Also, you cannot claim this credit if you claim the eligible dependant or other dependent tax credits in connection with the relative.

Deducting self-employment expenses

When you're self-employed, you can deduct a multitude of expenses from your income before calculating your taxable income. If you buy a computer or office furniture, you can deduct those expenses. (Sometimes they need to be gradually deducted, or *depreciated,* over time.) Salaries for your office supplies, rent or mortgage interest for your office space, and phone/communications expenses are generally deductible, as are salaries you pay to any employees and payments to casual or contract help.

Many self-employed folks don't take all the deductions they're eligible for. In some cases, people simply aren't aware of the wonderful world of deductions. Others are worried that large deductions will increase the risk of an audit. Spend some time finding out more about tax deductions; you'll be convinced that taking full advantage of your eligible deductions makes sense and saves you money.

The following are common mistakes made by people who are their own bosses:

- ✔ **Being an island unto yourself.** When you're self-employed, going it alone is usually a mistake when it comes to taxes. You must educate yourself to make the tax laws work for rather than against you. Hiring tax help is well worth your while. (See "Professional hired help," later in this chapter, for info on hiring tax advisers.)

- ✔ **Making administrative tax screwups.** As a self-employed individual, you're responsible for the correct and timely filing of all taxes owed on your income and employment taxes on your employees. You need to make estimated tax payments on a quarterly basis. And if you have employees, you also need to withhold taxes from each paycheque they receive and make timely payments to Canada Revenue Agency (CRA). In addition to federal and provincial income taxes, you also need to withhold and send in Canada Pension Plan (or QPP) contributions and Employment Insurance premiums.

✔ **Failing to document expenses.** When you pay with cash, following the paper trail for all the money you spent can be hard for you to do (and for the CRA, in the event you're ever audited). At the end of the year, how are you going to remember how much you spent for parking or client meals if you fail to keep a record? How will you survive a CRA audit without proper documentation?

Debit cards are accepted most places and provide a convenient paper trail. (Be careful about getting a debit card in your business's name, because some banks don't offer protection against fraudulent use of business debit cards.) Otherwise, you need a system or written record of your daily petty cash purchases. Most pocket calendars or daily organizers include ledgers that allow you to track these small purchases. If you aren't that organized, at least get receipts for cash transactions and stash them in a file folder in your desk. Or keep receipts in envelopes labelled with the month and year.

✔ **Failing to fund a retirement plan.** You should be saving money toward retirement anyway, and you can't beat the tax break. People who are self-employed are allowed to contribute up to 18 percent of their net income to an RRSP. (This amount is capped each year at a set dollar amount, which in 2009 was $21,000.) If they also belong to a registered pension plan, the maximum amount they are allowed to contribute is decreased by a pension adjustment. To find out more about RRSPs, see Chapter 11.

✔ **Failing to use numbers to help manage business.** If you're a small-business owner who doesn't track her income, expenses, staff performance, and customer data on a regular basis, your tax return may be the one and only time during the year when you take a financial snapshot of your business. After you go through all the time, trouble, and expense to file your tax return, make sure you reap the rewards of all your work; use those numbers to help analyze and manage your business.

Some bookkeepers and tax preparers can provide you with management information reports on your business from the tax data they compile for you. Just ask! See "Software and Web sites" later in this chapter for our recommendations.

✔ **Failing to pay family help.** If your children, spouse, or other relatives help with some aspect of your business, consider paying them for the work. Besides showing them that you value their work, this practice may reduce your family's tax liability. For example, children are usually in a lower tax bracket. By shifting some of your income to your child, you cut your tax bill.

Reducing Investment Income Taxes

The distributions and profits on investments that you hold outside of RRSPs and other tax-sheltered retirement plans are exposed to taxation when you receive them. Interest, dividends, and *capital gains* (profits from the sale of an investment at a price that's higher than the purchase price) are all taxed.

This section explains some of the best methods for reducing the taxes on investments exposed to taxation; see Chapter 13 to find out how and where to invest money held *outside* of tax-sheltered retirement plans.

Fill up those retirement plans

Taking advantage of opportunities to direct money into an RRSP and other retirement plans gives you two possible tax benefits. First, your contributions are generally immediately tax-deductible. Second, the distributions and growth of the investments in the retirement plans aren't generally taxed until withdrawal. (See Chapter 11 for details.)

Consider other tax-sheltered vehicles

Over the last few years, the government has introduced several new tax-sheltered accounts that are worth taking advantage of. We include all the details you need to make the most of them in other chapters, but here's a brief overview of these tax-saving options.

Registered Education Savings Plans (RESPs)

If you have children who you hope will go on to postsecondary education, you likely have also had your heart sink when you come across stories about the enormous costs involved. Let us assure you that the ultimate cost will likely not be anywhere near the excessive estimates some experts come up with. But we can't deny that education is a significant expense.

Planning a savings strategy will help you be able to carry some of the costs, and one of the best tools available is a Registered Education Savings Plan, or RESP. Unlike money contributed to an RRSP, money put into an RESP is not deductible from your taxable income. However, after it's inside the plan, the money can grow tax-free. Further, when the money is withdrawn it is treated as income for the child who will be using it for education expenses. As a result, little if any tax will likely have to be paid on it. What's more, contributions to an RESP earn you a grant of 20 percent of the first $2,500 you contribute each year, up to a lifetime maximum of $7,200 for each beneficiary. Be sure to read Chapter 14 for the details on saving for education expenses.

Tax-Free Savings Accounts (TFSAs)

Tax-Free Savings Accounts, or TFSAs, are exactly what their name suggests: A place to stash some cash and not have the gains the money earns taxed. As long as you're 18 or older, you can open a TFSA. These accounts are offered by virtually all financial institutions.

In essence, TFSAs are the mirror of RRSPS. Contributions to a TFSA can't be deducted from your taxable income when doing your taxes for that particular year. Money inside the plan can be invested in most common types of investments, including interest-bearing GICS and bonds as well as stocks and an enormous range of mutual funds.

Unlike RRSPS, any withdrawals you make are not taxed — this applies to both your original contributions and any gains you've earned. As a result, a TFSA is not only a great place to shelter any extra cash you have lying about, but also a valuable tool for both short- and long-term saving. You'll find all the details about TFSAs and how to make the most of them in Chapter 13.

Registered Disability Savings Plans (RDSPs)

Registered Disability Savings Plans, or RDSPs, offer individuals with a disability, and the parents or guardians of a disabled minor, an additional way to save and invest money in a tax-friendly account. To qualify, the disability must be "a severe and prolonged impairment that restricts your daily life and has lasted — or is expected to last — for at least twelve months."

RDSPs first became available in 2008 and are similar to TFSAs and RESPs. Money you put into an RDSP is not tax-deductible. But when sheltered inside the plan the money can be invested in a wide range of investments, and the interest or capital gains you earn aren't taxed.

No restrictions exist on who can contribute to the plan, nor is there a limit on how much money can be contributed in any one year. The only restriction is a lifetime maximum limit of $200,000. Contributions may also trigger a government grant to the plan, called a Canada Disability Savings Grant, or CDSG. This grant is similar to the grant that accompanies RESP contributions.

Payments from the plan must begin the year the beneficiary turns 60. The portion that comes from the original contributions isn't taxed, but profits earned inside the plan are taxed when they're paid out. You can find the full details on RDSPs in Chapter 13.

Select tax-friendly investments

Too often, when selecting investments, people mistakenly focus on past rates of return. Everyone knows that the past is no guarantee of the future. But choosing an investment with a reportedly high rate of return without considering tax consequences is an even worse mistake. What you get to keep — after taxes — is what matters in the long run.

For example, when comparing two similar funds, most people prefer a fund that averages returns of 14 percent per year to one that earns 12 percent per year. But what if the 14-percent-per-year fund, because of greater taxable distributions, causes you to pay a lot more in taxes? What if, after factoring in taxes, the 14-percent-per-year fund nets just 9 percent, but the 12-percent-per-year fund nets an effective 10 percent return? In such a case, you'd be unwise to choose a fund solely on the basis of the higher (pre-tax) reported rate of return.

We call investments that appreciate in value and don't distribute much in the way of highly taxed income *tax-friendly*. (Some in the investment business use the term *tax-efficient*.) See Chapter 10 for more information on tax-friendly stocks and stock mutual funds.

Stocks that pay dividends are one of the most tax-friendly investments. Typically, the after-tax yield of these investments is better than that on interest-paying GICs or bonds. The yield is not guaranteed, but major companies try to maintain their dividends, especially for preferred shares. If you're in the 34-percent tax bracket, you'll pay exactly the same rate on any interest income. However, the effective tax rate on qualifying dividends is just 14 percent.

If you are in the lower tax brackets, the effective tax rate on any dividends you receive may actually be negative. This happens due to the formula used to calculate the dividend tax credit. The dividend tax credit rate can actually be higher than the lowest one or two tax rates. In this case, the qualifying dividends you receive and the resulting tax credit can be used to reduce your other taxes payable. Real estate is another area that can provide tax-friendly returns. In addition to deductions allowed for mortgage interest and property taxes, you can depreciate rental property to reduce your taxable income. *Depreciation* is a special tax deduction allowed for the gradual wear and tear on rental real estate. See Chapter 15 for a crash course in real estate.

Make your profits long-term

As we discuss in Part III, when you buy growth investments such as stocks and real estate, you should do so for the long-term — ideally, ten or more years. The tax system rewards your patience with lower tax rates on your profits. With stocks, you don't have to pay taxes on your profits until you sell the shares. Similarly, when you invest in real estate, the value can rise substantially and for many years. That profit is taxable only if and when you sell the property.

Does funding an RRSP still make sense?

Historically, taking advantage of opportunities to direct money into RRSPs has given you two possible tax benefits. First, contributions to your RRSP are immediately tax-deductible (see Chapter 11 for details). Second, the returns on the investments inside RRSPs aren't generally taxed until withdrawal.

In the section "Reducing Investment Income Taxes," we mention tax breaks for stocks, dividends, and real estate. These breaks, unfortunately, really only matter on investments held outside of RRSPs. (If you realize a long-term capital gain or receive stock dividends inside an RRSP, those investment returns are taxed, upon withdrawal, at the relatively higher ordinary income tax rates.) As a result, some have argued you shouldn't fund RRSPs. In most cases, the people making the argument have a vested interest.

One good reason not to fund an RRSP is if you have a specific goal, such as saving to purchase a home or start a business, that necessitates having access to your money. (However, money inside an RRSP can be used by first-time homebuyers to purchase a home; see Chapter 11 for the details.) Generally only two atypical situations exist in which not funding an RRSP could make sense:

- ✔ **You're temporarily in a very low tax bracket.** This can happen, for example, if you lose your job for an extended period of time or are in school. In these cases, you're unlikely to have lots of spare money to contribute to an RRSP!

- ✔ **You have too much money socked away already.** If you have a large net worth inside your RRSP, which eventually will be taxed at your marginal tax bracket when you withdraw it, it may make sense to divert some of your savings into tax-friendly investments outside of an RRSP.

Getting Help from Tax Resources

All sorts of ways to prepare your tax return exist. Which approach makes sense for you depends on the complexity of your situation and your knowledge of taxes. Regardless of which approach you use, you should be taking financial moves during the year to reduce your taxes. By the time you actually file your return in the following year, it's often too late for you to take advantage of many tax-reduction strategies.

Not only is the tax system sprawling and often complicated, it's constantly changing. In the following sections we point you towards a number of sources for help and guidance in preparing your tax return.

Assistance from the Canada Revenue Agency

If you have a simple, straightforward tax return, filing it on your own using only the CRA instructions is fine. This approach is as cheap as you can get. The main costs are time, patience, photocopying expenses (always keep a copy for your files), and postage for mailing the completed tax return.

CRA publications don't have Warning or Tip icons. And the CRA has been known to give wrong information from time to time. When you call the CRA with a question, be sure to take notes about your conversation to protect yourself in the event of an audit. Date your notes and include the name and identification number of the tax employee you talked to, the questions you asked, and the employee's responses. File your notes in a folder with a copy of your completed return.

In addition to the standard instructions that come with your tax return, CRA offers a number of free and helpful tax guides that you can pick up at your nearest taxation centre (or call to request them). These guides serve as useful references and provide more detail and insight than the basic CRA publications. For the self-employed, many booklets are available depending on your occupation, including *Business and Professional Income, Farming Income, Fishing Income,* and *Rental Income.* Other guides deal with specific circumstances. To inquire about and request these documents, call 800-959-2221 (905-712-5813 in the Toronto area). You can also visit the CRA Web site at www.cra-arc.gc.ca.

Preparation and advice guides

Books about tax preparation and tax planning that highlight common problem areas and are written in clear, simple English are invaluable. They supplement the official instructions not only by helping you complete your return correctly but also by showing you how to save as much money as possible. Here are some of the books we recommend:

- ✔ *Tax Planning For You and Your Family* (prepared by KPMG and published by Thomson Carswell)

- ✔ *78 Tax Tips For Canadians For Dummies* (please excuse the shameless Dummies promotion, but this book has everything you need to prepare and save on your tax return)

- ✔ *101 Tax Secrets For Canadians* (written by Tim Cestnick and published by John Wiley & Sons Canada)

Software and Web sites

If you have access to a computer, good tax-preparation software can be helpful. One program that we rate highly is Studiotax, which despite its excellent quality and ease of use is absolutely free regardless of your income level. (The Ottawa-based developers do ask for a donation to help them maintain and improve the program.) QuickTax and Ufile are two other programs that we have reviewed and recommend. QuickTax has a slight edge in usability, but it is also more expensive than Ufile. If you go the software route, we highly recommend having a good tax advice book by your side.

For you Web surfers, the CRA Web site (www.cra-arc.gc.ca) is among the better Internet tax sites, believe it or not. The Certified General Accountants of Ontario Web site (www.cga-ontario.org) also has lots of resources.

Professional hired help

Competent tax preparers and advisers can save you money — sometimes more than enough to pay their fees — by identifying tax-reduction strategies you may overlook. They can also help reduce the likelihood of an audit, which can be triggered by blunders. Mediocre and lousy tax preparers, on the other hand, may make mistakes and not be aware of sound ways to reduce your tax bill.

Tax practitioners come with varying backgrounds, training, and credentials. One credential is not necessarily better than another. The four main types are preparers, certified general accountants (CGAs), chartered accountants (CAs), and tax lawyers (tricked ya — no acronym). The more training and specialization a tax practitioner has (and the more affluent his or her clients), the higher the hourly fee usually is. Fees and competence at all levels of the profession vary significantly. If you do hire a tax adviser and you're not sure of the quality of work performed and the soundness of the advice, try getting a second opinion.

Preparers

Preparers generally have the least amount of training of all the tax practitioners, and a greater proportion of them work part time. As with financial planners, no national regulations apply to preparers, and no licensing is required.

Preparers are appealing because they're relatively inexpensive — they can do most basic returns for around $100 or so. The drawback of using a preparer is that you may hire someone who doesn't know much more than you do.

Preparers make the most sense for folks who have relatively simple financial lives, who are budget minded, and who hate doing their own taxes. If you're not good about hanging on to receipts, or you don't want to keep your own files with background details about your taxes, you should definitely shop around for a tax preparer who's committed to the business. You may need all that stuff someday for an audit, and many tax preparers keep and organize their clients' documentation rather than return everything each year. Also, going with a firm that is open year-round may be a safer option (some small shops are open only during tax season) in case tax questions or problems arise.

Certified general accountants

CGAs are often a sound, economical choice for tax advice. Many certified general accountants have large personal income tax practices.

If you have moderately complex returns and don't necessarily need complicated tax-planning advice throughout the year, then CGAs are a good choice. Many CGAs also have expertise in preparing returns for small businesses. A professional who is familiar with the peculiarities of your industry may be able to give you more complete advice on opportunities for saving and how to organize your business to minimize your tax bill. What's more, he or she will likely be able to do your return more quickly, meaning a lower bill.

CGAs don't close down when the tax season ends. That means you can go to them for advice and help on your schedule, and you'll be able to get help if you have problems after filing your return. Fees for a straightforward return should be about $100, while more complex situations (for example, a part-time business or investment income) might mean a bill for several hundred dollars.

Chartered accountants (CAs)

CAs are the folks who audit public companies. They tend to have specialties in specific industries or types of businesses. Many CAs work for large firms that have international operations in both accounting and consulting, so they have the expertise to prepare complicated returns involving investments and earnings in different countries.

CA fees vary tremendously. Most charge around $100 per hour, but CAs at large companies and in high-cost-of-living areas tend to charge somewhat more. The cost of having a CA prepare your return can range anywhere from $150 to several thousand dollars.

If you have to file some of the more unusual and less user-friendly schedules, or have to file returns in several countries, a CA is generally your best bet. A typical CA user might be a Canadian who, because she works a portion of the year in the United States, has to file in both countries and who has numerous tax shelters and real estate investments.

If your return is uncomplicated and your financial situation is stable, hiring a high-priced CA year after year to fill in the blanks is a waste of money. Sometimes you'll be granted an initial interview with a partner, who then has a less qualified — and lower-paid — associate carry out the work. However, the bill you receive for the associate's advice often will reflect the CA's rate.

Paying for the additional cost of a CGA or CA on an ongoing basis makes sense if you can afford it and if your situation is reasonably complex or dynamic. If you're self-employed and/or file lots of other schedules, it may be worth hiring a CGA or CA. But you needn't do so year after year. If your situation grows complex one year and then stabilizes, consider getting help for the perplexing year and then using preparation guides, software, or a lower-cost preparer in the future.

Tax lawyers

Unless you're a super-high-income earner with a complex financial life, hiring a tax lawyer to prepare your annual return is prohibitively expensive. (In fact, many tax lawyers don't prepare returns as a normal practice.)

Tax lawyers deal with complicated tax problems and issues that usually have some legal angle. Because of their level of specialization and training, tax lawyers tend to have the highest hourly billing rates — $200 to $300+ per hour is not unusual.

Dealing with an Audit

On a list of real-life nightmares, most people would rank tax audits right up there with root canals, rectal exams, and court appearances. Many people are traumatized by audits because they feel like they're on trial and being accused of a crime. Take a deep breath and don't panic.

You may be getting audited simply because a business that reports tax information on you, or someone at the CRA, made an error regarding the data on your return. In the vast majority of cases, the CRA conducts its audit by corresponding with you through the mail.

Audits that require you to schlep to the local CRA office are the most feared type of audit. In these cases, a reasonable percentage of such audited returns are left unchanged by the audit — in other words, the taxpayer doesn't end up owing more money. In fact, if you're the lucky sort, you may be one of the few folks who actually gets a refund because the audit finds a mistake in your favour!

Unfortunately, you'll most likely be in the majority — meaning you'll end up owing more tax money. The amount of additional tax that you owe in interest and penalties hinges on how your audit goes.

Getting your act together

Preparing for an audit is sort of like preparing for a test at school. The CRA will let you know which sections of your tax return it wants to examine.

The first decision you face when you get an audit notice is whether to handle it yourself or hire a tax adviser to represent you. Hiring representation may help you save time, stress, and money.

If you normally prepare your own return and you're comfortable with your understanding of the areas being audited, handle the audit yourself. When the amount of tax money in question is small compared to the fee you'd pay the tax adviser to represent you, self-representation is probably your best option. However, if you're likely to turn into a babbling, intimidated fool and you're unsure of how to present your situation, hire a tax adviser to represent you. (See "Professional hired help," earlier in this chapter, for information about whom to hire.)

If you decide to handle the audit yourself, get your act together sooner rather than later. Don't wait until the night before to start gathering receipts and other documentation. You may need to contact others to get copies of documents you can't find.

You need to document and be ready to speak only about the areas the audit notice says are being investigated. Organize the various documents and receipts into folders. You want to make it as easy as possible for the auditor to review your materials. *Don't* show up, dump shopping bags full of receipts and paperwork on the auditor's desk, and say, "Here it is — *you* figure it out."

Whatever you do, *don't ignore your audit request letter.* The CRA is the ultimate bill-collection agency. And if you end up owing more money (the unhappy result of most audits), the sooner you pay, the less interest and penalties you'll owe.

Surviving the day of reckoning

Two people with identical situations can walk into an audit and come out with very different results. The loser can end up owing much more in taxes and have the audit expanded to include other parts of the return. The winner can end up owing no additional tax or even owing less.

Here's how to be a winner in your tax audit:

✔ **Treat the auditor as a human being.** This advice may be obvious, but it isn't practised by taxpayers very often. You may be resentful or angry about being audited. You may be tempted to gnash your teeth and tell the auditor how unfair it is that an honest taxpayer like you had to spend hours getting ready for this ordeal. You may feel like ranting and raving about how the government wastes too much of your tax money, or that the party in power is out to get you. Bite your tongue.

Believe it or not, most auditors are decent people just trying to do their jobs. They're well aware that taxpayers don't like seeing them. Don't suck up, either — just relax and be yourself. Behave as you would around a boss you like — with respect and congeniality.

✔ **Stick to the knitting.** Your audit is for discussing only the sections of your tax return that are in question. The more you talk about other areas or things that you're doing, the more likely the auditor will probe into other items. Don't bring documentation for parts of your return that aren't being audited. Besides creating more work for yourself, you may be opening up a can of worms that doesn't need to be opened. Should the auditor inquire about areas that aren't covered by the audit notice, politely say that you're not prepared to discuss those other issues and that another meeting should be scheduled.

✔ **Don't argue when you disagree.** State your case. When the auditor wants to disallow a deduction or otherwise increase the taxes you owe and you disagree, state once why you don't agree with her assessment. If the auditor won't budge, don't get into a knock-down, drag-out confrontation. She may not want to lose face and is inclined to find additional tax money — that's the auditor's job.

When necessary, you can plead your case with several people who work above your auditor. If this method fails and you still feel wronged, you can take your case to tax court.

✔ **Don't be intimidated.** The tax system is enormously complicated, and most auditors are not tax geniuses. The work is stressful — being in a job where people dislike seeing you is not easy. Turnover is quite high. Thus, many auditors are fairly young, just-out-of-school types who majored in something like English, history, or sociology. They may know less about tax and financial matters than you do. The basic CRA tax boot camp that auditors go through doesn't come close to covering all the technical details and nuances in the tax code. So you may not be at such a disadvantage in your tax knowledge after all, especially if you work with a tax adviser (some tax advisers know much more about the tax system than the average CRA auditor).

Part III
Building Wealth with Wise Investing

"Hey, Luke, I was just thinking — why don't we try investing some of the stolen loot in some mutual funds, bonds, maybe check out some international fund, or real estate,...shoot, what am I talking about? Let's just stash it in the old mine shaft like before."

In this part . . .

*W*e lay out the principles of investing and show you how to choose your investments wisely. Earning and saving are hard work, so you need to be careful where you invest the fruits of your labour. In this part you find out the real story about stocks, bonds, and mutual funds; the differences between investing in retirement plans and non-retirement accounts; how to invest for university; and how to buy a home and invest in other real estate.

Chapter 8

Considering Important Investment Concepts

In This Chapter

▶ Determining your investment goals

▶ Evaluating returns and risks

▶ Keeping your eggs in more than one basket: Asset allocation

▶ Distinguishing the best investment firms from the rest

Making wise investments doesn't have to be complicated. However, many investors get bogged down in the morass of the thousands of investment choices out there and the often-conflicting perspectives on how to invest. This chapter helps you grasp the important "bigger picture" issues that can help you ensure that your investment plan meshes with your needs and the realities of the investment marketplace.

Establishing Your Goals

Before you select a specific investment, first determine your investment needs and goals. Why are you saving money — what are you going to use it for? You don't need to earmark every dollar, but you should set some major objectives. Establishing objectives is important because the expected use of the money helps you determine how long to invest it. And that, in turn, helps you determine which investments to choose.

The risk level of your investments should factor in your time frame and your comfort level. Investing in high-risk vehicles doesn't make sense if you'll have to spend all your profits supporting your family because you've had to take a long and unpaid stress leave from work. For example, suppose you've been accumulating money for a down payment on a home you want to buy in a few years. You can't afford much risk with that money. You're going to need that money sooner rather than later. Putting that money in the stock market, then, is foolish. As we discuss later in this chapter, the stock market can drop a lot in a year or over several consecutive years. So stocks are probably too risky a place to invest money you plan to use soon.

Perhaps you're saving toward a longer-term goal, such as retirement, that's 20 or 30 years away. In this case, you're in a position to make riskier investments, because your holdings have more time to bounce back from temporary losses or setbacks. You may want to consider investing in growth investments, such as stocks, in a retirement plan that you leave alone for 20 years or longer. You can tolerate year-to-year volatility in the market — you have time on your side. If you haven't yet done so, take a tour through Chapter 4, which helps you contemplate and set your financial goals.

Understanding the Primary Investments

For a moment, forget all the buzzwords, jargon, and product names you've heard tossed around in the investment world — in many cases, they're only meant to obscure what an investment really is and to hide the hefty fees and commissions.

Imagine a world with only two investment flavours — think of chocolate and vanilla ice cream (or low-fat frozen yogurt for you health-minded folks). The investment world is really just as simple. You have only two major investment choices: You can be a lender or an owner. In other words, you can lend it to a person, a bank, or a business, or even a government. Or you can use it to buy a piece of something, from a rental building to a small business or a tiny piece of a very large business like one of the big banks.

Looking at lending investments

You're a lender when you invest your money in a bank guaranteed investment certificate (GIC), a Treasury bill, a term deposit, or a bond issued by a company like Bombardier. In each case, you lend your money to an organization — a bank, the federal government, or Canada's own maker of planes and trains. You're paid an agreed-upon rate of interest for lending your money. The organization also promises to have your original investment (the *principal*) returned to you on a specific date.

Getting paid all the interest in addition to your original investment (as promised) is the best that can happen with a lending investment. Given that the investment landscape is littered with carcasses of failed investments, this is not a result to take for granted.

The worst that can happen with a lending investment is that you don't get everything you're promised. Promises can be broken under extenuating circumstances. When a company goes bankrupt, for example, you can lose all or part of your original investment.

Another risk associated with lending investments is that even if you get what you were promised, the ravages of inflation may reduce the purchasing power of your money. Also, the value of a bond may drop below what you paid for it if interest rates rise or the quality/risk of the issuing company declines.

Table 8-1 shows the reduction in the purchasing power of your money at varying rates of inflation after just ten years.

Table 8-1	Reduction in Purchasing Power Due to Inflation
Inflation Rate	*Reduction in Purchasing Power after Ten Years*
6 percent	–44 percent
8 percent	–54 percent
10 percent	–61 percent

Some conservative-minded investors make the common mistake of thinking that they're diversifying their long-term investment money by buying several bonds, some GICs, and an annuity. The problem, however, is that all these investments pay a relatively low fixed rate of return that's exposed to the vagaries of inflation.

A final drawback to lending investments is that you don't share in the success of the organization to which you lend your money. If the company doubles or triples in size and profits, your principal and interest rate don't double or triple in size along with it; they stay the same. Of course, such success should ensure that you get your promised interest and principal.

Exploring ownership investments

You're an *owner* when you invest your money in an asset, such as a company or real estate, which has the ability to generate earnings or profits. Suppose you own 100 shares of Canadian National Railway stock. With hundreds of millions of shares of stock outstanding, CNR is a mighty big company — your 100 shares represent a tiny piece of it.

What do you get for your small slice of Canadian National? As a shareholder, although you don't get free train rides, you do share in the profits of the company in the form of annual dividends — a payout of some of the profits to shareowners — and an increase (you hope) in the stock price if the company grows and becomes more profitable. Of course, you receive these benefits when things are going well. If CN's business declines, your stock may be worth less (or even worth*less*!).

Real estate is another one of our favourite financially rewarding and time-honoured ownership investments. Real estate can produce profits when it's rented out for more than the expense of owning the property or sold at a price higher than what you paid for it. We know numerous successful real estate investors who have earned excellent long-term profits.

The value of real estate depends not only on the particulars of the individual property but also on the health and performance of the local economy. When companies in the community are growing and more jobs are being produced at higher wages, real estate often does well. When local employers are laying people off and excess housing is sitting vacant because of previous over-building, rent and property values fall, as they did in the late 2000s.

Finally, many Canadians have also built substantial wealth through small business. According to *Forbes* magazine, more of the world's wealthiest individuals have built their wealth through their stake in small businesses than through any other vehicle. Small business is the engine that drives much of North America's economic growth. One 2009 Industry Canada study estimated that businesses with less than 100 employees were responsible for creating some 36 percent of new jobs.

You can participate in small business in a variety of ways. You can start your own business, buy and operate an existing business, or simply invest in promising small businesses. In the chapters ahead, we explain each of these major investment types in detail.

Shunning Gambling Instruments and Behaviours

Although investing is often risky, it's not gambling. *Gambling* is putting your money into schemes that are sure to lose you money over time. That's not to say that everyone loses or that you lose every time you gamble. However, the deck is stacked against you. The house wins most of the time.

Horse-racing tracks, gambling casinos, and lotteries are set up to pay out 50 to 60 cents on the dollar. The rest goes to profits and the administration of the system — don't forget that these are businesses. Sure, your chosen horse may win a race or two, but in the long run, you're almost guaranteed to lose about 40 to 50 percent of what you bet. Would you put your money in an "investment" where your expected return was negative 40 percent?

Forsake futures, options, and other derivatives

Futures, options, and commodities are *derivatives,* or financial investments whose value is derived from the performance of another security, such as a stock or bond.

Say you hear a radio ad from the firm Fleecem, Cheatem, and Leavem advocating that you buy heating oil futures because of conflicts in the Middle East and the upcoming rise in heating oil usage due to the cold-weather months. You call the firm and are impressed by the smooth-talking vice president who spends so much time with little ol' you. His logic makes sense, and he spends a lot of time with you, so you send him a cheque for $10,000.

Buying futures isn't much different from blowing $10,000 at the craps tables in Las Vegas. Futures prices depend on short-term, highly volatile price movements. As with gambling, you occasionally win when the market moves the right way at the right time. But in the long run, you're gonna lose. In fact, you can lose it all.

Options are as risky as futures. With options, you're betting on the short-term movements of a specific security. If you have inside information (such as knowing in advance when a major corporate development is going to occur), you can get rich. But insider trading is illegal and may land you in jail.

Honest brokers who help their clients invest in stocks, bonds, and mutual funds will tell them the truth about commodities, futures, and options. Here's how one former broker we know who worked for various major brokerage firms for 12 years puts it: "I had just one client who made money in options, futures, or commodities, but the only reason he came out ahead was because he was forced to pull money out to close on a home purchase just when he happened to be ahead. The commissions were great for me, but there's no way a customer will make money in them." Remember these words if you're tempted to gamble with futures, options, and the like.

Futures and options are not always used for speculation and gambling. Some sophisticated professional investors actually use them to reduce the risk of their broad investment holdings, a strategy known as *hedging.* Even when futures and options are used in this fashion, things don't often work out the way that the pros hoped. You, the individual investor, should steer clear of futures and options.

Ditch daytrading

Daytrading — which is the rapid buying and selling of securities online — is a an equally foolish vehicle for individual investors to pursue that was born out of the quick access to information — and the opportunity to instantly buy and sell securities — brought in by the Internet. Placing trades online is far cheaper than the older methods of trading (such as telephoning a broker), but the more you trade, the more trading costs eat into your investment capital.

Frequent trading also increases your tax bill. If you sell a stock or other investment at a profit, you have to pay tax on your gains when you file that year's tax return. In contrast, as long as you hold on to an investment — no matter how much it rises in value — you put off having to pay any taxes on your gains (see Chapter 7). You certainly can make some profits when day-trading. However, over an extended period of time, you'll inevitably under-perform the broad market averages. In those rare instances where you may do a little better than the market averages, it's rarely worth the time and per-sonal sacrifices that you, your family, and your friendships endure.

Understanding Investment Returns

The previous sections describe the difference between ownership and lend-ing investments, and they help you distinguish gambling and speculation from investing. "That's all well and good," you say, "but how do I choose which type of investments to put my money into? How much can I make, and what are the risks?"

Good questions. We'll start with the returns you *might* make. We say "might" because we're looking at history, and history is a record of the past. Using history to predict the future — especially the near future — is dangerous. History may repeat itself, but not always in exactly the same fashion and not necessarily when you expect it to.

During this past century, ownership investments such as stocks and real estate returned around 10 percent per year, handily beating lending invest-ments such as bonds (around 5 to 7 percent) and savings accounts (roughly 3 to 4 percent) in the investment performance race. Inflation has averaged 3 percent per year.

If you already know that the stock market can be risky, you may be wondering why investing in stocks is worth the anxiety and potential losses. Why bother for a few extra percent per year? Well, over many years, a few extra percent per year can really magnify the growth of your money (see Table 8-2). The more years you have to invest, the greater the difference a few percent makes in your returns.

Table 8-2	The Difference a Few Percent Makes	
At This Rate of Return on $10,000 Invested	You'll Have This Much in 25 Years	You'll Have This Much in 40 Years
4% (savings account)	$26,658	$48,010
5% (bond)	$33,863	$70,400
10% (stocks and real estate)	$108,347	$452,592

Investing is not a spectator sport. You can't earn good returns on stocks and real estate if you keep your money in cash on the sidelines. If you invest in growth investments such as stocks and real estate, don't chase one new investment after another trying to beat the market average returns. *The biggest value is to be in the market, not to beat it.*

Sizing Investment Risks

Many investors have a simplistic understanding of what risk means and how to apply it to their investment decisions. For example, when compared to the yo-yo motions of the stock market, a bank savings account may seem like a less risky place to put your money. Over the long term, however, the stock market usually beats the rate of inflation, while the interest rate on a savings account does not. Thus, if you're saving your money for a long-term goal like retirement, a savings account can be a "riskier" place to put your money.

Before you invest, ask yourself these questions:

- ✔ **What am I saving and investing this money for?** In other words, what's my goal?

- ✔ **What is my timeline for this investment?** When will I use this money?

- ✔ **What is the historical volatility of the investment I'm considering?** Does that suit my comfort level and timeline for this investment?

After you answer these questions, you'll have a better understanding of risk and you'll be able to match your savings goals to their most appropriate investment vehicles. In Chapter 4, we help you consider your savings goals and timeline. We address investment risk and returns in the sections that follow.

Comparing the risks of stocks and bonds

Given the relatively higher historical returns we mention for ownership investments in the previous section, some people think that they should put all their money in stocks and real estate. So what's the catch?

The risk with ownership investments is the short-term fluctuations in their value. During the last century, stocks declined, on average, by more than 10 percent once every five years. Drops in stock prices of more than 20 percent occurred, on average, once every ten years. Real estate prices suffer similar periodic setbacks.

Therefore, in order to earn those generous long-term returns from ownership investments like stocks and real estate, you must be willing to tolerate volatility. You absolutely should not put all your money in the stock or real estate market. You should not invest your emergency money or money you expect to use within the next five years in such volatile investments.

The shorter the time period that you have for holding your money in an investment, the less likely growth-oriented investments like stocks are to beat out lending-type investments like bonds. Table 8-3 illustrates the historical relationship between stock and bond returns based on number of years held.

Table 8-3	Stocks versus Bonds
Number of Years Investment Held	*Likelihood of Stocks Beating Bonds*
1	60%
5	70%
10	80%
20	91%
30	99%

Some types of bonds have higher yields than others, but the risk–reward relationship remains intact (see Chapter 9 for more on bonds). A bond generally pays you a higher rate of interest when it has a:

- ✔ **Lower credit rating:** To compensate for the higher risk of default and the higher likelihood of losing your investment
- ✔ **Longer-term maturity:** To compensate for the risk that you'll be unhappy with the bond's set interest rate if the market level of interest rates moves up

Focusing on the risks you can control

When Eric taught a personal finance class at the University of California, he would ask his students to write down what they'd like to learn. Here's what one student had to say: "I want to learn what to invest my money in now, as the stock market is overvalued and interest rates are about to go up, so bonds are dicey and banks give lousy interest — HELP!"

This student recognized the risk of price fluctuations in her investments, but she also seemed to believe, like too many people, that you can predict what's going to happen. How did *she* know that the stock market was overvalued, and why hadn't the rest of the world figured it out? How did she know that interest rates were about to go up, and why hadn't the rest of the world figured that out, either?

When you invest in stocks and other growth-oriented investments, you must accept the volatility of these investments. That said, you can take several actions, which we discuss in this chapter and the remainder of Part III, to greatly reduce your risk when investing in these higher-potential-return investments. Invest the money that you have earmarked for the longer term in these vehicles. Minimize the risk of these investments through diversification. Don't buy just one or two stocks; buy a number of stocks. Later in this chapter, we discuss what you need to know about diversification.

Discovering low-risk, high-return investments

Despite what professors teach in the nation's leading business and finance graduate school programs, low-risk investments that almost certainly lead to high returns are available. We can think of at least four such investments:

✔ **Paying off consumer debt.** If you're paying 10-, 14-, or 20-percent interest or more on an outstanding credit card or other consumer loan, pay it off before investing. To get a comparable return through other investment vehicles (after the government takes its share of your profits), you'd have to start a new career as a loan shark. If you're in a 33-percent tax bracket and you're paying 14 percent interest on consumer debt, you need to annually earn a whopping pre-tax return of 21 percent on your investments to justify not paying off the debt. Good luck!

When your only source of funds for paying off debt is a small emergency reserve equal to a few months' living expenses, paying off your debt may involve some risk. Tap in to your emergency reserves only if you have a backup source — for example, the ability to borrow from a willing family member.

✔ **Investing in your health.** Eat healthy, exercise, and relax.

✔ **Investing in friends and family.** Invest time and effort in improving your relationships with loved ones.

✔ **Investing in personal and career development.** Pick up a new hobby, improve your communication skills, or read widely. Take an adult education course or go back to school for a degree. Your investment should lead to greater happiness and perhaps even higher paycheques.

Diversifying Your Investments

Diversification is one of the most powerful investment concepts. It refers to saving your eggs (or investments) in different baskets.

Diversification requires you to place your money in different investments with returns that are not completely correlated. This is a fancy way of saying that when some of your investments are down in value, odds are that others are up in value.

To decrease the chances of all your investments getting clobbered at the same time, you must put your money in different types of investments, such as bonds, stocks, real estate, and small business. (We cover all these investments and more in Chapter 9.) You can further diversify your investments by investing in domestic as well as international markets.

Within a given class of investments, such as stocks, investing in different types of that class (such as different types of stocks) that perform well under various economic conditions is important. For this reason, *mutual funds,* which are diversified portfolios of securities such as stocks or bonds, are a highly useful investment vehicle. When you buy into a mutual fund, your money is pooled with the money of many others and invested in a vast array of stocks or bonds.

You can look at the benefits of diversification in two ways:

- ✔ Diversification reduces the volatility in the value of your whole portfolio. In other words, your portfolio can achieve the same rate of return that a single investment can provide with less fluctuation in value.

- ✔ Diversification allows you to obtain a higher rate of return for a given level of risk.

Keep in mind that no one, no matter whom he works for or what credentials he has, can guarantee returns on an investment. You can do good research and get lucky, but no one is free from the risk of losing money. Diversification allows you to hedge the risk of your investments. See Figures 8-1, 8-2, and 8-3 to get an idea of how diversifying can reduce your risk. (The figures in these charts are adjusted for inflation.) Notice that different investments did better during different time periods. Because the future can't be predicted, diversifying your money into different investments is safer. (In the 1990s, stocks appreciated greatly, and bonds did pretty well, too, while gold and silver did poorly. In the 2000s, stocks treaded water (except those in emerging markets) while bonds and precious metals did well.

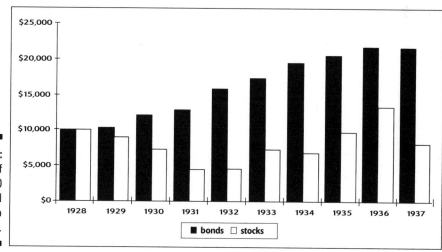

Figure 8-1: Value of $10,000 invested from 1928 to 1937.

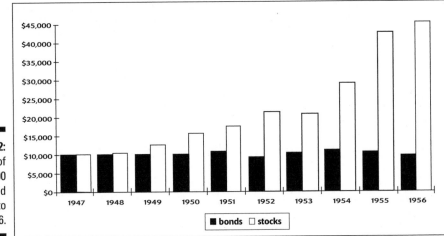

Figure 8-2:
Value of $10,000 invested from 1947 to 1956.

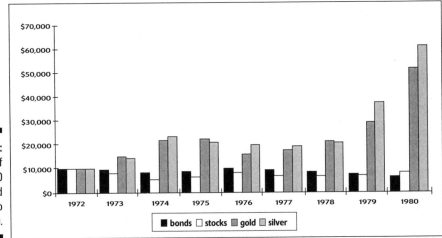

Figure 8-3:
Value of $10,000 invested from 1972 to 1980.

Spreading the wealth: Asset allocation

Asset allocation refers to how you spread your investing dollars among different investment options (stocks, bonds, GICs, savings accounts, and so on). Before you can intelligently decide how to allocate your assets, you need to ponder a number of issues, including your present financial situation, your goals and priorities, and the pros and cons of various investment options.

Although stocks and real estate offer attractive long-term returns, they can sometimes suffer significant declines. Thus, these investments are not suitable for money that you think you may want or need to use within, say, the next five years.

High-interest savings accounts, money market funds, and shorter-term bond investments are good places to keep money that you expect to use soon. Everyone should have a reserve of money — about three to six months' worth of living expenses — in a money market fund or high-interest savings account that they can access in an emergency. Shorter-term bonds or bond mutual funds can serve as a higher-yielding, secondary emergency cushion. (Refer to Chapter 4 for more on emergency reserves.)

Bonds can also be useful for some longer-term investing for diversification purposes. For example, when investing for retirement, placing a portion of your money in bonds helps buffer stock market declines. The remaining chapters in Part III detail your various investment options and explain how to select those that best meet your needs.

Allocating money for the long term

Investing money for retirement is a classic long-term goal that most people have. Your current age and the number of years until you retire are the biggest factors to consider when allocating money for long-term purposes. The younger you are and the more years you have before retirement, the more comfortable you should be with growth-oriented (and more volatile) investments, such as stocks and investment real estate.

One useful guideline for dividing or allocating your money between longer-term-oriented growth investments, such as stocks, and more-conservative lending investments, such as bonds, is to subtract your age from 110 (or 120 if you want to be aggressive; 100 to be more conservative) and invest the resulting percentage in stocks. You then invest the remaining amount in bonds.

For example, if you're 30 years old, you invest from 70 (100 – 30) to 90 (120 – 30) percent in stocks. The portion left over — 10 to 30 percent — is invested in bonds.

Table 8-4 lists some guidelines for allocating long-term money. All you need to figure out is how old you are and the level of risk you're comfortable with.

Table 8-4	Allocating Long-Term Money	
Your Investment Attitude	*Bond Allocation (%)*	*Stock Allocation (%)*
"Play it safer"	= Age	= 100 – age
"Middle-of-the-road"	= Age – 10	= 110 – age
"Aggressive"	= Age – 20	= 120 – age

For example, if you're the conservative sort who doesn't like a lot of risk but recognizes the value of striving for some growth and making your money work harder, you're a *middle-of-the-road* type. Using Table 8-4, if you're 40 years old, you may consider putting 30 percent (40 – 10) in bonds and 70 percent (110 – 40) in stocks.

In most employer retirement plans, mutual funds are the typical investment vehicle. If your employer's retirement plan includes more than one stock mutual fund as an option, you may want to try discerning which options are best by using the criteria we discuss in Chapter 10. In the event that all your retirement plan's stock fund options are good, you can simply divide your stock allocation among the choices.

When one or more of the choices is an international stock fund, consider allocating a percentage of your stock fund money to overseas investments: at least 20 percent for play-it-safe investors, 25 to 35 percent for middle-of-the-road investors, and as much as 35 to 50 percent for aggressive investors.

If the 40-year-old middle-of-the-roader from the previous example is investing 70 percent in stocks, about 25 to 35 percent of the stock fund investments (which works out to be about 18 to 24 percent of the total) can be invested in international stock funds.

Historically, most employees haven't had to make their own investing decisions with retirement money. Pension plans, in which the company directs the investments, were more common in previous years. It's interesting to note that in a typical pension plan, companies choose to allocate the majority of money to stocks (about 60 percent), with a bit less placed in bonds (about 35 percent) and other investments. For more information on investing in RRSPs and retirement plans, see Chapters 11 and 12.

Sticking with your allocations: Don't trade

The allocation of your investment dollars should be driven by your goals and desire to take risk. As you get older, gradually scaling back on the riskiness (and therefore growth potential) of your portfolio generally makes sense.

Don't tinker with your portfolio daily, weekly, monthly, or even annually. (Every three to five years or so, you may want to rebalance your holdings to get your mix to a desired asset allocation, as discussed in the previous section.) Don't engage in trading with the hopes of buying into a hot investment and selling your losers. Jumping onto a "winner" and dumping a "loser" may provide some short-term psychological comfort, but in the long term such an investment strategy often produces below-average returns.

When an investment gets front-page coverage and everyone is talking about its stunning rise, it's definitely time to take a reality check. The higher the value of an investment rises, the greater the danger that it's overpriced. Its next move may be downward. Don't follow the herd.

During the late 1990s, many technology (especially Internet) stocks had spectacular rises, thus attracting a lot of attention. However, the fact that the world's economy was becoming increasingly technology-based didn't mean that any price you paid for a technology stock was fine. Some investors who neglected to do basic research and bought into the attention-grabbing, high-flying technology stocks — the dot-coms — lost 80 percent or more of their investments in the early 2000s. Ouch!

Conversely, when things look bleak (as when stocks in general suffered significant losses in the early 2000s and then again in the late 2000s), giving up hope is easy — who wants to be associated with a loser? However, investors who forget about their overall asset allocation plan and panic and sell *after* a major decline miss out on a tremendous buying opportunity.

Many people like buying everything from clothing to cars to ketchup on sale — yet whenever the stock market has a clearance sale, most investors stampede for the exits instead of snatching up great buys. Demonstrate your courage; don't follow the herd.

Investing lump sums via dollar-cost averaging

When you have a large chunk of cash to invest — whether you received it from an accumulation of funds over the years, the sale of some of your investments, an inheritance, or a recent windfall from work you've done — you may have a problem deciding what to do with it. Many people, of course, would like to have your problem. (You're not complaining, right?) You want to invest your money, but you're a bit skittish, if not outright terrified, at the prospect of investing the lump of money all at once.

If the money is residing in a regular savings account or money market fund, you may feel like it's wasting away. You want to put it to work! Our first words of advice are "Don't rush." Nothing is wrong with earning a small return in a safe in account. (See Chapter 13 for our recommendations of the best money funds.) Remember that a bank account or money market fund beats the heck out of rushing into an investment in which you may lose 20 percent or more. We sometimes speak with people in a state of near panic. Typically, these folks have GICs coming due, and they feel that they must decide exactly where they want to invest the money in the 48 hours before the GIC matures.

Take a deep breath. You have absolutely no reason to rush into an important decision. Tell your friendly banker that when the GIC matures, you want to put the proceeds into the bank's highest-yielding savings account. That way, your money continues to earn interest while you buy yourself some breathing room.

One approach to investing is called *dollar-cost averaging* (DCA). With DCA, you invest your money in equal chunks on a regular basis — say, once a month — into a diversified group of investments.

For example, if you have $60,000 to invest, you can invest $2,500 per month until it's all invested, which takes a couple years. The money awaiting future investment isn't lying fallow; you keep it in a money market account so it can earn a bit of interest while waiting its turn.

The attraction of DCA is that it allows you to ease into riskier investments instead of jumping in all at once. If the price of the investment drops after some of your initial purchases, you can buy some later at a lower price. If you dump all your money into the "sure win" investment all at once and then it drops like a stone, you'll be kicking yourself for not waiting. (The flip side of DCA is that when your investment of choice appreciates in value, you may wish that you had invested your money faster.)

Another drawback of DCA is that you may get cold feet as you continue to pour money into an investment that's dropping in value. Many people who are attracted to DCA because they fear that they may buy before a price drop end up bailing out of what feels like a sinking ship.

DCA can also cause headaches with your taxes when the time comes to sell investments held outside retirement plans. When you buy an investment at many different times and prices, the accounting becomes muddied as you sell blocks of the investment.

DCA is most valuable when the money you want to invest represents a large portion of your total assets and you can stick to a schedule. Make DCA automatic so that you're less likely to chicken out should the investment fall after your initial purchases. Most of the investment firms we recommend in the next few chapters provide automatic investment services.

Keeping your investing wits during uncertain times

During times like the early 2000s and again in the late 2000s, some investors abandon the stock market for good. That's why the rebound from a severe bear market — and the down stock-market cycle in those years has been the worst in magnitude and duration in decades — sometimes takes time to develop. Although some people who get burned badly learn that they're not cut out for stock investing, everybody else should take stock of their investing approaches and adjust their practices and expectations.

In the early 2000s, the stock market began falling — with some growth stocks, especially technology stocks, plunging like stocks do in a depression. Layoffs mounted, and September 11 undermined consumer confidence. Then the general public learned that some major companies — Enron, WorldCom, and Global Crossing — pulled the wool over investors' eyes with shady accounting techniques that artificially inflated earnings. Concerns about further terrorist attacks, SARS, and war with Iraq (and perhaps other nations) hung like dark clouds on the horizon. Here in Canada, we had our own share of sketchy stock market promoters, including overhyped dot-coms like Book4Golf and Bid.com.

In the late 2000s, a global financial crisis brought on by risky mortgage investments made by financial service companies captured headlines and public attention. Major financial firms went bankrupt while others required large capital injections from the government for their survival. Most global stock markets plunged in value by the largest amounts since the Great Depression of the 1930s. And the wars in Iraq and Afghanistan and associated spending lingered on and depressed the public's mood, adding to a widening federal budget deficit.

Many similarities are apparent between the early 2000s and the early 1970s, when a multitude of unpredictable problems unfolded. The early '70s saw record trade and budget deficits and inflation rearing its ugly head, in addition to the invasion of Cambodia, the Arab oil embargo, gas lines, and that period's Arab–Israeli conflict — the Yom Kippur War. Vice President Spiro Agnew resigned over the exposure of his personal income tax evasion and acceptance of bribes while working in Maryland's government.

Then news of Watergate broke, and Nixon's impeachment hearings began. After flirting with the 1,000 level since 1966, the Dow Jones Industrial Average plunged below 600 after Nixon resigned in 1974. Here at home the Toronto Stock Exchange (TSE) also plummeted, falling 38 percent. Many investors soured on stocks and swore off the market forever. That reaction was unfortunate, because even with the recent, severe stock market decline, stocks are still 15-fold higher today than they were back at their lows in 1974.

The same chain of events occurred during the recession in the late nineties that was brought on by the sub-prime debt crisis. In late 2007 the stock markets started to fall; by early 2009 they had lost more than half their value. But if you had sold at the very bottom, you would have simply locked in your losses. In a little more than a year, the markets rose by more than 75 percent.

The lesson from all this is simple: Don't let a poor string of events sour you on stock investing. History has repeatedly proven that continuing to buy stocks during down markets increases your long-term returns. Throwing in the towel is the worst thing you can do in a slumping market. And don't waste time trying to find a way to beat the system. Buy and hold a diversified portfolio of stocks. Remember that the financial markets reward investors for accepting risk and uncertainty.

Acknowledging Differences among Investment Firms

Thousands of firms sell investments and manage money. Banks, mutual fund companies, securities brokerage firms, and even insurance companies all vie for your dollars.

Just to make matters more complicated, each industry plays in the others' backyards. You can find mutual fund companies that offer securities brokerage, insurance firms that are in the mutual fund business, and mutual fund companies that offer bank-like accounts and services. You may benefit from this competition and one-stop shopping convenience. On the other hand, some firms are novices at particular businesses and count on some people's shopping by brand-name recognition.

Focusing on the best firms

Make sure you do business with a firm that

- ✔ **Offers the best value investments in comparison to its competitors.** Value is the combination of performance (including service) and cost. Given the level of risk that you're comfortable with, you want investments that offer higher rates of return but you don't want to have to pay a small fortune for them. Commissions, management fees, maintenance fees, and other charges can turn a high-performance investment into a mediocre or poor one.

- ✔ **Employs representatives who do not have an inherent self-interest in steering you into a particular type of investment.** This criterion has nothing to do with whether an investment firm hires polite, well-educated, or well-dressed people. The most important factor is the way the company compensates its employees. If the investment firm's personnel are paid on commission, it can be a challenge for employees not to focus on their compensation. Give preference to investing firms that don't tempt their employees to push one investment over another in order to generate more fees.

No-load (commission-free) mutual fund companies

Mutual funds are an ideal investment vehicle for most investors. *No-load mutual fund companies* are firms through which you can invest in mutual funds without paying sales commissions. In other words, every dollar you invest goes to work in the mutual funds you choose — nothing is siphoned off to pay sales commissions. See Chapter 10 for details on investing in mutual funds.

Discount brokers

In one of the most beneficial changes for investors this past century, the Securities and Exchange Commission (SEC) deregulated the retail brokerage industry on May 1, 1975. (In 1983, the Toronto and Montreal stock exchanges followed suit.) Prior to this date, investors were charged fixed commissions when they bought or sold stocks, bonds, and other securities. In other words, no matter which brokerage firm an investor did business with, the cost of the firm's services was set (and the level of commissions was high). After deregulation, brokerage firms could charge people whatever their little hearts desired.

Competition inevitably resulted in more and better choices. Many new brokerage firms (that didn't do business the old way) opened. They were dubbed *discount brokers* because the fees they charged customers were substantially lower than what brokers charged under the old fixed-fee system.

Even more important than saving customers money, discount brokers established a vastly improved compensation system that greatly reduced conflicts of interest. Discount brokers generally pay the salaries of their brokers. The term *discount broker* is actually not an enlightening one. It's certainly true that this new breed of brokerage firm saves you lots of money when you invest. You can easily save 50 to 80 percent through the major discount brokers. But these firms' investments are not "on sale" or "second-rate." Discount brokers are simply brokers without major conflicts of interest. Of course, like any other for-profit enterprise, they're in business to make money, but they're much less likely to steer you wrong for their own benefit.

Places to consider avoiding

The worst places to invest are those that charge you a lot, have mediocre- or poor-performing investments, and have major conflicts of interest. The prime conflict of interest arises when investment firms pay their brokers commissions on the basis of what and how much they sell. The result: The investment firms sell lots of stuff that pays fat commissions, and they *churn,* or cause a rapid turnover of, your account. (Because each transaction has a fee, the more you buy and sell, the more money they make.)

Some folks who call themselves *financial planners* or *financial consultants* work on commission. In addition to working at the bigger brokerage firms, many of them belong to so-called *broker-dealer networks,* which provide back-office support and investment products to sell. When a person claiming to be a financial planner or adviser is part of a broker-dealer network, odds are quite high that you're dealing with an investment salesperson. See Chapter 18 for more background on the financial-planning industry and questions to ask an adviser you're thinking about hiring.

Commissions and their impact on human behaviour

Investment products bring in widely varying commissions. The products that bring in the highest commissions tend to be the ones that money-hungry brokers push the hardest.

Table 8-5 lists the commissions that you pay and that come out of your investment dollars when you work with brokers, financial consultants, and financial planners who work on commission.

Table 8-5	Investment Sales Commissions	
Investment Type	*Average Commission on $20,000 Investment*	*Average Commission on $100,000 Investment*
Annuities	$1,400	$7,000
Initial public offerings (new stock issue)	$1,000	$5,000
Limited partnerships	$1,800	$9,000
Load mutual funds	$1,200	$5,000
Options and futures	$2,000+	$10,000+

Besides the fact that you can never be sure you're getting an unbiased recommendation from a salesperson working on commission, you may be wasting money unnecessarily. The best investments can be bought on a *no-load* (commission-free) basis.

No-load mutual funds are a good example of an investment that can be purchased without paying a commission. Many discount brokers will also sell you load funds without a commission, charging only a relatively small transaction fee.

When you're unsure about an investment product that's being pitched to you (and even when you *are* sure), ask for a copy of the *prospectus*. In the first few pages, check out whether the investment includes a commission (also known as a *load*). Although salespeople can hide behind obscure titles such as vice president or financial consultant, a prospectus must detail whether the investment carries a commission.

Investment salespeople's conflicts of interest

Financial consultants (also known as stockbrokers), financial planners, and others who sell investment products can have enormous conflicts of interest when recommending strategies and specific investment products. Commissions and other financial incentives can't help but skew the advice of even the most earnest and otherwise well-intentioned salespeople.

Numerous conflicts of interest can damage your investment portfolio. The following are the most common conflicts to watch out for:

- **Pushing higher-commission products:** As we discuss earlier in this chapter, commissions on investment products vary tremendously. Products like limited partnerships, commodities, options, and futures are at the worst end of the spectrum for you (and the best end of the spectrum for a salesperson). Investments such as no-load mutual funds and Treasury bills that are 100-percent commission-free are at the best end of the spectrum for you (and, therefore, the worst end of the spectrum for a salesperson).

- **Recommending active trading:** Investment salespeople often advise you to trade frequently into and out of different securities. They usually base their advice on current news events or an analyst's comments on the security. Sometimes these moves are valid, but more often they're not. In extreme cases, brokers trade on a monthly basis. By the end of the year, they've churned through your entire portfolio. Needless to say, all these transactions cost you big money in trading fees.

  Diversified mutual funds (see Chapter 10) make more sense for most people. You can invest in mutual funds free of sales commissions. Besides saving money on commissions, you earn better long-term returns by having an expert money manager work for you.

- **Failing to recommend investing through a company retirement plan:** An investment salesperson is not likely to recommend that you contribute to your employer's retirement plan. Such contributions cut into the money you have available to invest with your friendly salesperson.

- **Pushing high-fee products:** Many of the brokerage firms that used to sell investment products only on commission moved into fee-based investment management. This change is an improvement for investors because it reduces some of the conflicts of interest caused by commissions.

  On the other hand, these brokers charge extraordinarily high fees, which are usually quoted as a percentage of assets under management, on their managed-investment (or wrap) accounts.

TIP

What to do when you're fleeced by a broker

You can't sue a broker just because you lose money on that person's investment recommendations. However, if you have been the victim of one of the following cardinal financial sins, you may have some legal recourse:

✔ **Misrepresentation and omission:** If you were told, for example, that a particular investment guaranteed returns of 15 percent per year and then the investment ended up plunging in value by 50 percent, you were misled. Misrepresentation can also be charged if you're sold an investment with hefty commissions after you were originally told that it was commission-free.

✔ **Unsuitable investments:** Retirees who need access to their capital are often advised to invest in limited partnerships (or LPs, discussed in Chapter 9) for safe, high yields. The yields on most LPs end up being anything but safe. LP investors have also discovered how *illiquid* (or not readily converted into cash) their investments are — some can't be liquidated for up to ten years or more.

✔ **Churning:** If your broker or financial planner is constantly trading your investments, odds are that his weekly commission cheque is benefiting at your expense.

✔ **Rogue elephant salespeople:** When your planner or broker buys or sells without your approval or ignores your request to make a change, you may be able to collect for losses caused by these actions.

Two major types of practitioners — securities lawyers and arbitration consultants — stand ready to help you recover your lost money. You can find securities lawyers by looking in the Yellow Pages or other business directory, or calling your local bar association for referrals. If your claim is for $100,000 or less, the Investment Industry Regulatory Organization of Canada (IIROC) offers an arbitration service. However, you generally have to pay a share of the arbitration fees. You can find out more by calling their complaints line (877-442-4322) or by visiting their Web site at www.iiroc.ca and looking under "Investor" information. Most lawyers and consultants will ask for a fee to be paid upfront — called a retainer — of anywhere from a few hundred to several thousand dollars as an advance to cover their time and expenses.

You may want to go to *arbitration* — an agreement you may have made (probably without realizing it) when you set up an account to work with the broker or planner. Arbitration is usually much quicker, cheaper, and easier than going to court. You can even choose to represent yourself. If you decide to prepare for arbitration by yourself, the nonprofit American Arbitration Association can send you a package of background materials to help with your case. Contact the association's headquarters (1633 Broadway, 10th Floor, New York, NY 10019; phone 212-716-5800; Web site www.adr.org). Although similar Canadian organizations exist, they are largely professional development bodies.

Valuing brokerage research

Brokerage firms and the brokers who work for them frequently argue that their research is better. With their insights and recommendations, they say, you'll do better and "beat the market averages."

Wall Street analysts are often overly optimistic when it comes to predicting corporate profits. If analysts were simply inaccurate or bad estimators, you'd expect that they'd sometimes underestimate and, at other times, overestimate companies' earnings. The discrepancy identifies yet another conflict of interest among many of the brokerage firms.

Brokerage firm analysts are generally reluctant to write a negative report about a company because the firms these analysts work for also solicit companies to issue new stock to the public. What better way to show businesses your potential for selling shares to the public at a high price than by showing how much you believe in certain companies and writing glowing reports about their future prospects?

Seeing through Experts Who Predict the Future

Believing that you can increase your investment returns by following the prognostications of certain gurus is a common mistake that some investors make, especially during more trying and uncertain times. Many people may want to believe that some experts can predict the future of the investment world and keep them out of harm's way. Believing in gurus makes it easier to accept the risk you know you're taking when trying to make your money grow. The sage predictions that you read in an investment newsletter or hear from an "expert" who is repeatedly quoted in financial publications make you feel protected — sort of like Linus and his security blanket.

Investment newsletter subscribers and guru followers would be better off buying a warm blanket instead — it has a lot more value and costs a whole lot less! No one can predict the future. If they could, they'd be so busy investing their own money and getting rich that they wouldn't have the time and desire to share their secrets with you.

Investment newsletters

Many investment newsletters purport to time the markets, telling you exactly the right time to get into and out of certain stocks or mutual funds (or the financial markets in general). Such an approach is doomed to failure in the long run. By failure, we mean that this approach won't beat the tried-and-true strategy of buy and hold.

We see people paying hundreds of dollars annually to subscribe to all sorts of market-timing and stock-picking newsletters. One person we know, a lawyer, subscribed to several newsletters. When asked why, he said that their marketing materials claimed that if you followed their advice, you would make a 20-percent-per-year return on your money. But in the four years that he'd followed their advice, he'd actually *lost* money, despite appreciating financial markets overall.

Before you even consider subscribing to any investment newsletter, examine its track record through avenues such as *Hulbert Financial Digest*. The investment newsletter's marketing materials typically hype the supposed returns that the publication's recommendations have produced. Sadly, newsletters seem to be able to make lots of bogus claims without suffering the timely wrath of securities regulators.

Don't get predictive advice from newsletters. If newsletter writers were so smart about the future of financial markets, they'd be making lots more money as money managers. The only types of investment newsletters and periodicals that you should consider subscribing to are those that offer research and information rather than predictions. We discuss the investment newsletters that fit the bill in the subsequent investment chapters. Eric's Web site, www.erictyson.com, provides excerpts and updates from some of the best newsletters. Also check out the "Guru Watch" section for evaluations of commonly quoted gurus.

Investment gurus

Investment gurus come and go. Some of them get their 15 minutes of fame on the basis of one or two successful predictions that someone in the press remembers (and makes famous).

During the financial crisis of 2008 and 2009, all sorts of pundits were coming out of the woodwork claiming that they had predicted what was unfolding. Chief among them was an economist named Nouriel Roubini, whom few people had previously heard of.

Many news services credited Roubini for supposedly predicting the recession. It's true that Roubini had indeed predicted a recession. The only problem, however, is that Roubini predicted a recession in 2004, 2005, 2006, and 2007. So he was wrong for four long years in a row. In 2008, his prediction of a recession finally came true.

When the stock market dropped sharply and the recession worsened in late 2008, Roubini maintained a breakneck schedule with the news media. So he made even more predictions. For example, in late October, Roubini predicted that "hundreds of hedge funds are poised to fail as frantic investors rush to redeem their assets and force managers into a fire sale of assets. . . . We've reached a situation of sheer panic. Don't be surprised if policymakers need to close down markets for a week or two in coming days." This prediction sounded absurd to us, and of course never happened. Roubini was wrong.

In January 2009, Roubini predicted oil prices would stay below $40 per barrel for all of 2009. It didn't take long for that prediction to be proven wrong: Oil jumped above $50 per barrel by April and $70 by June.

When the Dow Jones Industrial Average fell to 6,500 in early 2009, Roubini said the market was likely to fall much further, and he described any rally from that level as a "sucker's rally." Those who panicked and sold in early 2009 because of Roubini's dire prediction were soon disappointed again as the stock market rebounded sharply.

The sad part about hyped articles with hyped predictions is that they cause some individual investors to panic and do the wrong thing — selling good assets like stocks at depressed prices. The media shouldn't irresponsibly publicize hyped predictions, especially without clearly and accurately disclosing the predictor's track record. Don't fall victim to such hype.

Commentators and experts who publish predictive commentaries and newsletters and who are interviewed in the media can't predict the future. Ignore the predictions and speculations of self-proclaimed gurus and investment soothsayers. The few people who have a slight leg up on everyone else aren't going to share their investment secrets — they're too busy investing their own money! If you have to believe in something to offset your fears, believe in good information and proven investment managers. And don't forget the value of optimism, faith, and hope — regardless of *what* or *whom* you believe in!

Leaving You with Some Final Advice

We cover a lot of ground in this chapter. In the remaining chapters in this part, we detail different investment choices and accounts and how to build a champion portfolio! Keep several issues in mind as you make important investing choices:

- ✔ **Don't invest based on sales solicitations.** Companies that advertise and solicit prospective customers aggressively with tactics such as telemarketing offer some of the worst financial products with the highest fees. Companies with great products don't have to reach their potential customers this way. Of course, all companies have to do some promotion. But the companies with the best investment offerings don't have to use the hard-sell approach; they get plenty of new business through the word-of-mouth recommendations of satisfied customers.

- ✔ **Don't invest in what you don't understand.** The mistake of not understanding the investments you purchase usually follows from the preceding no-no — buying into a sales pitch. When you don't understand an investment, odds are good that it won't be right for you. Slick-tongued brokers (who may call themselves financial consultants, advisers, or planners) who earn commissions based on what they sell can talk you into inappropriate investments. Before you invest in anything, you should know its track record, its true costs, and how liquid (easily convertible to cash) it is.

- ✔ **Minimize fees.** Avoid investments that carry high sales commissions and management expenses (usually disclosed in a prospectus). Virtually all investments today can be purchased without a salesperson. Besides paying unnecessary commissions, the bigger danger in investing through a salesperson is that you may be directed to a path that's not in your best interests. Management fees create a real drag on investment returns. Not surprisingly, higher-fee investments, on average, perform worse than alternatives with lower fees. High ongoing management fees often go toward lavish offices, glossy brochures, and skyscraper salaries, or toward propping up small, inefficient operations. Do you want your hard-earned dollars to support either of these types of businesses?

- ✔ **Pay attention to tax consequences.** Even if you never become an investment expert, you're smart enough to know that the more money you pay in taxes, the less you have for investing and playing with. See Chapter 12 for info on how retirement plans can help boost your investment returns. For investments outside retirement plans, you need to match the types of investments to your tax situation (see Chapter 13).

Wrap (or managed) accounts

Wrap accounts (also called managed accounts) remain very popular among commission-based brokerage firms. These accounts go by a variety of names, but they're all similar in that they charge a fixed percentage of the assets under management to invest your money through money managers.

Wrap accounts can be poor investments because their management expenses may be extraordinarily high — up to 3 percent per year (some even higher) of assets under management. Remember that in the long haul, stocks can return about 10 percent per year before taxes. So if you're paying 3 percent per year to have your money managed in stocks, 30 percent of your return (before taxes) is siphoned off. But don't forget — because the government sure won't — that you pay a good chunk of money in taxes on your 10 percent return as well. So the 3 percent wrap actually ends up depleting 40 to 50 percent of your after-tax profits!

The best no-load (commission-free) mutual funds offer investors access to the nation's best investment managers for a fraction of the cost of wrap accounts. You can invest in dozens of top-performing funds for an annual expense of 2 percent per year or less. Some of the best fund companies offer excellent funds for a cost as low as 0.3 to 1.5 percent (see Chapter 10).

You may be told, in the marketing of wrap accounts, that you're getting access to investment managers who don't normally take money from small-fry investors like you. Not a single study shows that the performance of money managers has anything to do with the minimum account they handle. Besides, no-load mutual funds hire many of the same managers who work at other money management firms.

You also may be told that you'll earn a higher rate of return, so the extra cost is worth it. "You could have earned 18 to 25 percent per year," they say, "had you invested with the 'Star of Yesterday' investment management company." The key word here is had. History is history. Many of yesterday's winners become tomorrow's losers or mediocre performers.

You also need to remember that wrap account performance records may include marketing hype. Showing only the performance of selected accounts — those that performed the best — is the most common ploy.

Chapter 9

Understanding Your Investment Choices

In This Chapter

▶ Playing it safe: Bank and money market accounts and bonds

▶ Growing your wealth: Stocks, real estate, and small business

▶ Eyeballing oddball investments: Precious metals, annuities, and collectibles

*W*hich vehicle you choose for your investment journey depends on where you're going, how fast you want to get there, and what risks you're willing to take. If you haven't yet read Chapter 8, please do so now. In it, we cover a number of investment concepts, such as the difference between lending and ownership investments, that will enhance your ability to choose among the common investment vehicles we discuss in this chapter.

Slow and Steady Investments

Everyone should have some money in stable, safe investment vehicles. For example, this would include money that you've earmarked for bills you need to pay in the near future, both expected and unexpected. Likewise, if you're saving money for a home purchase within the next few years, you certainly don't want to risk that money on the roller coaster of the stock market.

The investment options that follow are appropriate for money you don't want to put at great risk.

Transaction/chequing accounts

Transaction/chequing accounts are best used for depositing your monthly income and paying for your expenditures. If you want to have unlimited cheque-writing privileges and access to your money with a bank (ABM) card, chequing accounts at the bigger banks are often your best bet.

Here's how not to be taken by banks:

✓ **Consider small banks and credit unions.** You may get a better chequing account deal at a credit union or a smaller bank. Because you can easily obtain cash through ABM outlets, you may not need to do business with Big City Bank, which has ABM and branch offices at every intersection.

✓ **Shop around.** Some banks don't require you to maintain a minimum balance to avoid a monthly service charge when you direct deposit your paycheques. Make sure you shop around for accounts that don't ding you $1.50 here for the use of an ABM and $12 there for a low balance.

✓ **Limit the amount you keep in chequing.** Keep only enough money in the account for your monthly bill payment needs. If you consistently keep more than a few thousand dollars in a chequing account, get the excess out. You can earn more in a savings, high interest, or money market account, which we describe in the following section.

Savings accounts and money market funds

Savings accounts are available at banks and a number of other institutions such as President's Choice Financial and ING Direct. Money market funds are available through mutual fund companies and most larger financial institutions. The major difference is that money market funds and the high-interest accounts offered by President's Choice Financial, ING Direct, and others generally pay a much better rate of interest than comparable accounts from the major banks, although the high-interest accounts now being offered by the big banks are often competitive. The interest rate paid to you, also known as the *yield,* fluctuates over time depending on the level of interest rates in the overall economy. In addition, the high-interest accounts typically have no transaction fees.

The Canada Deposit Insurance Corporation (CDIC) backs most bank accounts. We wouldn't suggest you give preference to a traditional bank just because your investment (your *principal*) is insured, and because of the psychological comfort some people derive from seeing branches of their bank on every second street corner. The high-interest accounts offered by ING Direct and President's Choice Financial are also covered by CDIC insurance. Your money is just as safe as it is with a traditional bank, as long as you don't have more on deposit than the maximum insured by CDIC. And the lack of bricks-and-mortar outlets shouldn't bother you. In fact, not having the extra expenses of branches and tellers to serve you is a major reason why these companies can pay such high interest rates on your savings.

In addition to current rates, you can find contact information, along with links to take you to the relevant account sign-up pages.

Here's how to reach some of our favourite high-interest-account offerers:

- ✔ ING Direct (888-464-3232 or `www.ingdirect.ca`)
- ✔ President's Choice Financial (888-872-4724 or `www.pcfinancial.ca`)

Although money market funds are not covered by CDIC insurance they *are* regulated, and dozens of money market funds invest billions of dollars of individuals' and institutions' money. We haven't heard of the industry causing an individual to lose even a penny of principal. The risk difference versus a bank account is nil. General-purpose money market funds invest in safe, short-term bank guaranteed investment certificates (GICs), Government of Canada Treasury bills, provincial treasury bills, and corporate commercial paper (short-term debt), which is issued by the largest and most creditworthy companies.

Money market fund investments generally must have an average maturity of less than 90 days. In the unlikely event that an investment in a money market fund's portfolio goes sour, the mutual fund company that stands behind the money market fund would almost certainly cover the loss.

If the lack of insurance on money market funds still spooks you, here's a way to get the best of both worlds: Select a money market fund that invests exclusively in Canadian government securities, which are virtually risk-free because they are backed by the full strength and credit of the federal government. These types of accounts typically pay around a quarter-percent less interest than other money market funds.

Bonds

When you invest in a bond, you effectively lend your money to an organization. When a bond is issued, it includes a specified maturity date at which time the principal will be repaid. Bonds are also issued at a particular interest rate, or what's known as a *coupon*. This rate is fixed on most bonds. So, for example, if you buy a five-year, 6-percent bond issued by Bombardier, you're lending your money to Bombardier for five years at an interest rate of 6 percent per year. (Bond interest is usually paid in two equal, semi-annual installments.)

The value of a bond generally moves opposite the directional change in interest rates. For example, if you're holding a bond issued at 6 percent and rates increase to 8 percent on comparable, newly issued bonds, your bond decreases in value. (Why would anyone want to buy your bond at the price you paid if it yields just 6 percent and 8 percent can be obtained elsewhere?)

The overused GIC

A guaranteed investment certificate (GIC) is another type of bond that is issued by a bank. With a GIC, as with a real bond, you agree to lend your money to an organization (in this case, a bank) for a predetermined number of months or years. Generally, the longer you agree to lock up your money, the higher the interest rate you receive.

With most GICs, you pay a penalty for early withdrawal. If you want your money back before the end of the GIC's term, you'll get whacked with the loss of a number of months' worth of interest. Some GICs don't let you cash out early, period. Others may offer you the option of getting your money back before the GIC matures, but at the cost of a lower interest rate. Also, GICs generally don't tend to pay very competitive interest rates. You can usually beat the interest rate on shorter-term GICs (those that mature within a year or so) with the best high-interest savings accounts and money market mutual funds, which also give you access to your money without any penalty.

Some bonds are tied to variable interest rates. For example, you can buy bonds that are adjustable-rate mortgages, on which the interest rate can fluctuate. As an investor, you're actually lending your money to a mortgage borrower — indirectly, you're the banker making a loan to someone buying a home.

Bonds differ from one another in the following major ways:

✔ **The type of institution to which you're lending your money:** With municipal bonds, you lend your money to local governments; with Treasury bills, you lend your money to the federal government; with mortgage-backed securities, you lend your money to a mortgage holder; with corporate bonds, you lend your money to a corporation.

✔ **The credit quality of the borrower to whom you lend your money:** This refers to the probability that the borrower will pay you the interest and return your principal as agreed.

✔ **The length of maturity of the bond:** Short-term bonds mature within a few years, intermediate bonds within 7 to 10 years, and long-term bonds within 30 years. Longer-term bonds generally pay higher yields but fluctuate more with changes in interest rates.

Bonds are rated by major credit-rating agencies for their safety, usually on a scale where AAA is the highest possible rating. For example, high-grade corporate bonds (AAA or AA) are considered the safest (that is, most likely to pay you back). Next in safety are general bonds (A or BBB), which are still safe but just a little less so. Junk bonds (rated BB or lower), are actually not all that junky; they're just lower in quality and have a slight (1 or 2 percent) probability of default over long periods of time.

Some bonds are *callable,* which means that the bond's issuer can decide to pay you back earlier than the previously agreed-upon date. This event usually occurs when interest rates fall and the lender wants to issue new, lower-interest-rate bonds to replace the higher-rate bonds outstanding. To compensate you for early repayment, the lender typically gives you a small premium over what the bond is currently valued at.

Building Wealth with Ownership Vehicles

The three best legal ways to build wealth are to invest in stocks, real estate, and small business. We've found this to be true from observing many investors and from our own personal experiences. Check out the following sections for more details about these three options.

Socking your money away in stocks

Stocks, which represent shares of ownership in a company, are the most common ownership investment vehicle. When companies *go public,* they issue shares of stock that people like you can purchase on the major stock exchanges, such as the Toronto Stock Exchange, the New York Stock Exchange, and NASDAQ (National Association of Securities Dealers Automated Quotations), or on the over-the-counter market.

As the economy grows and companies grow with it and earn greater profits, stock prices (and dividend payouts on those stocks) generally follow suit. Stock prices and dividends don't move in lockstep with earnings, but over the years the relationship is pretty close. In fact, the *price–earnings ratio* — which measures the level of stock prices relative to (or divided by) company earnings — of stocks has averaged approximately 15 (although it has tended to be higher during periods of low inflation). A price–earnings ratio of 15 simply means that stock prices per share, on average, are selling at about 15 times those companies' earnings per share.

Companies that issue stock (called *publicly held* companies) include automobile manufacturers, computer software producers, fast-food restaurants, hotels, publishers, supermarkets, wineries, zipper manufacturers, and everything in between! (You can even invest overseas — see the "International stocks" sidebar.) By contrast, some companies are *privately held,* which means that they've elected to have their stock owned by senior management and a small number of affluent investors. Privately held companies' stocks do not trade on a stock exchange, so folks like you and us can't buy stock in such firms.

International stocks

Not only can you invest in company stocks that trade on the Canadian stock exchanges, but you can also invest in stocks in the U.S. and overseas. Aside from folks with business connections abroad, why would the average citizen want to do so?

We can give you several reasons. First, many investing opportunities exist outside of our borders. If you look at the total value of all stocks outstanding worldwide, the value of Canadian stocks is less than 3 percent of the total.

Another reason for investing in international stocks is that when you confine your investing to Canadian securities, you miss a world of opportunities, not only because of business growth available in other countries but also because you get the opportunity to diversify your portfolio even further. International securities markets don't move in tandem with Canadian markets. During various Canadian stock market drops, some international stock markets drop less, while others actually rise in value.

Some people hesitate to invest in overseas securities out of concern that overseas investing hurts the Canadian economy and contributes to a loss of jobs here at home. We have some counterarguments. First, if you don't profit from the growth of economies overseas, someone else will. If money is to be made, Canadians may as well be there to participate. Profits from a foreign company are distributed to all shareholders, no matter where they live. Dividends and stock price appreciation know no national boundaries.

Also, recognize that you already live in a global economy — making a distinction between Canadian and non-Canadian companies is no longer appropriate. Many companies that are headquartered in Canada also have overseas operations. Some Canadian firms derive a large portion of their revenue from their international divisions. Conversely, many firms based overseas also have Canadian operations. An increasing number of companies are worldwide operations.

Companies differ in what industry or line of business they're in and also in size. In the financial press, you often hear companies referred to by their *market capitalization,* which is the value of their outstanding stock (the number of total shares multiplied by the market price per share). When describing the sizes of companies, Wall Street has done away with such practical adjectives as *big* and *small* and replaced them with expressions like *large cap* and *small cap* (where *cap* stands for *capitalization*). Such is the language of financial geekiness.

Investing in the stock market involves occasional setbacks and difficult moments (just like raising children or going mountain climbing), but the overall journey should be worth the effort. Over the past two centuries, for example, the U.S. stock market (for which decades more data exists than for the Canadian stock market) has produced an annual average rate of return of about 10 percent. However, the market, as measured by the Dow Jones Industrial Average, fell more than 20 percent during 16 different periods in the 20th century. On average, these periods of decline lasted less than two years. So if you can withstand a temporary setback over a few years, the stock market is a proven place to invest for long-term growth.

You can invest in stocks by making your own selection of individual stocks or by letting a mutual (or exchange-traded) fund (discussed in Chapter 10) do it for you.

Discovering the relative advantages of mutual funds

Efficiently managed mutual funds offer investors of both modest and substantial means low-cost access to high-quality money managers. Mutual funds span the spectrum of risk and potential returns, from non-fluctuating money market funds (which are similar to savings accounts) to bond funds (which generally pay higher yields than money market funds but fluctuate with changes in interest rates) to stock funds (which offer the greatest potential for appreciation but also the greatest short-term volatility).

Investing in individual securities should be done only by those who really enjoy doing it and are aware of and willing to accept the risks. Mutual funds and exchange-traded funds, if properly selected, are a low-cost, quality way to hire professional money managers. Over the long haul, you're not going to beat full-time professional managers who are investing in the securities of the same type and risk level. Chapter 10 is devoted to mutual funds.

Understanding exchange-traded funds, hedge funds, and managed accounts

Mutual funds aren't the only game in town when it comes to hiring a professional money manager. Three additional options you may hear about include:

- ✔ **Exchange-traded funds (ETFs):** These are the most similar to mutual funds except that they trade on a major stock exchange and, unlike mutual funds, can be bought and sold during the trading day. The best ETFs have low fees, and like an index fund (see Chapter 10), they invest to track the performance of a stock market index.

- ✔ **Hedge funds:** These privately managed funds are for wealthier investors and generally take more risk (some even go bankrupt) than a typical mutual fund. The fees can be steep — typically 20 percent of the hedge fund's annual returns as well as an annual management fee of 1 percent or so. We generally do not recommend them.

- ✔ **Managed accounts:** The major brokerage firms, which employ brokers on commission, offer access to private money managers. In reality, this option isn't really different from getting access to fund managers via mutual funds, but you'll generally pay a much higher fee, which reduces this option's attractiveness.

Investing in individual stocks

Our experience is that plenty of people choose to invest in individual securities because they think they're smarter or luckier than the rest. We don't know you personally, but it's safe to say that in the long run, your investment choices aren't going to outperform those of the best full-time investment professionals and index funds.

Speaking with many folks about how they approach investing, we've noticed a distinct difference between the sexes on this issue. Perhaps because of the differences in how people are raised, testosterone levels, or whatever, men tend to have more of a problem swallowing their egos and admitting that they're better off not selecting their own individual securities. Maybe the desire to be a stock picker is genetically linked to not wanting to ask for directions!

Investing in individual stocks entails numerous drawbacks and pitfalls:

- ✔ **You should spend a significant amount of time doing research.** When you're considering the purchase of an individual security, you should know a lot about the company in which you're thinking about investing. Relevant questions to ask about the company include: What products does it sell? What are its prospects for future growth and profitability? How much debt does the company have? You need to do your homework not only before you make your initial investment but also on an ongoing basis for as long as you hold the investment. Research takes your valuable free time and sometimes costs money.

    Don't fool yourself or let others fool you into thinking that picking and following individual companies and their stocks is simple and requires little time.

- ✔ **Your emotions will probably get in your way.** Analyzing financial statements, corporate strategy, and competitive position requires great intellect and insight. However, those skills aren't nearly enough. Will you have the stomach to hold on after what you thought was a sure-win stock plunges 50 percent? Will you have the courage to dump such a stock if your new research suggests that the plummet is the beginning of the end rather than just a big bump in the road? When your money is on the line, emotions often kick in and undermine your ability to make sound long-term decisions. Few people have the psychological constitution to handle and outfox the financial markets.

- ✔ **You're less likely to diversify.** Unless you have tens of thousands of dollars to invest in different stocks, you probably can't cost-effectively afford to develop a diversified portfolio. For example, when you're investing in stocks, you should hold companies in different industries, different companies within an industry, and so on. By not diversifying, you unnecessarily add to your risk.

- ✔ **You'll face accounting and bookkeeping hassles.** When you invest in individual securities outside retirement plans, every time you sell a specific security you must report that transaction on your tax return. Even if you pay someone else to complete your tax return, you still have the hassle of keeping track of statements and receipts.

Individual stock dividend reinvestment plans

Many corporations allow existing shareholders to reinvest their dividends (their share in company profits) in more shares of stock without paying brokerage commissions. In some cases, companies allow you to make additional cash purchases of more shares of stock, also commission-free.

In order to qualify, you must first generally buy some shares of stock through a broker (although some companies allow the initial purchases to be made directly from them). Ideally, you should purchase these initial shares through a discount broker to keep your commission burden as low as possible. Some investment associations — including ShareOwner (`www.shareowner.`

`com`) — also have plans that allow you to buy one or just a few shares to get started.

We're not enamoured of these plans, because this type of investing is generally available and cost-effective for investments held only outside RRSPs and RRIFs. You typically need to complete a lot of paperwork to invest in a number of different companies' stock. Life is too short to bother with these plans for this reason alone.

Finally, even with those companies that do sell stock directly without charging an explicit commission like a brokerage firm, you pay plenty of other fees. Many plans charge an upfront enrollment fee, fees for reinvesting dividends, and a fee when you want to sell.

Of course, you may find some people (with a vested interest) who try to convince you that picking your own stocks and managing your own portfolio of stocks is easy and more profitable than investing in, say, a mutual fund. In our experience, such stock-picking cheerleaders fall into at least one of the following categories:

✔ **Newsletter writers:** Whether in print, on television, or on a Web site, some pundits pitch the notion that professional money managers are just overpaid buffoons and that you can handily trounce the pros with little investment of your time by simply putting your money into the pundits' stock picks. Of course, what these self-anointed gurus are really selling is either an ongoing newsletter (which can run upwards of several hundred dollars per year) or your required daily visitation of their advertising-stuffed Web sites. How else will you be able to keep up with their announced buy-and-sell recommendations? These supposed experts want you to be dependent on continually following their advice. (We discuss investment newsletters in Chapter 8 and Web sites in Chapter 20.)

✔ **Book authors:** Go into any bookstore with a decent-sized investing section and you'll find plenty of books claiming that they can teach you a stock-picking strategy for beating the system. Never mind the fact that the author has no independently audited track record demonstrating her success! The book publisher of at least one investment group was successfully sued over hyping and distorting the group's actual investment success.

✔ **Stockbrokers:** Some brokers steer you toward individual stocks for several reasons that benefit the broker and not you. First, as we discuss in Chapter 8, the high-commission brokerage firms can make handsome profits for themselves by getting you to buy stocks. Secondly, brokers can use changes in the company's situation to encourage you to then sell and buy different stocks, generating even more commissions. Lastly, as with newsletter writers, this whole process forces you to be dependent on the broker, leaving you broker!

Researching individual stocks can be more than a full-time job, and if you choose to take this path, remember that you'll be competing against the professionals who do so on a full-time basis. If you derive pleasure from picking and following your own stocks, or you want an independent opinion of some stocks you currently own, useful research reports are available from ShareOwner (800-268-6881; www.shareowner.com) or Value Line (800-833-0046; www.valueline.com). We also recommend that you limit your individual stock picking to no more than 20 percent of your overall investments.

Generating wealth with real estate

Over the generations, real estate owners and investors have enjoyed rates of return comparable to those produced by the stock market, thus making real estate another time-tested method for building wealth. However, like stocks, real estate goes through good and bad performance periods. Most people who make money investing in real estate do so because they invest over many years and do their homework when they buy to ensure that they purchase good property at an attractive price.

Buying your own home is the best place to start investing in real estate. The *equity* (the difference between the market value of the home and the loan owed on it) in your home that builds over the years can become a significant part of your net worth. Among other things, this equity can be tapped to help finance other important money and personal goals, such as retirement, university, and starting or buying a business. Moreover, throughout your adult life, owning a home should be less expensive than renting a comparable home. See Chapter 15 for the best ways to buy and finance real estate.

Real estate: Not your ordinary investment

Besides providing solid rates of return, real estate also differs from most other investments in several other respects. Here's what makes real estate unique as an investment:

✔ **Usability:** You can't live in a stock, bond, or mutual fund (although we suppose you could glue together a substantial fortress with all the paper these companies fill your mailbox with each year). Real estate is the only investment you can use (living in or renting out) to produce income.

✔ **Land is in limited supply:** The percentage of the Earth occupied by land is relatively constant. And because humans like to reproduce, the demand for land and housing continues to grow. Consider the areas that have the most expensive real estate prices in the world — Hong Kong, Tokyo, Hawaii, San Francisco, and Manhattan. In these densely populated areas, virtually no new land is available for building new housing.

✔ **Zoning shapes potential value:** Local government regulates the zoning of property, and zoning determines what a property can be used for. In most communities these days, local zoning boards are against big growth. This position bodes well for future real estate values. Also know that in some cases, a particular property may not have been developed to its full potential. If you can figure out how to develop the property, you can reap large profits.

✔ **Leverage:** Real estate is also different from other investments because you can borrow a lot of money to buy it — up to 80 to 90 percent or more of the value of the property. This borrowing is known as exercising *leverage:* With only a small investment of 10 to 25 percent down, you're able to purchase and own a much larger investment. When the value of your real estate goes up, you make money on your investment and on all the money you borrowed. (In case you're curious, you can leverage stock and bond investments held outside registered accounts such as an RRSP or RRIF through borrowing *on margin.* However, you have to make a much larger "down payment" — about double to triple when compared with buying real estate.)

For example, suppose that you plunk down $20,000 to purchase a property for $100,000. If the property appreciates to $120,000, you make a profit of $20,000 (on paper) on your investment of just $20,000. In other words, you make a 100-percent return on your investment. But leverage cuts both ways. If your $100,000 property decreases in value to $80,000, you actually lose (on paper) 100 percent of your original $20,000 investment, even though the property value drops only 20 percent.

✔ **Hidden values:** In an *efficient market,* the price of an investment accurately reflects its true worth. Some investment markets are more efficient than others because of the large number of transactions and easily accessible information. Real estate markets can be inefficient at times. Information is not always easy to come by, and you may find an ultra-motivated or uninformed seller. If you're willing to do some homework, you may be able to purchase a property below its fair market value (perhaps by as much as 10 to 20 percent).

Just as with any other investment, real estate has its drawbacks. For starters, buying or selling a property generally takes time and significant cost. When you're renting property, you discover firsthand the occasional headaches of being a landlord. And especially in the early years of rental property ownership, the property's expenses may exceed the rental income, producing a net cash drain.

Comparing real estate and stocks

Real estate and stocks have historically produced comparable returns. Deciding between the two depends less on the performance of the markets than on you and your situation. Consider the following major issues when deciding which investment may be better for you:

- The first and most important question to ask yourself is whether you're cut out to handle the responsibilities that come with being a landlord. Real estate is a time-intensive investment (property managers can help, but their cost takes a sizable chunk of your rental income). Investing in stocks can be time-intensive as well, but it doesn't have to be if you use professionally managed mutual funds (see Chapter 10).

- An often-overlooked drawback to investing in real estate is that you earn no tax benefits while you're accumulating your down payment. Registered retirement plans (see Chapter 11) give you an immediate tax deduction as you contribute money to them. If you haven't exhausted your contributions

to these plans, consider doing so before chasing after investment real estate.

- Ask yourself which investments you have a better understanding of. Some folks feel uncomfortable with stocks and mutual funds because they don't understand them. If you have a better handle on what makes real estate tick, you have a good reason to consider investing in it.

- Figure out what will make you happy. Some people enjoy the challenge that comes with managing and improving rental property; it can be a bit like running a small business. If you're good at it and you have some good fortune, you can make money and derive endless hours of enjoyment.

Although few will admit it, some real estate investors get an ego rush from a tangible display of their wealth. Sufferers of this "edifice complex" can't obtain similar pleasure from a stock portfolio detailed on a piece of paper (although others have been known to boast of their stock-picking prowess).

The best real estate investment options

Although real estate is in some ways unique, it's also like other types of investments in that prices are driven by supply and demand. You can invest in homes or small apartment buildings and then rent them out. In the long run, investment-property buyers hope that their rent income and the value of their properties will increase faster than their expenses.

When selecting real estate for investment purposes, remember that local economic growth is the fuel for housing demand. In addition to a vibrant and diverse job base, you want to look for limited supplies of both existing housing and land on which to build. When you identify potential properties in which you may want to invest, run the numbers to understand the cash demands of owning the property and the likely profitability. See Chapter 15 for help determining the costs of real estate ownership.

When you want to invest directly in real estate, residential housing — such as single-family homes or small multi-unit buildings — may be an attractive investment. Buying properties close to home offers the advantage of allowing you to more easily monitor and manage what's going on. The downside is that you'll be less diversified — more of your investments will be dependent on the local economy.

If you don't want to be a landlord — one of the biggest drawbacks of investment real estate — consider investing in real estate through real estate investment trusts (REITs). *REITs* are diversified real estate investment companies that purchase and manage rental real estate for investors. A typical REIT invests in different types of property, such as shopping centres, apartments, and other rental buildings. You can invest in REITs either by purchasing them directly on the major stock exchanges or by investing in a real estate mutual fund (see Chapter 10) that invests in numerous REITs.

The worst real estate investments

Not all real estate investments are good; some aren't even real investments. The bad ones are characterized by burdensome costs and problematic economic fundamentals:

✔ **Limited partnerships:** Avoid limited partnerships (LPs) sold through brokers and financial consultants. LPs are inferior investment vehicles. They're so burdened with high sales commissions and ongoing management fees that deplete your investment that you can do better elsewhere. The salesperson who sells you such an investment stands to earn a commission of up to 10 percent or more — so only 90 cents of each dollar gets invested. Each year, LPs typically siphon off another several percent for management and other expenses. Most partnerships have little or no incentive to control costs. In fact, they have a conflict of interest that forces them to charge more to enrich the managing partners.

Unlike a mutual fund, you can't vote with your dollars. If the partnership is poorly run and expensive, you're stuck. LPs are *illiquid* (not readily convertible into cash without a substantial loss). You can't access your money until the partnership is liquidated, typically seven to ten years after you buy in.

Brokers who sell LPs often tell you that while your investment is growing at 20 percent or more per year, you get handsome dividends of 8 percent or so annually. Many of the yields on LPs have turned out to be bogus. In some cases, partnerships prop up their yields by paying back investors' principals (without telling them, of course). As for returns — well — most LP investors of a decade ago are lucky to have half their original investment left. The only thing limited about a limited partnership is its ability to make you money.

✔ **Timeshares:** Timeshares are another nearly certain money loser. With a timeshare, you buy a week or two of ownership, or usage, of a particular unit (usually a condominium in a resort location) per year. If, for example, you pay $8,000 for a week (in addition to ongoing maintenance fees), you're paying the equivalent of more than $400,000 for the whole unit, when a comparable unit nearby may sell for only $150,000. The extra markup pays the salespeople's commissions, administrative expenses, and profits for the timeshare development company.

People usually get enticed into buying a timeshare when they're enjoying a vacation someplace. They're easy prey for salespeople who want to sell them a souvenir of the trip. The "cheese in the mousetrap" is an offer of something free (for example, a free night's stay in a unit) for going through the sales presentation.

If you can't live without a timeshare, consider buying a used one. Many previous buyers, who more than likely have lost a good chunk of money, are trying to dump their shares (which should tell you something). In this case, you may be able to buy a timeshare at a fair price. But why commit yourself to taking a vacation in the same location and building at the same time each year? Many timeshares let you trade your weeks for other times and other places; however, doing so is a hassle — you're charged an extra fee, and your choices are usually limited to time slots that other people don't want (that's why they're trading them!).

✔ **Second homes:** The weekend getaway is a sometimes romantic notion and a dream of many Canadians — a place you can escape to a couple of times a month. When your cottage or cabin is not in use, you may be able to rent it out and earn some income to help defray the expense of keeping it up.

If you can realistically afford the additional costs of a second (or vacation) home, we're not going to tell you how to spend your extra cash. But please don't make the all-too-common mistake of viewing a second home as an investment. The way most people use them, they're not. Most second-home owners seldom rent out their property — they typically do so 10 percent or less of the time. As a result, second homes are usually money drains.

The supposed tax benefits are part of the attraction of a second home. Even when you qualify for some or all of them, tax benefits only partially reduce the cost of owning a property. In some cases, the second home is such a cash drain that it prevents its owners from contributing to and taking advantage of tax-deductible retirement savings plans.

If you aren't going to rent out a second home most of the time, ask yourself whether you can afford such a luxury. Can you accomplish your other financial goals — saving for retirement, paying for the home in which you live, and so on — with this added expense? Keeping a second home is more of a consumption than investment decision. Few people can afford more than one home.

Investing in small business (and your career)

With what type of investment have people built the greatest wealth? If you said the stock market or real estate, you're wrong. The answer is small business. You can invest in small business by starting one yourself (and thus finding yourself the best boss you've probably ever had), buying an existing business, or investing in someone else's small business. Even if small business doesn't interest you, your own job should, so we present some tips on making the most of your career.

Launching your own enterprise

When you have self-discipline and a product or service you can sell, starting your own business can be both profitable and fulfilling. Consider first what skills and expertise you possess that you can use in your business. You don't need a "eureka"-type idea or invention to start a small business. Millions of people operate successful businesses that are hardly unique, such as dry cleaners, restaurants, tax preparation firms, and so on.

Begin exploring your idea by first developing a written business plan. Such a plan should detail your product or service, how you're going to market it, your potential customers and competitors, and the economics of the business, including the start-up costs.

Of all the small-business investment options, starting your own business involves the most work. Although you can do this work on a part-time basis in the beginning, most people end up running their business full-time — it's your new job, career, or whatever you want to call it.

We've both been running our own businesses for most of our working years, and we wouldn't trade that experience for the corporate life. That's not to say that running our own businesses doesn't have its drawbacks and down moments. But in our experience dealing with small-business owners, we've seen many people of varied backgrounds, interests, and skills succeed and be happy with running their own businesses.

In most people's eyes, starting a new business is the riskiest of all small-business investment options. But if you're going into a business that uses your skills and expertise, the risk isn't nearly as great as you may think. Many businesses can be started with little cash by leveraging your existing skills and expertise. You can build a valuable company and job if you have the time to devote. As long as you check out the competition and offer a valued service at a reasonable cost, the principal risk with your business comes from not doing a good job marketing what you have to offer. If you can market your skills, you're home free.

As long as you're thinking about the risks of starting a business, consider the risks of staying in a job you don't enjoy or that doesn't challenge or fulfill you. If you never take the plunge, you may regret that you didn't pursue your dreams.

Buying an existing business

If you don't have a specific product or service you want to sell but you're skilled at managing and improving the operations of a company, buying a small business may be for you. Finding and buying a good small business takes much time and patience, so be willing to devote at least several months to the search. You may also need to enlist financial and legal advisers to help inspect the company, look over its financial statements, and hammer out a contract.

Although you don't have to go through the riskier start-up period if you buy a small business, you'll likely need more capital to buy an established enterprise. You'll also need to be able to deal with stickier personnel and management issues. The history of the organization and the way things work will predate your ownership of the business. If you don't like making hard decisions, firing people who don't fit with your plans, and coercing people into changing the way they do things, buying an existing business likely isn't for you.

Some people perceive buying an existing business as being safer than starting a new one. Buying someone else's business can actually be riskier. You're likely to shell out far more money upfront, in the form of a down payment, to buy an existing business. If you don't have the ability to run the business and it does poorly, you have more to lose financially. In addition, the business may be for sale for a reason — it may not be very profitable, it may be in decline, or it may generally be a pain in the neck to operate.

Good businesses don't come cheap. If the business is a success, the current owner has already removed the start-up risk from the business, so the price of the business should be at a premium to reflect this lack of risk. When you have the capital to buy an established business and you have the skills to run it, consider going this route.

Investing in someone else's small business

Are you someone who likes the idea of profiting from successful small businesses but doesn't want the day-to-day headaches of being responsible for managing the enterprise? Then investing in someone else's small business may be for you. Although this route may seem easier, few people are actually cut out to be investors in other people's businesses. The reason: Finding and analyzing opportunities aren't easy.

Are you astute at evaluating corporate financial statements and business strategies? Investing in a small, privately held company has much in common with investing in a publicly traded firm (as is the case when you buy stock), but it also has a few differences. One difference is that private firms aren't required to produce comprehensive, audited financial statements that adhere to certain accounting principles. Thus, you have a greater risk of not having sufficient or accurate information when evaluating a small, private firm.

Another difference is that unearthing private, small-business investing opportunities is harder. The best private companies that are seeking investors generally don't advertise. Instead, they find prospective investors through networking with people such as business advisers. You can increase your chances of finding private companies to invest in by speaking with tax, legal, and financial advisers who work with small businesses. You can also find interesting opportunities through your own contacts or experience within a given industry.

Don't consider investing in someone else's business unless you can afford to lose all of what you're investing. Also, you should have sufficient assets so that what you're investing in small, privately held companies represents only a small portion (20 percent or less) of your total financial assets.

Investing in your career

In working with clients over the years and from observing friends and colleagues, we've witnessed plenty of people succeed working for employers. So we don't want to leave you with the impression that financial success equates with starting, buying, or investing in someone else's small business.

You can and should invest in your career. Some time-tested, proven ways to do that include

- ✔ **Networking:** Some people wait to network until they've been laid off or are really hungry to change jobs. Take an interest in what others do for a living and you'll learn and grow from the experience, even if you choose to stay with your current employer or in your chosen field.

- ✔ **Making sure you keep learning:** Whether it's reading quality books or other publications or taking some night courses, find ways to build on your knowledge base.

- ✔ **Considering the risk in the status quo:** Many folks are resistant to change and get anxious thinking about what could go wrong when taking a new risk. We know when we walked away from our own jobs with prestigious firms and opened our own businesses, a number of relatives and friends thought we'd lost our marbles. We're glad we didn't listen to their fears and worries!

Off the Beaten Path: Investment Odds and Ends

The investments that we discuss in this section sometimes belong on their own planet (because they're not an ownership or lending vehicle). Here are the basics on these other common, but odd, investments.

Precious metals

Gold and silver have been used by many civilizations as currency or a medium of exchange. One advantage of precious metals as a currency is that they can't be debased by the government. With paper currency, such as the Canadian or U.S. dollar, governments can simply print more. This process can lead to the devaluation of a currency and inflation. It takes a whole lot more work to make more gold. Just ask Rumpelstiltskin.

Holdings of gold and silver can provide a so-called *hedge* against inflation. In the late 1970s and early 1980s, inflation rose dramatically in North America. This largely unexpected rise in inflation depressed stocks and bonds. Gold and silver, however, rose tremendously in value — in fact, more than 500 percent (even after adjusting for inflation) from 1972 to 1980 (see Chapter 8). Such periods are unusual. Precious metals produced decent returns in the 2000s. Over many decades, precious metals have tended to be lousy investments. Their rate of return tends to keep up with the rate of inflation but not surpass it.

When you want to invest in precious metals as an inflation hedge, your best option is to do so through mutual funds (see Chapter 10). Don't purchase precious metals futures. They're not investments; they're short-term gambles on which way gold or silver prices may head over a short period of time. You should also stay away from firms and shops that sell coins and *bullion* (not the soup, but bars of gold or silver). Even if you can find a legitimate firm (not an easy task), the cost of storing and insuring gold and silver is quite costly. You won't get good value for your money. We hate to tell you this, but the Gold Rush is over.

Annuities

Annuities are a peculiar type of insurance and investment product. They're a sort of savings-type account with slightly higher yields that are backed by insurance companies.

As with other types of retirement plans, money placed in an annuity compounds without taxation until it's withdrawn. However, unlike RRSPs, you don't receive upfront tax breaks on contributions you make to an annuity. Ongoing investment expenses also tend to be much higher than in RRSPs. Therefore, consider an annuity only after you fully fund tax-deductible retirement plans. (For more help on deciding whether to invest in an annuity, read Chapter 13.)

Collectibles

The collectibles category is a catchall for antiques, art, autographs, baseball cards, clocks, coins, comic books, diamonds, dolls, gems, photographs, rare books, rugs, stamps, vintage wine, and writing utensils — in other words, any material object that, through some kind of human manipulation, has become more valuable to certain humans.

Notwithstanding the few people who discover on the *Antiques Roadshow* that they own an antique of significant value, collectibles are generally lousy investment vehicles. Dealer markups are enormous, maintenance and protection costs are draining, research is time-consuming, and people's tastes are quite fickle. All this for returns that, after you factor in the huge markups, rarely keep up with inflation.

Buy collectibles for your love of the object, not for financial gain. Treat collecting as a hobby, not as an investment. When buying a collectible, try to avoid the big markups by cutting out the intermediaries. Buy directly from the artist or producer when you can.

Chapter 10

Investing in Funds

. . . .

In This Chapter

▶ Grasping the advantages of mutual funds

▶ Checking out the different types of funds

▶ Choosing the best funds

▶ Evaluating your fund's performance

▶ Monitoring and selling your funds

. . . .

*W*hen you invest in a mutual fund, an investment company pools your money with the money of many other like-minded individuals and invests it in stocks, bonds, and other securities. Think of it as a big investment club without the meetings! When you invest through a typical mutual fund, several hundred million to billions of dollars are typically invested along with your money.

If you're thinking of joining the club, read on to discover the benefits of investing in mutual funds and exchange-traded funds and the types of funds available (see Chapter 9 for a discussion of mutual fund alternatives). In this chapter, we advise you on analyzing and choosing your funds, explain how to track your investments, and help you decide when to sell.

Understanding the Benefits of Mutual Funds

Mutual funds rank right up there with microwave ovens, sticky notes, and plastic wrap as one of the best modern inventions. To understand their success is to grasp how and why funds can work for you. Here are the benefits you receive when you invest in mutual funds:

✔ **Professional management:** Mutual funds are managed by a portfolio manager and research team whose full-time jobs are to screen the universe of investments for those that best meet the stated objectives of the fund. These professionals call and visit companies, analyze companies' financial statements, and speak with companies' suppliers and customers. In short, the team does more research and analysis than you could ever hope to do in your free time.

Fund managers are typically graduates of the top business and finance schools in the country, where they learn the principles of portfolio management and securities valuation and selection. The best fund managers typically have a decade of experience or more in analyzing and selecting investments, and many measure their experience in decades rather than years.

✔ **Low fees:** The most efficiently managed stock mutual funds cost less than 2 percent per year in fees (bond and money market funds cost much less). Because mutual funds typically buy or sell tens of thousands of shares of a security at a time, the percentage commissions these funds pay are far less than what you pay to buy or sell a few hundred shares on your own. In addition, when you buy a *no-load fund,* you avoid paying sales commissions (known as *loads*) on your transactions. We discuss these types of funds throughout this chapter.

✔ **Diversification:** Mutual fund investing enables you to achieve a level of diversification that is difficult to reach without tens of thousands of dollars and a lot of time to invest. If you go it alone, you should invest money in at least 8 to 12 different securities in different industries to ensure that your portfolio can withstand a downturn in one or more of the investments. Proper diversification allows a mutual fund to receive the highest possible return at the lowest possible risk given its objectives. The most unfortunate investors during major stock market downswings have been individuals who had all their money riding on only a few stocks that plunged in price by 90 percent or more.

✔ **Low cost of entry:** Most mutual funds have low minimum-investment requirements, especially if you're investing inside an RRSP. Even if you have a lot of money to invest, you should also consider mutual funds for the low-cost, high-quality money-management services that they provide.

✔ **Audited performance records and expenses:** In their prospectuses, all mutual funds are required to disclose historical data on returns, operating expenses, and other fees. Each province's securities regulators check these disclosures for accuracy. Also, several organizations (such as Globefund and Morningstar) report hundreds of fund statistics, allowing comparisons of performance, risk, and many other factors.

✔ **Flexibility in risk level:** Among the different mutual funds, you can choose a level of risk that you're comfortable with and that meets your personal and financial goals. If you want your money to grow over a long period of time, you may want to select funds that invest more heavily in stocks. If you need current income and don't want investments that fluctuate in value as widely as stocks, you may choose more-conservative bond funds. If you want to be sure that your invested principal doesn't drop in value (perhaps because you may need your money in the short term), you can select a money market fund.

Exploring Various Fund Types

One of the major misconceptions about mutual funds is that they're all invested in stocks. They're not. Table 10-1 shows how the money currently invested in mutual funds breaks down.

As you can see, the majority of mutual fund money is *not* invested in stocks. When you hear folks talk about the riskiness of mutual funds, you know that they're overlooking this fact: All mutual funds are not created equal. Some funds, such as money market funds, carry virtually no risk that your investment will decline in value.

When mutual fund companies package and market funds, the names they give their funds aren't always completely accurate or comprehensive. For example, a stock fund may not be *totally* invested in stocks. Twenty percent of it may be invested in bonds. Don't assume that a fund invests exclusively in Canadian companies, either — it may invest in international firms as well.

Table 10-1	How Mutual Fund Assets Are Invested
Fund Type	*Percentage of Total*
Canadian equity	22%
Global and international equity	11%
U.S. equity	4%
Sector equity funds	2.5%
Balanced	40%
Fixed income	12%
Specialty	1%
Bond and income	7.5%

Note: If you haven't yet read Chapters 8 and 9, which provide an overview of investment concepts and vehicles, doing so can enhance your understanding of the rest of this chapter.

Money market funds

Money market funds are the safest type of mutual funds for people concerned about losing their invested dollars. As with bank savings accounts, the value of your original investment does not fluctuate. (For more background on the advantages of money funds, see Chapter 9.)

General-purpose money market funds invest in safe, short-term bank guaranteed investment certificates (GICs), Government of Canada Treasury bills, and *corporate commercial paper* (short-term debt), which is issued by the largest and most creditworthy companies.

Since their origination in the early 1970s, money market funds have been extremely safe. The risk difference versus a bank account is nil. Hundreds of billions of dollars have flowed into and out of money funds over the decades without any retail investors losing principal.

Money market fund investments can exist only in the most creditworthy securities and must have an average maturity of less than 90 days. In the unlikely event that an investment in a money market fund's portfolio goes sour, the mutual fund company that stands behind the money market fund will almost certainly cover the loss.

If the lack of insurance on money market funds still spooks you, select a money market fund that invests exclusively in Government of Canada securities, which are virtually risk-free because they're backed by the full strength and credit of the federal government.

Bond funds

Bonds are IOUs. When you buy a newly issued bond, you lend your money typically to a corporation or government agency. A *bond mutual fund* is nothing more than a large group (pack, herd, gaggle, whatever) of bonds.

Bond funds typically invest in bonds of similar *maturity* (the number of years that elapse before the borrower must pay back the money you lend). The names of most bond funds include a word or two that provides clues about the average length of maturity of their bonds. For example, a *short-term bond fund* typically concentrates its investments in bonds maturing in the next one to three years. An *intermediate-term fund* generally holds bonds that come due within three to ten years. The bonds in a *long-term fund* usually mature in more than ten years.

In contrast to an individual bond that you buy and hold until it matures, a bond fund is always replacing bonds in its portfolio to maintain its average maturity objective. Therefore, if you know that you absolutely, positively must have a certain principal amount back on a particular date, individual bonds may be more appropriate than a bond fund.

Bond funds are useful when you want to live off dividend income or you don't want to put all your money in riskier investments such as stocks and real estate (perhaps because you plan to use the money soon). Also, making small incremental investments in a bond fund is easier, as opposed to the cost of buying a single individual bond, which can be many thousands of dollars.

Stock funds

Stock mutual funds, as their name implies, invest in stocks. These funds are often referred to as *equity funds. Equity* — not to be confused with equity in real estate — is another word for stocks. Stock mutual funds are often categorized by the type of stocks they primarily invest in.

Stock types are first defined by size of company (small, medium, or large). The total market value (*capitalization*) of a company's outstanding stock determines its size. Small- and mid-sized Canadian company stocks, for example, are usually defined as companies with total market capitalization of less than $500 million.

Stocks are further categorized as growth or value. *Growth stocks* represent companies that are experiencing rapidly expanding revenues and profits and typically have high stock prices relative to their current earnings or asset (book) values. These companies tend to reinvest most of their earnings back into their infrastructure to fuel future expansion. Thus, growth stocks typically pay low dividends. (See the "Dividends" section for more information.)

Value stocks are at the other end of the spectrum. Value stock investors look for good buys. They want to invest in stocks that are cheaply priced in relation to the profits per share and book value (assets less liabilities) of the company. Value stocks are usually less volatile than growth stocks.

These categories are combined in various ways to describe how a mutual fund invests its money. One fund may focus on large-company growth stocks, while another fund may limit itself to small-company value stocks. Funds are further classified by the geographical focus of their investments: Canadian, U.S., international, worldwide, and so on (see the section "Canadian, U.S., international, and global funds").

Balancing bonds and stocks: Hybrid funds

Hybrid funds invest in a mixture of different types of securities. Most commonly, they invest in bonds and stocks. These funds are usually less risky and volatile than funds that invest exclusively in stocks. In an economic downturn, bonds usually hold up in value better than stocks do. However, during good economic times when the stock market is booming, the bond portions of these funds tend to drag down their performance a bit.

Hybrid mutual funds are typically known as balanced funds or asset allocation funds. *Balanced funds* generally try to maintain a fairly constant percentage of investments in stocks and bonds. *Asset allocation funds* tend to adjust the mix of different investments according to the portfolio manager's expectations of the market. Of course, exceptions do exist — some balanced funds make major shifts in their allocations, whereas some asset allocation funds maintain a relatively fixed mix. Note that most funds that shift money around instead of staying put in good investments rarely beat the market averages over a number of years.

Increasing numbers of *target-maturity funds* also now exist, which tend to decrease their risk (and stock allocation) over time. Such funds appeal to investors who are approaching a particular future goal, such as retirement or a child's university education, and want their fund to automatically adjust as that date approaches.

Hybrid funds are a way to make fund investing simple. They give you extensive diversification across a variety of investing options. They also make it easier for stock-skittish investors to invest in stocks while avoiding the high volatility of pure stock funds.

Canadian, U.S., international, and global funds

Unless they have words like *international, global, worldwide,* or *world* in their names, most Canadian mutual funds focus their investments in Canada. But even funds without one of these terms attached may invest money internationally.

The only way to know for sure where a fund is currently invested (or where the fund may invest in the future) is to ask. You can start by calling the toll-free number of the mutual fund company you're interested in. A fund's annual report (which often can be found on the fund company's Web site) also details where the fund is investing.

When a fund has the term *international* or *foreign* in its name, it typically means that the fund invests anywhere in the world except Canada. The term *worldwide* or *global* generally implies that a fund invests everywhere in the world, including Canada. We generally recommend avoiding worldwide or global funds for two reasons. First, thoroughly following the financial markets and companies is hard enough for a fund manager to do solely in Canada or a specific international market; following the markets and companies in both is even more difficult. Second, most of these funds charge high operating expenses — some in excess of 3 percent per year — which puts a drag on returns.

Index funds

Index funds are funds that can be (and are, for the most part) managed by a computer. An index fund's assets are invested to replicate an existing market index such as the Toronto Stock Exchange's S&P/TSX index, or the Standard & Poor's 500, an index of 500 large U.S. company stocks.

Over long periods (ten years or more), index funds outperform about three-quarters of their peers! How is that possible? How can a computer making mindless, predictable decisions beat an intelligent, creative, MBA-endowed portfolio manager with a crack team of research analysts scouring the market for the best securities? The answer is largely cost. The computer does not demand a high salary or need a big corner office. And index funds don't need a team of research analysts.

Most active fund managers can't overcome the handicap of high operating expenses that pull down their funds' rates of return. As we discuss later in this chapter, operating expenses include all the fees and profit that a mutual fund extracts from a fund's returns before the returns are paid to you. For example, the average Canadian stock fund has an operating expense ratio of about 2.5 percent per year. So a Canadian stock index fund (or its peer exchange-traded fund, which is an index fund that trades on a stock exchange) with an expense ratio of just 1 percent per year has an advantage of 1.5 percent per year.

Another not-so-inconsequential advantage of index funds is that you can't underperform the market. Some funds do just that because of the burden of high fees and/or poor management. For money invested outside retirement plans, index funds have an added advantage: Lower taxable capital gains distributions are made to shareholders because less trading of securities is conducted and a more stable portfolio is maintained.

Identifying socially responsible funds

Select mutual funds label themselves *socially responsible*. This term means different things to different people. In most cases, though, it implies that the fund avoids investing in companies whose products or services harm people or the world at large — tobacco manufacturers, for example. Because cigarettes and other tobacco products kill hundreds of thousands of people and add billions of dollars to healthcare costs, most socially responsible funds shun tobacco companies.

Socially responsible investing presents challenges. For example, your definition of social responsibility may not match the definition offered by the investment manager who's running a fund. Another problem is that even if you can agree on what's socially irresponsible (such as selling tobacco products), funds aren't always as clean as you would think or hope. Even though a fund avoids tobacco manufacturers, it may well invest in retailers that sell tobacco products, such as drug stores.

If you want to consider a socially responsible fund, review the fund's recent annual report that lists the specific investments the fund owns. Also consider giving directly to charities (and getting a tax deduction) instead.

Yes, index funds may seem downright boring. When you invest in them, you give up the opportunity to brag to others about your shrewd investments that beat the market averages. On the other hand, with a low-cost index fund you have no chance of doing much worse than the market (which more than a few mutual fund managers do).

Index funds and exchange-traded funds make sense for a portion of your investments, because beating the market is difficult for portfolio managers. At the time we wrote this edition, TD e-Series Funds were among the lowest-cost versions, and are available for purchase online at www.tdcanadatrust.com.

Specialty (sector) funds

Specialty funds don't fit neatly into the previous categories. These funds are often known as *sector funds,* because they tend to invest in securities in specific industries.

In most cases, you should avoid investing in specialty funds. Investing in stocks of a single industry defeats one of the major purposes of investing in mutual funds — diversification. Another good reason to avoid specialty funds is that they tend to carry much higher expenses than other mutual funds.

Specialty funds that invest in real estate or precious metals may make sense for a small portion (10 percent or less) of your investment portfolio. These types of funds can help diversify your portfolio, because they can do better during times of higher inflation.

Selecting the Best Mutual Funds

When you go camping in the wilderness, you can do a number of things to maximize your chances for happiness and success. You can take maps and a GPS to keep you on course, food for nourishment, proper clothing to stay dry and warm, and some first-aid gear to treat minor injuries. But regardless of how much advance preparation you do, you may have a problematic experience. You may take the wrong trail, trip on a rock and break your ankle, or lose your food to a tenacious bear that comes romping through camp one night.

And so it is with mutual funds. Although most mutual fund investors are rewarded for their efforts, you get no guarantees. You can, however, follow some simple, common-sense guidelines to help keep you on the trail and increase your odds of investment success and happiness. The issues in the following sections are the main ones to consider.

Reading prospectuses and annual reports

Mutual fund companies produce information that can help you make decisions about mutual fund investments. Every fund is required to issue a *prospectus*. This legal document is reviewed and audited by securities regulators. Most of what's written isn't worth your time to slog through it.

The most valuable information — the fund's investment objectives, costs, and performance history — is summarized in the first few pages of the prospectus. Make sure that you read this part. Skip the rest, which mostly comprises tedious legal details.

Funds also produce *annual reports* that discuss how the fund has been doing and provide details on the specific investments a fund holds. If, for example, you want to know which countries an international fund invests in, you can find this information in the fund's annual report.

Keeping costs low

The charges you pay to buy or sell a fund, as well as the ongoing fund operating expenses, can have a big impact on the rate of return you earn on your investments. Many novice investors pay too much attention to a mutual fund's prior performance (in the case of stock funds) or to the fund's current yield (in the case of bond funds) and too little attention to fees. Doing so is dangerous because a fund can inflate its return or yield in many (risky) ways. And what worked yesterday may flop tomorrow.

Fund costs are an important factor in the return you earn from a mutual fund. Fees are deducted from your investment. All other things being equal, high fees and other charges depress your returns. What are a fund's fees, you ask? Good question — read on to find the answers.

Eliminating loads

Loads are upfront commissions paid to brokers who sell mutual funds. Loads typically range from 2 percent to as high as 6 or 7 percent of your investment. Sales loads have two problems:

- ✔ **Sales loads are an extra cost that drags down your investment returns.** Because commissions are paid to the salesperson and not to the fund manager, the manager of a load fund doesn't work any harder and isn't any more qualified than a manager of a no-load fund. Common sense suggests, and studies confirm, that load funds perform *worse,* on average, than no-loads when factoring in the load because the load charge is subtracted from your payment before being invested.

- ✔ **The power of self-interest can bias your broker's advice.** Although this issue is rarely discussed, it's even more problematic than the issue of extra sales costs. Brokers who work for a commission are interested in selling you commission-based investment products; therefore, their best interests often conflict with your best interests.

Although you may be mired in high-interest debt or underfunding your retirement plan, salespeople almost never advise you to pay off your credit cards or put more money into your employer's pension plan. To get you to buy, they tend to exaggerate the potential benefits and obscure the risks and drawbacks of what they sell. They don't take the time to educate investors. We've seen too many people purchase investment products through brokers without understanding what they're buying, how much risk they're taking, and how these investments will affect their overall financial lives.

Invest in no-load (commission-free) funds. The only way to be sure that a fund is truly no-load is to look at the prospectus for the fund. Only there, in black and white and without marketing hype, must the truth be told about sales charges and other fund fees. When you want investing advice, hire a financial adviser on a fee-for-service basis (see Chapter 19), which should cost less and minimize potential conflicts of interest.

Decreasing operating expenses

All mutual funds charge ongoing fees. The fees pay for the operational costs of running the fund — employees' salaries, marketing, servicing the toll-free phone lines, printing and mailing published materials, computers for tracking investments and account balances, accounting fees, and so on. Despite being labelled "expenses," the profit a fund company earns for running the fund is added to the tab as well.

The fund's operating expenses are quoted as an annual percentage of your investment and are essentially invisible to you, because they're deducted before you're paid any return. The expenses are charged on a daily basis, so you don't need to worry about trying to get out of a fund before these fees are deducted.

You can find a fund's operating expenses in the fund's prospectus. Look in the expenses section and find a line that says something like "Total Fund Operating Expenses." You can also call the fund's toll-free number and ask a representative.

Within a given sector of mutual funds (for example, money market, short-term bonds, or international stock), funds with low annual operating fees can more easily produce higher total returns for you. Although expenses matter on all funds, some types of funds are more sensitive to high expenses than others. Expenses are critical on money market mutual funds and very important on bond funds. Fund managers already have a hard time beating the averages in these markets; with higher expenses added on, beating the averages is nearly impossible.

With stock funds, expenses are a less important (but still significant) factor in a fund's performance. Don't forget that, over time, stocks average returns of about 10 percent per year. So if one stock fund charges 1 percent more in operating expenses than another fund, you're already giving up an extra 10 percent of your expected returns.

Some people argue that stock funds that charge high expenses may be justified in doing so if they generate higher rates of return. Evidence doesn't show that these stock funds actually generate higher returns. In fact, funds with higher operating expenses tend to produce *lower* rates of return. This trend makes sense, because operating expenses are deducted from the returns a fund generates.

Stick with funds that maintain low total operating expenses and don't charge loads (commissions). Both types of fees come out of your pocket and reduce your rate of return. You have no reason to pay a lot for the best funds. (In Chapters 12 and 13, we provide some specific fund recommendations as well as sample portfolios for investors in different situations.)

Evaluating historical performance

A fund's *performance,* or historical rate of return, is another factor to weigh when selecting a mutual fund. As all mutual funds are supposed to tell you, past performance is no guarantee of future results. An analysis of historical mutual fund performance proves that some of yesterday's stars turn into tomorrow's skid-row bums.

Many former high-return funds achieved their results by taking on high risk. Funds that assume higher risk should produce higher rates of return. But high-risk funds usually decline in price faster during major market declines. Thus, in order for a fund to be considered a *best* fund, it must consistently deliver a favourable rate of return given the degree of risk it takes.

When assessing an individual fund, compare its performance and volatility over an extended period of time (five or ten years will do) to a relevant market index. For example, compare funds that focus on investing in large Canadian companies to the S&P/TSX index. For large U.S. companies, look at the Standard & Poor's 500 index; for funds that invest in U.S. stocks of all sizes, check out the Wilshire 5000 index. Indexes also exist for bonds, foreign stock markets, and almost any other type of security you can imagine.

Assessing fund manager and fund family reputations

Much is made of who manages a specific mutual fund. As Peter Lynch, the retired and famous former manager of the Fidelity Magellan fund, said, "The financial press made us Wall Street types into celebrities, a notoriety that was largely undeserved. Stock stars were treated as rock stars. . . ."

Although the individual fund manager is important, no fund manager is an island. The resources and capabilities of the parent company are equally important. Different companies have different capabilities and levels of expertise in relation to the different types of funds. When you're considering a particular fund — for example, the Barnum & Barney High-Flying Foreign

Stock fund — examine the performance history and fees not only of that fund but also of similar foreign stock funds at the Barnum & Barney company. If Barnum's other foreign stock funds have done poorly, or Barnum & Barney offers no other such funds because it's focused on its circus business, those are strikes against its High-Flying fund. Also be aware that "star" fund managers tend to be associated with higher-expense funds to help pay their rock-star salaries.

Rating tax friendliness

Investors often overlook tax implications when selecting mutual funds to hold outside tax-sheltered accounts such as an RRSP, RRIF, RESP, or TFSA. Numerous mutual funds effectively reduce their shareholders' returns because of their tendency to produce more taxable distributions — that is, capital gains and dividends. (See the "Dividends" and "Capital gains" sections later in this chapter.)

Mutual fund capital gains distributions have an impact on an investor's after-tax rate of return. All mutual fund managers buy and sell stocks over the course of a year. Whenever a mutual fund manager sells securities, any gain or loss from those securities must be distributed to fund shareholders. Securities sold at a loss can offset securities sold at a profit within the fund.

When a fund manager has a tendency to cash in more winners than losers, investors in the fund receive taxable gains. So, even though some funds can lay claim to producing higher total returns, *after* you factor in taxes they actually may not produce higher total returns.

Choosing mutual funds that minimize capital gains distributions helps you defer taxes on your profits. By allowing your capital to continue compounding as it would in a registered retirement plan, you receive a higher total return. When you're a long-term investor, you benefit most from choosing mutual funds that minimize capital gains distributions. The more years that appreciation can compound without being taxed, the greater the value to you as the investor.

 Investors who purchase mutual funds outside tax-sheltered plans should also consider the time of year they purchase shares in funds. December is the most common month in which mutual funds make capital gains distributions. When making purchases late in the year, ask if and when the fund may make a significant capital gains distribution. Consider delaying purchases in such funds until after the distribution date.

Determining your needs and goals

Selecting the best funds for you requires an understanding of your investment goals and risk tolerance. What may be a good fund for your next-door neighbour may not necessarily be a good fund for you. You have a unique financial profile.

If you've already determined your needs and goals — terrific! If you haven't, refer to Chapter 4. Understanding yourself is a good part of the battle. But don't shortchange yourself by not being educated about the investment you're considering. If you don't understand what you're investing in and how much risk you're taking, stay out of the game.

Deciphering Your Fund's Performance

Mutual fund statements confuse most investors. Getting a handle on how you're doing is the hardest part. Most people want to know (and have a hard time figuring out) how much they made or lost on their investment.

You can't simply calculate your return by comparing the share price of the fund today to the share price you originally paid. Why not? Because mutual funds make distributions (of dividends and capital gains), which gives you more shares of the fund.

Distributions create an accounting problem, because they reduce the share price of a fund. (Otherwise you could make a profit from the distribution by buying into it just before a distribution is made.) Therefore, over time, following just the share price of your fund doesn't tell you how much money you made or lost.

The only way to figure out exactly how much you made or lost on your investment is to compare the total value of your holdings in the fund today with the total dollar amount you originally invested. If you invested chunks of money at various points in time and you want to factor in the timing of your various investments, this exercise becomes complicated. (Check out our investment software recommendations in Chapter 20 if you want your computer to help you crunch the numbers.)

The *total return* of a fund is the percentage change of your investment over a specified period. For example, a fund may tell you that in 2010, its total return was 15 percent. Therefore, if you invested $10,000 in the fund on the last day of 2009, your investment would be worth $11,500 at the end of 2010. To find out a fund's total return, you can call the fund company's toll-free number, visit the company's Web site, or read the fund's annual report.

The following three components make up your total return on a fund:

- Interest and dividends
- Capital gains distributions
- Share price changes

Interest and dividends

Interest and dividends are income paid by investments. Bond funds and stocks can pay out both. The interest from bond funds (the interest paid by the individual bonds in a fund) tends to be higher (as a percentage of the amount you have invested in a fund). When a distribution is made, you can receive it as cash (which is good if you need money to live on) or reinvest it into more shares in the fund. In either case, the share price of the fund drops to offset the payout. So if you're hoping to strike it rich by buying into a bunch of funds just before their dividends are paid, don't bother. You'll just end up paying more in income taxes.

If you hold your mutual fund outside a tax-sheltered plan or account, the distributions are taxable. You have to pay tax on these gains whether you receive them in the form or cash or you reinvest them as additional shares in the fund.

Interest is taxed at your full marginal tax rate. Dividends, however, are taxed at a much lower rate thanks to the dividend tax credit. As a result, dividend funds are a good bet if you're investing to earn income outside of a tax-sheltered plan, such as an RRSP. (See Chapter 6 for more on how different types of investments are taxed.)

Capital gains

When a mutual fund manager sells a security in the fund, net gains realized from that sale (the difference from the purchase price) must be distributed to you as a *capital gain*. Typically, funds make one annual capital gains distribution in December, but distributions can be paid multiple times per year.

As with a dividend distribution, you can receive your capital gains distribution as cash or as more shares in the fund. In either case, the share price of the fund drops to offset the distribution.

For funds held outside registered retirement plans, your capital gains distribution is taxable. As with dividends, capital gains are taxable whether or not you reinvest them in additional shares in the fund.

If you want to avoid making an investment in a fund that is about to make a capital gains distribution, check with the fund to determine when capital gains are distributed. Capital gains distributions increase your current-year tax liability for investments made outside of retirement plans. (We discuss this concept in more detail in Chapter 13.)

Share price changes

You also make money with a mutual fund when the share price increases. This occurrence is just like investing in a stock or piece of real estate. If the mutual fund is worth more today than it was when you bought it, you made a profit (on paper, at least). In order to realize or lock in this profit, you need to sell your shares in the fund.

There you have it. Here are the components of a mutual fund's total return:

```
    Interest and dividends distribution
  + Capital gains
  + Share price changes
  = Total return
```

Evaluating and Selling Your Funds

How closely you follow your funds is up to you, depending on what makes you happy and comfortable. We don't recommend tracking the share prices of your funds (or other investments, for that matter) on a daily basis; it's time-consuming and nerve-racking, and it can make you lose sight of the long-term picture. When you track your investments too closely, you're more likely to panic when times get tough. And with investments held outside of registered retirement plans, every time you sell an investment at a profit, you get hit with taxes.

A monthly or quarterly check-in is more than frequent enough for following your funds. Many publications carry total return numbers over varying periods so you can determine the exact rate of return you're earning.

Trying to time and trade the markets so that you buy at lows and sell at highs rarely works. Yet an entire industry of investment newsletters, hotlines, online services, and the like purport to be able to tell you when to buy and sell. Don't waste your time and money on such predictive nonsense. (See Chapter 8 for more info about gurus and newsletters.)

Consider selling a fund when it no longer meets the criteria mentioned in "Selecting the Best Mutual Funds," earlier in this chapter. If a fund underperforms its peers for at least a two-year period, or if a fund jacks up its management fees, it may be a good time to sell. But if you do your homework and buy good funds from good fund companies, you shouldn't have to do much trading.

Finding and investing in good funds isn't rocket science. Chapters 12 and 13 recommend some specific mutual funds using the criteria discussed earlier in this chapter.

Chapter 11

Registered Retirement Savings Plans

. . . .

In This Chapter

▶ Figuring out RRSPs

▶ Learning how to make the most of the investments in your RRSPs

▶ Making sense of the contribution rules

▶ Looking at the different types of RRSPs

▶ Withdrawing funds from your RRSP before retirement

▶ Assessing your options for when your RRSP matures

. . . .

*T*he phrase Registered Retirement Savings Plan, or RRSP, is perhaps the best-known financial term in the country. Unfortunately, it's also one of the most often misunderstood. For example, many people think of an RRSP as an investment. The reality is that an RRSP is a special holding account where you can place most generally available Canadian and foreign investments.

An RRSP is the single best, easiest, and most efficient way to save for retirement. RRSPs also offer one of the best ways to reduce the tax you pay. To make the most out of RRSPs, it's wise to know not only how to use them, but also how they work and what their benefits are.

Understanding How RRSPs Work

When you open an RRSP, you basically make a deal with the government. By "registering" your retirement savings plan, you agree to put money away for your retirement and not spend it. In return, the government gives you two valuable benefits:

✔ Money that you contribute to your RRSP is deductible from your taxable income. This means that any income you contribute to your savings plan is not taxed.

✔ The government lets the savings in your RRSP grow tax-free. Any profits your RRSP investments earn are not taxable until you collapse your plan and withdraw the funds.

The benefits of tax-deductible contributions and tax-deferred growth combine to supercharge your retirement savings. In this section we look at the powerful impact they can have on your ability to save for the future.

The benefits of tax-deductible contributions

Money you contribute to an RRSP can be deducted from your income before your income tax is calculated for the year. Say you made $50,000 and contributed $5,000 to your RRSP. If you claimed that $5,000 as a deduction on your tax return, your income tax would be calculated as though you had made only $45,000 that year.

Suppose you're in a 42-percent tax bracket, which means the government takes 42 cents of the last dollar you earn. If you contribute $1,000 to your RRSP, you save yourself $420 in tax. So the *real* out-of-pocket cost of a $1,000 contribution is only $580. Contributing $1,000 to your RRSP only leaves you short $580 in after-tax money you can put your hands on.

The tax savings from contributing to an RRSP are substantial regardless of your tax bracket, as Table 11-1 shows.

Table 11-1	Short-Term Benefits of Tax-Deductible RRSP Contributions			
Where	*Investment Amount*	*Tax Rate*	*Tax Reduction*	*After-Tax Cost in Dollars*
Outside RRSP	$5,000	All	$0	$5,000
Inside RRSP	$5,000	24%	$1,200	$3,800
Inside RRSP	$5,000	36%	$1,800	$3,200
Inside RRSP	$5,000	42%	$2,100	$2,900
Inside RRSP	$5,000	46%	$2,300	$2,700

The payoff from tax-deferred compound growth

When you put your money into an RRSP, any profits you earn with that money aren't taxed until you take the money out of your plan. As a result, you can reinvest those profits and have them earn their own profits.

When interest and earnings on investments aren't taxed, the full value is added to the original amount. This new, larger amount then earns further gains, which again are added to, or compounded with, your investments. This phenomenon is called *compound growth,* and over time it will lead to your retirement savings growing exponentially.

Just how well does compound growth work? A good guideline to remember is the "Rule of 72." Take 72, divide it by your rate of return, and the result is the approximate number of years it will take for your investment to double in value. For example, an investment earning 7 percent will double in about ten years.

The benefits of tax-deductible contributions increase over time. Suppose you're 35 and you invest $5,000 of your salary this year outside an RRSP. Assuming that given your province's tax rate you're in a combined federal and provincial tax bracket of 40 percent, the Canada Revenue Agency would first take $2,000 in tax, leaving you with $3,000. You invest that $3,000 in a mutual fund that earns a 10-percent compound return. After 30 years, you would have amassed a tidy $52,000. (This doesn't take into account the taxes you would likely have to pay each year on the distribution of capital gains, dividends, and interest, which would further reduce your average compound return outside an RRSP.)

Now, how would the numbers look if you had contributed that money to your RRSP? Because the Canada Revenue Agency doesn't take any tax off your contributions, you can invest the full $5,000. Right away, that puts you $2,000 ahead. (In the real world, of course, you would have had the tax already taken off your income as it was earned. But you would then receive a $2,000 tax rebate for your $5,000 contribution, so, at the end of the day, the real cost is only $3,000.)

If you invest that $5,000 in the same mutual fund inside an RRSP earning an average 10-percent compound return for 30 years, you're left with $87,000, or almost $35,000 more than you would have if you had put the money in a mutual fund. Table 11-2 shows just how valuable a tax-sheltered RRSP contribution can be to the long-term growth of your savings.

Table 11-2		Long-Term Payoff of Tax-Favoured RRSP Contributions	
Where	*Savings*	*Available for Investment (with 10-percent growth)*	*Value in 30 Years*
Inside RRSP	$5,000	$5,000	$87,000
Outside RRSP	$5,000	$3,000	$52,000

As Table 11-2 demonstrates, the message is simple: The more money you invest to begin with, the more money you end up with for any given investment.

Maximizing Your RRSP's Growth

You can maximize the growth of your RRSP in two simple steps:

✔ Begin contributing as early as you can in life, and

✔ Try to maximize your RRSP's returns.

The payoff from starting an RRSP early

Your RRSP needs a good, long runway to get off the ground, but when it takes flight it will gain altitude quickly. The real value in starting as early in life as possible is not simply the total amount of the extra contributions you manage to put in. It's that the longer you have money in an RRSP, the more time your savings have to compound.

Take someone who starts an RRSP when she is 28, making annual $2,000 contributions each year until she's 65. If she puts her money into a family of mutual funds that earns an average return of 10 percent, the total accumulation would be about $660,000.

But she could have accumulated that same amount if she had begun putting $2,000 a year into an RRSP when she was 21 — and contributed for only seven years (see Table 11-3).

Even if you're just 25 and have only $1,000 to spare, put it in an RRSP! If you earn an average of 10 percent a year, you'll have an extra $45,000 in your plan when you retire at 65.

Table 11-3	The Money-Earning Potential of Starting an RRSP When You're Young			
Annual Contribution	**Age Beginning**	**Age Ended**	**Total Years**	**Final Value at Age 65**
$2,000	21	27	7	$664,000
$2,000	28	65	37	$660,000

Note: Table 11-3 assumes a 10-percent annual rate of return.

Examples like the previous one are commonly used to sell the benefits of putting money into an RRSP from an early age. The problem is that if you aren't young, these examples can be unsettling. If you didn't find out about the benefits of RRSPs when you were young or didn't have money to contribute, you likely find it dispiriting to realize the tax savings and compound growth you missed out on. Whatever you do, don't let that stop you from taking action today. To rework that old cliché, today is the first day of the rest of your financial life!

Increasing your returns

Choosing appropriate investments is critical in maximizing the growth of your RRSP. And the more years you have before you have to collapse your plan, the larger the impact of boosting your returns by even just 1 or 2 percent.

Say you contribute $5,000 a year to your plan for 30 years, and you earn an average return of 8 percent. The final value of your plan would be just over $566,000.

But consider the results if you had taken a little more time in choosing your RRSP investments and you had managed to earn 9 percent a year — just 1 percent more. In 30 years' time, your plan would be worth more than $681,000.

By improving your fund's performance by only 1 percent, you would end up with an extra $115,000! (See Table 11-4.)

How to get motivated to make RRSP contributions

To help stem your appetite for a large expense that you may desperately want but not necessarily need, it can help to get a firm grip on the substantial payoff from contributing to an RRSP.

For example, suppose you were able to put $6,000 every year into your RRSP and earned an average return of 9 percent. After 30 years, you would have accumulated an impressive $817,845.

But what if you put in only $4,500 annually, using the extra $1,500 to give yourself a week in the sun? Your total would still be a respectable $613,384. But look at it another way. Indulging yourself a little today will cost you more than $200,000 in your retirement. Are your sunfests really worth having $200,000 less when you retire?

Do you find it tough to come up with anywhere near your maximum allowable contribution when the RRSP deadline comes around? Try an automatic deduction plan. You can tell your financial institution or RRSP holder to take a certain amount out of your bank account every few weeks — for example, when your paycheque comes in. You likely won't miss the money, and you'll be surprised at how much more you can put away.

Table 11-4	The Payoff from Profitable Investing: How a $5,000 Annual Contribution Will Grow	
Value at Growth Rate of . . . Years	*8%*	*9%*
5	$29,333	$29,924
10	$72,433	$75,965
30	$566,416	$681,538

Examining the Contribution Rules

As long as you are 71 years or younger and you have received income from a job, running a business, or even net rental income — that is, as long as you've received *earned income* — you generally can contribute to an RRSP. No minimum age requirement applies — even a child can have an RRSP, as long as he or she has earned income.

Making the most of your unused contributions

If you don't contribute the full amount you're allowed to in a given year — or don't make a contribution at all — the unused portion can be carried forward and used in later years.

For example, if you were allowed to contribute $7,000 this year and contributed only $5,000, you would have $2,000 of what's called unused contribution room to use in the future. Say the next year your income meant that you could contribute an additional $10,000. The total amount you could contribute to your RRSP in that year would be $12,000 — the $2,000 of allowable contributions brought forward from the previous year, and the $10,000 allowable contribution for the current year. In the jargon of RRSPs, this amount is not called your allowable contribution, but your contribution room. If you've saved enough money for a contribution that uses contribution room you haven't been able to take advantage of in the past, congratulations are in order.

You don't have to deduct contributions to an RRSP from your taxable income in the same year they're made. In fact, it often makes sense not to claim some or even all of your contribution on this year's tax return. Why would you not want to deduct your contributions as soon as possible? When you deduct an RRSP contribution, the tax you save is determined by your marginal tax bracket. If your income fluctuates or is unusually low (perhaps you've taken time off to care for a baby, start a new business, or just smell the roses), you may save more in taxes by putting off claiming the deduction for some or even all of a contribution until your income is higher. By doing so, you'll be in a higher marginal bracket, which means your deduction will save you that much more in taxes.

Also, a large deduction can decrease your taxable income so that you actually drop a tax bracket. For example, suppose you earn $44,000, which means your marginal tax rate is approximately 36 percent. But only the last $3,000 of your income is taxed at this rate. Income below about $41,000 down to $10,300 is taxed at only about 24 percent. You could maximize your tax savings from a large RRSP contribution by claiming only about $3,000 — just enough to reduce your taxable income so that none of it is taxed at 36 percent. You could then use the same strategy for the remainder of the contribution in future years.

Checking out the contribution limits

Three factors determine the maximum you can contribute to your RRSP in any year.

✔ **The absolute maximum amount that anyone can contribute in any one year:** The maximum for the 2009 tax year was $21,000, and for 2010 it was $22,000. After 2010, the absolute maximum amount will be increased at the same rate as the cost of living, or indexed.

What's earned income?

Now, you probably quite naturally believe that when it comes to your income, you've earned all of it — but the government has other ideas. When determining what qualifies as your "earned income," certain types of earnings are excluded.

Earned income includes only income sources such as these:

✔ Salary

✔ Net self-employment income

✔ Bonuses and commissions

✔ Net business income

✔ Taxable alimony, maintenance, and child-support payments you receive

✔ Net rental income

✔ Royalties

✔ Disability pension received under the Canada Pension Plan or Quebec Pension Plan

✔ Employee profit-sharing plan income

✔ Unemployment benefits

✔ Some types of taxable employment incomes, including disability and sick benefits

The following reduce your earned income:

✔ Deductible alimony, maintenance, and child-support payments you make

✔ Most deductible employment-related expenses, including travel expenses and union dues

✔ Rental losses

✔ Union or professional dues

Finally, many types of income are simply excluded from your earned income. In addition to most income from investments, including interest, dividends, and capital gains, you may not include pension benefits, retiring allowances or severance pay, death benefits, or money received from an RRSP, RRIF, or deferred profit-sharing plan (DPSP).

✔ **Your income:** Regardless of the absolute ceiling on contributions, the amount you earn the right to contribute to your RRSP in any year is also limited to 18 percent of your earned income from the previous year (see the sidebar "What's earned income?" for more information about what qualifies as earned income). For example, the most you could contribute in the 2011 tax year would be 18 percent of your 2010 earned income.

✔ **Membership in a company pension plan or a deferred profit-sharing plan (DPSP):** The employer makes an estimate of the value of the pension you earned in the previous year. This amount, called your pension adjustment (PA), is subtracted from whichever is lower, the dollar maximum contribution allowable or 18 percent of your earned income, to arrive at the most you can put into your RRSP.

In the spring or summer of each year, the Canada Revenue Agency sends all taxpayers a Notice of Assessment for the previous year. Your contribution limit for the current year is included on the statement. For example, if you've filed your 2010 tax return you'll find your allowable contribution for 2011 on your assessment statement, which you should receive in the first half of 2011.

Review your allowable maximum contribution to ensure the government has come up with the right figure. If the CRA's number is too high and you over-contribute, you may risk having to pay a penalty. If the figure is too low, your plan will suffer because you won't have maximized your contribution.

How much can you contribute?

To begin with, realize that the government puts absolute maximums on how much people, regardless of situation, can contribute each year — the *allowable contribution.*

The most you can contribute in any given year, then, is the lowest of

✔ The annual maximum amount for that year (see the previous section), or

✔ 18 percent of your earned income in the previous year

(If no one in your family has a company pension plan, you can skip this next section. Those with plans, please stay with the program.)

If you belong to a pension plan or deferred profit-sharing plan (DPSP), the government further scales back the amount it lets you contribute. The thinking is that because you have alternative sources of retirement income, you shouldn't get the full tax break allotted to people without pensions.

The government reduces your otherwise maximum allowable contribution by the value attributed for the contributions that both you and your employer make to your pension or DPSP. This figure is called your *pension adjustment,* or *PA factor.* How that figure is arrived at depends on the type of plan you belong to.

Your pension adjustment is then subtracted from the lower of 18 percent of your earned income or the year's maximum to arrive at your RRSP limit. Your pension adjustment is listed on your T4 slip, which you should receive from your employer before the end of every February. In general, the higher your pension the larger your pension adjustment and the lower your maximum allowable contribution.

The contribution deadline

For any given tax year, you can make a contribution any time up to and including the 60th day in the next year. The last day you are allowed to contribute for the 2010 tax year, for example, is March 1, 2011. You could contribute as early as January 1, 2010, of course. The exception is that in the year in which you turn 71 you must contribute to your plan before December 31.

The only positive thing that can be said about leaving your contribution to the last minute is that it's probably good for an adrenaline rush. But consider this: If you plan ahead and make your contributions well in advance, you'll likely earn enough in extra interest over the years to pay for hours of heart-stopping bungee jumping and skydiving when you retire.

Every February, many people dash around trying to get their RRSP contribution in before the deadline. Rushed contributions, however, are usually made without considering investment options.

If you can't avoid making your contribution at the last minute, put off making any major investment decisions. Consider putting your money into a money market mutual fund or other cash-like investment, and then moving your money into better-performing investments when you have the time and energy to consider your options. By carefully assessing your RRSP investments, you can greatly boost the value of your plan, which translates directly into thousands of dollars more income to live on during retirement.

If you belong to a defined-benefit pension plan

With a defined-benefit pension plan, the amount you receive when you retire is based upon your years of service and your income level. When you belong to this kind of plan, your pension adjustment (PA factor) is based on a calculation of the future value attributed to your pension of your previous year of employment. Your maximum contribution for 2010, for example, would be 18 percent of your 2009 earned income to a maximum of $22,000, less your 2009 PA factor.

If you belong to a money-purchase pension plan

Your pension adjustment under this kind of pension plan is the total combined amount put into your pension by both you and your employer for the previous year. Your maximum contribution for 2010, for example, would be 18 percent of your 2009 earned income to a maximum of $22,000, less all the 2009 pension contributions (PA factor).

If you belong to a deferred profit-sharing plan

If your employer contributes money to a deferred profit-sharing plan on your behalf, your pension adjustment equals the total of the contributions made (up to the maximum allowable DPSP contribution) for the previous year. For example, your 2010 maximum would be 18 percent of your 2009 earned income to a maximum of $22,000, minus your 2009 PA factor.

Types of RRSPs

You can get an RRSP just about anywhere — your local bank, trust company, brokerage house, insurance company, credit union, or mutual fund company. You'll often hear about three different types — *guaranteed, mutual fund,* and *self-directed* or *brokerage-house RRSPs.* The names are often partly dictated by the financial institution that is offering them.

You aren't limited to a specific number of RRSPs. You could, for example, open up a handful of RRSPs, each in different types of investments with different companies. Drawbacks do exist to having several plans, however. The paperwork can be burdensome, and it can become a real chore to follow your investments. If you invest with a number of different mutual fund companies, the trustee fees can start to add up.

Here's how to interpret what the different names mean.

Guaranteed RRSPs

Guaranteed plans are really just RRSPs in which you put your money into investments where your principal is protected, such as guaranteed investment certificates (GICs). When you do so, you lend your money to a bank or other financial institution in return for regular interest payments. Guaranteed plans pay fixed returns, and your money, if invested in GICs, is usually protected by the Canada Deposit Insurance Corporation's deposit protection.

Mutual fund RRSPs

The second basic type of RRSP is an investment in mutual funds. Mutual fund RRSPs offer two benefits. First, by using funds, you can invest your money in stocks and bonds, which over the long haul will handily beat the returns from guaranteed investments. Second, if you set up an RRSP with a mutual fund company, you can diversify your savings by putting them into several different types of funds with the same company. Some mutual fund companies charge an annual trustee fee ranging from $25 to $50 a year for RRSP accounts.

Reducing your family's tax bill with a spousal RRSP

A spousal RRSP can help reduce your household's future tax bill if you're married or living common-law and anticipate a big gap between your income and your spouse's income when you both retire.

A spousal RRSP is simply a special kind of RRSP to which one spouse makes the contributions and is able to claim the tax deduction. However, the money then belongs to the other spouse. (Although this change in official ownership worries some potential contributing partners, it shouldn't. In most cases the money in RRSPs is simply counted as part of your combined assets and divided equally between you and your spouse if you get separated or divorced.) A spousal RRSP allows you to move some future income out of the hands of the person in the higher tax bracket, and into the hands of the spouse with the lower retirement income and therefore the lower tax bracket.

You need to know some specific rules. The total contributions made by a spouse to both his or her own plan and a spousal RRSP can't exceed that individual's allowable maximum individual contribution. In addition, restrictions exist that prevent the higher-earning spouse from contributing to a spousal plan, claiming the deduction against income that is taxed at a high marginal rate, and then having the lower-earning spouse remove the money from the plan and being taxed at the lower marginal rate. If you contribute to a spousal plan, the money immediately belongs to your spouse. However, if he or she withdraws any of the contribution in that year or during the next two calendar years, the withdrawal is treated as though you had earned it, and taxed at your marginal rate. (This rule does not apply if you and your spouse are separated or divorced.)

Also, you have to close down your RRSP by the end of the year in which you turn 71. But if you have earned income in any year, that still earns your RRSP contribution room. If your spouse is 71 or younger, you can contribute to the spousal RRSP and claim a deduction.

Self-directed and brokerage-house RRSPs

The third type of RRSP includes self-directed plans and RRSPs you open with brokerage houses. This type of plan allows you to invest in a wide range of securities. In addition to GICs and mutual funds, you can invest in individual stocks and bonds and a wide range of other securities.

You can set up a self-directed plan with most investment dealers and discount brokerages. Some of these companies charge an annual fee, which typically runs around $100. Some institutions are willing to reduce or eliminate their fees for self-directed plans. The discount brokerages run by the big banks and trust companies often waive the first-year fee for new plans. If you do have to pay a fee, make sure you pay it out of your regular savings, not out of the funds in your plan.

Taking Money Out of Your RRSP before Retirement

It's called a *retirement* savings plan, but you don't have to wait until you've left the working world to take money out of an RRSP.

In fact, you're allowed to withdraw money out of your RRSP whenever you like. When you do, though, the government will want to collect the taxes it had earlier forgone on your contributions (with two exceptions, which we discuss in the section "Special circumstances").

Regular withdrawals before retirement

When you withdraw money from your RRSP, the planholder is required to withhold taxes on your withdrawals. As of 2005, the rates in all provinces (except Quebec) were 10 percent on amounts up to $5,000, 20 percent on the next $10,000, and 30 percent on withdrawals of more than $15,000. In Quebec, for any single withdrawal, the amount withheld is one-half of the federal withholding rates listed above, plus another 16 percent.

When you prepare your next income tax return, you have to declare your withdrawals as income in the year you took the money out of your plan. For most people, that will mean an additional tax bill because the withholding rates in most cases are lower than the marginal tax rate.

The withholding tax rates are calculated on each individual withdrawal. If you do need to get at your RRSP funds, take out separate withdrawals of no more than $5,000 each time to minimize the amount of withholding tax.

Special circumstances

In two cases, you can withdraw funds from your RRSP without paying taxes: to help purchase a house or to pay for an education.

The Home Buyers' Plan

You can tap your RRSP when you're younger to help get a down payment together for a home under the Home Buyers' Plan. You can borrow up to $25,000 from your RRSP to buy — or build — a home. Under the plan, this is not treated as a regular withdrawal and so is not taxed. However, you have to repay this loan over 15 years, beginning in the second year after you've taken the money out. For the full details of the plan, see Chapter 15.

Pensions and your contribution limits

Sometimes, pension benefits under a defined-benefit pension plan are improved retroactively. If this happens, your RRSP contribution limit may be further reduced by a past-service pension adjustment (PSPA).

On the other hand, you may find your contribution limits increased. For example, you may work for a company that has a pension plan. As a result, your RRSP contribution limits will be reduced by your pension adjustment. However, you may leave the company before you fully earn the rights to those benefits — before they vest. To give you back some of the RRSP contribution room that had been taken away because of the supposed pension benefits you were due to receive, you will get a pension adjustment reversal (PAR). A PAR increases your allowable RRSP contribution in the year you leave that particular job.

The Lifelong Learning Plan

You can also use your RRSP savings to help pay for an education. Under the Lifelong Learning Plan, you can take a loan out from your RRSP to help pay for postsecondary education or full-time training. You — or your spouse — can withdraw up to a maximum of $10,000 a year over a four-year period. The total withdrawn can't be more than $20,000. Like the Home Buyers' Plan, the money must be repaid.

The Lifelong Learning Plan repayments must start in the fifth year after the first withdrawal was made, and the full amount must be put back into your RRSP within ten years. For more details on the Lifelong Learning Plan, see Chapter 14.

Closing Down Your RRSP

You must close out, or *mature,* your RRSP by the end of the year during which you turn 71. You can make a final contribution to your plan in that year; however, instead of having 60 days into the next year to get your money in, the deadline for your final contribution is December 31.

Deciding just when to fold your plan and what to do with your funds are two of the most important financial decisions you'll ever make. Time your moves correctly and make some astute choices, and you'll find you have a much larger financial comfort zone than you expected. However, if you make your decisions at the last minute without doing your homework, you may find that your lack of attention costs you in terms of a lower standard of living.

Although you can close out your RRSP earlier than the year in which you celebrate your 71st birthday, the best strategy for most people is to leave your RRSP intact for as long as you're allowed. This is almost always the case if you decide to turn it into a *Registered Retirement Income Fund (RRIF)*. If you choose to go the *annuity* route, collapsing your plan a year or two early can make sense. If interest rates are relatively high, closing your plan out early may make sense if it allows you to lock in a higher-than-average return.

You have three basic options to choose from when your RRSP matures:

- ✔ Cash out — take all the money right out of your RRSP and do what you will with it. The Canada Revenue Agency will treat the sum total of your plan as taxable income in that year. The resulting tax bill will lop off anywhere from one-third to half of your retirement savings, right then and there. Ughh! (Because we don't think this is a sensible decision, this is all we'll say about this option.)

- ✔ Convert your RRSP into another sort of registered plan — called a Registered Retirement Income Fund (or RRIF), they allow you to continue to enjoy tax-deferred compounding. However, RRIFs require that you take out a certain minimum amount every year.

- ✔ Use the funds to buy an annuity — hand over your money to a financial institution (usually an insurance company), which then pays out regular sums to you for a period of time that you choose. This can be as short as ten years or as long as the rest of your life.

You aren't limited to just one of these three options. You can choose to split your RRSP funds and use two or even all three of these different strategies.

To make the right decision for your individual circumstances, you have to consider a lot more than simply how much cash flow each option will bring in. Each strategy has its own specific tax burden and a different schedule on when those tax bills will come due to consider. Further, you need to decide how much control you want to have over how your funds are invested, and whether you want to have access to your funds. Finally, each option offers different levels of estate or survivorship protections.

Registered Retirement Income Funds (RRIFs)

An RRIF is similar in many ways to an RRSP. An RRIF allows your money to continue to grow tax-deferred, and you can invest your funds in most of the eligible RRSP investments, from money market funds to individual stocks. Also, as with an RRSP, you can have one, two, or a handful of different RRIFs.

The only difference between an RRIF and an RRSP is that you aren't allowed to put any money into your RRIF. Instead, you're required to take out a certain minimum amount each year. The amount is a percentage of the value of your RRIF at the start of the year. The percentage increases slightly each year depending on your age, and levels out the year you turn 94.

These minimum payments are required to start the year after you set up your RRIF. You can choose monthly, quarterly, semi-annual, or annual payments. What's more, you don't have to take your payments in cash. You can move any investment out of your RRIF without selling it. However, you must pay tax on the fair market value at the time of the withdrawal, just as if it had been taken out as income.

The main benefit of an RRIF is that you continue to have control over how and where your money is invested. This control gives you the best chance of earning healthier returns on your money. In particular, it allows you to invest in equities and bonds.

RRIFs also let you have a say about how much income you have. As long as you withdraw the required minimums, you can take out as little or as much as you wish in any given year. If you suddenly come into some money, you can leave your RRIF essentially untouched and keep ringing up tax-free growth. If you have a medical emergency, you can quickly get your hands on as much as you need at the time.

RRIFs are usually a good choice if you:

- ✔ Enjoy managing your money.
- ✔ Have an indexed company pension plan that guarantees you a basic level of income.
- ✔ Don't immediately need to start drawing on your funds. Another advantage of RRIFs is that you can convert them to an annuity at any time, whereas an annuity is for life: After you sign up for an annuity, you can't change your mind. Further, with an RRIF you have a lot more control over what happens to your money at your death.

Prior to 1993, you were required to have withdrawn all your money from your RRIF by the time you were 90. The rules changed in 1992 to allow you to maintain your RRIF as long as you live. If you opened an RRIF before 1993, your minimum withdrawals are determined by the pre-1993 rules until you hit 78 or, if you have a younger spouse, when he or she turns 78.

Your minimum withdrawals are a percentage of the market value of your RRIF at the end of the previous year. The requirement for each year is determined by your age on January 1 of that year (see Table 11-5).

Table 11-5	Minimum RRIF Withdrawals	
Age	**RRIF Opened before 1993**	**RRIF Opened 1993 and Later**
64	3.85%	3.85%
65	4.00%	4.00%
66	4.17%	4.17%
67	4.35%	4.35%
68	4.55%	4.55%
69	4.76%	4.76%
70	5.00%	5.00%
71	5.26%	7.38%
72	5.56%	7.48%
73	5.88%	7.59%
74	6.25%	7.71%
75	6.67%	7.85%
76	7.14%	7.99%
77	7.69%	8.15%
78	8.33%	8.33%
79	8.53%	8.53%
80	8.75%	8.75%
81	8.99%	8.99%
82	9.27%	9.27%
83	9.58%	9.58%
84	9.93%	9.93%
85	10.33%	10.33%
86	10.79%	10.79%
87	11.33%	11.33%
88	11.96%	11.96%
89	12.71%	12.71%
90	13.62%	13.62%
91	14.73%	14.73%
92	16.12%	16.12%
93	17.92%	17.92%
94 and up	20.00%	20.00%

Annuities

When you use your RRSP funds to buy an annuity, you transfer your funds over to a financial institution (usually an insurance company), which then pays them back to you a little bit at a time. You don't pay tax on any RRSP funds at the time you turn them into an annuity. The regular payments from the annuity, though, are taxable and treated by the Canada Revenue Agency as "pension" income. If you have no other pension income, up to $2,000 of the annuity payments will qualify for the Pension Income Tax Credit.

The biggest decision when buying an annuity is the length of time you want your payments to run for. One option is to pick a specific number of years, such as 5, 10, or 20. At the end of the specific time, your payments end and your annuity is fully depleted. Another choice is a *life annuity,* which provides you with payments for the rest of your life; a *joint-life annuity* continues payments as long as you or your spouse is still alive.

If you select a life annuity, the size of your payments depends on your age and sex. Men tend to die at an earlier age than women do, so life annuity payments for males are generally higher because the funds have to last for fewer years. And, obviously, the younger you are the smaller your payments will be, because (we hope) your payments will have to stretch far into the future.

You can also add a couple of wrinkles to your annuity. If you choose a life annuity, even if you die the very next week the insurance company gets to keep all the money. But if you choose a *guaranteed annuity,* you ensure that if you die before a certain number of years have passed the payments will continue and will go to your beneficiaries. You can also choose to have your payments increase gradually from year to year. Such *indexed annuities* help your income keep up with inflation.

Just how much your funds will pay you, how long you want them to continue, and the options you want are all put through complex calculations by the technical climbers of the accounting world, actuaries. After you decide on your options, your payments can be calculated by using the statistics of how long you're likely to live and the likelihood of your dying at various ages. (Don't ask to see these numbers, because you probably don't want to know.) After you select your options, they can never be changed; they will remain in place until the annuity contract ends with your death or, if you choose the spousal survivor option, when your spouse dies.

This means that options such as indexing and guarantees all come at a price. Because these features mean that the insurance company will in all likelihood have to pay out more money, your regular payments will be lower than if you chose to go with a basic, stripped-down *defined-term annuity.*

Unlocking locked-in RRSPs and retirement accounts

If you leave a company in which you were a member of a pension plan, you may have earned the right to your pension benefits. However, you may not be allowed to gain access to those benefits due to the pension regulations (locking-in legislation). In this case, your pension benefits may be transferred to a special type of RRSP called a locked-in RRSP or locked-in retirement account (LIRA), depending on the province you live in.

When you're ready to start drawing on this money, you have two options. You can take the money and purchase an annuity. The other option is to convert such locked-in plans and accounts into a life income fund (LIF) or locked-

in retirement income fund (LRIF), depending on your province. These accounts are similar to an RRIF, but with a few extra wrinkles. Like an RRIF, you have to withdraw a set minimum as a percentage of the funds in your LRIF or LIF every year. However, unlike an RRIF, on which no maximums exist, there's also a ceiling on how much you can withdraw each year. (Until recently, a number of provinces required that you convert an LIF into an annuity in the year in which you turned 80. However, Newfoundland is now the only remaining province in which this rule applies. In all other provinces, an LIF can be maintained until age 90, at which point all the money in the plan has to be withdrawn.)0

Annuities are usually best when you:

- ✔ Have small retirement savings that absolutely need to last a number of years, especially if you're young and your family has a history of living a long time.

- ✔ Must have the peace of mind that comes with knowing just how much you have to live on.

- ✔ Don't want to have to make ongoing decisions about how to invest your money.

On the flip side of these advantages are several drawbacks, including these:

- ✔ You lose all control of your savings.

- ✔ Your rate of return is fixed when you buy your plan and will likely be lower than what you could earn investing in good mutual funds. If the investment world suddenly becomes littered with far more profitable options, you'll just have to lump it.

- ✔ If you don't accept lower payments in return for an indexed annuity, you may be faced with having less buying power over the years if inflation takes off.

✔ If you don't take out a guarantee, or you die after the guarantee period expires, your family or other beneficiaries won't get anything on your death.

The largest drawback to annuities is that you lose all input in how your money is invested and in how much it earns for you. You also have to accept lower initial payments if you want your annuity to increase with the cost of living.

Chapter 12

Investing in Retirement Plans

In This Chapter

▶ Determining how to allocate money in RRSPs and retirement plans

▶ Looking at investments to avoid in RRSPs and retirement plans

▶ Moving your retirement plan to a new firm

*T*his chapter helps you decide how to invest money you currently hold inside — or plan to contribute to — an RRSP or other retirement plan.

When compared to the often-overwhelming world of investing outside retirement plans, investing inside tax-sheltered retirement plans — RRSPs, RRIFs, and company plans — is less complicated for two reasons:

✔ **The range of possible retirement plan investments is more limited.** Direct investments, such as real estate and investments in small, privately owned companies, aren't generally available or accessible in most retirement plans.

✔ **When you invest in a tax-sheltered retirement plan, your returns aren't taxed as you earn them.** Money inside retirement plans compounds and grows without taxation. You generally pay taxes on these funds only when you withdraw money from the account. (Direct transfers to registered retirement plans at another investment firm are not withdrawals, so they're not taxed.) So when you choose an investment for your retirement plan, don't rack your brain over dividends and capital gains; save all that worry for the money you invest in non-retirement accounts.

Allocating Your Money in Retirement Plans

With good reason, people are concerned about placing their retirement money in investments that can decline in value. You may feel that you're gambling with dollars intended for the security of your golden years.

Most working folks need to make their money work hard in order for it to grow fast enough to provide this security. This involves taking some risk; you have no way around it. Luckily, if you have 15 to 20 years or more before you need to draw on the bulk of your retirement plan assets, time is on your side. As long as the value of your investments has time to recover, what's the big deal if some of your investments drop a bit over a year or two? The more years you have before you're going to retire, the greater your ability to take risk.

Think of your retirement plans as part of your overall plan to generate retirement income. Then allocate different types of investments between your tax-deferred retirement plans and other taxable investment accounts to get the maximum benefit of tax deferral. This section helps you determine how to distribute your money in retirement plans. Chapter 9 can help you decide how to divide your money among different non-retirement investment options based on your time frame and risk tolerance.

Understanding the difference between an RRSP and the investments inside your RRSP

Many people get confused when discussing the investments they make in retirement plans, especially those held inside RRSPs. Often, they don't realize that you can have an RRSP at a variety of financial institutions (for example, a mutual fund company or brokerage firm). At each financial institution, you can choose among the firm's investment options for putting your RRSP money to work.

No-load, or commission-free, mutual fund and discount brokerage firms are your best bet for establishing an RRSP. For more specifics, see our recommendations in Chapter 10.

Prioritizing retirement contributions

When you have access to various retirement plans, prioritize which account you're going to use first by determining how much each gives you in return. Your first contributions should be to employer-based plans that match your contributions. After that, contribute to any other employer plans that allow tax-deductible contributions or to a self-directed RRSP. After you contribute as much as possible to these tax-deductible plans, consider an annuity (see "Annuities: An Odd Investment," in this chapter). For information on how to set up an RRSP, refer to Chapter 11.

Inappropriate retirement plan investments

Some investments, such as those that are treated favourably by the tax man, often don't make a lot of sense inside retirement plans.

Although annuities (refer to Chapter 9) are retirement vehicles, they have no place inside retirement plans. Annuities allow your investment dollars to compound without taxation. In comparison to other investments that don't allow such tax deferral, annuities carry much higher annual operating expenses, which depress your returns.

Purchasing an annuity inside an RRSP is like wearing a belt and suspenders together. Either you have a peculiar sense of style, or you're spending too much time worrying about your pants falling down. In our experience, many people who mistakenly invest in annuities inside retirement plans have been misled by investment salespeople.

Limited partnerships are treacherous, high-commission, high-cost (and hence low-return) investments sold through investment salespeople. Part of their supposed allure, however, is the tax benefits they generate. But when you buy and hold a limited partnership in an RRSP or other retirement plan, you lose the ability to take advantage of many of the tax deductions. The illiquidity of LPs may also mean that you can't make required retirement plan withdrawals when needed. These are just some of the many reasons to avoid investing in limited partnerships. (For more reasons, see Chapter 9.)

Allocating money when your employer selects the investment options

In some company-sponsored plans, you're limited to the predetermined investment options your employer offers. In the following sections, we discuss typical investment options for employer-sponsored plans in order of increasing risk and, hence, likely return. Then we follow with examples for how to allocate your money across the different types of common employer retirement plan options.

Money market/savings accounts

For regular contributions that come out of your paycheque, the money market or savings account option makes little sense. Some people who are skittish about the stock and bond markets are attracted to money market and savings accounts because they can't drop in value. However, the returns are low — so low that you have a great risk that your investment will not stay ahead of, or even keep up with, inflation and taxes (which are due upon withdrawal of your money from the retirement plan).

Don't be tempted to use a money market fund as a parking place until the time when you think stocks and bonds are cheap. In the long run, you won't be doing yourself any favours. As we discuss in Chapter 8, timing your investments to attempt to catch the lows and avoid the peaks isn't possible.

You may need to keep money in the money market investment option if you utilize the borrowing feature that some retirement plans allow. Check with your employee benefits department for more details. After you retire, you may also want to use a money market account to hold money you expect to withdraw and spend within a year or so.

Bond mutual funds

Bond mutual funds (which we describe in Chapter 10) invest in a mixture of typically high-quality bonds. Bonds pay a higher rate of interest or dividends than money funds. Depending on whether your plan's option is a short-term, intermediate-term, or long-term fund (maybe you have more than one type), the bond fund's current yield is probably a percent or two higher than the money market fund's yield. (*Note:* During certain time periods, such as the late 2000s, the yield difference may be more; during other time periods, such as the mid-2000s, it may be less.)

Bond funds carry higher yields than money market funds, but they also carry greater risk, because their value can fall if interest rates increase. However, bonds tend to be more stable in value over the shorter term (such as a few years) than stocks.

Aggressive, younger investors should keep a minimum amount of money in bond funds. Older folks who want to invest conservatively can place more money in bonds (see the asset allocation discussion in Chapter 8).

Guaranteed investment certificates

Guaranteed investment certificates (GICs) are backed by a bank, trust company, or insurance company, and they typically quote a rate of return for anywhere from thirty days to five years or more. The positive return is certain — so you don't have the uncertainty you normally face with bond or stock investments.

The attraction of these investments is that your account value does not fluctuate (at least, not that you can see). Financial institutions normally invest your money mostly in bonds and maybe a bit in stocks. The difference between what these investments generate for the issuer and what they pay in interest to investors is how they make a profit. (Institutions also lend your money to borrowers, and share those borrowers a higher interest rate than that which they pay you.) A GIC's yield is usually comparable to that of a bond fund.

For people who hit the eject button the moment that a bond fund slides a bit in value, GICs are soothing to the nerves. And they're certainly higher yielding than a money market or savings account.

Like bonds, however, GICs don't give you the opportunity for much long-term growth above the rate of inflation. Over the long haul, you should earn a better return in a mixture of bond and stock investments. In GICs, you pay for the peace of mind of a guaranteed return with lower long-term returns.

Balanced mutual funds

Balanced mutual funds invest primarily in a mixture of stocks and bonds. This one-stop-shopping concept makes investing easier and smoothes out fluctuations in the value of your investments — funds investing exclusively in stocks or in bonds make for a rougher ride. These funds are solid options and, in fact, can be used for a significant portion of your retirement plan contributions. See Chapter 10 to find out more about balanced funds.

Watch out for the higher fees that some fund companies charge on their balanced funds.

Stock mutual funds

Stock mutual funds invest in stocks, which often provide greater long-term growth potential but also wider fluctuations in value from year to year. Some companies offer a number of different stock funds, including funds that invest overseas. Unless you plan to borrow against your RRSP funds to purchase a home, you should have a healthy helping of stock funds. See Chapter 10 for an explanation of the different types of stock funds as well as for details on how to evaluate a stock fund.

Shares in the company you work for

Some companies offer employees the option of investing in the company's stock. We generally advocate avoiding this option for the simple reason that your future income and other employee benefits are already riding on the success of the company. If the company hits the skids, you may lose your job and your benefits. You certainly don't want the value of your retirement savings to depend on the same factors.

In the early 2000s, you may have heard all the hubbub about companies such as Enron going under and its employees losing piles of money in their retirement savings plans. Enron's bankruptcy in and of itself shouldn't have caused direct problems in the company's pension plan. The problem was that Enron required employees to hold substantial amounts of Enron company stock. Thus, when the company tanked, employees lost their jobs *and* their retirement savings balances.

If you think that your company has its act together and the stock is a good buy, investing a portion of your retirement savings is fine — but no more than 25 percent. Now, if your company is on the verge of hitting it big and the stock is soon to soar, you'll of course be kicking yourself for not putting more of your money into the company's stock. But when you place a big bet on your company's stock, be prepared to suffer the consequences if the stock tanks. Consider all those Nortel employees who piled their savings into Nortel stock, only to watch Nortel's shares drop from $120 to under a buck and then eventually become worthless. Don't forget that lots of smart investors track companies' prospects, so odds are that the current value of your company's stock is reasonably fair.

Some employers offer employees an additional option to buy company stock at a discount, sometimes as much as 15 percent, when compared to its current market value. If your company offers a discount on its stock, take advantage of it. When you sell the stock you usually will be able to lock in a decent profit over your purchase price.

Some asset allocation examples

Using the methodology that we outline in Chapter 8 for allocating money, Table 12-1 shows a couple examples of how people in different employer plans may choose to allocate their retirement investments among the plan's investment options.

Please note that making allocation decisions is not a science. Use the formulas in Chapter 8 as a guideline.

Table 12-1 Allocating Company Pension Plan Investments			
	25-Year-Old, Aggressive Risk Investor	*45-Year-Old, Moderate Risk Investor*	*60-Year-Old, Moderate Risk Investor*
Bond Fund	5%	35%	50%
Balanced Fund (50% stock/50% bond)	10%	0%	0%
Blue Chip/Larger Company Stock Fund(s)	30–40%	25–30%	25%
Smaller Company Stock Fund(s)	20%	15%	10%
International Stock Fund(s)	25–35%	20–25%	15%

Allocating money in RRSPs

With RRSPs, you may select the investment options as well as the allocation of money among them. In the sections that follow, we give some specific recipes that you may find useful for investing at some of the premier investment companies.

To establish an RRSP at one of these firms, simply pick up your telephone, dial the company's toll-free number, and ask the representative to mail you an account application. You can also have the company mail you background information on specific mutual funds. (If you're less patient, and you're a fan of the Internet, many investment firms provide downloadable account applications. However, downloading an application can be a tedious process, especially if you also need other information such as investment prospectuses and annual reports.)

Note: In the examples, we recommend a conservative portfolio and an aggressive portfolio for each firm. We use the terms *conservative* and *aggressive* in a relative sense. Because some of the funds we recommend do not maintain fixed percentages of their different types of investments, the actual percentage of stocks and bonds that you end up with may vary slightly from the targeted percentages. Don't sweat it.

Where you have more than one fund choice, you can pick one or split the suggested percentage among them. If you don't have enough money today to divvy up your portfolio as we suggest, you can achieve the desired split over time as you add more money to your RRSP.

Beutel Goodman & Co.

The following two Beutel Goodman (800-897-7282; www.beutel-can.com) recommendations are for a conservative mix and an aggressive mix, respectively.

A conservative portfolio with 50 percent stocks, 50 percent bonds

If you don't want to risk too much, try this:

- ✔ Beutel Goodman Canadian Equity — 25 percent
- ✔ Beutel Goodman Income — 30 percent
- ✔ Beutel Goodman Long Term Bond — 10 percent
- ✔ Beutel Goodman Balanced — 20 percent
- ✔ Beutel Goodman World Focus Equity — 15 percent

An aggressive portfolio with 80 percent stocks, 20 percent bonds

If you can afford to be aggressive, try this:

- ✔ Beutel Goodman Canadian Equity — 30 percent
- ✔ Beutel Goodman Income — 20 percent
- ✔ Beutel Goodman Canadian Dividend — 10 percent
- ✔ Beutel Goodman Small Cap — 20 percent
- ✔ Beutel Goodman World Focus Equity — 20 percent

Mawer

The following two Mawer (800-889-6248; www.mawer.com) recommendations are for a conservative mix and an aggressive mix, respectively.

A conservative portfolio with 50 percent stocks, 50 percent bonds

If you don't want to risk too much, try this:

- ✔ Mawer Canadian Equity — 20 percent
- ✔ Mawer Canadian Bond — 35 percent
- ✔ Mawer Canadian Balanced Retirement Savings — 30 percent
- ✔ Mawer U.S. Equity — 5 percent
- ✔ Mawer Global Equity — 10 percent

An aggressive portfolio with 80 percent stocks, 20 percent bonds

If you can afford to be aggressive, try this:

- ✔ Mawer Canadian Equity — 30 percent
- ✔ Mawer New Canada — 10 percent
- ✔ Mawer Global Small Cap — 10 percent
- ✔ Mawer U.S. Equity — 15 percent
- ✔ Mawer Global Equity — 15 percent
- ✔ Mawer Canadian Bond — 20 percent

Phillips, Hager & North

The following two Phillips, Hager & North (800-661-6141; www.phn.com) recommendations are for a conservative mix and an aggressive mix, respectively.

A conservative portfolio with 50 percent stocks, 50 percent bonds

If you don't want to risk too much, try this:

- ✔ PH&N Canadian Equity — 15 percent
- ✔ PH&N Bond — 35 percent
- ✔ PH&N Balanced — 30 percent
- ✔ PH&N Dividend — 10 percent
- ✔ PH&N Global Equity Portfolio — 10 percent

Should I use more than one investment firm?

The firms we recommend in this chapter offer a large enough variety of investment options, managed by different fund managers, that you can feel comfortable concentrating your money at one firm. Your investments aren't at risk based on the financial health of the fund company itself. Discovering the nuances and choices of just one firm rather than several and having fewer administrative hassles are the advantages of a focused approach.

If you like the idea of spreading your money around, you may want to invest through a number of different firms using a discount brokerage account (see Chapter 8). You can diversify across different mutual fund companies through one brokerage firm. However, you'll pay small transaction fees on some of your purchases and sales of funds.

An aggressive portfolio with 80 percent stocks, 20 percent bonds

If you can afford to be aggressive, try this:

- ✔ PH&N Canadian Equity — 30 percent
- ✔ PH&N Canadian Growth — 10 percent
- ✔ PH&N Dividend — 10 percent
- ✔ PH&N U.S. Equity — 15 percent
- ✔ PH&N Global Equity — 15 percent
- ✔ PH&N Bond — 20 percent

Discount brokers

As we discuss in Chapter 8, a discount brokerage account can allow you centralized, one-stop shopping and the ability to hold mutual funds from a variety of leading fund companies. Some funds are available without transaction fees, although most of the better funds require you to pay a small transaction fee when you buy funds through a discount broker. The reason: The discounter is an intermediary between you and the fund companies. You have to weigh the convenience of being able to buy and hold funds from multiple fund companies in a single account versus the lower cost of buying funds directly from their providers. A $25 to $30 transaction fee can gobble a sizeable chunk of what you have to invest, especially if you're investing smaller amounts.

You don't have to set up your RRSP with one particular mutual fund company. Discount brokerages offer self-directed RRSPs in which you can choose from a huge range of investments — including mutual funds. When you buy through discount brokerages, you can buy hundreds of different mutual funds without paying transaction fees. However, there may be a charge for switching funds or selling within a certain period. Here is a suggested conservative portfolio and an aggressive portfolio using a basket of funds from different fund companies.

A conservative portfolio with 50 percent stocks, 50 percent bonds

If you don't want to risk too much, try this:

- Mawer Canadian Equity — 25 percent
- Mawer World Investment — 15 percent
- Mac Cundill Value — 10 percent
- PH&N Bond or TD Canadian Bond — 35 percent
- RBC Global Bond — 15 percent

An aggressive portfolio with 80 percent stocks, 20 percent bonds

If you can afford to be aggressive, try this:

- Sceptre Canadian Equity or Mawer Canadian Equity — 20 percent
- Altamira Tactical Asset Allocation Fund — 10 percent
- Sceptre Equity Growth or GBC Canadian Growth — 10 percent
- Fidelity Growth America — 15 percent
- RBC O'Shaughnessy U.S. Value — 15 percent
- Mawer World Investment — 10 percent
- Altamira Bond or TD Canadian Bond — 20 percent

Annuities: An Odd Investment

Annuities are peculiar investment products. They're contracts that are backed by an insurance company. If you, the annuity holder (investor), die during the so-called *accumulation phase* (that is, prior to receiving payments from the annuity), your designated beneficiary is guaranteed to receive the amount of your contribution. In this sense, annuities look a bit like life insurance.

Annuities, like RRSPs, allow your capital to grow and compound without taxation. You defer taxes until withdrawal. Unlike an RRSP that has an annual contribution limit, you can deposit as much as you want into an annuity in any year — even a million dollars or more if you have it!

Contributing to an annuity may make sense if

✔ **You have exhausted contributions to RRSPs and employer-sponsored and self-employed plans.** Your contributions to these retirement plans are tax-deductible; annuity contributions are not.

✔ **You expect to leave the money compounding in the annuity for at least 15 years.** It typically takes this long for the benefits of tax-deferred compounding to outweigh the higher annuity fees and treatment of all withdrawn annuity earnings at the higher ordinary income tax rates. If you're close to or are actually in retirement, tax-friendly investments made outside of retirement plans are preferable.

For details about other investment options and the best places to purchase annuities, see Chapter 13, where we discuss investing money outside of retirement plans.

Transferring Retirement Plans

With the exception of plans maintained by your employer that limit your investment options, you can move your money held in RRSPs or RRIFs (Registered Retirement Income Funds) to almost any major investment firm or mutual funds company. Moving the money is pretty simple; if you can fill out a couple of short forms and send them back in a postage-paid envelope, you can transfer an account. The investment firm to which you are transferring your account does the rest.

Transferring accounts you control

Here's a step-by-step list of what you need to do to transfer a retirement savings plan to another investment firm. Even if you're working with a financial adviser, you should be aware of this process (called a *direct trustee-to-trustee transfer*) to ensure that no hanky-panky takes place on the adviser's part.

1. **Decide where you want to move the account.**

   We recommend several investment companies in this chapter, along with some sample portfolios within those firms. You may also want to consult the latest edition of our other book, *Investing For Canadians For Dummies.*

2. **Obtain an account application and asset transfer form.**

   Call the toll-free number of the firm you're transferring the money to and ask for an account application and asset transfer form for the type of account you're transferring. You can also visit the firm's Web site, but for this type of request we think most people find it easier to speak directly to someone.

Ask for the form for the *same* type of account you currently have at the company from which you're transferring the money. You can determine the account type by looking at a recent account statement — the account type should appear near the top of the form or in the section with your name and address. If you can't figure out the account type on a cryptic statement, call the firm where the account is currently held and ask a representative to tell you what kind of account you have.

Never, ever sign over assets such as cheques and security certificates to a financial adviser, no matter how trustworthy and honest she may seem. The adviser could bolt with them quicker than you can say "Bonnie and Clyde." Transfers should not be completed this way. Besides, you'll find it easier to handle the transfer by following the information in this section.

3. **Figure out which securities you want to transfer and which need to be liquidated.**

   Transferring existing investments in your account to a new investment firm can sometimes be a little sticky. Transferring such assets as cash (money market funds) or securities that trade on any of the major stock exchanges is not a problem.

If you own publicly traded securities, transferring them as is (also known as transferring them *in kind*) to your new investment firm is better, especially if the firm offers discount brokerage services. You can then sell your securities through that firm more cheaply.

If you own mutual funds unique to the institution you're leaving, check with your new firm to see whether it can accept them. If not, you need to contact the firm that currently holds them to sell them.

GICs are tricky to transfer. Ideally, you should send in the transfer forms several weeks or so before the GICs mature — few people do this. If the GIC matures soon, call the bank and say that when the GIC matures you want to invest the funds in a savings or money market account that you can access without penalty when your transfer request lands in the bank's mailbox.

4. **Complete and mail the account application and asset transfer form.**

   Completing these for your new investment firm opens your new account and authorizes the transfer.

You shouldn't take possession of the money in your retirement plan when moving it over to the new firm. The tax authorities impose huge penalties if you perform a transfer incorrectly. For example, if you make the mistake of withdrawing your investments from an RRSP during the transfer process, the full amount gets included in your taxable income for that year, and you'll have to pay tax on it at your marginal tax rate. Let the company to which you're transferring the money do the transfer for you. If you have questions or problems, the firm(s) to which you're transferring your account has armies of capable employees waiting to help you. Remember, these firms know that you're transferring your money to them, so they should roll out the red carpet.

5. Let the firm from which you're transferring the money know that you're doing so. (This step is optional.)

If the place you're transferring the money from doesn't assign a specific person to your account, you can definitely skip this step. When you're moving your investments from a brokerage firm where you dealt with a particular broker, deciding whether to follow this step can be more difficult.

Most people feel obligated to let their representative know that they're moving their money. In our experience, calling the person with the "bad news" is usually a mistake. Brokers or others who have a direct financial stake in your decision to move your money will try to sell you on staying. Some may try to make you feel guilty for leaving, and some may even try to bully you.

Writing a letter may seem like the coward's way out, but writing usually makes leaving your broker easier for both of you. You can polish what you have to say, and you don't put the broker on the defensive. Although we don't want to encourage lying, not telling the *whole* truth may be an even better idea. Excuses, such as that you have a family member in the investment business who will manage your money for free, may help you avoid an uncomfortable confrontation.

Then again, telling an investment firm that its charges are too high or that it misrepresented and sold you a bunch of lousy investments may help the firm improve in the future. Don't fret too much — do what's best for you and what you're comfortable with. Brokers are not your friends. Even though the broker may know your kids' names, your favourite hobbies, and your birthday, you have a *business* relationship with him.

Transferring your existing assets typically takes a month to complete. If the transfer is not completed within one month, get in touch with your new investment firm to determine the problem. If your old company isn't cooperating, call a manager there to help get the ball rolling.

The unfortunate reality is that an investment firm will cheerfully set up a new account to *accept* your money on a moment's notice, but it will drag its feet, sometimes for months, when the time comes to relinquish your money. To light a fire under the behinds of the folks at the investment firm, tell a manager at the old firm that you're going to send a letter to the provincial securities regulator if it doesn't complete your transfer within the next week.

Moving money from an employer's plan

When you leave a job, particularly if you're retiring or being laid off after many years of service, money-hungry brokers and financial planners probably will be on you like a pack of bears on a tree leaking sweet honey. If you seek financial help, tread carefully — Chapter 19 helps you avoid the pitfalls of hiring such assistance.

When you leave a job, you're confronted with a slightly different transfer challenge: If you've earned the right to some or all of your pension benefits (called vesting), you have the option of moving them into a special account called a locked-in retirement account (LIRA). In some provinces, these are called locked-in RRSPs. (As long as your employer allows it, you may be able to leave your money in your old employer's plan. Evaluate the quality of the investment choices using the information we provide in this part of the book.)

Never take personal possession of money from your employer's retirement plan. If you want to transfer your pension funds, simply inform your employer of where you want your money to be sent. Prior to doing so, establish an appropriate account at the investment firm you intend to use. Then tell your employer's benefits department where you would like your retirement money transferred. You can send your employer the Canada Revenue Agency forms and lock-in agreement (if required) that have been signed by the investment firm's retirement plan trustee. These forms will contain the investment firm's mailing address and your account number.

Chapter 13

Investing Outside Retirement Plans

In This Chapter

▶ Making sure you've explored your options

▶ Taking advantage of Tax-Free Savings Accounts

▶ Making the most of Registered Disability Savings Plans

▶ Factoring taxes into your investment decisions

▶ Bolstering your emergency reserves

▶ Examining recommended longer-term investments

*I*n this chapter, we discuss investment options for money held outside registered retirement plans, and we include some sample portfolio recommendations. (Chapter 12 reviews investments for money *inside* retirement plans.) This distinction may seem somewhat odd — it's not one that's made in most financial books and articles. However, thinking of these two types of investments differently can be useful because

✔ **Investments held outside registered retirement plans are subject to taxation.** You have a whole range of different investment options to consider when taxes come into play.

✔ **Money held outside registered retirement plans is more likely to be used sooner than funds held inside retirement plans.** Why? Because you'll generally have to pay far more in income taxes to access money inside rather than outside retirement plans.

✔ **Funds held inside registered retirement plans have their own nuances.** For example, when you invest through your employer's retirement plan, your investment options are usually limited to a handful of choices. And special rules govern transfer of your retirement plan balances.

Getting Started

Suppose you have some money sitting in a bank savings account or money market mutual fund, earning a small amount of interest, and you want to invest it more profitably. You need to remember two things about investing this type of money:

- ✓ **Earning a little is better than losing 20 to 50 percent or more.** Just talk to anyone who bought a lousy investment. Be patient. Educate yourself *before* you invest.

- ✓ **To earn a higher rate of return, you must be willing to take more risk.** In order to earn a better rate of return, you need to consider investments that fluctuate in value — of course, the value can drop as well as rise.

You approach the vast sea of investment options and start stringing up your rod to go fishing. You hear stories of people catching big ones — cashing in big on stocks or real estate that they bought years ago. Even if you don't have delusions of grandeur, you'd at least like your money to grow faster than the cost of living.

But before you cast your investment line, consider the following often overlooked ways to put your money to work and earn higher returns without much risk. These options may not be as exciting as hunting the big fish out there, but they should easily improve your financial health.

Paying off high-interest debt

Many folks have credit card or other consumer debt that costs more than 10 percent per year in interest. Paying off this debt with savings is like putting your money in an investment with a guaranteed return that's equal to the rate you're paying on the debt.

For example, if you have credit card debt outstanding at 25 percent interest, paying off that loan is the same as putting your money to work in an investment with a sure 25 percent annual return. Remember that the interest on consumer debt is not tax-deductible, so you actually need to earn *more* than 25 percent investing your money elsewhere in order to net 25 percent after paying taxes. (See Chapter 5 for more details if you're still not convinced.)

Paying off some of or your entire mortgage may make sense, too. This financial move isn't as clear as erasing consumer debt, because the mortgage interest rate is lower than it is on consumer debt.

Taking advantage of tax breaks

Make sure you take advantage of the tax benefits offered on RRSPs and other plans. If you work for a company that offers to match your contributions to a retirement savings plan, try to fund it at the highest level you can manage. (Refer to Chapters 11 and 12 for more about RRSPs.)

If you need to save money outside retirement plans for shorter-term goals (for example, to buy a car or a home, or to start or buy a small business), then by all means, save money outside retirement plans. This chapter will show you how to save and invest money in two valuable tax-friendly accounts, Tax-Free Savings Accounts and Registered Disability Savings Plans. You'll also learn the best ways to invest in taxable accounts (non-retirement plans that are exposed to taxation).

Taking Advantage of Tax-Free Savings Accounts (TFSAs)

If you're 18 or older, and have more than enough in a savings or chequing account to handle your regular ongoing cash needs and bill payments — say, a few thousand dollars — take advantage of a Tax-Free Savings Account, or TFSA.

Think of a TFSA as being the reverse of an RRSP. Unlike an RRSP, you don't get to deduct money you put into a TFSA from your taxable income. However, any funds withdrawn aren't taxed.

Any interest, dividends, and capital gains you earn on the money and investments inside your TFSA are tax-free. That means your money can enjoy compound growth without the headwind of taxes slowing it down. TFSAs are easy to understand, a breeze to set up, and they'll help you save on taxes and help your money grow faster. What's not to like?

You can take out your money — and your profits — at any time, tax-free. Thus, a TFSA can help you reach both your short-term and long-term goals.

Understanding how much you can contribute

Starting in 2009, you automatically earn the right to contribute a maximum of $5,000 into a TFSA each year. (Beginning in 2010, the allowable annual $5,000 contribution amount will be indexed to inflation.) Unlike RRSPs, the allowable contribution is not affected in any way by your level of income or whether you are a member of a pension plan.

If you don't contribute the maximum allowed in any given year, the unused portion gets added to a running total of what you can contribute in any year in the future. In the jargon of the tax world, this is known as *carrying forward* your *unused contribution room*.

You can hold more than one TFSA, but the contribution ceiling applies to the total amount contributed, not the contributions made to each individual account.

If you are married or living in common-law, TFSAs offer an additional way to save on your taxes. If one spouse earns more than the other, the higher-earning spouse can give money to their partner, which the partner can use to make contributions to their own TFSA. (The maximum amounts are governed by the available contribution room of the person making the contribution.)

Normally, when you give money to your spouse and he or she then invests it, the Canada Revenue Agency (CRA) treats any gains as though you had earned them. In other words, the CRA attributes the gains to the giver, under the logically named *attribution income rules*. However, the attribution rules do not apply to funds put into a TFSA. This means that if in total a couple can come up with $10,000, they can contribute that full amount regardless of who put up what (each investing $5,000 into a TFSA), and enjoy tax-free growth on the full amount.

Understanding your TFSA investment choices

Most of the common types of investments that are allowed inside an RRSP are also eligible for use in a TFSA. This includes cash, term deposits, and guaranteed investment certificates (GICs). Exchange-traded funds (ETFs), mutual funds, bonds, and stocks are also allowed, as are shares of small business corporations in certain cases. Regardless of the type of investment, your gains are not taxable. (Note that if you sell an investment inside a TFSA at a loss, that loss can't be used to reduce taxes on the gains on other investments outside your account.)

If you don't have actual cash on hand, you can start building up your TFSA if you own investments that aren't inside a registered plan. Most investments, including GICs, stocks, and units of mutual funds, can be contributed to a TFSA in the place of cash.

If you do contribute an investment that has appreciated in value since you bought it, moving that investment into your TFSA will trigger a tax bill. When you do this — called making a *contribution in kind* — the tax department assesses your gains, and taxes them, by using the value you originally paid for the investment and the value of the investment at the time you transfer it into your TFSA.

Making withdrawals from a TFSA

You can make withdrawals of any size from your TFSA at any time, and your withdrawals won't be taxed. One valuable wrinkle in the TFSA rules to be aware of is that the dollar amount of any withdrawal is added on to your available contribution room for the following year. This means you can take money out of your TFSA when needed and, beginning with the start of the next year, "re-contribute" that same amount of money at any point in the future. This rule not only applies to your original contributions, but also works with any profits you've earned inside your account and subsequently withdrawn.

The ability to re-contribute withdrawn funds opens up some potentially valuable strategies. In essence, you can enjoy tax-free gains, get access to those profits if you need them, and still leave yourself with the option of replacing the full amount you've withdrawn in future years. For example, say you invested $5,000 in a mutual fund inside your TFSA. The fund has a lucky streak, and in a few years' time it's worth $8,500. You could sell the units, withdraw the $8,500, and at any point in the future have the right to put the full $8,500 back into your account. This is in addition to the annual $5,000 allowed, along with any other contribution room you've built up.

Although you can replace any money you've taken out of a TFSA, you have to wait until the next calendar year. If you re-contribute money in the same year you've withdrawn it, that contribution will be added to any other contributions you've made that year. If the total is more than your allowable contribution, you'll be hit with a 1 percent a month penalty on the overcontribution amount.

Understanding Registered Disability Savings Plans (RDSPs)

If you or someone in your family has a disability, a Registered Disability Savings Plan (RDSP) is a valuable tool to help you provide for the longer-term financial needs you — or he or she — will face.

RDSPs work in a similar fashion to Registered Education Savings Plans (RESPs), which we explore in Chapter 14. Similar to RESPs and TFSAs (which we investigate in the previous section), your contributions aren't tax-deductible. In other words, contributions have to be made with after-tax dollars. Inside the plan, your contributions can be invested in most common investments and any interest or gains you then earn aren't taxed.

Determining whether you're eligible for an RDSP

In order to open up an RDSP for yourself you must be eligible for the disability tax credit, which in turn requires that the disability must be a severe and prolonged impairment that restricts your daily life and has lasted, or is expected to last, for at least 12 months. Parents or guardians can also open up an RDSP for a minor child with a disability that meets this definition.

The only restriction on contributions is a lifetime maximum limit of $200,000. Until that limit is reached, you can contribute as much as you like at any time, and no annual maximums exist.

Unlike all other special tax-friendly savings accounts and plans, no restrictions exist on who can put money into an RDSP. Beyond the beneficiary and their family, this means even distant relatives and friends can make contributions after an RDSP is set up.

Earning disability grants for an RDSP

Contributions to an RDSP earn the plan a government grant called the Canada Disability Savings Grant, or CDSG. This grant is similar to the grant that accompanies RESP contributions (see Chapter 14). The grant isn't provided automatically — you have to apply for it through the financial institution where you have your RDSP.

If your family's net income is less than a set amount (in 2010 it was $77,664), the grant is worth $3 for every $1 contributed, up to the first $500 contributed in the year. The next $1,000 of contributions earns a grant of $2 for every $1 put in. If your family's net income is over the ceiling, you'll earn a grant of $1 for every $1 put in for the first $1,000 of contributions each year. The maximum lifetime grant is $70,000. One important point is that, for some reason, the grant is available only to those under the age of 49.

Lower-income families may qualify for a grant of Canada Disability Savings Bonds up to a value of $1,000 every year. The lifetime maximum is $20,000.

Withdrawing funds from an RDSP

Two different types of withdrawals, or *payments from an RDSP,* exist. Regardless of the method chosen, an annual maximum is placed on how much can be taken out.

It's important to watch the timing of these payments in order to protect the money received from government contributions to the plan. When payments from an RDSP are made, any grants or bonds that have been received in the previous ten years have to be returned to the government.

Lifetime Disability Assistance Payment

One way to withdraw funds from an RDSP is through recurring annual payments. These are referred to as *lifetime disability assistance payments,* or LDAPs. They can be started at any age, but at the latest must begin the year the beneficiary turns 60. After they are started, they have to be continued until the death of the beneficiary. The maximum that can be paid out each year is capped by an amusingly complex — and a tad too real — calculation. The formula is:

$$\frac{\text{current value of plan}}{3 + \text{life expectancy}} - \text{current age}$$

For example, take a plan where the beneficiary is 65, has a life expectancy of 80, and the plan is worth $100,000. The value of the plan ($100,000) is divided by 18 (3 + 80 – 65), making the maximum allowable annual payments $5,555.

Disability Assistance Payments

The second way that money can be paid out from an RDSP is through individual lump-sum payments called *disability assistance payments,* or DAPs. A maximum exists for any single DAP, which is determined using the same formula as for LDAPs.

Understanding Taxes on Your Investments

When you invest money outside of a retirement plan, *investment distributions* — such as interest, dividends, and capital gains — are subject to current taxation. Too many folks (and too many of their financial advisers) ignore the tax impact of their investment strategies. You need to pay attention to the tax implications of your investment decisions *before* you invest your money.

Consider a person with a moderate income who is in a 34-percent tax bracket (combined federal and provincial) and who keeps extra cash in a bond paying 3 percent interest. If she pays 34 percent of her interest earnings in taxes, she ends up making just 2 percent. If she weren't using that money as an emergency fund, she might consider putting it into a dividend-producing investment, such as a dividend mutual fund. The effective tax rates on dividend income are much lower than those for interest income. For someone in a 34-percent tax bracket, the effective tax rate on dividends is just a few percent. For those in the top marginal tax rate, the effective tax on dividend income is about 21 to 23 percent.

In the sections that follow, we give specific advice about investing your money while keeping an eye on taxes.

Fortifying Your Emergency Reserves

In Chapter 4, we explain the importance of keeping sufficient money in an emergency reserve account. From such an account, you need two things:

- **Accessibility:** When you need to get your hands on the money for an emergency, you want to be able to do so quickly and without penalty.

- **Highest possible return:** You want to get the highest rate of return possible without risking your principal. This doesn't mean that you should simply pick the money market or savings option with the highest yield, because other issues, such as taxes, are a consideration. What good is earning a slightly higher yield if you pay a lot more in taxes?

The following sections give you information on investments that are suitable for emergency reserves.

Bank and credit union accounts

When you have a few thousand dollars or less, your best and easiest path is to keep this excess savings in a local bank or credit union. Look first to the institution where you keep your chequing account.

Keeping this stash of money in your chequing account, rather than in a separate savings account, makes financial sense if the extra money helps you avoid monthly service charges when your balance occasionally dips below the minimum. Compare the service charges on your chequing account with the interest earnings from a savings account.

For example, suppose you're keeping $2,000 in a savings account to earn 2 percent interest versus earning no interest on your chequing account money.

Over the course of a year, you earn $40 interest on that savings account. If you incur a $9 per month service charge on your chequing account, you pay $108 per year. So keeping your extra $2,000 in a chequing account may be better if it keeps you above a minimum balance and erases that monthly service charge. (However, if you're more likely to spend the extra money in your chequing account, keeping it in a separate savings account where you won't be tempted to spend it may be better.)

High-interest savings accounts

Another good choice for your short-term savings or emergency funds is a high-interest savings account. High-interest savings accounts fill the gap between a bank account, where you park a little money to cover your regular bill payments and cash needs, and mutual funds and other investments in which you invest your savings for the longer term. These accounts usually don't offer all the usual features of regular bank accounts such as bank machine access, bill payments, cheque-writing, and so on, but in return you're rewarded with a much better interest rate.

You can arrange to have your paycheque deposited directly to a high-interest savings account, and have the account set up in conjunction with a chequing account.

Unlike money market funds, you don't have to make a minimum deposit, nor do you have to worry about getting dinged with commissions, charges, or fees for withdrawing your money within a certain time frame of making a deposit. Another big plus is that, unlike a money market fund, you can get at your money quickly (although this may require first transferring it into a regular account) as long as your money has been in the account the required number of days. Most of these accounts allow you to access your cash simply by using a bank card at an ABM.

Some of the best deals in high-interest savings accounts are with companies that don't have any actual branches in your neighbourhood or town. Although this may be somewhat unnerving, your money is generally just as safe as if it were in a traditional savings account. Just be sure to check that, like companies we mention in the following sections, the institution is a member of the CDIC, an insurance program that protects your savings up to $100,000. We recommend a few high-interest savings accounts below.

President's Choice Financial

Loblaw Companies Limited took its well-known President's Choice brand of food products, hooked up with Canadian Imperial Bank of Commerce, and developed the President's Choice Financial line of financial products, which now includes banking accounts, mortgages, GICs, and insurance.

The President's Choice Financial Interest Plus savings account is a stripped-down affair that doesn't include a bank card or ABM access to your funds. However, you can check your balance and transfer money from other accounts into an Interest Plus account by phone, online, or by using a President's Choice or CIBC bank machine. If you keep a minimum balance of $1,000, you get a competitive interest rate and a small yearly bonus.

President's Choice also offers the Interest First savings account. This account has a slightly lower interest rate than the Interest Plus account, but has no required minimum balance.

To get at your money quickly, you'll need to also have a PC chequing account, which comes with a bank card. You can use this card at any CIBC bank machine without getting nicked for fees. You can also use the card at any other ABMs, but you'll have to pay the Interac transaction fee. A President's Choice Financial chequing account can also be used to pay bills, which you can arrange to have done automatically.

ING Direct

ING Direct is part of the Amsterdam-based ING Group. ING's Investment Savings Account typically pays the same rate as one-year GICs, far beyond what you would earn in a regular savings account.

No minimum balance is required, and you won't have to pay any fees. The only restriction you'll face is that you have to wait five days after making a deposit before you can withdraw those funds. Interest is earned daily on your balances, and compounded monthly. You also get a bank card with your account. Although the card can be used to withdraw money at any ABM, a transaction fee is applied each time you use it.

Canadian Tire Financial Services

In addition to engine oil, wrench sets, and bike locks, Canadian Tire now offers financial products, including a high-interest savings account. The interest rate is generally competitive with the other financial institutions mentioned above. The account comes with no monthly fees, and no minimum required balance.

Money market mutual funds

Money market funds, a type of mutual fund (see Chapter 10), are just like bank savings accounts — but better, in most cases. The best money market funds pay higher yields than bank savings accounts.

The yield on a money market fund is an important consideration. The operating expenses deducted before payment of dividends is the single biggest determinant of yield. All other things being equal (which they usually are with different money market funds), lower operating expenses translate into higher yields for you. With interest rates as low as they are these days, seeking out money funds with the lowest operating expenses is now more vital than ever.

Doing most or all of your fund shopping (money-market and otherwise) at one good fund company can reduce the clutter in your investing life. Chasing after a slightly higher yield offered by another company is sometimes not worth the extra paperwork and administrative hassle. On the other hand, as long as you don't mind the extra paperwork you can invest in funds at multiple firms, using each for its relative strengths.

Most mutual fund companies don't have many local branch offices, so you may have to open and maintain your money market mutual fund through the fund's toll-free phone line, Web site, or the mail. Distance has its advantages. Because you can conduct business by mail, the Internet, and the phone, you don't need to go schlepping into a local branch office to make deposits and withdrawals.

Despite the distance between you and your mutual fund company, you can usually have money transferred to your local bank on any business day, as well as having the fund company simply mail you a cheque. Don't fret about a deposit being lost in the mail; it rarely happens, and no one can legally cash a cheque made payable to you, anyway. Just be sure to endorse the cheque with the notation "for deposit only" under your signature.

(For that matter, driving or walking to your local bank isn't 100-percent safe. Imagine all the things that could happen to you or your money en route to the bank. You could slip on a banana peel, drop your deposit down a sewer grate, get mugged, walk into a bank holdup, get run over by a bakery truck. . . .)

Recommended money market mutual funds

In this section, we recommend good money market mutual funds.

- ✔ Beutel Goodman Money Market (800-461-4551; www.beutel-can.com)

- ✔ Legg Mason T-Bill Plus (800-565-6781; www.leggmasoncanada.com)

- ✔ Mackenzie Sentinel Cash Management (800-387-0614; www.mackenziefinancial.com)

- ✔ Mawer Canadian Money Market (800-889-6248; www.mawer.com)

- ✔ McLean Budden Money Market (800-884-0436; www.mcleanbudden.com)

- ✔ Phillips, Hager & North Money Market (800-661-6141; www.phn.com)

- ✔ Sceptre Money Market (800-265-1888; www.sceptre.ca)

- ✔ TD Canadian Money Market (866-567-8888; www.tdcanadatrust.com/mutualfunds)

Recommended T-bill money market mutual funds

Canadian Treasury bill (T-bill) money market funds are appropriate if you prefer a fund that invests solely in government-issued debt, which has the safety of government backing. Note that some of these funds are permitted to invest in other money market securities. If the additional security is important to you, call the specific fund to ensure it is 100 percent in T-bills before you invest.

- ✔ BMO T-Bill (800-665-7700; www.bmo.com)
- ✔ Franklin Templeton Treasury Bill (800-387-0830; www.templeton.ca)
- ✔ RBC Canadian T-Bill (800-463-3863; www.rbcam.com)
- ✔ Scotia T-bill (800-268-9269; www.scotiabank.com)

Investing for the Longer Term (A Few Years or More)

Important note: This section (together with its recommended investments) assumes that you have a sufficient emergency reserve stashed away and are taking advantage of tax-deductible retirement plan contributions. (Please see Chapter 3 for more on these goals.)

Asset allocation refers to the process of figuring out what portion of your wealth you should invest in different types of investments. You often (and most appropriately) practice asset allocation with retirement plans, because this money is earmarked for the long term. Ideally, more of your saving and investing should be conducted through tax-sheltered retirement plans. These accounts generally offer the best way to lower your long-term tax burden (see Chapters 11 and 12 for details).

If you plan to invest outside retirement plans, asset allocation for these accounts should depend on how comfortable you are with risk. But your choice of investments should also be suited to how much *time* you have until you plan to use the money. That's not because you won't be able to sell these investments on short notice if necessary (in most cases, you can). Investing money in a more volatile investment is simply riskier if you need to liquidate it in the short term.

For example, suppose you're saving money for a down payment on a house and are about one to two years away from having enough to make your foray into the real estate market. If you had put this "home" money into the stock market near the beginning of one of the stock market's 20- to 50-percent corrections (such as what happened in the early 2000s and then again in the late 2000s), you'd have been mighty unhappy. You would have seen a substantial portion of your money *vanish* in short order, and witnessed your home dreams put on hold.

Defining your time horizons

The different investment options in the remainder of this chapter are organized by time frame. All the recommended investment funds that follow assume you have *at least* a several-year time frame, and they're all *no-load* (commission-free) mutual funds. Mutual funds can be sold on any business day, usually with a simple phone call. Funds come with all different levels of risk, so you can choose funds that match your time frame and desire to take risk. (Chapter 10 discusses all the basics of mutual funds.)

The recommended investments are also organized by your tax situation. (If you don't know your current tax bracket, be sure to review Chapter 7.) Following are summaries of the different time frames associated with each type of fund:

- ✔ **Short-term investments:** These investments are suitable for a period of a few years — perhaps you're saving money for a home or some other major purchase in the near future. When investing for the short term, look for liquidity and stability — features that rule out real estate and stocks.

  Recommended investments include shorter-term bond funds, which are higher-yielding alternatives to high-interest savings accounts and money market funds. If interest rates increase, these funds drop slightly in value — a couple percent or so (unless rates rise tremendously). We also discuss Treasury bonds and guaranteed investment certificates (GICs) later in this chapter.

- ✔ **Intermediate-term investments:** These investments are appropriate for more than a few years but less than ten years. Investments that fit the bill are intermediate-term bonds and well-diversified hybrid funds (which include some stocks as well as bonds).

- ✔ **Long-term investments:** If you have a decade or more for investing your money, you can consider potentially higher-return (and therefore riskier) investments. Stocks, real estate, and other growth-oriented investments can earn the most money if you're comfortable with the risk involved. See Chapter 8 for information on investing the portion you intend to hold for the long term.

Bonds and bond funds

Bond funds pay taxable distributions (mostly interest) that generally are taxed at your full marginal tax rate. Just like interest earned from a savings account, you have to pay tax on any interest generated by bond funds each year, whether the interest is distributed to you or reinvested in your fund. As a result, you're far better off holding bond funds inside your RRSP, where the interest isn't taxed and the full amount of your earnings can be reinvested.

Here are some of our favourite short-term bond funds:

- ✔ CIBC Canadian Short-Term Bond Index (800-465-3863; www.cibc.com)
- ✔ HSBC Mortgage (888-310-4722; www.hsbc.ca)
- ✔ National Bank Mortgage (888-835-6281; www.nbc.ca)
- ✔ Phillips, Hager & North Short Term Bond and Mortgage (800-661-6141; www.phn.com)
- ✔ Scotia Mortgage Income (800-268-9269; www.scotiabank.com)
- ✔ TD Short-Term Bond, TD Mortgage Income (800-465-5463; www.tdwaterhouse.ca)

Here are our long-term bond fund picks:

- ✔ Beutel Goodman Income (800-461-4551; www.beutel-can.com)
- ✔ Mawer Canadian Bond Fund (800-889-6248; www.mawer.com)
- ✔ McLean Budden Fixed Income (800-884-0436; www.mcleanbudden.com)
- ✔ Phillips, Hager & North Bond (800-661-6141; www.phn.com)
- ✔ TD Canadian Bond (800-465-5463; www.tdwaterhouse.ca)

Guaranteed investment certificates (GICs)

For generations, *guaranteed investment certificates* (GICs) have been a popular investment for folks with some extra cash that isn't needed in the near future. With a GIC, you get a higher rate of return than you get on a bank savings account. And unlike with bond funds, your principal does not fluctuate in value.

Inflation-indexed Treasury bonds

Like a handful of other nations, the government of Canada now offers *inflation-indexed* government bonds. Because a portion of these bonds' return is pegged to the rate of inflation, the bonds offer investors a safer type of bond investment option.

To understand the relative advantages of an inflation-indexed bond, take a brief look at the relationship between inflation and a normal bond. When an investor purchases a normal bond, he's committing himself to a fixed yield over a set period of time — for example, a bond that matures in ten years and pays 6 percent interest. However, changes in the cost of living (inflation) are not fixed, so they're difficult to predict.

Suppose an investor put $10,000 into a regular bond in the 1970s. During the life of his bond, he would've unhappily watched escalating inflation. During the time he held the bond, and by the time his bond matured, he would've witnessed the erosion of the purchasing power of his $600 of annual interest and $10,000 of returned principal.

Enter the inflation-indexed Treasury bond. Say you have $10,000 to invest and you buy a ten-year, inflation-indexed bond that pays you a real rate of return (this is the return above and beyond the rate of inflation) of, say, 2 percent (or $200). This portion of your return is paid out in interest. The other portion of your return is from the inflation adjustment to the principal you invested. The inflation portion of the return gets put back into principal. So if inflation were running at about 2 percent, as it has in recent years, your $10,000 of principal would be indexed upward after one year to $10,200. In the second year of holding this bond, the 2 percent real return of interest ($204), would be paid on the increased ($10,200) principal base.

If inflation skyrocketed and was running at, say, 8 percent rather than 2 percent per year, your principal balance would grow 8 percent per year, and you'd still get your 2 percent real rate of return on top of that. Thus, an inflation-indexed Treasury bond investor would not see the purchasing power of his invested principal or annual interest earnings eroded by unexpected inflation.

The inflation-indexed Treasuries can be a good investment for conservative, inflation-worried bond investors, as well as taxpayers who want to hold the government accountable for increases in inflation. The downside: Inflation-indexed bonds can yield slightly lower returns, because they're less risky compared to regular Treasury bonds.

Compared to bonds, however, GICs have a couple of drawbacks:

- ✔ **Inaccessibility:** In a GIC, your money is not accessible unless you cough up a fairly big penalty — typically six months' interest. With a no-load (commission-free) bond fund, you can access your money without penalty — whether you need some or all of your money next week, next month, or next year.

- ✔ **Taxability:** A good deal of your earnings on GICs usually ends up in Canada Revenue Agency's hands. Unless you hold them in your RRSP, the interest earned on a GIC is taxed at your full marginal tax rate, the same rate as your salary.

In the long run, you should earn more — perhaps 1 to 2 percent more per year — and have better access to your money in bond funds than in GICs.

One final piece of advice: Don't buy GICs simply for the CDIC (Canada Deposit Insurance Corporation) insurance. Much is made, particularly by bankers, of the CDIC insurance that comes with bank GICs. The lack of this insurance on high-quality bonds shouldn't be a big concern for you. High-quality bonds rarely default; even if a fund held a bond that defaulted, it would probably represent only a tiny fraction (less than 1 percent) of the value of the fund, having little overall impact.

Besides, the CDIC itself is no Rock of Gibraltar. Banks have failed, and will continue to fail. Yes, you are insured if you have less than $100,000 in a bank. However, if the bank crashes, you may have to wait a long time and settle for less interest than you thought you were getting. You're not immune from harm, CDIC or no CDIC.

If the insurance you receive through the CDIC allows you to sleep better, you can invest in T-bills (see "Bond funds" earlier in this chapter), which are government-backed bonds.

Stocks and stock funds

Stocks have stood the test of time for building wealth. (In Chapter 9, we discuss picking individual stocks versus investing through stock mutual funds.) Remember that when you invest in stocks in taxable (non-retirement) accounts, all the distributions on those stocks, such as dividends and capital gains, are taxable. However, stock dividends and long-term capital gains benefit from lower tax rates.

Additionally, increasing numbers of fund companies offer *tax-friendly* stock funds, which are appropriate if you don't want current income or are in a high tax bracket and seek to minimize receiving taxable distributions on your funds. In general, the less a fund turns over (sells some holdings to buy different stocks), the lower the capital gains distributed to you each year, and the lower the amount of tax you'll have to pay on the fund's gains. As a result, index funds tend to have the best returns after taxes are accounted for.

Here are some of our other favourite tax-friendly stock funds:

- ✔ Altamira Canadian Equity Growth (888-270-394; www.nbc.ca)

- ✔ HSBC Equity (888-310-4722; www.hsbc.ca)

- ✔ McLean Budden Canadian Equity Value (800-884-0436; www.mclean budden.com)

- ✔ RBC O'Shaughnessy All Canadian Equity and RBC O'Shaughnessy Canadian Equity (800-463-3863; www.rbcam.com)

Alternatively, you can invest in a wider variety of diversified stock funds inside an annuity (see the following section). Also consider some of the stock funds we recommend in Chapter 12.

Annuities

As we discuss in Chapter 12, *annuities* are accounts that are partly insurance but mostly investment. Consider contributing to an annuity only after you exhaust contributions to all your available retirement plans. Because annuities carry higher annual operating expenses than comparable mutual funds, consider them only if you plan to leave your money invested, preferably, for 15 years or more. Even if you leave your money invested for that long, the tax-friendly funds discussed in the previous sections of this chapter can allow your money to grow without excessive annual taxation.

Real estate

Real estate can be a financially and psychologically rewarding investment. It can also be a money pit and a real headache if you buy the wrong property or get a "tenant from hell." (We discuss the investment particulars of real estate in Chapter 9 and the nuts and bolts of buying real estate in Chapter 15.)

Small-business investments

Investing in your own business or someone else's established small business can be a high-risk but potentially high-return investment. The best options are those you understand well. See Chapter 9 for more information about small-business investments.

Chapter 14

Investing for Educational Expenses

In This Chapter

▶ Understanding the financial aid system

▶ Examining the right and wrong ways to save for university and college

▶ Figuring out how much you need to save

▶ Finding ways to pay for university or college when the time comes

▶ Exploring educational investment options

*I*f you're like most parents (or potential future parents), just turning to this chapter makes you anxious. Such trepidation is understandable. According to much of what you read about educational expenses (particularly university expenses), if costs keep rising at the current rate you'll have to spend upward of tens of thousands of dollars to give your youngster a quality postsecondary education.

Whether you're about to begin a regular education investment plan or you've already started saving, your emotions may lead you astray. The hype about educational costs may scare you into taking a financially detrimental path. However, quality education for your child doesn't have to — and probably won't — cost you as much as those gargantuan projections suggest. In this chapter, we explain the inner workings of the financial aid system, help you gauge how much money you'll need, and discuss educational investment options so that you can keep a cool head (and some money in your pocket) when all is said and done.

Strategizing to Pay for Educational Expenses

We don't have just one solution to paying for your kids' education, because how you help pay for your child's university costs depends on your own unique situation. However, in most cases you may have to borrow *some* money, even if you have some available cash that can be directed to pay the university bills as you receive them.

By concentrating on contributing to your RRSP or company pension plan and paying down your mortgage today, you'll have a number of options when your kids graduate from high school. If you've paid down some — or all — of your mortgage, you can borrow against the paid-up value of your home (your *home equity*), usually at or near the lowest interest rate available (the *prime rate*).

You'll already have some strong momentum and compounding going on if you've been building up your retirement savings. You've also established a savings habit. When your kids get close to university age, you can divert your RRSP or other retirement plan contributions to help pay their education costs. When they graduate, you can easily resume your RRSP contributions.

You can even take advantage of the allowable RRSP contributions you missed out on because you're allowed to carry forward unused contributions indefinitely. (Canada Revenue Agency tracks this for you. You'll find a summary on the income tax return assessment notice you receive every year.) This will leave you in much better financial shape than if you had forgone contributions to your RRSP or company retirement savings plan when you were younger in order to start an educational savings program.

Further, when your kids are ready to go to university you'll likely be in your peak earning years, so some extra funds will probably be available.

Estimating university or college costs

University or college can cost a lot. The total costs — including tuition, fees, books, supplies, room, board, and transportation — vary substantially from school to school. The total average annual cost is running around $8,000 to $12,000 per year. The more expensive schools can cost up to one-third to half as much again. If you have younger children, you'll be interested to hear that some estimates put the cost of a four-year degree, including tuition and living costs, at close to $100,000 or more by 2020. Ouch!

Is all this expense worth it? Although many critics of higher education claim that the cost shouldn't be rising faster than inflation and that costs can, and should, be contained, denying the value of going to university is hard. Whether you're considering a local community college, your friendly nearby university, or a select high-end business school, investing in education is usually worth the effort and the cost.

An *investment* is an outlay of money for an expected profit. Unlike a car, which depreciates in value, an investment in education yields monetary, social, and intellectual profits. A car is more tangible in the short term, but an investment in education (even if it means borrowing money) gives you more bang for your buck in the long run.

Universities and colleges are now subject to the same types of competition that companies confront. As a result, many schools are clamping down on rising costs. As with any other product or service purchase, it pays to shop around. You can find good values — schools that offer competitive pricing *and* provide a quality education. Although you don't want your son or daughter to choose a university simply because it costs the least, you also shouldn't allow a university choice without any consideration or recognition of cost.

Setting realistic savings goals

If you have money left over *after* taking advantage of retirement plans, by all means try to save for your children's university costs.

Be realistic about what you can afford for university expenses given your other financial goals, especially saving for retirement (see Chapter 4). Being able to personally pay 100 percent of the cost of a university education is a luxury of the very affluent. If you're not a high-income earner, consider trying to save enough to pay a third or, at most, half of the cost. You can make up the balance through loans, your child's employment before and during university, and the like.

Use Table 14-1 to help get a handle on how much you should be saving for university.

Table 14-1	How Much to Save for University or College*
Figure Out This	*Write It Here*
1. **Cost of the school you think your child will attend	$_____
2. Percentage of costs you'd like to pay (for example, 20% or 40%)	× _____ %
3. Line 1 times line 2 (the amount you'll pay in today's dollars)	= $ _____
4. Number of months until your child reaches university or college age	÷ _____ months
5. ***Line 3 divided by line 4 (amount to save per month in today's dollars)	= $ _____ / month

* Don't worry about correcting the overall analysis for inflation. This worksheet takes care of that through the assumptions made on the returns of your investments as well as the amount that you save over time. This way of doing the calculations works because you assume that the money you're saving will grow at the rate of inflation of education costs. (In the happy event that your investment return exceeds the rate of university or college inflation, you end up with a little more than you expected.)
** The average cost of a four-year university education today is about $50,000.
*** The amount you need to save (calculated in line 5) needs to be increased once per year to reflect the increase in university or college inflation — 5 or 6 percent should do.

Strategies for Saving for Education Expenses

If you have sufficient funds to take care of your other needs, such as contributing to an RRSP, terrific! You can also start putting money away for your children's postsecondary education. Just as important as the specific investments you choose is the way in which you organize your savings efforts.

Two basic ways to set up an effective savings plan for postsecondary education expenses exist:

- *Registered Education Savings Plans* (RESPs): For many people, an RESP is a great way to save, thanks in part to a generous government grant program.

- *In-trust accounts*: Under an in-trust account arrangement, you put money into a special account and invest it on your child's behalf. If your children might not attend university or college, this could be a better choice.

Registered Education Savings Plans (RESPs)

If you're familiar with RRSPs (see Chapter 11 for all the details), then RESPs will be fairly easy to grasp. However, a few major differences between these two savings plans exist.

One of the big attractions of an RESP is that, as with an RRSP, money inside the plan can grow without being taxed. As a result, all your profits, whether interest, dividends, or capital gains from the appreciation in the value of stocks and mutual funds, can be put right back to work for you to deliver further gains.

Unlike contributions to an RRSP, however, your contributions to an RESP are not exempt from taxation. You don't get to deduct the money you put into an RESP when arriving at your taxable income.

But one other — and very valuable — difference between RRSPs and RESPs exists. Money put into an RESP earns you a contribution to your plan in the form of a grant from the federal government. The official name of the grant is the Canada Education Savings Grant (CESG). The CESG can make a sizeable dent in the cost of postsecondary education particularly if you start contributing to an RESP when your children are young.

To qualify for the grant, the RESP beneficiary must be a resident of Canada and be age 17 or under. They must also have a social insurance number. These can take several weeks to obtain. Contact Human Resources and Skills Development Canada for an application. (For more information, see "Maximizing RESP grants" later in this section.) The government doesn't limit how much you can contribute to an RESP within a year. (Prior to 2007, there was a yearly maximum of $4,000 a year for each child.) The total lifetime contribution limit per child is $50,000.

You're allowed to contribute money for up to 31 years. The plan can be kept open — and the money inside earning tax-sheltered gains — for another four years. However, the maximum lifespan of an RESP is 35 years, after which the plan must be wound up.

You'll find two basic types of RESPs. The first are so-called "scholarship" plans. Because these plans are limited to mostly guaranteed investments, the rate of return on your plan is mediocre.

A much better choice is self-directed or mutual fund RESPs. You can open these with most brokerage and mutual fund firms, often at no charge. A self-directed or mutual fund RESP allows you to choose from a wide range of investments. If you start an RESP when your children are still in diapers, these plans are a much better choice because they allow you to benefit from the larger earnings potential of equities and equity mutual funds.

Making withdrawals

Money that you contribute to an RESP isn't tax-deductible, but any gains inside the plan are not taxed. When your child is ready to go to school, money from the plan can be taken out tax-free and used for a variety of education-related expenses.

Investigating what happens if your child doesn't go to university

In the past, a major drawback to RESPs was that if your child didn't go to a postsecondary institution you forfeited the earnings — either to another child, to an educational institution, or, in the case of pooled or "scholarship" RESPs, to other children in the program.

The rules have been greatly relaxed, however. You can now transfer up to $50,000 of the earnings from an RESP to your RRSP or your spouse's RRSP, as long as you have the contribution room available. The tax deduction you get on the money going into your RRSP offsets the tax on the funds you withdraw from the RESP. In order to transfer out profits from an RESP in this way, the plan must have been running for a minimum of ten years, with none of the beneficiaries postsecondary students by age 21. And while any grants received under the CESG program must be repaid, any money earned inside the plan on the grants can be kept.

For an individual RESP, another option is to name a sibling as a replacement for the original beneficiary. (For a family plan, another child can be added.) If this is done, the grant doesn't have to be repaid, and can be used by the new beneficiary for their post-secondary education.

Any earnings that can't be transferred in this way can still be moved out of the RESP, but they're taxed at your marginal tax rate plus an additional 20-percent penalty. (You can take out your original contributions — your principal — without any penalties or restrictions.)

Also, you can open a family plan, into which you can make contributions for several children. If one of the children in the plan chooses not to pursue a postsecondary education, both the money you've contributed to the plan for that child, as well as any gains it has rung up, can be used by the other children in the plan.

Maximizing RESP grants

Under the CESG program, the government will make a contribution to the RESP of 20 percent of the first $2,500 of contributions you make in a year. The maximum grant (as of 2010) was $500 per year per child for each year the beneficiary is under 18.

Grant rates for lower- and middle-income families are enhanced. For 2010, families with incomes of $37,000 or less earned a 40-percent CESG on their first $500 of RESP contributions. Families with incomes between $37,000 and $74,000 earned a 30-percent CESG on the first $500 they contributed. The maximum CESG payable each year is also increased to accommodate the enhanced grants.

If you don't contribute enough in any year to get the full $500 grant, you can earn the unused portion in later years. (For the years 1998 to 2006, the annual CESG contribution room was $2,000.) However, regardless of how much unused CESG you have, the maximum per beneficiary in any one year is capped at whichever is lower, $1,000 or 20 percent of any unused RESP room. The total lifetime maximum you can receive under this program is $7,200.

The government has removed the ceiling on how much you can contribute to an RESP in any given year, as long as you don't exceed the overall lifetime limit of $50,000. However, before contributing more than the amount needed to earn the maximum CESG for the year, weigh the extra profits a large lump-sum contribution can earn over time against the loss of potential grants. The problem is that if you contribute in excess of what's needed to earn you the maximum grant in one year, that "overcontribution" can't be used to earn a grant in future years.

Neglecting RRSPs: A big mistake

You want what's best for your children. As a parent, that's a given. Not only do you want to be able to provide good learning opportunities for them when they are young, but you also want to give them choices. When little Dweezil and Moon Unit fill out their university applications, you don't want to have to say that you can't afford to send them to their dream school.

We know you're going to think that our advice sounds selfish. But consider this reality: You have to provide for your own financial security before saving for your child. Let us explain.

If you're a frequent flyer, think back to your most recent trip by airplane. Remember what the flight attendants instructed you to do in an emergency? In the event of a loss of air pressure that necessitates the use of oxygen masks, put your own oxygen mask on *first*. Only then should you help your children with their oxygen masks.

Consider for a moment why airlines recommend this approach. Although your instinct may be to ensure that your children are safe before taking care of yourself, by taking care of yourself first, you're stronger and better able to help your children.

Similarly, in regard to your personal finances, you need to take care of yourself first. You should save and invest through an RRSP or other retirement savings plan that gives you significant tax benefits.

Take care of your long-term financial needs first (for example, by saving through an RRSP). By doing so, you strengthen your financial health, which better enables you in the long run to help your kids with their educational expenses. (See Chapters 7 and 11 to learn how to reduce your taxes and save for retirement.)

In-trust accounts

In-trust accounts — also known as informal trusts — allow you to save money for your child's future and have a portion of your earnings compound tax-free. These accounts also go by the name ITF (which stands for "in trust for") accounts. The account is "in trust" because minors can't enter into financial contracts. No restrictions exist on contributions to an in-trust account. You can put in as much or as little you wish at any time.

When money is inside an informal trust, it belongs to the child. All profits on investments inside the trust are taxed. The person who contributes the money pays taxes on the dividends and income, but the child is responsible for paying taxes on any capital gains. Because most children have insufficient income to actually have to pay any tax, that portion of the account can compound tax-free. Because of this, the best investments for an in-trust account, especially when many years are left before the child will need the money, are equity mutual funds, where most of the profits are in the form of capital gains.

Using your RRSP savings to pay university or college expenses

You can use the money inside an RRSP to help finance a postsecondary education or full-time training for either yourself or your spouse. Under the federal government's Lifelong Learning Plan, you can withdraw up to $10,000 a year from your RRSP for four years. The maximum amount you can withdraw over that time is $20,000.

Much like the RRSP Home Buyers' Plan (which we discuss in Chapter 15), using your RRSP to fund an education has several drawbacks. Although the withdrawals are not taxed, you have to repay the money to your RRSP in equal instalments over ten years. The first payment has to be made within 60 days after the end of the fifth year after your first withdrawal.

Any repayments not made are included in the taxable income of the person who made the withdrawal. In addition, you will likely find it difficult to repay what you've taken out for education expenses as well as continue your regular contributions. In that case, you will have to be able to get by on less if you have been factoring your tax rebate from a regular RRSP contribution into your cash flow, because your repayments don't earn you a deduction. Further, borrowing money from your plan, as well as delaying new contributions while you repay those funds, will significantly reduce the long-term growth of your retirement savings.

If you set up an in-trust account and contribute only Child Tax Benefit payments, the above tax rules don't apply. All the gains, whether in the form of capital gains, interest, or dividends, are taxed to the child.

The big drawback to informal trusts is that when the child turns 18, the money and all the profits legally become hers to spend as she wishes. No rules specify what the money must be spent on, so your child could use it for purposes other than an education, such as starting his or her own small business. Although you can hope that little Johnny or Jenny will spend the money wisely, you can't do anything if, on the day of his 18th birthday, Johnny empties his account and buys a convertible.

Certain steps are involved in setting up an in-trust account. When you open the account you must clearly delineate the role of everybody involved. The person who puts money into the account is known as the "settler" or contributor. The law requires that a different person have the responsibility of overseeing how the money is invested (the trustee) on behalf of the child (the beneficiary). When you set up an account, ensure that you use the proper phrasing: your name (if you are the trustee) followed by "in trust for" and then your child's name.

Obtaining Loans, Grants, and Scholarships

A host of financial aid programs, including a number of loan programs, enable you to borrow at fair interest rates. Additionally, a wide range of grants and scholarships are available from schools, service clubs, local companies, and other sources.

Your child can work and save money during high school and university. In fact, if your child qualifies for financial aid he or she may be expected to contribute a certain amount to education costs from savings and from employment during the school year or summer breaks. Besides giving your child a stake in his or her own future, this training encourages sound personal financial management down the road.

Government student loans program

The Canada Student Loans Program (CSLP) is the largest source of college and university student loans in the country. The program is run by the federal government in conjunction with the provinces. The provinces administer the loans through their own separate student aid offices.

Each province also has its own loan scheme that's rolled in with the CSLP. (You can find out more by following the link to your province's student loan program at `www.canlearn.ca`.)

To qualify, students must be citizens or permanent residents of Canada, attend an institution recognized by the program, and meet the criteria for being either part-time or full-time students. Students must also live in a province that participates in the Canada Student Loans Program (if your province doesn't, it will run its own distinct loans program to which the federal government contributes).

You generally need to submit only one application to receive loans from both programs, although interest and conditions on the federal loan and the provincial loan differ slightly. Regardless of where they're going to go to school, your kids must apply to the province in which they live. Applications can be obtained from any university or college or by calling your provincial student loans program. Find the number online.

Part of the assessment process involves examining your entire family's income. The assessment is based solely on cash flow — assets don't come into the picture at all. As a result, it doesn't pay to neglect contributing to your RRSP or company retirement savings plan, or paying down your mortgage.

The loan programs demand that parents assist in paying the education costs of any dependent children. Even if parents absolutely refuse to assist their children, their ability to pay will still be taken into account when the application is assessed. In order not to be classified as a dependant, a child must have graduated from high school at least four years earlier or have been in the workforce for at least 24 months.

If the loan is approved, your children should go to the financial aid office when they enrol at their university or college. They'll be given some loan documents, which they can then take to the bank of their choice. (The loans are administered through the big banks, but the provincial and federal governments guarantee them.) A number of credit unions and *caisses populaires* are also approved student loan providers. The maximum amount available varies depending on which province the student lives in.

The interest rate on the two components is calculated differently. The rate on the federal part of the loan is fixed once a year at a percentage or so above the best rates offered by financial institutions (the prime rate). The provinces tend to use a floating rate. For example, a province might charge prime plus 1 percent on its loans, with the rate rising and falling along with the going prime rate.

The federal and provincial governments pay the interest on the debt until the student either graduates or withdraws. At that point, the federal government stops paying its share of the interest, and the student is responsible for the debt. Some provinces, however, will continue to pay the debt costs on their part of the loan for an additional six months.

Even though the federal government stops paying the interest on its portion of the combined loan at graduation, students aren't required to start repaying the federal or provincial component of their loan until six months after graduation. Generally, this due date falls on November 1. At that time, students must negotiate a schedule with their bank. Although students are largely free to choose whatever repayment time frame they like, both the federal and provincial loans must be completely paid off within 114 months (ten years minus six months). After the student signs agreements for the two separate loans, most institutions will consolidate the debts and work out a single payment schedule.

Both Ottawa and the provinces have become aggressive in tracking down delinquents and getting their money back. The federal government can even take what it's owed out of the tax refunds of those who are behind on their payments. Worse yet, many past-due student loans are now routinely handed over to collection agencies, and the students end up with a nick on their credit rating.

In addition to the negative impact it will have on the student's credit rating, declaring bankruptcy if student loans become overwhelming comes with strict conditions. Changes to the bankruptcy rules in the late 2000s mean that a student who declares bankruptcy after July 7, 2008 cannot have his or her loans discharged until seven years after he or she finished attending school. (This may be reduced to five years in the case of extreme financial hardships.)

Canada Access Grants

The Canada Access Grants program offers grants that do not have to be repaid. (Although they are considered taxable income, in most cases the student's overall income will be low enough that the tax bill will be minimal or non-existent.)

These grants are available to a wide variety of students. Depending on their circumstances, students may be eligible if they are from a low- or middle-income family, have dependants, are studying part-time, or have a disability. Students can qualify for more than one type of grant. A student from a middle-income family, for instance, may be eligible for $100 for each month he is studying at the undergraduate level, up to a maximum of $1,200 for the year. Meanwhile, a student with permanent disabilities and who faces extra education-related costs may qualify for $8,000 annually. (**Note:** Grant amounts are from 2010.)

Tips for getting loans, grants, and scholarships

A number of grant programs are available through schools and the government as well as through independent sources. Employers, banks, credit unions, and community groups also offer grants and scholarships. In addition to the aid offices at universities and colleges, look into directories and databases at your local library, and speak with your child's school counselling department. Also try local organizations, churches, employers, and so on. You or your child has a better chance of getting scholarship money through these avenues.

Postsecondary scholarship search services are generally a waste of money; in some cases, they're scams. Some of these services charge up to $100 or more just to tell you about scholarships that either you're already being considered for or that you aren't even eligible for.

Investing Educational Funds

Financial companies pour millions of dollars into advertising for investment and insurance products that they claim are best for making your money grow for your children. Don't get sucked in by these ads.

What makes for good and bad investments in general applies to investments for educational expenses, too. Stick with basic, proven, lower-cost investments. (Chapter 9 explains what you generally need to look for and beware of.) The following sections focus on considerations specific to investing to pay for university or college.

Good investments: No-load mutual funds

As we discuss in Chapter 10, the professional management and efficiency of the best no-load mutual funds makes them a tough investment to beat. Chapters 12 and 13 provide recommendations for investing money in funds both inside and outside tax-sheltered retirement plans.

Gearing the investments to the time frame involved until your children will need to use the money is the most important issue with no-load mutual funds. The closer your child gets to attending university or college and using the money saved, the more conservatively the money should be invested.

Bad investments

Life insurance policies that have cash values are some of the most oversold investments for funding university costs. Here's the usual pitch: "Because you need life insurance to protect your family, why not buy a policy that you can borrow against to pay for university?"

The reason you shouldn't invest in this type of policy to fund university costs is that you're better off contributing to an RRSP that gives you an immediate tax deduction — which saving through life insurance doesn't offer. Because life insurance that comes with a cash value is more expensive, parents are also more likely to make another mistake — not buying enough coverage. If you need and want life insurance, you're better off buying lower-cost term life insurance (see Chapter 17).

Another poor investment for university expenses is one that fails to keep you ahead of inflation, such as savings or money market accounts. You need your money to grow so that you can afford educational costs down the road.

Prepaid tuition plans — offered by a few U.S. schools — should generally be avoided. The allure of these plans is that by paying today, you eliminate the worry of not being able to afford rising costs in the future.

This logic doesn't work for several reasons. First, odds are quite high that you don't have the money today to pay in advance. Second, putting money into such plans reduces your eligibility for financial aid dollar for dollar. If you have that kind of extra dough around, you're better off using it for other purposes (and you're not likely to worry about rising costs anyway). You can invest your own money — that's what the school's going to do with it, anyway.

Besides, how do you know which school your child will want to attend and how long it may take her to finish? Coercing your child into the school you've already paid for is a sure ticket to long-term problems in your relationship.

Overlooked investments

Too often, we see parents knocking themselves out to make more money so that they can afford to buy a bigger home, purchase more expensive cars, take better vacations, and send their kids to more expensive (and therefore supposedly better) private schools. Families stretch themselves with outrageous mortgages or complicated living arrangements so that they can get into neighbourhoods with top-rated public schools or send their kids to expensive private elementary schools.

The best school in the world for your child is you and your home. The reason many people we know were able to attend some of the top educational institutions in this country is that their concerned parents worked hard — not just at their jobs, but at spending time with the kids when they were growing up. Rather than working to make more money (with the best of intentions of buying educational games or trips, or sending the kids to better schools), try focusing more attention on your kids. In our humble opinion, you can do more for your kids by spending more time with them.

We see parents scratching their heads about their child's lack of academic interest and achievement — they blame the school, TV, video games, or society at large. These factors may contribute to the problem, but education begins in the home. Schools can't do it alone.

Living within your means not only allows you to save more of your income but also frees up more of your time for raising and educating your children. Don't underestimate the value of spending more time with your kids and giving them your attention.

Chapter 15

Investing in Real Estate: Your Home and Beyond

In This Chapter

▶ Choosing between buying and renting

▶ Determining how to finance your real estate purchase

▶ Finding a great property

▶ Working successfully with real estate agents

▶ Negotiating your best deal

▶ Handling financial issues after you buy

*B*uying a home or investing in real estate can be financially and psychologically rewarding. Perhaps you're looking to escape your rented apartment and buy your first home. Or maybe you're interested in cornering the local real estate market and making millions in investment property. In either case, you can learn many lessons from real estate buyers who've travelled before you.

Note: Although this chapter focuses primarily on real estate in which you're going to live — otherwise known by those in the trade as *owner-occupied property* — much of what this chapter covers is relevant to real estate investors. (For additional information on buying *investment real estate* — property that you rent out to others — see Chapter 9. And if you want even more information, check out the latest editions of *Buying & Selling a Home For Canadians For Dummies* and *Real Estate Investing For Canadians For Dummies* [Wiley]).

Deciding Whether to Buy or Rent

You may be tired of moving from rental to rental. Perhaps your landlord doesn't adequately keep up the place, or you have to ask permission to hang a picture on the wall. You may desire the financial security and rewards that seem to come with home ownership. Or maybe you just want a place to call your own.

Any one of these reasons is "good enough" to *want* to buy a home. But you should take stock of your life and your financial health *before* you decide to buy so you can decide whether you still want to buy a home and how much you can really afford to spend. You need to ask yourself some bigger questions.

Assessing your timeline

From a financial standpoint, you really shouldn't buy a place unless you can anticipate being there for at least three years (preferably five or more). Buying and selling a property entails a load of expenses, which can include getting an inspection, moving costs, land transfer tax, HST (for new homes), lawyers' fees, and real estate agents' commissions. To cover these transaction costs plus the additional costs of ownership, a property needs to appreciate about 10 to 15 percent.

If you need or want to move in a couple years, counting on that kind of appreciation is risky. If you're fortunate and you happen to buy before a sharp upturn in housing prices, you may get it. If you're unlucky, you'll probably lose money on the deal.

Some people are willing to invest in real estate even when they don't expect to live in it for long and would consider turning their home into a rental. Doing so can work well financially in the long haul, but don't underestimate the responsibilities that come with being a landlord. Also, most people need to sell their first home in order to tap all the cash that they have in it so that they can buy the next one.

Determining what you can afford

Although buying and owning your own home can be a wise financial move in the long run, it's a major purchase that can send shock waves through the rest of your personal finances. You'll probably have to take out a mortgage — really just a loan secured by the property you're buying — where the payments are spread out, or *amortized* (typically over 25 years), to finance your purchase. And the home you buy will need maintenance over the years.

We've seen too many people fall in love with a home and make a rash decision without taking a hard look at the financial ramifications. Take stock of your overall financial health (especially where you stand in terms of retirement planning) *before* you buy property and agree to a particular mortgage. Don't let the financial burdens of a home control your financial future.

Don't trust a lender when he tells you what you can "afford" according to some formulas the bank uses to figure out what kind of a credit risk you are. To determine how much a potential home buyer can borrow, lenders look primarily at annual income; they pay no attention to some major aspects of a borrower's overall financial situation. Even if you don't have money tucked away into retirement savings, or you have several children to clothe, feed, and help put through university, you still qualify for the same size loan as other people with the same income (assuming equal outstanding debts). Only you can figure out how much you can afford, because only you know what your other financial goals are and how important they are to you.

Here are some important financial questions that no lender will ask or care about but that you should ask yourself before buying a home:

- ✔ Are you saving enough money monthly to reach your retirement goals?

- ✔ How much do you spend (and want to continue spending) on fun things such as travel and entertainment?

- ✔ How willing are you to budget your expenses in order to meet your monthly mortgage payments and other housing expenses?

- ✔ How much of your children's expected post-secondary educational expenses do you want to be able to pay for?

The other chapters in this book can help you answer these important questions.

Calculating how much you can borrow

Mortgage lenders want to know your ability to repay the money you borrow. So you have to pass a few tests that calculate the maximum amount the lender is willing to lend you. For a home in which you'll reside, lenders total up your monthly housing expenses. They define your housing costs as

```
mortgage payment + property taxes + insurance
```

Lenders typically loan you about 30 to 32 percent of your monthly gross (before taxes) income for the housing expense. If you're self-employed, getting a mortgage is a lot more complicated. Lenders will often want to see your financial statements and your income tax returns from the last several years, and many decide on a case-by-case basis.

Lenders also consider your other debts when deciding how much to lend you. These other debts diminish the funds available to pay your housing expenses. Lenders add the amount you need to pay down your other consumer debts (for example, auto loans and credit cards) to your monthly housing expense. The monthly total costs of these debt payments plus your housing costs typically cannot exceed 40 percent. This test is called the *total debt-service ratio*.

One general rule says that you can borrow up to three times (or two and one-half times) your annual income when buying a home. But this rule is a really rough estimate. The maximum that a mortgage lender will loan you depends on interest rates. If rates fall, the monthly payment on a mortgage of a given size also drops. Thus, lower interest rates make real estate more affordable.

Table 15-1 gives you an estimate of the maximum amount you may be eligible to borrow. Multiply your gross annual income by the number in the second column to determine the approximate maximum you may be able to borrow. For example, if you're getting a mortgage with a rate around 7 percent and your annual income is $50,000, multiply 3.5 by $50,000 to get $175,000 — the approximate maximum mortgage allowed.

Table 15-1	The Approximate Maximum You Can Borrow
When Mortgage Rates Are	*Multiply Your Gross Annual Income* by This Figure*
4%	4.6
5%	4.2
6%	3.8
7%	3.5
8%	3.2
9%	2.9
10%	2.7
11%	2.5

*If you're self-employed, this is your net business income (before taxes).

Comparing the costs of owning versus renting

The cost of owning a home is an important financial consideration for many renters. Some people assume that owning costs more. In fact, owning a home doesn't have to cost a truckload of money; it may even cost less than renting.

On the surface, buying a place seems a lot more expensive than renting. You're probably comparing your monthly rent (measured in hundreds of dollars to more than $1,000, depending on where you live) to the purchase price of a property, which is usually a much larger number — perhaps $150,000 to $500,000 or more. When you consider a home purchase, you're forced to think about your housing expenses in one huge chunk rather than in small monthly instalments (like a rent cheque).

Tallying up the costs of owning a place can be a useful and not-too-complicated exercise. To make a fair comparison between ownership and rental costs, you need to figure what it will cost on a *monthly basis* to buy a place you desire versus what it will cost to rent a *comparable* place. The worksheet in Table 15-2 enables you to do such a comparison. ***Note:*** In the interest of reducing the number of variables, all this "figuring" assumes a fixed-rate mortgage. (For more info on mortgages, see "Financing Your Home," later in this chapter.)

Also, we ignore what economists call the *opportunity cost of owning.* In other words, when you buy, the money you put into your home can't be invested elsewhere, and the forgone investment return on that money, say some economists, should be considered a cost of owning a home. We choose to ignore this concept for two reasons. First, and most importantly, we don't agree with this line of thinking. When you buy a home, you're investing your money in real estate, which historically has offered solid returns over the decades (see Chapter 8). And second, we have you ignore opportunity cost because it greatly complicates the analysis.

Table 15-2	Monthly Expenses: Renting versus Owning
Figure Out This	*Write It Here (\$ per Month)*
1. Monthly mortgage payment (see "Mortgage")	$_____
2. Plus monthly property taxes (see "Property taxes")	+ $_____
3. Equals total monthly mortgage plus property taxes	= $_____
4. Plus insurance ($30 to $150/mo., depending on property value)	+ $_____
5. Plus maintenance (1% of property cost divided by 12 months)	+ $_____
6. Equals total costs of owning (add lines 3, 4, and 5)	= $_____

Now compare line 6 in Table 15-2 with the monthly rent on a comparable place to see which costs more — owning or renting.

Mortgage

To determine the monthly payment on your mortgage, simply multiply the relevant number (or multiplier) from Table 15-3 by the size of your mortgage expressed in thousands of dollars (divided by 1,000). For example, if you're taking out a $100,000, 8-percent mortgage amortized over 25 years, you multiply 100 by 7.63 for a $632 monthly payment.

Table 15-3	Your Monthly Mortgage Payment Multiplier	
Interest Rate	*15-Year Amortization*	*25-Year Amortization*
5.0%	7.88	5.82
5.5%	8.14	6.10
6.0%	8.40	6.40
6.5%	8.66	6.70
7.0%	8.93	7.00
7.5%	9.21	7.32
8.0%	9.49	7.63
8.5%	9.77	7.96
9.0%	10.05	8.27
9.5%	10.34	8.61
10.0%	10.62	8.94
10.5%	10.92	9.29
11.0%	11.21	9.62
11.5%	11.51	9.97
12.0%	11.81	10.32

Property taxes

You can ask a real estate person, mortgage lender, or your local assessor's office what your annual property tax bill would be for a house of similar value to the one you're considering buying. Divide this amount by 12 to arrive at your monthly property tax bill.

Considering the long-term costs of renting

When you crunch the numbers to find out what owning rather than renting a comparable place may cost you on a monthly basis, you may discover that owning isn't as expensive as you thought. Or you may find that owning costs more than renting. This discovery may tempt you to think that, financially speaking, renting is cheaper than owning.

Be careful not to jump to conclusions. Remember that you're looking at the cost of owning versus renting *today.* What about 5, 10, 20, or 30 years from now? As an owner, your biggest monthly expense, the mortgage payment, doesn't rise steadily — it fluctuates, and only if interest rates are at a different level when your mortgage term expires and you renew. If interest rates are higher or lower at that time, your payments will rise — or fall — accordingly. Your property taxes, homeowner's insurance, and maintenance expenses — which are generally far less than your mortgage payment — increase with the cost of living.

When you rent, however, your entire monthly rent is subject to the vagaries of inflation. Living in a rent-controlled unit, where the annual increase allowed in your rent is capped, is the exception to this rule. Rent control does not eliminate price hikes; it just limits them.

Suppose you're comparing the costs of owning a home that costs $200,000 to renting that same home for $1,200 a month. Table 15-4 compares the cost of owning the home to your rental costs over 25 years. The comparison assumes that you take out a mortgage loan equal to 75 percent of the cost of the property at a fixed interest rate of 7.5 percent, meaning your mortgage payments would be $1,097 (rounded up to $1,100) and that the rate of inflation of your homeowner's insurance, property taxes, maintenance (which for the ownership example starts off at $450 a month), and rent is 4 percent per year. (This is higher than inflation has been running the last few years, but inflation can and does rise quickly.)

Table 15-4	Cost of Owning versus Renting over 25 Years	
Year	*Ownership Cost per Month*	*Rental Cost per Month*
1	$1,550	$1,200
5	$1,626	$1,404
10	$1,740	$1,708
20	$2,048	$2,528
25	$2,253	$3,076

As you can see in Table 15-4, in the first few years, owning a home costs a little more than renting it. In the long run, however, owning is less expensive, because more of your rental expenses increase with inflation. And don't forget that as a homeowner you're building equity in your property; that equity will be quite substantial by the time you have your mortgage paid off.

You may be thinking that if inflation doesn't rise 4 percent per year, renting could end up being cheaper. This is not necessarily so. Suppose inflation didn't exist. Your rent wouldn't escalate, but home ownership expenses wouldn't either. And with no inflation, you could probably refinance your mortgage at a rate lower than 7 percent. If you do the math, owning would still cost less in the long run with lower inflation, but the advantage of owning is less than during periods of higher inflation.

Recognizing advantages to renting

Although owning a home and investing in real estate generally pay off handsomely over the long term, to be fair and balanced we must say that renting has its advantages. Some of the financially successful renters we've seen include people who pay low rent, either because they made housing sacrifices or they live in a rent-controlled building. If you're consistently able to save 10 percent or more of your earnings, you're probably well on your way to achieving your future financial goals.

As a renter, you can avoid worrying about or being responsible for fixing up the property — that's your landlord's responsibility. You also have more financial and psychological flexibility as a renter. If you want to move, you can generally do so a lot easier as a renter than you can as a homeowner.

Having a lot of your money tied up in your home is another challenge that you don't face when renting over the long haul. Some people enter their retirement years with a substantial portion of their wealth in their homes. As a renter, you can have all your money in financial assets that you can tap in to more easily. Homeowners who have a major chunk of equity tied up in a home at retirement can downsize to a less costly property to free up cash and/or take out a reverse mortgage (which we discuss later in this chapter) on their home equity.

Financing Your Home

After you look at your financial health, figure out your timeline, and compare renting costs to owning costs, you need to confront the tough task of taking on debt to buy a home (unless you're independently wealthy). A mortgage loan from a bank or other source makes up the difference between the cash you intend to put into the purchase and the agreed-upon selling price of the real estate. This section reviews the different options you have for financing your home.

Understanding mortgage essentials

Like many other financial products, you have more different types and configurations of mortgages to choose from than you could ever possibly evaluate. The differences can be important or trivial, expensive or not. We'll begin with the big differences.

Familiarize yourself with the following three main features:

- ✔ The total amount of time you want to take to pay your loan back. This is called the *amortization*.

- ✔ The term that your mortgage agreement runs for. This typically will range from six months to five years or more.

- ✔ Whether you can pay off the balance of your mortgage at any time — called an *open* mortgage — or have to continue making your payments until the end of the term, called a *closed* mortgage.

Weigh the pros and cons of each mortgage type and decide what's best for your situation before you go out to purchase a piece of real estate or refinance a loan. In the real world, however, most people ignore this advice. The excitement of purchasing a home tends to cloud one's judgment. Our experience has been that few people look at their entire financial picture before making major real estate decisions. You may end up with a mortgage that could someday seriously overshadow your delight in your little English herb garden out back.

We help you understand your choices on these three fronts in the following sections.

Understanding amortization

If you take out a consumer loan to buy a car, you have to decide how long you will take to pay the money back. Say you choose four years. Over that time, you'll have to pay back the full amount you originally borrowed, plus interest. When the four years is up, you'll have paid your lender all the money you borrowed, and all the interest on the borrowed funds. Mortgages are similar, in that instead of a car, you're borrowing to buy a home. But one significant difference exists.

When your mortgage payments are calculated, you can choose the number of years over which you want to stretch out the repayment of the principal, with your interest costs being calculated over that period and included in your regular payments. The number of years you choose to spread your home loan out over is called the *amortization*. This is the period used to calculate your monthly payments, given the interest rate you accept.

Most mortgages in Canada are amortized over 25 years. You can, however, choose a shorter or sometimes longer period. These typically range from 5 to as many as 35 years.

Understanding your mortgage term

The *term* is the length of time you want your loan agreement with a particular lender to run. (The length of the amortization you choose is distinct and separate from the *term*.)

When the term expires, your loan expires. You can choose to sign up for another loan for whatever term you like, either with the same lender or a different financial institution. You can pay off some of or your entire mortgage at that point if you have the money available. You can even alter the amortization at that point.

For instance, you could take out a mortgage with the total cost spread out — amortized — over 25 years, with the actual mortgage agreement lasting for only two years. When those two years are up, you could renew your mortgage and change the loan arrangement. This time, for instance, you could decide to choose a shorter amortization of just 15 years, but sign up for a five-year term.

Comparing short-term and long-term mortgages

You can typically choose a term of anywhere from six months or a year to five years. Seven and even ten-year terms are also available from some lenders.

Generally, the longer the term you choose, the higher your interest rate. Lenders charge you more as a way to protect themselves should rates rise. The longer your term, the longer you have a lower rate locked in, and the more the lender loses out on what they could make off you if you had to renew earlier at a higher interest rate.

In contrast, a short term means that you have to renew much more frequently, putting you at the mercy of current interest rates. If rates have moved up by the time your term ends and you have to renew, your monthly payments will also be higher. If rates stay level, though, your payments will be less than what they would be with a longer-term mortgage, which generally comes with a higher interest rate. Of course, if rates have fallen when you come to renew, you'll be even farther ahead.

Is a short-term or long-term mortgage best for you?

When choosing your term, you're making a trade-off. If you choose a short term, you risk having rates rise between now and your next renewal date. If you go long and rates don't rise, you pay more than you need to.

Selecting a long term (four to five years or longer) guarantees your payments for that entire period, often an important consideration for those who are on tightly controlled budgets. This approach is often a good choice if you are in the early years of home ownership. When you're locked in, you know exactly how much your mortgage will cost for years to come. You don't have to make any new decisions about your home loan for a long time. And your heart won't jump every time interest rates do. But this peace of mind comes at a price.

Five-year rates, for example, typically range anywhere from 1 percent to more than 3 percent higher than six-month rates. You pay a kind of insurance premium to protect yourself against the possibility of higher rates in the future. Ask yourself if the cost is worth it. Often, you'll find that both the financial and security risks of going short are not as great as you think.

Longer terms are also worth considering if you're just starting out, or you find your finances stretched to the limit. If an unexpected jump in rates would push your payments beyond what you can comfortably handle, then lock in at a rate you know you can afford for several years.

When is it generally wise to consider a shorter term? When rates are at historical all-time highs. Remember, the reason for going long is to lock in a rate that protects you from renewing at an even higher rate. Otherwise, everyone would select a short term. Sure, it's hard to know if rates have peaked. But by staying short, you can quickly capture the gains when rates fall back down again.

If you choose a short term, you'll have to take your chances at the mortgage rate roulette wheel more often. If you can handle the uncertainty — both psychologically and financially — you'll be rewarded by rates that are consistently lower than long-term rates. Making decisions more often also allows you to fine-tune your strategy and gives you more opportunity to reduce your principal.

Be warned, however, that interest rates fluctuate. If they jump quickly, they can just as easily fall back to where they started or even lower. The moral of the story is don't base your decisions on short-term movements. Make sure you have enough of a financial cushion to afford the higher payments that you'll have to make if rates have risen by the time your renewal date rolls around.

How to select your mortgage term

Your decision depends on your ability to live with risk. Staying short means more uncertainty, but you're almost certain to have lower mortgage costs unless rates keep marching up without coming back down. Choose long and you may sleep better, but you pay a premium for those worry-free nights.

If you're still unsure about which route to follow, don't worry. It's something that everybody goes through. Next time you're at a party, just start asking people about the choices they've made with their mortgages. You're bound to hear all sorts of tales about thousands of dollars lost or saved.

Open and closed mortgages

A *closed* mortgage means you're stuck with the terms of the deal until your loan agreement ends, or matures. You can refinance only if your lender lets you, and often that can involve paying stiff penalties. The upside of a closed mortgage is that, because the lender knows it can depend on your regular payments, your rates are lower.

Growing competition, however, has forced lenders to build in ways for you to pay off significant portions of your loan even within a closed mortgage. For example, the right to pay off 10 percent of your initial principal amount on each anniversary of your agreement is common.

An *open* mortgage, on the other hand, allows you to pay off part or all of the loan at any time without penalty. That can be a valuable option if you expect to come into a substantial sum of money or if you know you'll sell your home shortly. By completely paying off an open mortgage, you effectively terminate your contract with the lender. An open loan gives you flexibility to adapt your loan to changes in your financial picture or the economic situation. You have to pay more for this feature, usually a percent or so.

If falling rates are too tough to resist, but you want something less risky than a variable rate (which we describe in the next section), consider a fixed open mortgage. Your rate is guaranteed, but if rates fall to an even more attractive level you can lock in at that point without any penalty. If you want to play the interest game, this allows you to keep your options open while still protecting you should rates go up instead of down. It's usually not worth paying the premium that lenders charge for open mortgages, though, and you have other options.

Today's numerous prepayment options allow you to pay down significant sums during the life of your mortgage. In addition, more and more homeowners opt for shorter and shorter terms. Simply rolling over six-month terms, for example, can be a sensible strategy. At the end of each term, you're free to pick whatever term you like, from whatever lender you want, if you meet the lender's basic requirements. You also have the option of paying off any amount of your principal that you choose.

Otherwise, however, if you're trying to take advantage of low or falling rates, a much better alternative is now available, called a six-month convertible. We talk more about convertible mortgages later in this chapter.

Examining the difference between fixed- and variable-rate mortgages

With a *fixed-rate mortgage,* your payments won't change during your mortgage term. You lock in an interest rate that's fixed for the entire length of your term — nothing complicated to track, and no uncertainty. If you like getting your daily newspaper delivered at the same time every day, you're gonna like fixed-rate mortgages.

A *variable-rate mortgage* (sometimes referred to as an *adjustable mortgage*) carries an interest rate that (no surprise here!) varies. Usually tied to the lender's prime rate, it moves, jumps, rises, falls, and otherwise can't sit still, just like a fidgeting child.

The return for putting up with this volatility is that the rate is usually the lowest available at any point in time. Variable rates generally are set at, or slightly above, the lender's prime rate, and they rise and fall accordingly.

Some lenders offer protection from soaring rates by putting an absolute ceiling on how high your rate can go. You pay a slightly higher rate for a capped variable, usually around 1 percent above that of a regular variable.

If rates are on their way up, you're better off locking in to a fixed-rate mortgage before the rates go any higher. And if rates are going down, you should select a variable rate and go along for the ride. So, some people ask, "Shouldn't the likelihood of interest rates going up or down determine whether I take a fixed-rate or variable-rate mortgage?"

Good question. The problem is that there really is no accurate way to predict which way rates are going. If you feel strongly that rates are likely to fall and you prefer the variable option, you should understand the risks involved. A rise in interest rates can mean that at some point your monthly payment won't even cover the interest cost of your loan. If this happens, the outstanding interest is added to your balance. When that figure hits about 105 to 110 percent of the original loan amount, you can expect to hear from your lender. You'll either have to make a lump-sum payment against your principal or lock in to a fixed term.

If you decide that a variable-rate mortgage is the way to go, you also have to pass some extra tests. Due to their volatility, variable-rate mortgages often have lower lending limits. Many lenders won't let you borrow more than 70 percent of your property's appraised value. In some cases, you must also select an amortization period of 20 years or less. And in 2010, the federal government brought in a new rule requiring that borrowers qualify for a five-year, fixed-rate mortgage in order to take out a mortgage, even if the actual mortgage selected has a lower interest rate or a shorter term, and thus lower payments.

Convertible mortgages

Although the bells and whistles of convertible mortgages vary from lender to lender, the basic principle remains the same. You get a mortgage with a term of six months — or sometimes a year — typically with the same interest rate available for fixed mortgages for the same term. This is generally the best mortgage rate available.

At any point during the term of your convertible mortgage, you can "convert" your mortgage to a different term; you can also choose between an open or closed loan.

The benefit of a convertible mortgage is that it allows you to avoid paying a premium for longer-term fixed rates. You're also protected against rapidly rising rates because you can lock in at any time, rather than having to wait until your term expires or paying a hefty penalty. If rates should suddenly move up, you can simply lock in a longer-term rate. Meanwhile, you also save yourself the extra premium for an open mortgage.

If rates are falling, you can lock in the lower rates at any point. It often pays to simply ride out the term and, if rates are still falling at that point, to just sign up for another six-month convertible.

The important point with a convertible loan is to check the fine print for specific conditions. One institution, for example, allows you to convert only to a five-year term. Even if you let the six months elapse, you're automatically signed up. In essence, this is really a 5½-year mortgage, with the possibility of lower rates for a maximum of the first six months.

Most lenders allow you to convert at any time to any term you wish. The only across-the-board restriction is that you can't convert during the term to another six-month convertible. The other drawback to convertibles is that if you want to renew part way through the six months, you can't change lenders. That means losing some bargaining power, which can cost you a quarter or a half percentage point.

Variables are variable in another way: No other type of mortgage differs so much from lender to lender. Every aspect, from the terms available to whether you can pay the loan off early, varies widely depending on the institution. It's important to ask specific questions about any variable mortgage — and make sure that the answers are there on paper — before signing on the dotted line.

A relatively unpromoted player on the mortgage scene can save you from having to decide whether the potential savings from lower rates is worth all this worry. It's called a *convertible mortgage,* and it's one of the best-kept secrets in the mortgage game. A convertible loan offers many of the benefits of a variable-rate mortgage, with very little downside. For more information, see the sidebar on "Convertible mortgages."

Avoiding the down payment blues

You can generally qualify for the most favourable mortgage terms by making a down payment of at least 20 percent of the purchase price of the property.

Why? Because you can generally qualify for the most favourable terms on a mortgage with such a down payment, and you can avoid the added cost of mortgage insurance. Mortgage insurance protects lenders against losing money in the event you default on your loan, and can cost several hundred dollars per year on a typical mortgage.

Many people don't have the equivalent of 20 percent or more of the purchase price of a home to avoid paying private mortgage insurance. Here are a number of solutions for coming up with that 20 percent faster or buying with less money down:

- ✔ **Go on a spending diet.** One sure way to come up with a down payment is to raise your savings rate by slashing your spending. Take a tour through Chapter 6 to find strategies for cutting back on your spending.

- ✔ **Consider lower-priced properties.** Some first-time home buyers have expectations that are too grand. Smaller properties and ones that need some work can help keep down the purchase price and, therefore, the required down payment.

- ✔ **Find partners.** You can often get more home for your money when you buy a building in partnership with one, two, or a few people. Make sure you write up a legal contract to specify what's going to happen if a partner wants out, divorces, or passes away.

- ✔ **Seek reduced-down-payment financing.** Some lenders will offer you a mortgage even though you may be able to put down only as little as 5 to 10 percent of the purchase price. You can't be as picky about properties because not as many are available under these terms — many need work or haven't yet sold for other reasons.

- ✔ **Get assistance from family.** If your parents, grandparents, or other relatives have money dozing away in a savings account or a GIC, they may be willing to lend (or even give) you the down payment. You can pay them an interest rate higher than the rate they're currently earning but lower than what you'd pay to borrow from a bank — a win/win situation. Lenders generally ask whether any portion of the down payment is borrowed and will reduce the maximum amount they're willing to loan you accordingly.

Checking out the RRSP Home Buyers' Plan

You can borrow up to $25,000 from your RRSP to buy a house without paying any extra taxes or penalties under the federal government's Home Buyers' Plan (up to January 28, 2009, the maximum was $20,000). For hopeful home buyers the plan can be useful, but it is by no means perfect. The plan has a number of strict conditions and some potentially big costs, too.

Home equity loans

Home equity loans, or home equity lines of credit, can be a useful source of financing to help buy or improve a home. When established, home equity loans allow you to tap in to your credit line as you need or want to so you can use the money for many purposes, including a home remodel, university expenses for your kids, or as an emergency source of funds.

Home equity lines of credit have their downsides. The biggest negative in our experience is that they encourage homeowners to view their homes as piggybanks from which they can keep borrowing. The interest rate can increase instantaneously. Also beware that lenders can generally cancel your home equity line of credit at their discretion, for example if the value of your home falls too much or your credit score deteriorates.

Understand all the specifics, despite their positively desert-like aridity. Knowing what you're getting into now can save you a lot of financial worries down the road.

One important restriction is that the funds that you're withdrawing from your RRSP for the Home Buyers' Plan must have been in your RRSP for at least 90 days. The government doesn't want people to put money into their plan, get the tax break, and then draw on the same funds to use as part of a down payment. If you've been making regular contributions to your RRSP, and you've been building the tax refund into your budget, you need to prepare for this loss in cash flow.

Repayment rules

Strict rules govern how quickly you have to repay the money you've borrowed from your RRSP. You must repay the money into your RRSP within 16 years. The minimum you have to repay each year starting with the second year after you make your withdrawal is the equivalent of $\frac{1}{15}$ of the amount borrowed.

Keep in mind those payments aren't considered RRSP contributions, and you don't get any tax write-offs for them. And if you miss a payment or part of a payment, the government treats that money as if you had withdrawn it directly from your RRSP. The sum is included as part of your income for that year, and you have to pay tax on it. Ouch!

If you're currently finding it tough to put money into your RRSP, it will be twice as hard if you use your retirement funds for a down payment. Before you can even think of making a fresh contribution, you have to replace the required portion of the borrowed funds for that year. If that leaves you unable to make a direct RRSP contribution for that year, you miss out on a big tax break and a large tax refund. You also forgo the tax-free compound growth you could have earned from that new contribution.

Loss of potential growth in your RRSP

By taking money out, you lose all the potential growth from those funds as long as that money isn't in your plan. The younger you are, the higher the cost is to you. Unfortunately, the only way to understand the dangers this option poses for your RRSP is to do battle with a few numbers.

Suppose you're 30 and you borrow $18,000 from your plan to buy a home. You have to repay $1,200 a year, or $100 a month, for the next 15 years. The alternative would have been to borrow the money, say, as a second mortgage. If you borrowed the money at 10 percent and spread the loan over 15 years, the monthly payments would be $193.50. So the extra cost of borrowing the money from a bank or trust company instead of your RRSP is $93.50 a month.

But you have to balance that off against the gains possible by leaving that $18,000 in your RRSP. Earning an average of 10 percent a year, in 40 years that money would grow to more than $800,000. By comparison, if it were left in for 35 years, it would be worth just over $500,000.

This is an extreme example, but it amply demonstrates the true cost of borrowing "free" from your RRSP. The actual cost depends on how old you are and how quickly you're able to repay the borrowings. In general, if you're over 40 the price may not be too steep. In addition, if you use the plan to buy a home and it appreciates steadily, the growth on the value of your house will offset some of the forgone growth in your RRSP. You may be able to get the best of both worlds by borrowing from your RRSP and repaying the loan quickly, say in the first three or four years after you have settled into your new home.

Beware of prepayment penalties

Avoid loans with prepayment penalties. You pay this charge, usually 2 to 3 percent of the loan amount, when you pay off your loan before you're supposed to.

Prepayment penalties can also apply when you pay off a loan because you sell the property. (These penalties may be waived if you are selling to buy another property on which you take out a new mortgage with your current lender.) But if you refinance such a loan in order to take advantage of lower interest rates, you almost always get hit by the prepayment penalties if the loan calls for such penalties.

The only way to know whether a loan has a prepayment penalty is to ask. If the answer is yes, find yourself another mortgage.

Obtaining a high-ratio mortgage

If you have a down payment of at least 5 percent of the purchase price, you can obtain a high-ratio mortgage from most lenders. However, you're required to buy special mortgage insurance. If your application is approved, your lender will generally organize this for you. The insurance is provided either by the Canada Mortgage and Housing Corporation (CMHC), which is run by the federal government, or Genworth (formerly GE Capital). The insurance is there to protect your lender — not you — in case you fail to meet your payments.

Your down payment determines your insurance rate, which can run from 0.5 percent to 3.25 percent. You pay the premium only once — when you take out your mortgage. You're required to insure the entire loan, not just the difference between your down payment and the 20 percent required for a conventional loan. On a $100,000 mortgage, an insurance rate of 2.5 would mean paying $2,500 in insurance. If you don't have the money, you can ask your lender to add the insurance premium to your loan. Of course, that means you'll likely end up paying twice or three times that amount back over the life of the mortgage when all the interest costs have been added in.

In general, you're probably better off borrowing the money, even if that means taking out a second mortgage or a high-ratio mortgage. Just make sure you can afford the higher interest rate charges or the mortgage insurance premium.

Finding the best lender

As with other financial purchases, you can save a lot of money by shopping around. It doesn't matter whether you shop around on your own or hire someone to help you. On a 25-year, $150,000 mortgage, for example, getting a mortgage that costs 0.5 percent less per year saves you about $14,000 in interest over the life of the loan (given current interest rates).

Shopping for a lender on your own

In most areas, you can find many mortgage lenders. Although having a large number of lenders to choose from is good for competition, it also makes shopping a chore.

Large banks whose names you recognize from their advertising usually don't offer the best rates. Make sure that you check out some of the smaller lending institutions in your area, as well as credit unions and alternative lenders such as President's Choice Financial and ING Direct.

Real estate agents can also refer you to lenders with whom they've previously done business. These lenders may not necessarily offer the most competitive rates — the agent simply may have done business with them in the past.

You can also look in the weekend real estate section of one of the larger newspapers (and their associated Web sites) in your area for charts of selected lender interest rates. These tables are by no means comprehensive or reflective of the best rates available. In fact, many of them are sent to newspapers for free by firms that distribute mortgage information to mortgage brokers. Use the tables as a starting point by calling the lenders who list the best rates.

Adding up lender fees

Lenders can nickel and dime you with a number of fees other than points. Actually, you pay more than nickels and dimes — $300 here and $50 there add up in a hurry! Try to determine whether the lenders you're considering will charge you for the following:

- ✔ **Application and processing fees:** Most lenders charge several hundred dollars to complete your paperwork and process it through their underwriting (loan evaluation) department. The justification for this fee is that if your loan is rejected or you decide not to take it, the lender needs to cover the costs. Some lenders return this fee to you upon closing if you go with their loan (after you're approved).

- ✔ **Credit report:** Many lenders charge a modest fee (about $50 to $75) for obtaining a copy of your credit report. This report tells the lender whether you've been naughty or nice to other lenders in the past. If you have problems on your credit report, clean them up before you apply (see "Increasing your approval chances," later in this chapter; also look at Chapter 2 for info on checking your credit report).

- ✔ **Appraisal:** The property for which you're borrowing money needs to be valued. If you default on your mortgage, your lender doesn't want to get stuck with a property worth less than you owe. For most residential properties, the appraisal cost is typically several hundred dollars.

Get a written itemization of charges from all lenders you are seriously considering so that you can more readily compare different lenders' mortgages, and so that you have no surprises when you close on your loan. And to minimize your chances of throwing money away on a loan for which you may not qualify, ask the lender if you may not be approved for some reason. Be sure to disclose any problems you're aware of on your credit report or with the property.

Hiring a mortgage broker

Insurance agents peddle insurance, real estate agents sell real estate, and mortgage brokers deal in mortgages. They buy mortgages at wholesale from lenders and then mark them up to retail before selling them to you. The mortgage brokers get their income from the difference, or *spread,* in the form of a commission. The terms of the loan obtained through a broker are generally the same as the terms you obtain from the lender directly.

Mortgage brokers get paid a percentage of the loan amount — typically 0.5 to 1 or 2 percent. This commission is negotiable, especially on larger loans that are more lucrative. Ask a mortgage broker what his cut is. Many people don't ask for this information, so some brokers may act taken aback when you inquire. Remember, it's your money!

The chief advantage of using a mortgage broker is that the broker can shop among lenders to get you a good deal. If you're too busy or disinterested to shop around for a good deal on a mortgage, a competent mortgage broker can probably save you money. A broker can also help you through the tedious process of filling out all those horrible documents lenders demand before giving you a loan. And if you have credit problems or an unusual property you're financing, a broker may be able to match you up with a hard-to-find lender who's willing to offer you a mortgage.

When evaluating a mortgage broker, be on guard for those who are lazy and don't continually shop the market looking for the best mortgage lenders. Some brokers place their business with the same lenders all the time, and those lenders don't necessarily offer the best rates. Also watch out for salespeople who earn big commissions pushing certain loan programs that aren't in your best interests. These brokers aren't interested in taking the time to understand your needs and discuss your options. Thoroughly check a broker's references before doing business.

When a loan broker quotes you a really good deal, ask who the lender is. (Most brokers refuse to reveal this information until you pay the few hundred dollars to cover the appraisal and credit report.) You can check with the actual lender to verify the interest rate and points the broker quotes you and make sure that you're eligible for the loan.

Increasing your approval chances

A lender can take several weeks to complete your property appraisal and an evaluation of your loan package. When you're under contract to buy a property, having your loan denied after waiting several weeks can mean that you lose the property as well as the money you spent applying for the loan and having the property inspected. Some property sellers may be willing to give you an extension, but others won't.

Here's how to increase your chances of having your mortgage approved:

✓ **Get your finances in shape before you shop.** You won't have a good handle on what you can afford to spend on a home until you whip your personal finances into shape. Do so before you begin to make offers on properties. This book can help you. If you have consumer debt, eliminate it — the more credit card, auto loan, and other consumer debt you rack up, the less mortgage you qualify for. In addition to the high interest rate and the fact that it encourages you to live beyond your means, you now have a third reason to get rid of consumer debt. Hang onto the dream of owning a home, and plug away at paying off consumer debts.

✓ **Clear up credit report problems.** If you think you may have errors on your credit report, get a copy before you apply for a mortgage. Chapter 2 explains how to obtain a free copy of your credit report, as well as correct any mistakes or clear up blemishes.

✓ **Get preapproved or prequalified.** When you get *prequalified,* a lender speaks with you about your financial situation and then calculates the maximum amount he's willing to lend you based on what you tell him. *Preapproval* is much more in-depth and includes a lender's review of your financial statements. Just be sure not to waste your time and money getting preapproved if you're not really ready to get serious about buying.

✓ **Be upfront about problems.** Late payments, missed payments, or debts that you never bothered to pay can come back to haunt you. The best defence against loan rejection is to avoid it in the first place. You can sometimes head off potential rejection by disclosing to your lender anything that may cause a problem before you apply for the loan. That way, you have more time to correct problems and find alternate solutions. Mortgage brokers (see the preceding section) can also help you shop for lenders who are willing to offer you a loan despite credit problems.

✓ **Work around low/unstable income.** When you've been changing jobs or you're self-employed, your recent economic history may be as unstable as a country undergoing a regime change. Making a larger down payment is one way around this problem. You may try getting a co-signer, such as a relative or good friend. As long as he isn't borrowed up to his eyeballs, he can help you qualify for a larger loan than you can get on your own. Be sure that all parties understand the terms of the agreement, including who's responsible for monthly payments!

✓ **Consider a backup loan.** You certainly should shop among different lenders, and you may want to apply to more than one for a mortgage. Although applying for a second loan means additional fees and work, it can increase your chances of getting a mortgage if you're attempting to buy a difficult-to-finance property or if your financial situation makes some lenders leery. Be sure to disclose to each lender what you're doing — the second lender to pull your credit report will see that another lender has already done so.

Finding the Right Property

Shopping for a home can be fun. You get to peek inside other people's cupboards and closets. But for most people, finding the right house at the right price can take a lot of time. When you're buying with partners or a spouse (or children, if you choose to share the decision-making with them), finding the right place can also entail a lot of compromise. A good agent (or several who specialize in different areas) can help with the legwork. The following sections cover the main things you need to consider when shopping for a home to call your own.

Determining the right type of property

Some people's image of a home is a single-family dwelling — a stand-alone house with a lawn and white picket fence. In some areas, however — particularly in higher-cost neighbourhoods — you find *condominiums* (you own the unit and a share of everything else), *town homes* (attached or row houses), and *cooperatives* (you own a share of the entire building).

The allure of such higher-density housing is that it's generally less expensive. In some cases, you don't have to worry about some of the general maintenance, because the owner's association (which you pay for, directly or indirectly) takes care of it.

If you don't have the time, energy, or desire to keep up a property, shared housing may make sense for you. You generally get more living space for your dollar, and it may also provide you with more security than a stand-alone home.

As investments, however, single-family homes generally do better in the long run. Shared housing is easier to build and hence easier to *over*build; on the other hand, single-family houses are harder to put up because more land is required. But most people, when they can afford it, still prefer a stand-alone home.

With that being said, remember that a rising tide raises all boats. In a good real estate market all types of housing appreciate, although single-family homes tend to do better. Shared housing values tend to increase the most in densely populated urban areas with little available land for new building.

From an investment return perspective, if you can afford a smaller single-family home instead of a larger shared-housing unit, buy the single-family home. Be especially wary of buying shared housing in suburban areas with lots of developable land.

Casting a broad net

You may have an idea about the type of property and location you're interested in or think you can afford before you start your search. You may think, for example, that you can afford only a condominium in the neighbourhood you're interested in. But if you take the time to check out other communities, you may be surprised to find one that meets most of your needs and also has affordable single-family homes.

Even if you've lived in an area for a while and you think you know it well, look at different types of properties in a number of communities before you narrow your search. Be open-minded, and figure out which of your many criteria are essential for a home you *really* care about.

Finding out actual sale prices

Don't look at just a few of the homes listed at a particular price and then get depressed because they're all dogs or you can't afford what you really want. Before you decide to renew your apartment lease, remember that properties often sell for less than the price at which they're listed.

Find out what the places you look at eventually sell for. Doing so gives you a better sense of what you can really afford as well as what places are really worth. Ask the agent or owner who sold the property what the sale price was, or contact the town's assessor's office for information on how to obtain property sale price information.

Researching the area

Even (and especially) if you fall in love with a house at first sight, go back to the neighbourhood at various times of the day and on different days of the week. Travel to and from your prospective new home during commute hours to see how long your commute will really take. Knock on a few doors and meet your potential neighbours. You may discover, for example, that a flock of chickens lives in the backyard next door or that the street and basement frequently flood.

What are the schools like? Go visit them. Don't rely on statistics about test scores. Talk to parents and teachers. What's really going on at the school? Even if you don't have kids, the quality of the local school has direct bearing on the value of your property. Is crime a problem? Call the local police department. Will future development be allowed? If so, what type? Talk to the planning department. What are your property taxes going to be? Is the property located in an area susceptible to major risks, such as floods, mudslides, fires, or earthquakes? Consider these issues even if they're not important to you, because they can affect the resale value of your property. Make sure you know what you're getting yourself into *before* you buy.

Working with Real Estate Agents

When you buy (or sell) a home, you'll probably work with a real estate agent. Real estate agents earn their living on commission. As such, their incentives can be at odds with what's best for you.

A top-notch real estate agent can be a significant help when you purchase or sell a property. On the other hand, a mediocre, incompetent, or greedy agent can be a real liability. The following sections help you sort the good from the bad.

Recognizing conflicts of interest

Real estate agents, because they work on commission, face numerous conflicts of interest. Some agents may not even recognize the conflicts in what they're doing. The following list presents the most common conflicts of interest that you need to watch out for:

- ✔ Because agents work on commission, it costs them when they spend time with you and you don't buy or sell. They want you to complete a deal, and they want that deal as soon as possible — otherwise, they don't get paid. Don't expect an agent to give you objective advice about what you should do given your overall financial situation. Examine your overall financial situation *before* you decide to begin working with an agent.

- ✔ Because real estate agents get a percentage of the sales price of a property, they have a built-in incentive to encourage you to spend more.

- ✔ Agents often receive a higher commission when they sell listings that belong to other agents in their office. Beware. Sometimes the same agent represents both the property seller and the property buyer in the transaction — a real problem. Agents who are holding open houses for sale may try to sell to an unrepresented buyer they meet at the open house. No way can one person represent the best interests of both sides.

✔ Because agents work on commission and get paid a percentage of the sales price of the property, many are not interested in working with you if you can't or simply don't want to spend a lot. Some agents may reluctantly take you on as a customer and then give you little attention and time. Before you hire an agent, check references to make sure that he works well with buyers like you.

✔ Real estate agents typically work a specific territory. As a result, they usually can't objectively tell you the pros and cons of the surrounding region. Most won't admit that you may be better able to meet your needs by looking in another area where they don't normally work. Before you settle on an agent (or an area), spend time figuring out the pros and cons of different territories on your own. If you want to seriously look in more than one area, find agents who specialize in each area.

✔ If you don't get approved for a mortgage loan, your entire real estate deal may unravel. So some agents may refer you to a more expensive lender who has the virtue of high approval rates. Be sure to shop around — you can probably get a loan more cheaply. Be especially wary of agents who refer you to mortgage lenders and mortgage brokers who pay agents referral fees. Such payments clearly bias a real estate agent's "advice."

✔ Home inspectors are supposed to be objective third parties who are hired by prospective buyers to evaluate the condition of a property. Some agents may encourage you to use a particular inspector with a reputation of being "easy" — meaning he may not "find" all the house's defects.

✔ Some agents, under pressure to get a house listed for sale, agree to be accomplices and avoid disclosing known defects or problems with the property. In most cover-up cases, it seems, the seller doesn't explicitly ask an agent to help cover up a problem; the agent just looks the other way or avoids telling the whole truth. Never buy a home without having a home inspector look it over from top to bottom.

Looking for the right qualities in real estate agents

When you hire a real estate agent, you want to find someone who's competent and with whom you can get along. Working with an agent costs a lot of money — so make sure you get your money's worth.

Interview several agents. Check references. Ask agents for the names and phone numbers of at least three clients they've worked with in the past six months (in the geographical area in which you're looking). You should look for the following traits in any agent you work with:

✔ **Full-time employment:** Some agents work in real estate as a second or even third job. Information in this field changes constantly. The best agents work at it full time so that they can stay on top of the market.

✔ **Experience:** Hiring someone with experience doesn't necessarily mean looking for an agent who's been kicking around for decades. Many of the best agents come into the field from other occupations, such as business or teaching. Some sales, marketing, negotiation, and communication skills can certainly be picked up in other fields, but experience in buying and selling real estate does count.

✔ **Honesty and integrity:** You trust your agent with a lot. If your agent doesn't level with you about what a neighbourhood or particular property is really like, you suffer the consequences.

✔ **Interpersonal skills:** An agent has to be able to get along not only with you but also with a whole host of other people who are typically involved in a real estate deal: other agents, property sellers, inspectors, mortgage lenders, and so on. An agent doesn't have to be Mr. Congeniality, but he should be able to put your interests first without upsetting others.

✔ **Negotiation skills:** Putting a real estate deal together involves negotiation. Is your agent going to exhaust all avenues to get you the best deal possible? Be sure to ask the agent's references how well the agent negotiated for them.

✔ **High quality standards:** Sloppy work can lead to big legal or logistical problems down the road. If an agent neglects to recommend thorough and complete inspections, for example, you may be stuck with undiscovered problems after the deal is done.

Agents sometimes market themselves as *top producers,* which means that they sell a relatively large volume of real estate. This title doesn't count for much for you, the buyer. In fact, it may be a red flag for an agent who focuses on completing as many deals as possible. When you're buying a home, you need an agent who has the following additional traits:

✔ **Patience:** When you're buying a home, the last thing you want is an agent who tries to push you into making a deal. You need an agent who's patient and willing to allow you the necessary time it takes to get educated and make the best decision for yourself.

✔ **Local market and community knowledge:** When you're looking to buy a home in an area in which you're not currently living, an informed agent can have a big impact on your decision.

✔ **Financing knowledge:** As a buyer (especially a first-time buyer or someone with credit problems), you should look for an agent who knows which lenders can best handle your type of situation.

Buying real estate requires somewhat different skills than selling real estate. Few agents can do both equally well. No law or rule says that you must use the same agent when you sell a property as you do when you buy a property.

Putting Your Deal Together

After you do your homework on your personal finances, discover how to choose a mortgage, and research neighbourhoods and home prices, you'll hopefully be ready to close in on your goal. Eventually you'll find a home you want to buy. Before you make that first offer, though, you need to understand the importance of negotiations, inspections, and the other elements of a real estate deal.

Negotiating 101

When you work with an agent, the agent usually handles the negotiation process. But you need to have a plan and strategy in mind; otherwise, you may end up overpaying for your home. Here are some recommendations for getting a good deal:

✔ **Never fall in love with a property.** If you have money to burn and can't imagine life without the home you just discovered, pay what you will. Otherwise, remind yourself that other good properties are out there. Having a backup property in mind can help.

✔ **Find out about the property and owner before you make your offer.** How long has the property been on the market? What are its flaws? Why is the owner selling? For example, if the seller is moving because he got a job in another town and is about to close on a home purchase, he may be willing to reduce the price to get his money out of the home. The more you understand about the property and the seller's motivations, the better able you'll be to draft an offer that meets both parties' needs.

✔ **Get comparable sales data to support your price.** Too often, home buyers and their agents pick a number out of the air when making an offer. But if the offer has no substance behind it, the seller will hardly be persuaded to lower his asking price. Pointing to recent and comparable home sales to justify your offer price strengthens your case.

✔ **Remember that price is only one of several negotiable items.** Sometimes sellers get fixated on selling their homes for a certain amount. Perhaps they want to get at least what they paid for it years ago. You may be able to get a seller to pay for certain repairs or improvements, to pay some of your closing costs, or to offer you an attractive loan without the extra loan fees that a bank would charge. Likewise, the real estate agent's commission is negotiable.

Inspecting before you buy

When you buy a home, you may be making one of the biggest (if not *the* biggest) purchases of your life. Unless you build homes and do contracting work, you probably have no idea what you're getting yourself into when it comes to furnaces and termites.

Spend the time and money to locate and hire good inspectors and other experts to evaluate the major systems and potential problem areas of the home. Areas that you want to check include

- ✔ Overall condition of the property
- ✔ Electrical, heating, and plumbing systems
- ✔ Foundation
- ✔ Roof
- ✔ Pest control and dry rot
- ✔ Seismic/slide/flood risk

Inspection fees often pay for themselves. When problems that you weren't aware of are uncovered, the inspection reports give you the information you need to go back and ask the property seller to fix the problems or reduce the purchase price of the property to compensate you for correcting the deficiencies yourself.

As with other professionals whose services you retain, you need to make sure that you interview at least a few inspection companies. Ask which systems they inspect and how detailed a report they're going to prepare for you (ask for a sample copy). Ask them for names and phone numbers of three people who have used their service within the past six months.

Never accept a seller's inspection report as your only source of information. When a seller hires an inspector, he may hire someone who won't be as diligent and critical of the property. What if the inspector is a buddy of the seller or his agent? By all means, review the seller's inspection reports if available, but get your own as well.

And here's one more inspection for you to do: The day before you close on the purchase, do a brief walk-through of the property. Make sure that everything is still in good order and that all the fixtures, appliances, curtains, and other items that were to be left per the contract are still there. Sometimes sellers (and their movers) "forget" what they're supposed to leave or try to test your powers of observation.

Remembering title insurance

Everything from clerical errors and misrepresentations to outright fraud can turn owning a home into a legal nightmare. The role of title insurance is to provide you with some legal protection against these kinds of problems.

The major purpose of title insurance is to protect you against someone else claiming legal title to your property. This claim can happen, for example, when a husband and wife split up and the one who remains in the home decides to sell and take off with the money. If both spouses are listed as owners on the title, the spouse who sells the property (possibly by forging the other's signature) has no legal right to do so.

Both you and the lender can get stuck holding the bag if you buy the home that one spouse of this divided couple is selling. But title insurance acts as the salvation for you and your lender. Title insurance protects you against the risk that the spouse whose name was forged will come back and reclaim rights to the home after it's sold.

In addition to problems of who actually owns title to the property, title insurance can help you if problems crop up with your survey. This coverage can also protect you against smaller annoyances, such as vendors not having paid utility bills they claim to have settled, or not receiving a parking spot the seller asserted you were entitled to as part of your purchase.

 When you call around for title insurance quotes, make sure you understand all the fees. Many companies tack on all sorts of charges for things such as courier fees and express mail. If you find a company with lower prices and want to use it, ask for an itemization in writing so that you don't have any surprises.

Real estate agents and mortgage lenders can be a good starting point for referrals because they usually have a broader perspective on the cost and service quality of different companies. Call other companies as well. Agents and lenders may be biased toward a company simply because they're in the habit of using it or they've referred clients to it before.

After You Buy

After you buy a home, you'll make a number of important decisions over the months and years ahead. This section discusses the key issues you need to deal with as a homeowner and tells what you need to know to make the best decision for each of them.

Refinancing your mortgage

Three reasons motivate people to *refinance,* or obtain a new mortgage to replace an old one. One is obvious: to save money because interest rates have dropped. Lower rates look very appealing when you look at how much more money would stay in your bank account every month by cutting your mortgage payments. That's hard cash you could put toward other purposes or use to pay down your principal. Refinancing can also be a way to raise capital for some other purpose. You can use refinancing to get out of one type of loan and into another.

The following sections can help you to decide on the best option in each case.

Options for open and closed mortgages

If you have an open mortgage, of course, you can renew whenever current rates are more attractive. Find a new term you're comfortable with and sit back and count your savings. Better yet, keep your payments at the previous level and use the drop in rates to take years off your mortgage. And remember: When you refinance, you terminate your deal with your current lender. You're free to shop around your mortgage to other lenders. Or you could get a few offers to use as leverage to get your current lender to chop a quarter or even half a percent off its published rates.

Most mortgages, however, are closed. And although your lender may be willing to allow you to refinance early, it will want to be compensated for some — or all — of its losses. After all, if you want to refinance to reduce your rate from 11 percent to 8 percent, the banks aren't exactly going to leap at the chance to make 3 percent less on your loan, now are they?

The first step is to get your mortgage agreement out and read the fine print. Growing competition means that some lenders have made it easier for you to get out of your current loan. But this is a marketing edge they don't particularly want to tout unless they have to. After all, if you don't read your agreement and simply assume that you're stuck paying higher rates than you may need to, you don't really expect banks and trust companies to bring that to your attention — do you?

The three months' interest penalty

Your mortgage agreement may allow you to refinance your loan by paying the equivalent of three months' interest on your outstanding balance. By law, any mortgage with a term longer than five years also becomes open on the fifth anniversary, with the same three-month penalty applying.

Although they don't widely promote the fact, several of the big banks now also allow you to refinance under the same terms at any point after the third anniversary of your present agreement. But remember, it's unlikely that your lenders will alert you to the money you could be saving.

Whether the three-month penalty is worth paying is different in every case. It depends on the difference between your existing rate and what current rates are as well as on how much remains in your principal. Your best bet is to ask your lender to work the numbers out for you. The lender may not be that happy about doing so, but you should get the answers you need.

The interest-rate-differential (IRD) penalty

The most common penalty is something called the *interest-rate differential* (IRD). The IRD is the value today of the income the lender gives up by allowing you to refinance.

Say you're paying 10 percent and have two years left in your term. Your lender calculates how much it can make by taking the balance of your loan and lending it out elsewhere. Then it will ask you to make up the difference so that it can break even on the deal. The problem is that paying the IRD leaves you breaking even as well. The money you save with lower rates will be wiped out by the compensation you'll have to pay.

Another potential problem is that nobody can say with certainty where interest rates are headed. You lose out if rates fall and are lower at the end of your present term. If that happens, you've gone through an awful lot of tedious paperwork only to be locked in at a higher term than you would be paying if you had simply sat tight.

Mortgage life insurance

Shortly after you buy a home or close on a mortgage, you start getting mail from all kinds of organizations that keep track of publicly available information about mortgages. Most of these organizations want to sell you something, and they don't tend to beat around the bush. "What will your dependants do if you meet with an untimely demise and they're left with a gargantuan mortgage?" these organizations ask. In fact, this is a good financial-planning question. If your family is dependent on your income, can it survive financially if you pass away?

Don't waste your money on mortgage life insurance. You may need life insurance to provide for your family and help meet large obligations such as mortgage payments or educational expenses for your children, but mortgage life insurance is typically grossly overpriced. (Check out the life insurance section in Chapter 17 for advice about term life insurance.) Consider mortgage life insurance only if you have a health problem and the mortgage life insurer does not require a physical examination. Be sure to compare it with term life options.

Is a reverse mortgage a good idea?

An increasing number of homeowners are finding, particularly in their later years of retirement, that they lack cash. The home in which they live is usually their largest asset. Unlike other investments, such as bank accounts, bonds, or stocks, a home does not provide any income to the owner unless he decides to rent out a room or two.

A *reverse mortgage* allows a homeowner who's low on cash to tap in to home equity. For an elderly homeowner, tapping in to home equity can be a difficult thing to do psychologically. Most people work hard to feed a mortgage month after month, year after year, until it's finally all paid off. What a feat and what a relief after all those years!

Taking out a reverse mortgage reverses this process. Each month, the reverse mortgage lender sends you a cheque that you can spend on food, clothing, travel, or whatever suits your fancy. The money you receive each month is really a loan from the bank against the value of your home, which makes the monthly cheque free from taxation. A reverse mortgage also allows you to stay in your home and use its equity to supplement your monthly income.

The main drawback of a reverse mortgage is that it can diminish the estate that you may want to pass on to your heirs or use for some other purpose. Also, some loans require repayment within a certain number of years. The fees and the effective interest rate you're charged to borrow the money can be quite high.

Because some loans require the lender to make monthly payments to you as long as you live in the home, lenders assume you'll live many years in your home so that they won't lose money when making these loans. If you end up keeping the loan for only a few years because you move, for example, the cost of the loan is extremely high.

You may be able to create a reverse mortgage within your own family network. This technique can work if you have family members who are financially able to provide you with monthly income in exchange for ownership of the home when you pass away.

You have other alternatives to tapping the equity in your home. Simply selling your home and buying a less expensive property (or renting) is one option. Generally, any profit you make on the sale of the home you live in is not taxable.

Selling Your House

The day will someday come when you want to sell your house. If you're going to sell, make sure you can afford to buy the next home you desire. Be especially careful if you're a trade-up buyer — that is, if you're going to buy an even more expensive home. All the affordability issues discussed at the beginning of this chapter apply. You also need to consider the following issues.

Selling through an agent

When you're selling a property, you want an agent who can get the job done efficiently and for as high a price as possible. As a seller, you need to seek an agent who has marketing and sales expertise and is willing to put in the time and money necessary to sell your house. Don't necessarily be impressed by an agent who works for a large company. What matters more is what the agent will do to market your property.

When you list your house for sale, the contract you sign with the listing agent includes specification of the commission to be paid if the agent is successful in selling your house. In most areas of the country, agents usually ask for a 6-percent commission. In an area that has lower-cost housing, they may ask for 7 percent.

Regardless of what an agent says is "typical," "standard," or "what my manager requires," *always* remember that commissions are negotiable. Because the commission is a percentage, you have a much greater possibility of getting a lower commission on a higher-priced house. If an agent makes 6 percent selling both a $200,000 house and a $100,000 house, the agent makes twice as much on the $200,000 house. Yet selling the higher-priced house does not take twice as much work. (Selling a $400,000 house certainly doesn't take four times the effort of selling a $100,000 house.)

If you're selling a higher-priced home (above $350,000), you have no reason to pay more than a 5-percent commission. For expensive properties ($750,000 and up), a 4-percent commission may be reasonable. You may find, however, that your ability to negotiate a lower commission is greatest when an offer is on the table. Because you don't want to give other agents (working with buyers) a reason not to sell your house, have your listing agent cut his take rather than reduce the commission that you advertise you're willing to pay to an agent who brings you a buyer.

In terms of the length of the listing sales agreement you make with an agent, three months is reasonable. When you give an agent a listing that's too long (6 to 12 months) in duration, the agent may simply toss your listing into the multiple listing book and expend little effort to sell your property. Practically speaking, if your home hasn't sold, you can fire your agent whenever you want, regardless of the length of the listing agreement. However, a shorter listing may be more motivating for your agent.

Selling without a real estate agent

You may be tempted to sell without an agent so that you can save the commission that's deducted from your house's sale price. If you have the time, energy, and marketing experience and you can take the time to properly value your home, you can sell your house without an agent and possibly save some money. The major problem with attempting to sell your house on your own is that agents who are working with buyers don't generally look for or show their clients properties that are for sale by owner.

Besides saving you time, a good agent can help ensure that you're not sued for failing to disclose the known defects of your property. If you decide to sell your house on your own, make sure you have access to a legal adviser who can review the contracts.

Determining whether you should keep your home until prices go up

Many homeowners are tempted to hold on to their properties (when they need to move) if the property is worth less than when they bought it or if the real estate market is soft. Renting out your property is probably not worth the hassle, and holding on to it is probably not worth the financial gamble. If you need to move, you're better off, in most cases, selling your house.

If house prices are low, you may reason that, in a few years (during which you'd rent the property), the real estate storm clouds will clear, and you'll be able to sell your property at a much higher price. Here are three risks associated with this line of thinking:

> ✔ You can't know whether property prices in the next few years are going to rebound, stay the same, or drop even further. A property generally needs to appreciate at least a few percent per year just to make up for all the costs of holding and maintaining it.

✔ You may be unprepared for legal issues and dealings with your tenants. If you've never been a landlord, don't underestimate the hassle and headaches associated with this job.

✔ If you convert your home into a rental property in the meantime and it appreciates in value, you're going to pay capital gains tax on your profit when you sell it (and the profit can be bolstered if you have depreciated for rental property use). This tax wipes out much of the advantage of having held on to the property until prices recovered.

However, if you would realize little cash from selling *and* you lack other money for the down payment to purchase your next property, you have good reason for holding on to a home that has dropped in value.

Considering keeping your home as an investment property after you move

Converting your home into rental property is worth considering if you need or want to move. Don't consider doing so unless it really is a long-term proposition (ten years or more). As discussed in the preceding section, selling rental property has tax consequences.

If you want to convert your home into an investment property, you have an advantage over someone who's looking to buy an investment property, because you already own your home. Locating and buying investment property takes time and money. You also know what you have with your current home. If you go out and purchase a property to rent, you're starting from scratch.

If your property is in good condition, consider what damage renters may do to it; few renters will take care of your home the way that you would. Also consider whether you're cut out to be a landlord. For more information, see the section on real estate as an investment in Chapter 9.

Part IV
Insurance: Protecting What You Have

The 5th Wave   By Rich Tennant

@RICHTENNANT

"Frankly sir, issuing you reasonably priced auto insurance isn't going to be easy given the number of crashes you've been involved in."

In this part . . .

Just because insurance is boring doesn't mean you can ignore it! We show you how to obtain the right kind of insurance to shield you from the brunt of unexpected major expenses and protect your assets and future earnings. We also reveal which types of insurance you do and do not need, explain what to include and what not to include in your policies, and tell you how much of which things you should insure. Plus, we help you face other morbid but important stuff such as wills, probate, and estate planning.

Chapter 16

Insurance: Getting What You Need at the Best Price

In This Chapter

▶ Understanding our three laws of buying insurance

▶ What to do if you're denied coverage

▶ Getting your claim money

*U*nless you work in the insurance industry, you may find the topic dreadfully boring. Most people associate insurance with disease, death, and disaster and would rather do just about anything other than review or spend money on insurance. But because you won't want to deal with money hassles when you're coping with catastrophes — illness, disability, death, fires, floods, earthquakes, and so on — you should secure insurance well before you need it.

Insurance is probably the most misunderstood and least monitored area of personal finance. Studies by the U.S. non-profit National Insurance Consumer Organization show that more than nine in ten people purchase and carry the wrong types and amounts of insurance coverage. Most people are overwhelmed by all the jargon in sales and policy statements. Thus, they pay more than necessary for their policies and fail to get coverage through the best companies.

In this chapter, we tell you how to determine what kinds of insurance you need, explain what you can do if you're denied coverage, and give you advice on getting your claims filed. Later chapters discuss types of insurance in detail, including insurance on people (Chapter 17) and on possessions (Chapter 18).

Discovering Our Three Laws of Buying Insurance

We know your patience and interest in finding out about insurance may be limited, so in this section we boil the subject down to three fairly simple but powerful concepts that can easily save you big bucks. And though you're saving money, you can still get the quality coverage you need in order to avoid a financial catastrophe.

Law 1: Insure for the big stuff; don't sweat the small stuff

Imagine, for a moment, that you're offered a chance to buy insurance that reimburses you for the cost of a magazine subscription in the event that the magazine folds and you don't get all the issues you paid for. Because a magazine subscription doesn't cost much, we don't think you'd buy that insurance.

The point of insurance is to protect against losses that would be financially catastrophic to you, not to smooth out the bumps of everyday life. The preceding example is silly, but some people buy equally foolish policies without knowing it. In the following sections, we tell you how to get the most appropriate insurance coverage for your money. We start off with the "biggies" that are worth your money, and then we work down to some insurance options that are less worthy of your dollars.

Buy insurance to cover financial catastrophes

You should insure against what could be a huge financial loss for you or your dependants. The price of insurance isn't cheap, but it is relatively small in comparison to the potential total loss from a financial catastrophe.

The beauty of insurance is that it spreads risks over millions of other people. Should your home burn to the ground, paying the rebuilding cost out of your own pocket probably would be a financial catastrophe. If you have insurance, the premiums paid by you and all the other homeowners collectively can easily pay the bills.

Think for a moment about what your most valuable assets are. (No, we don't mean your dry wit or your charming personality.) Also consider potential large expenses. Perhaps they include the following:

✔ **Future income:** During your working years, your most valuable asset is probably your future earnings, and by extension, your ability to continue working so you can earn that money. If you were disabled and unable to work, what would you live on? Long-term disability insurance exists to help you handle this type of situation. If you have a family that's financially dependent on your earnings, how would your family manage if you died? Life insurance can fill the monetary void left by your death.

✔ **Business:** If you're a business owner, what would happen if you were sued for hundreds of thousands of dollars or a million dollars or more for negligence in some work that you messed up? Liability insurance can bail you out.

✔ **Health:** In this age of soaring medical costs, you can easily rack up significant bills in short order. Depending on your situation, it may pay to buy extended medical health insurance coverage that covers you for expenses your provincial plan doesn't, such as prescription drugs, dental care, physical therapists, and counselling. (See Chapter 17 for more on health insurance.)

Psychologically, buying insurance coverage for the little things that are more likely to occur is tempting. You don't want to feel like you're wasting your insurance dollars. You want to get some of your money back, darn it! You're more *likely* to get into a fender-bender with your car or have a package lost in the mail than you are to lose your home to fire or suffer a long-term disability. But if the fender-bender costs $500 (which you end up paying out of your pocket because you took our advice to take a high deductible), or Canada Post loses a package worth $50 or $100, it won't be a financial disaster.

On the other hand, if you lose your ability to earn an income because of a disability, or if you're sued for $1 million and you're not insured against such catastrophes, not only will you be extremely unhappy, but you'll also face financial ruin. "Yes, but what are the odds," we hear people rationalize, "that I'll suffer a long-term disability or that I'll be sued for $1 million?" We agree that the odds are quite low, but the risk is there. The problem is that you just don't know what, or when, bad luck may befall you.

And don't make the mistake of thinking you can figure the odds better than the insurance companies can. The insurance companies predict the probability of your making a claim, large or small, with a great deal of accuracy. They employ armies of number-crunching experts called *actuaries* to calculate the odds that bad things will happen and the frequency of current policyholders making particular types of claims. The companies then price their policies accordingly.

Buying (or not buying) insurance based on your perception of the likelihood of needing the coverage is foolish. Insurance companies aren't stupid; in fact, they're ruthlessly smart! When insurance companies price policies, they look at a number of factors to determine the likelihood of your filing a claim. Take the example of auto insurance. Who do you think will pay more for auto insurance — a single male who's age 20, lives the fast life in a high-crime city, drives a macho, turbo sports car, and has received two speeding tickets in the past year? Or a couple in their 40s, living in a low-crime area, driving a four-door sedan, and having a clean driving record?

Take the highest deductible you can afford

Most insurance policies have *deductibles* — the maximum amount you must pay in the event of a loss before your insurance coverage kicks in and begins paying out. On many policies, such as auto and homeowner's/renter's coverage, most folks opt for a $100 to $250 deductible.

Two benefits to taking a higher deductible are that:

- ✔ **You save premium dollars.** Year in and year out, you can enjoy the lower cost of an insurance policy with a high deductible. You may be able to shave 15 to 20 percent off the cost of your policy. Suppose, for example, that you can reduce the cost of your policy by $150 per year by raising your deductible from $250 to $1,000. That $750 worth of coverage is costing you $150 per year. Thus, you'd need to have a claim of $1,000 or more every five years — highly unlikely — to come out ahead. If you're that accident-prone, guess what — the insurance company will raise your premiums!

- ✔ **You don't have the hassles of filing small claims.** If you have a $300 loss on a policy with a $100 deductible, you need to file a claim to get your $200 (the amount you're covered for after your deductible). Filing an insurance claim can be an aggravating experience that takes hours of time. In some cases, you may even have your claim denied after jumping through all the necessary hoops. Getting your due may require prolonged haggling.

When you have low deductibles, you may end up filing more claims (although this doesn't necessarily mean that you'll get more money). After filing more claims, you may be "rewarded" with higher premiums — in addition to the headache you get from preparing all those blasted forms! Filing more claims may even cause cancellation of your coverage!

Avoid small-potatoes policies

A good insurance policy can seem expensive. A policy that doesn't cost much, on the other hand, can fool you into thinking that you're getting something for next to nothing. Policies that cost little also cover little — they're priced low because they don't cover large potential losses.

This section lists some examples of common "small-potatoes" insurance policies that are generally a waste of your hard-earned dollars. As you read through this list, you may find examples of policies you've bought and that you feel paid for themselves. We can hear you saying, "But I collected on that policy you're telling me not to buy!" Sure, getting "reimbursed" for the hassle of having something go wrong is comforting. But consider all such policies that you bought or may buy over the course of your life. You're not going to come out ahead in the aggregate — if you did, insurance companies would lose money! These policies aren't worth the cost relative to the small potential benefit. On average, insurance companies pay out just 60 cents in benefits on every dollar collected. Many of the following policies pay back even less — around 20 cents in benefits (claims) for every insurance premium dollar spent:

- **Extended warranty and repair plans:** Isn't it ironic that right after the salesperson persuades you to buy a television, computer, or car — in part by saying how reliable the product is — she tries to convince you to spend more money to insure against the failure of the item? If the product is so good, why do you need such insurance?

 Extended warranty and repair plans are expensive and unnecessary insurance policies. Product manufacturers' warranties typically cover any problems that occur in the first year to several years. After that, paying for a repair out of your own pocket won't be a financial catastrophe. Reputable manufacturers often fix problems or replace the product without charge after a warranty has expired (within a reasonable time period). Some credit card issuers automatically double the manufacturer's warranty without additional charge on items purchased with their card. However, the cards that do this typically are higher-cost premium cards so this is no free lunch — you're paying in terms of higher fees.

- **Home warranty plans:** A third-party new-home warranty is mandatory for most buyers in Ontario, Quebec, and British Columbia. In other provinces (as of at least 2010), they're still optional. If you're buying a new home in another province, and your real estate agent or the seller of a home wants to pay the cost of a home warranty plan for you, turning down the offer would be ungracious. (As grandma would say, you shouldn't look a gift horse in the mouth.) But don't buy this type of plan for yourself, unless you're required to by provincial regulations. In addition to requiring some sort of fee (around $50) if you need a contractor to come out and look at a problem, home warranty plans generally have a number of limits on how much they'll pay.

 Your money is best spent hiring a competent inspector to uncover problems and have them fixed *before* you purchase the home. If you're buying a house, expect to spend money on repairs and maintenance; don't waste money purchasing insurance for such expenses.

✔ **Dental insurance:** If your employer pays for dental insurance, take advantage of it. But you shouldn't pay for this coverage on your own. Dental insurance generally covers a couple teeth cleanings each year and limits payments for more expensive work.

✔ **Credit life and credit disability policies:** *Credit life policies* pay a small benefit if you die with an outstanding loan. *Credit disability policies* pay a small monthly income in the event of a disability. Banks and their credit card divisions usually sell these policies. Some companies sell insurance to pay off your credit card bill in the event of your death or disability, or to cover minimum monthly payments for a temporary period during specified life transition events (such as loss of job, divorce, and so on).

The cost of such insurance seems low, but that's because the potential benefits are relatively small. In fact, given what little insurance you're buying, these policies are usually extraordinarily expensive. If you need life or disability insurance, purchase it. But get enough coverage, and buy it in a separate, cost-effective policy (see Chapter 17 for more details).

If you're in poor health and you can buy these insurance policies without a medical evaluation, you represent an exception to the "don't buy it" rule. In this case, these policies may be the only ones to which you have access — another reason these policies are expensive. If you're in good health, you're paying for the people with poor health who can enroll without a medical examination and who undoubtedly file more claims.

✔ **Insuring packages in the mail:** You buy a $40 gift for a friend, and when you go to the post office to ship it, the friendly postal clerk asks whether you want to insure it. For a few bucks, you think, "Why not?" Canada Post rarely loses or damages things. Go spend your money on something else — or better yet, invest it.

✔ **Contact lens insurance:** The things that people come up with to waste money on just astound us. Contact lens insurance really does exist! The money goes to replace your contacts if you lose or tear them. Lenses are cheap. Don't waste your money on this kind of insurance.

✔ **Little-stuff riders:** Many policies that are worth buying, such as auto and disability insurance, can have all sorts of riders added on. These *riders* are extra bells and whistles that insurance agents and companies like to sell because of the high profit margin they provide (for *them*). On auto insurance policies, for example, you can buy a rider for a few bucks per year that pays you $25 each time your car needs to be towed. Having your vehicle towed isn't going to bankrupt you, so it isn't worth insuring against.

Likewise, small insurance policies that are sold as add-ons to bigger insurance policies are usually unnecessary and overpriced. For example, you can buy some disability insurance policies with a small amount of life insurance added on. If you need life insurance, purchasing a sufficient amount in a separate policy is less costly.

Law 11: Buy broad coverage

Purchasing coverage that's too narrow is another major mistake people make when buying insurance. Such policies often seem like cheap ways to put your fears to rest. For example, instead of buying life insurance, some folks buy flight insurance at an airport self-service kiosk. They seem to worry more about their mortality when getting on an airplane than they do when getting into a car. If they die on the flight, their beneficiaries collect. But should they die the next day in an auto accident or get some dreaded disease — which is statistically far more likely than going down in a jumbo jet — the beneficiaries get nothing from flight insurance. Buy life insurance (broad coverage to protect your loved ones financially in the event of your death no matter how you die), not flight insurance (narrow coverage).

The medical equivalent of flight insurance is cancer insurance. Older people, who are fearful of having their life savings depleted by a long battle with this dreaded disease, are easy prey for this narrow insurance. If you get cancer, cancer insurance pays the bills. But what if you get heart disease, diabetes, or some other disease? Cancer insurance won't pay these costs. Purchase major medical coverage, not cancer insurance.

Recognizing fears

Fears, such as getting cancer, are natural and inescapable. Although you may not have control over the emotions that your fears invoke, you must often ignore those emotions in order to make rational insurance decisions. In other words, getting shaky in the knees and sweaty in the palms when boarding an airplane is okay, but letting your fear of flying cause you to make poor insurance decisions is not okay, especially when those decisions affect the financial security of your loved ones.

Preparing for natural disasters — insurance and otherwise

In the chapters following this one, in which we discuss specific types of insurance such as disability insurance and homeowner's insurance, we highlight the fact that you may find it nearly impossible to buy broad coverage. For example, when purchasing homeowner's coverage, you find that losses from floods and earthquakes are excluded. You can secure such coverage in separate policies, which you should do if you live in an area subject to such risks (see more on this in Chapter 18). Many people don't understand these risks, and it's annoying and troubling that the insurance industry doesn't do more to educate customers about such gaping holes in their policies.

In addition to filling those voids, you should also think and plan for the non-financial issues that inevitably arise in a catastrophe. For example, make sure you have:

- ✔ A meeting place for you and your loved ones if you're separated during a disaster

- ✔ An escape plan should your area be hit with flooding or some other natural disaster (tornado, hurricane, earthquake, fire, or mudslide)

- ✔ The security of having taken steps to make your home safer in the event of an earthquake or fire (for instance, securing shelving and heavy objects from falling and tipping, and installing smoke detectors and fire extinguishers)

- ✔ A plan for what you'll do for food, clothing, and shelter should your home become uninhabitable

You get the idea. Although you can't possibly predict what's going to happen and when, you can find out about the risks of your area. In addition to buying the broadest possible coverage, you should also make contingency plans for disasters.

Law 111: Shop around and buy direct

Whether you're looking at auto, home, life, disability, or other types of coverage, some companies may charge double or triple the rates that other companies charge for the same coverage. Insurers that charge the higher rates may not be better about paying claims, however. You may even end up with the worst of both possible worlds — high prices *and* lousy service.

Most insurance is sold through agents and brokers who earn commissions based on what they sell. The commissions, of course, can bias what they recommend.

Not surprisingly, policies that pay agents the biggest commissions also tend to be more costly. In fact, insurance companies compete for the attention of agents by offering bigger commissions. Browse through publications targeted to insurance agents, and you'll often see ads in which the largest text is the commission percentage offered to agents who sell the advertiser's products.

Besides the attraction of policies that pay higher commissions, agents also get hooked, financially speaking, on companies whose policies they sell frequently. After an agent sells a certain amount of a company's insurance policies, she is rewarded with higher commission percentages (and other perks) on any future sales. Just as airlines bribe frequent fliers with mileage bonuses, insurers bribe agents with fatter commissions and awards such as trips and costly goods.

Shopping around is a challenge not only because most insurance is sold by agents working on commission but also because insurers set their rates in mysterious ways. Every company has a different way of analyzing how much of a risk you are; one company may offer low rates to you but not your neighbour, and vice versa.

Choosing financially stable insurers

In addition to the price of the policy and the insurer's reputation and track record for paying claims, an insurer's financial health is important to consider when choosing a company. If you faithfully pay your premium dollars year after year, you're going to be upset if the insurer goes bankrupt right before you have a major claim.

Insurance companies can fail just like any other company, and dozens do in a typical year. A number of organizations evaluate and rate, with some sort of letter grade, the financial viability and stability of insurance companies. The major rating agencies include A. M. Best Canada, Dominion Bond Rating Service, Fitch, Moody's, Standard & Poor's, and Weiss.

The rating agencies' letter-grade system works just the way it does in high school: A is better than B or C. Each company uses a different scale. Some companies have AAA as their highest rating, and then AA, A, BBB, BB, and so on. Others use A+, A, A–, B+, B, B, and so on.

Just as getting more than one medical opinion is a good idea, getting two or three financial ratings can give you a better sense of the safety of an insurance company. Stick with companies that are in the top two — or, at worst, three — levels on the different rating scales.

You can obtain current rating information about insurance companies, free of charge, by asking your agent for a listing of the current ratings. If you're interested in a policy sold without the involvement of an agent, you can request the current ratings from the insurer itself.

Although the financial health of an insurance company is important, it's not as big a deal as some insurers (usually those with the highest ratings) and agents make it out to be. Just as financially unhealthy banks are taken over and merged into viable ones, sickly insurers usually follow a similar path under the direction of insurance regulators.

With most insurance company failures, claims still get paid. The people who had money invested in life insurance or annuities with the failed insurer are the ones who usually lose out. Even then, you typically get back 80 cents to 90 cents on the dollar of your account value with the insurer, but you may have to wait years to get it.

Despite the obstacles, several strategies exist for obtaining low-cost, high-quality policies. The following sections offer smart ways to shop for insurance. (Chapters 17 and 18 recommend how and where to get the best deals on specific types of policies.)

Employer and other group plans

When you buy insurance as part of a larger group, you generally get a lower price because of the purchasing power of the group. Most of the health and disability policies that you can access through your employer are less costly than equivalent coverage you can buy on your own.

Likewise, many occupations have professional associations through which you may be able to obtain lower-cost policies. Not all associations offer better deals on insurance — compare their policy features and costs with other options.

Life insurance is the one exception to the rule that states that group policies offer better value than individual policies. Group life insurance plans usually aren't cheaper than the best life insurance policies that you can buy individually. However, group policies may have the attraction of convenience (ease of enrollment and avoidance of lengthy sales pitches from life insurance salespeople). Group life insurance policies that allow you to enroll without a medical evaluation are probably going to be more expensive, because such plans attract more people with health problems who can't get coverage on their own. If you're in good health, you should definitely shop around for life insurance (see Chapter 17 to find out how).

On the other hand, these policies may actually offer good value if you are in poor health, or have a disease or condition such as diabetes or serious heart problems. Some insurance companies may be willing to sell you coverage — although at a much, much higher cost than normal — and others may simply refuse to sell you a policy at any price. If you can purchase coverage through a group policy without having to submit your medical details or undergo any assessments, your coverage will often cost less than a policy that takes your state of health into consideration.

Insurance agents who want to sell you an individual policy can come up with 101 reasons why buying from them is preferable to buying through your employer or some other group. In most cases, agents' arguments for buying an individual policy from them include a lot of self-serving hype. In some cases, agents tell outright lies (which are hard to detect if you're not insurance-savvy).

One valid issue that agents raise is that if you leave your job, you'll lose your group coverage. Sometimes that may be true. For example, if you know that you're going to be leaving your job to become self-employed, securing an individual disability policy before you leave your job makes sense. However, your employer's health insurer may allow you to buy an individual policy when you leave.

In the chapter that follows, we explain what you need in the policies you're looking for so that you can determine whether a group plan meets your needs. In most cases, group plans, especially through an employer, offer good benefits. So as long as the group policy is cheaper than a comparable individual policy, you'll save money overall buying through the group plan.

Insurance without sales commissions

Buying policies from the increasing number of companies that are selling their policies directly to the public without the insurance agent and the agent's commission is your best bet for getting a good insurance value. Just as you can purchase no-load mutual funds directly from an investment company without paying any sales commission (see Chapter 10), you also can buy no-load insurance. Be sure to read Chapters 17 and 18 for more specifics on how to buy insurance directly from insurance companies.

The straight scoop on commissions

The commission paid to an insurance agent is never disclosed through any of the documents or materials that you receive when buying insurance. The only way you can know what the commission is and how it compares with other policies is to ask the agent. Nothing is wrong or impolite about asking. After all, your money pays the commission. You need to know whether a particular policy is being pitched harder because of its higher commission.

Commissions are typically paid as a percentage of the first year's premium on the insurance policy. (Many policies pay smaller commissions on subsequent years' premiums.) With life and disability insurance policies, for example, a 50-percent commission on the first year's premium is not unusual. With life insurance policies that have a cash value, commissions of 80 to 100 percent of your first year's premium are possible. Commissions on health insurance are lower but generally not as low as commissions on auto and homeowner's insurance.

Annuities, investment/insurance products traditionally sold through insurance agents, are also now available directly to the customer, without commission.

Dealing with Insurance Problems

When you seek out insurance or have insurance policies, sooner or later you're bound to hit a roadblock. Although insurance problems can be among the more frustrating in life, in the following sections we explain how to successfully deal with the more common obstacles.

Knowing what to do if you're denied coverage

Just as you can be turned down when you apply for a loan, you can also be turned down when applying for insurance. With medical, life, or disability insurance, a company may reject you if you have an existing medical problem (a preexisting condition) and are therefore more likely to file a claim. When it comes to insuring assets such as a home, you may have difficulty getting coverage if the property is deemed to be in a high-risk area.

Here are some strategies to employ if you're denied coverage:

✓ **Ask the insurer why you were denied.** Perhaps the company made a mistake or misinterpreted some information that you provided in your application. If you're denied coverage because of a medical condition, find out what information the company has on you and determine whether it's accurate.

✓ **Request a copy of your medical information file.** Just as you have a credit report file that details your use (and misuse) of credit, you also have a medical information report. Once per year, you can request a free copy of your medical information file (which typically highlights only the more significant problems over the past seven years, not your entire medical file or history) by calling 416-597-0590 or visiting `www.mib.com/html/request_your_record_can.html`). If you find a mistake on your report, you have the right to request that it be fixed. However, the burden is on you to prove that the information in your file is incorrect. Proving that your file contains errors can be a major hassle — you may even need to contact physicians you saw in the past, because their medical records may be the source of the incorrect information.

✓ **Shop other companies.** Just because one company denies you coverage, that doesn't mean all insurance companies will deny you coverage. Some insurers better understand certain medical conditions and are more comfortable accepting applicants with those conditions. Although most insurers charge higher rates to people with blemished medical histories than they do to people with perfect health records, some companies penalize them less than others. An agent who sells policies from multiple insurers, called an *independent agent,* can be helpful, because she can shop among a number of different companies.

✓ **Find out about provincial high-risk pools.** A number of provinces act as the insurer of last resort and provide insurance for those who can't get it from insurance companies. Provincial high-risk-pool coverage is usually bare bones, but it beats going without any coverage. If you're turned down for health or property insurance, check with your provincial department of insurance (see the "Government" section of your local phone directory).

✓ **Check for coverage availability before you buy.** If you're considering buying a home, for example, and you can't get coverage, the insurance companies are trying to tell you something. What they're effectively saying is, "We think that property is so high-risk, we're not willing to insure it even if you pay a high premium."

Dealing with insurance company problems

In the event that you suffer a loss and file an insurance claim, you may hope that your insurance company is going to cheerfully and expeditiously pay your claims. Given all the money that you shelled out for coverage and all the hoops you jumped through to get approved for coverage in the first place, that's a reasonable expectation.

Insurance companies may refuse to pay you what you think they owe you for many reasons, however. In some cases, your claim may not be covered under the terms of the policy. At a minimum, the insurer wants documentation and proof of your loss. Other people who have come before you have been known to cheat, so insurers won't simply take your word, no matter how honest and ethical you are.

Some insurers view paying claims as an adversarial situation and take a "negotiate tough" stance. Thinking that all insurance companies are going to pay you a fair and reasonable amount even if you don't make your voice heard is a mistake.

The tips that we discuss in this section can help you ensure that you get paid what your policy entitles you to.

Documenting your assets and case

When you're insuring assets, such as your home and its contents, having a record of what you own can be helpful if you need to file a claim. The best defence is a good offence. If you keep records of valuables and can document their cost, you should be in good shape.

A video is the most efficient record for documenting your assets, but a hand-written list detailing your possessions works, too. Just remember to keep this record someplace away from your home — if your home burns to the ground, you'll lose your documentation, too!

If you're robbed or are the victim of an accident, get the names, addresses, and phone numbers of witnesses. Take pictures of property damage and solicit estimates for the cost of repairing or replacing whatever has been lost or damaged. File police reports when appropriate, if for no other reason than to bolster your documentation for the insurance claim.

Preparing your case

Filing a claim should be viewed the same way as preparing for a court trial or a tax audit. Any information you provide verbally or in writing can and will be used against you to deny your claim. First, you should understand whether your policy covers your claim (this is why getting the broadest possible coverage helps). Unfortunately, the only way to find out whether the policy covers your claim is to read it. Policies are hard to read because they use legal language in non-user-friendly ways.

A possible alternative to reading your policy is to call the claims department and, *without* providing your name (*and* using caller ID blocking on your phone if you're calling from home), ask a representative whether a particular loss (such as the one that you just suffered) is covered under its policy. You have no need to lie to the company, but you don't have to tell the representative who you are and that you're about to file a claim, either. Your call is so you can understand what your policy covers. However, some companies aren't willing to provide detailed information unless a specific case is cited.

After you initiate the claims process, keep records of all conversations and copies of all the documents you give to the insurer's claims department. If you have problems down the road, this "evidence" may bail you out.

For property damage, get at least a couple of reputable contractors' estimates. Demonstrate to the insurance company that you're trying to shop for a low price, but don't agree to use a low-cost contractor without knowing that she can do quality work.

Approaching your claim as a negotiation

To get what you're owed on an insurance claim, you must approach most claims' filings for what they are — a negotiation that is often not cooperative. And the bigger the claim, the more your insurer will play the part of adversary.

A number of years ago, when Eric filed a homeowner's insurance claim after a major rain and wind storm significantly damaged his backyard fence, he was greeted on a weekday by a perky, smiley adjuster. When the adjuster entered his yard and started to peruse the damage, her demeanour changed dramatically. She had a combative, hard-bargainer type attitude that he last witnessed when he worked on some labour–management negotiations during his days as a consultant.

The adjuster stood on his back porch, a good distance away from the fences that had been blown over by wind and crushed by two large trees, and said that his insurer preferred to repair damaged fences rather than replace them. "With your deductible of $1,000, I doubt this will be worth filing a claim for," she said.

The fence that had blown over, she reasoned, could have new posts set in concrete. Because he had already begun to clean up some of the damage for safety reasons, he presented to her some pictures of what the yard looked like right after the storm; she refused to take them. She took some measurements and said that she'd have her settlement cheque to him in a couple of days. The settlement she faxed was for $1,119 — nowhere near what it would cost to fix the damage that was done.

Practising persistency

When you take an insurance company's first offer and don't fight for what you're due, you may be leaving a lot of money on the table. To make his long fence-repair story somewhat shorter, after *five* rounds of haggling with the adjusters, supervisors, and finally managers, Eric was awarded payment to replace the fences and clean up most of the damage. Even though all the contractors he contacted recommended that the work be done this way, the insurance adjuster discredited their recommendations by saying, "Contractors try to jack up the price and recommended work once they know an insurer is involved."

His final total settlement came to $4,888, more than $3,700 higher than the insurer's first offer. Interestingly, his insurer backed off its preference for repairing the fence when the contractor's estimates for doing that work exceeded the cost of a new fence.

Eric was understandably disappointed with the behaviour of that insurance company. But his homeowner's insurance company (at that time) was not unusual in its adversarial strategy, especially with larger claims. And to think that this insurer at the time had one of the better track records for paying claims!

Enlisting support

If you're doing your homework and you're not making progress with the insurer's adjuster, ask to speak with supervisors and managers. This is the strategy Eric used to get the additional $3,700 needed to get things back to where they were before the storm.

The agent who sold you the policy may be helpful in preparing and filing the claim. A good agent can help increase your chances of getting paid — and getting paid sooner. If you're having difficulty with a claim for a policy obtained through your employer or other group, speak with the benefits department or a person responsible for interacting with the insurer. These folks have a lot of clout, because the agent and/or insurer doesn't want to lose the entire account.

If, after following the steps we detail, you still haven't been able to resolve a problem with an insurance company, don't give up. Help is available, and best of all, it's free. Two independent insurance dispute resolution agencies will assist you in clarifying your situation, and also will provide mediation and adjudication services, all at no charge.

Problems with home, automobile, and business insurance

If you've been unsuccessful in your attempts to find a solution to a problem with an insurance company over a home, automobile, or business policy, your next step is to contact the General Insurance OmbudService (GIO).

The General Insurance OmbudService is an independent dispute resolution service. The agency's mandate is to provide consumers of car, home, and business insurance in Canada with a cost-free, independent, and impartial process for resolving their complaints.

After you've explained your particular situation, the GIO may begin by sending your insurer a written summary of your complaint, and discuss unresolved issues with the company's Complaint Liaison Officer. This will lead to a *Final Position Letter* explaining what the insurance company will do to resolve your complaint. If this is not to your satisfaction, you then move on to either mediation or *senior adjudication*.

If you choose mediation, the GIO will help you find a mediator. Their mediators are all independent and experienced in mediating disputes with insurance companies. You'll then meet with a representative from your insurance company and the mediator, who will try to resolve the issue.

If a resolution still isn't possible, you can then move on to senior adjudication. (You can also proceed to this stage without first going through mediation should you so desire.) Your case gets taken over by a *senior adjudicative officer* from the GIO. The officer may follow up with you as well as the insurance company for clarifications, but you don't have to meet with the company representative. The officer will review your case and deliver a report containing a non-binding recommendation.

If mediation fails, or if either you or the insurance company rejects the adjudicator's recommendation, then you can still pursue legal action.

You can begin the process by using the GIO's online submission form on its Web site. Here's how to reach them:

> General Insurance OmbudService
> 10 Milner Court, Suite 701
> Toronto, ON M1B 3C6
> 877-225-0446
> www.giocanada.org

Problems with life and health insurance

If you run into difficulties with your life or health insurance, the OmbudService for Life & Health Insurance (OLHI) may be able to help. (The name was changed from "Canadian Life and Health Insurance OmbudService" in 2009.)

The OLHI is a free national independent complaint resolution and information service for consumers. In addition to life and health insurance products and services, they also handle cases involving disability insurance, employee health benefits, and travel insurance, as well as insurance investment products such as annuities and segregated funds.

The agency will begin by reviewing your situation and clearing up any misunderstandings. Your case may then be referred to an OmbudService officer, who will act a conciliator/mediator and try to help you reach a voluntary resolution of your complaint with your insurer. In some cases, your complaint may be referred for a further review. This review results in a non-binding settlement recommendation to your and your insurance company.

You can reach the OLHI at 888-295-8112 (English) or 866-582-2088 (French). You can find more information and even start the process online at the OLHI's Web site at www.olhi.ca. You can also reach them by mail at

OmbudService for Life & Health Insurance
401 Bay St., P.O. Box 7
Toronto, ON M5H 2Y4

In Quebec, they can be reached at

OmbudService for Life & Health Insurance
1001, boul. De Maisonneuve O., Bureau 640
Montreal, PQ H3A 3C8

Seeking professional help

If the OmbudService isn't successful in helping you resolve your complaint, you still have two further options to pursue.

Hiring a public adjuster who, for a percentage of the payment (typically 5 to 10 percent), can negotiate with insurers on your behalf is one alternative. Adjusters understand insurance companies and their process for dealing with complaints. Best of all, they can negotiate on your behalf, which at this stage in the game most people find difficult because of the ever-increasing frustration, not to mention the time and effort it takes.

When all else fails and you have a major claim at stake, try contacting a lawyer who specializes in insurance matters. You can find these specialists in the yellow pages under "Lawyers — Insurance Law." Expect to pay around $150+ per hour. Look for a lawyer who's willing to negotiate on your behalf, help draft letters, and perform other necessary tasks on an hourly basis without filing a lawsuit. Your provincial insurance departments, the local bar association, or other legal, accounting, or financial practitioners also may be able to refer you to someone.

Chapter 17

Insurance on You: Life, Disability, and Health

. . . .

In This Chapter

▶ Looking into life insurance

▶ Debating disability insurance

▶ Selecting the best health insurance

▶ Considering overlooked insurance

. . . .

*D*uring your working years, multiplying your typical annual income by the number of years you plan to continue working produces a pretty big number. That dollar amount equals what is probably your most valuable asset — your ability to earn an income. You need to protect this asset by purchasing some insurance on *you.*

This chapter explains the ins and outs of buying insurance to protect your income: life insurance in case of death and disability insurance in case of an accident or severe medical condition that prevents you from working. We tell you what coverage you should have, where to look for it, and what to avoid.

In addition to protecting your income, you also need to insure against financially catastrophic expenses. We're not talking about December's credit card bill — you're on your own with that one. We're talking about the type of bills that are racked up from a major surgery and a multi-week stay in the hospital. Medical expenses today can make even the most indulgent shopping sprees look dirt-cheap. Even if you're covered by your province's health plan, you need to assess whether you should also have additional health insurance.

Providing for Your Loved Ones: Life Insurance

You generally need life insurance only when other people depend on your income. The following folks don't need life insurance to protect their incomes:

✔ Single people with no children

✔ Working couples who could maintain a lifestyle acceptable to them on one of their incomes

✔ Independently wealthy people who don't need to work

✔ Retired people who are living off their retirement nest egg

✔ Minor children (are you financially dependent upon your children?)

If others are either fully or partly dependent on your paycheque (usually a spouse and/or child) you should buy life insurance, especially if you have major financial commitments such as a mortgage or years of child-rearing ahead. You may also want to consider life insurance if an extended family member is currently or is likely to be dependent on your future income.

Determining how much life insurance to buy

Determining how much life insurance to buy is as much a subjective decision as it is a quantitative decision. We've seen some worksheets that are incredibly long and tedious (some are worse than your tax returns). No need to get fancy. If you're like us, your eyes start to glaze over when you have to complete 20-plus lines of calculations. Figuring out how much life insurance you need doesn't have to be that complicated.

The main purpose of life insurance is to provide a lump-sum payment to replace the deceased person's income. Ask yourself how many years of income you want to replace. Table 17-1 provides a simple way to figure how much life insurance you need to consider purchasing. To replace a certain number of years' worth of income, simply multiply the appropriate number in the table by your annual after-tax income.

Table 17-1	Life Insurance Calculation
Years of Income to Replace	*Multiply Annual After-Tax Income* By*
5	4.5
10	8.5
20	15
30	20

*You can roughly determine your annual after-tax income by getting out last year's tax return and subtracting the federal, provincial, and other payroll deductions you paid from your gross employment income.

Another way to determine the amount of life insurance to buy is to think about how much you'll need to pay for major debts or expenditures, such as your mortgage, other loans, and university for your children. For example, suppose you want your spouse to have enough of a life insurance death benefit to pay off your mortgage and half of your children's university education. Simply add your mortgage amount to half of your children's estimated university costs (see Chapter 14 for approximate numbers) and then buy that amount of life insurance.

Looking at the Canada Pension Plan's survivor benefits

If you're covered, the Canada Pension Plan (or Quebec Pension Plan) can provide *survivor benefits* to your spouse and children. However, your surviving spouse is going to get little if any survivor benefits if he or she is working and earning even a modest amount of money.

If you're already receiving your own CPP retirement pension or disability benefits, your survivor benefits will be combined with what you are already receiving into one monthly payment. This new combined total amount can't exceed the maximum retirement pension. If you are receiving a disability benefit, the total, after your survivor benefits are added in, can't exceed the maximum disability benefit.

The Guaranteed Income Supplement (GIS) and Allowance benefits are calculated using a couple's combined income. If you are receiving these benefits and your spouse or common-law partner dies, the monthly payments will be recalculated using your own income. If you start receiving a CPP survivor benefit, that is included in your income for the purposes of calculating your eligibility for GIS or Allowance benefits in the following year.

Examining "other" life insurance

Contemplating the possibility of your untimely demise is surely depressing. You'll likely feel some peace of mind when purchasing a life insurance policy to provide for your dependants. However, let's take things a step further. Suppose you (or your spouse) pass away. Do you think that simply buying a life insurance policy will be sufficient "help" for the loved ones you leave behind? Surely your contribution to your household involves far more than being a breadwinner.

For starters, you should make sure that all your important financial documents — RRSP, RESP, and investment account statements, insurance policies, employee benefits materials, small-business accounting records, and so on — are kept in one place (such as a file drawer) that your loved ones know about.

Do you have a will? See Chapter 18 for more details on wills and other estate-planning documents.

You may also want to consider providing a list of key contacts — such as who you recommend calling (or what you recommend reading) in the event of legal, financial, or tax quandaries.

So, in addition to trying to provide financially for your dependants, you also need to take some time to reflect on what else you can do to help point them in the right direction on matters you normally handle. With most couples, it's natural for one spouse to take more responsibility for money management. That's fine; just make sure to talk about what's being done so that in the event the responsible spouse dies, the surviving person knows how to jump into the driver's seat.

If you have kids (and even if you don't), you may want to give some thought to sentimental leave-behinds for your loved ones. These leave-behinds can be something like a short note telling them how much they meant to you and what you'd like them to remember about you.

What you will get as a survivor benefit depends on many factors, including whether your spouse was receiving a CPP retirement or disability pension, how long and how much they had paid into the plan, and your age.

Children of a contributor to the CPP may also be eligible for payments called the CPP Children's Benefit. If a child is under the age of 18, the benefit is normally paid to the parent. The monthly benefit is a flat amount. The average monthly payment in 2010 was about $214. Children between the ages of 18 and 25 who are attending school full-time are also eligible, as are part-time students in certain cases.

Some couples choose to split one of their CPP payments as a way to balance out their income and thus reduce their household's overall tax bill. This has no impact on the surviving spouse's benefits. If one spouse dies, the survivor benefits are calculated as if the splitting (officially called *assigning*) of benefits never took place.

Service Canada can tell you how much your survivors will receive per month in the event of your death. You can find this information online at www.service canada.ca; click on the link for seniors. You can also request information by mail. You'll find the address for the regional office nearest you at the Service

Canada Web site. You can also reach them by phone at 800-277-9914 (English), or 800-277-9915 (French).

Factor this benefit into the amount of life insurance that you calculate in Table 17-1. For example, suppose your annual after-tax income is $15,000, and the CPP will pay you a survivor benefit of $8,000 annually. For the purposes of Table 17-1, you should determine the amount of life insurance needed to replace $7,000 annually ($15,000 – $8,000), not $15,000.

Comparing term life insurance to cash-value life insurance

We're going to tell you how you can save hours of time and thousands of dollars. Ready? *Buy term life insurance.* (An exception is if you have a high net worth — several million bucks or more — in which case you may want to *consider* other options. See the estate-planning section in Chapter 18.) If you've already figured out how much life insurance to purchase and this is all the advice you need to go ahead, you can skip the rest of this section and the next and jump to the "Buying term insurance" section that follows.

If you want the details behind our recommendation for term insurance, the following information is for you. Or maybe you've heard (and have already fallen prey to) the sales pitches from life insurance agents, most of whom love selling cash-value life insurance because of its huge commissions.

Despite the variety of names that life insurance marketing departments have cooked up for policies, life insurance comes in two basic flavours:

- ✔ **Term insurance:** This insurance is pure life insurance. You pay an annual premium for which you receive a particular amount of life insurance protection. If you, the insured person, pass away, your beneficiaries collect; otherwise, the premium is gone, but you're grateful to be alive!

- ✔ **Cash-value insurance:** All other life insurance policies (whole, universal, variable, and so on) combine life insurance with a supposed savings feature. Not only do your premiums pay for life insurance, but some of your dollars are also credited to an account that grows in value over time, assuming you keep paying your premiums. On the surface, this sounds potentially attractive. People don't like to feel that all their premium dollars are getting tossed away.

  But cash-value insurance has a big catch. For the same amount of coverage (for example, for $100,000 of life insurance benefits), cash-value policies cost you about eight times (800 percent) more than comparable term policies.

Insurance salespeople know the buttons to push to get you interested in buying the wrong kind of life insurance. In the following sections, we give you some of the typical arguments they make for purchasing cash-value polices, followed by our perspective on each one.

"Cash-value policies are all paid up after X years. You don't want to be paying life insurance premiums for the rest of your life, do you?"

Agents who pitch cash-value life insurance present projections that imply that after the first ten or so years of paying your premiums, you don't need to pay more premiums to keep the life insurance in force. The only reason you may be able to stop paying premiums is because you poured a lot of extra money into the policy in the early years. Remember that cash-value life insurance costs about eight times as much as term insurance.

Imagine that you're currently paying $500 a year for auto insurance and that an insurance company comes along and offers you a policy for $4,000 per year. The representative tells you that after ten years, you can stop paying and still keep your same coverage. We're sure that you wouldn't fall for this sales tactic, but many people do when they buy cash-value life insurance.

You also need to be wary of the projections, because they often include unrealistic and lofty assumptions about the investment return that your cash balance can earn. When you stop paying into a cash-value policy, the cost of each year's life insurance is deducted from the remaining cash value. If the rate of return on the cash balance is not sufficient to pay the insurance cost, the cash balance declines, and eventually you receive notices saying that your policy needs more funding to keep the life insurance in force.

"You won't be able to afford term insurance when you're older."

As you get older, the cost of term insurance increases because the risk of dying rises. But life insurance is not something you need all your life! It's typically bought in a person's younger years when financial commitments and obligations outweigh financial assets. Twenty or thirty years later, the reverse should be true — if you use the principles in this book!

When you retire, you don't need life insurance to protect your employment income, because there isn't any to protect! You may need life insurance when you're raising a family and/or you have a substantial mortgage to pay off, but by the time you retire, the kids should be out on their own (you hope!), and the mortgage should be paid down.

In the meantime, term insurance saves you a tremendous amount of money. For most people, it takes 20 to 30 years for the premium they're paying on a term insurance policy to finally catch up to (equal) the premium they've been paying all along on a comparable amount of cash-value life insurance.

"You can borrow against the cash value at a low interest rate."

Such a deal! It's your money in the policy, remember? If you deposited money in a savings account or money market fund, how would you like to pay for the privilege of borrowing your own money back? Borrowing on your cash-value policy is potentially dangerous: You increase the chances that the policy will lapse — leaving you with nothing to show for your premiums.

"Your cash value grows tax-deferred."

Ah, a glimmer of truth at last. The cash-value portion of your policy grows without taxation until you withdraw it, but if you want tax deferral of your investment balances, you should first take advantage of your RRSP. An RRSP gives you an immediate tax deduction for your current contributions in addition to growth without taxation until withdrawal. The money you pay into a cash-value life policy gives you no upfront tax deductions. (See Chapter 11 for details on retirement plans.)

Life insurance tends to be a mediocre investment. The insurance company generally quotes you an interest rate for the first year; after that, the company changes the rate annually. If you don't like the future interest rates, you can be penalized for quitting the policy. Would you ever invest your money in a bank account that quoted an interest rate for the first year and then penalized you for moving your money within the next seven to ten years?

"Cash-value policies are forced savings."

Many agents argue that a cash-value plan is better than nothing — at least it's forcing you to save. This line of thinking is silly because so many people drop cash-value life insurance policies after just a few years of paying into them because the premiums are too high to keep paying.

You can accomplish "forced savings" without using life insurance. You can arrange to have money automatically transferred from your chequing account into your RRSP, for example. Your employer may also offer the option of having contributions to an RRSP or company pension plan come from your paycheque — and it doesn't take a commission! You can also set up monthly electronic transfers from your bank account to contribute to mutual funds (see Chapter 10).

Making your decision

Insurance salespeople aggressively push cash-value policies because of the high commissions that insurance companies pay them. Commissions on cash-value life insurance range from 50 to 100 percent of your first year's premium. An insurance salesperson, therefore, can make *eight to ten times more money* (yes, you read that right) selling you a cash-value policy than he can selling you term insurance.

Ultimately, when you purchase cash-value life insurance, you pay the high commissions that are built in to these policies. As you can see in the policy's cash-value table, you don't get back any of the money that you dump into the policy if you quit the policy in the first few years. The insurance company can't afford to give you any of your money back in those early years because so much of it has been paid to the selling agent as commission. That's why these policies explicitly penalize you for withdrawing your cash balance within the first seven to ten years.

Because of the high cost of cash-value policies relative to the cost of term, you're more likely to buy less life insurance coverage than you need — that's the sad part of the insurance industry's pushing of this stuff. *The vast majority of life insurance buyers need more protection than they can afford to buy with cash-value coverage.*

Cash-value life insurance is the most oversold insurance and financial product in the history of the financial services industry. Cash-value life insurance makes sense for a small percentage of people, such as small-business owners who own a business worth at least several million dollars and don't want their heirs to be forced to sell their business to pay estate taxes in the event of their death. (See "Considering the purchase of cash-value life insurance," later in this chapter.)

Purchase low-cost term insurance and do your investing separately. Life insurance is rarely a permanent need; over time, you can reduce the amount of term insurance you carry as your financial obligations lessen and you accumulate more assets.

Buying term insurance

Term insurance policies have several features from which to choose. We cover the important elements of term insurance in this section so you can make an informed decision about purchasing it.

Selecting how often your premium adjusts

Term insurance can be purchased so that your premium adjusts (increases) annually or after 5, 10, 15, or 20 years. The less frequently your premium adjusts, the higher the initial premium and its incremental increases will be. (Remember, as you get older, the risk of dying increases, so the cost of your insurance goes up.)

The advantage of a premium that locks in for, say, 15 years is that you have the security of knowing how much you'll be paying each year for the next 15 years. You also don't need to go through medical evaluations as frequently to qualify for the lowest rate possible.

The disadvantage of a policy with a long-term rate lock is that you pay more in the early years than you do on a policy that adjusts more frequently. In addition, you may want to change the amount of insurance you carry as your circumstances change. Thus, you may throw money away when you dump a policy with a long-term premium guarantee before its rate is set to change.

Policies that adjust the premium every five to ten years offer a happy medium between price and predictability.

Ensuring guaranteed renewability

Guaranteed renewability, which is standard practice on the better policies, assures that the policy can't be cancelled because of poor health. Don't buy a life insurance policy without this feature unless you expect that your life insurance needs will disappear when the policy is up for renewal.

Investigating guaranteed renewal rates

When assessing the price tag of a policy, what really matters is the overall amount you'll pay for your coverage for all the years that you'll require life insurance. Be sure that the premiums you'll pay each time you renew are guaranteed and laid out term by term in your policy. To evaluate different policies, have the agent do a *present-value comparison* of the total amount you'll pay in premiums over the period you estimate you'll require life insurance. This figure represents what a policy would cost if you had to pay for all your years of coverage in a single payment today.

Deciding where to buy term insurance

A number of sound ways to obtain high-quality, low-cost term insurance are available. You may choose to buy through a local agent because you know him or prefer to buy from someone close to home. However, you should invest a few minutes of your time getting quotes from one or two of the following sources to get a sense of what's available in the insurance market. Gaining familiarity with the market can prevent an agent from selling you an overpriced, high-commission policy.

In addition to sample rates from the best value providers, you can also get free, no-commitment quotes from a number of different companies. (For some types of insurance, you'll need to provide information such as your date of birth, whether you smoke, some basic health questions, and how much coverage you want.)

Other sources for high-quality, low-cost term insurance include:

- ✔ **Blue Cross** (you can find a phone number for Blue Cross in your province on the Web site, www.bluecross.ca)
- ✔ **Canadian Automobile Association** (877-942-4222; www.caa.ca)

See Chapter 20 for information on how to use your computer when making life insurance decisions.

Getting rid of cash-value life insurance

If you were snookered into buying a cash-value life insurance policy and you want to part ways with it, go ahead and do so. *But don't cancel the coverage until you first secure new term coverage.* When you need life insurance, you don't want to have a period when you're not covered (Murphy's Law says *that's* when disaster will strike).

Ending a cash-value life insurance policy has tax consequences. For most of these policies, you must pay tax on the amount you receive in excess of the premiums you paid over the life of the policy. If you want to withdraw the cash balance in your life insurance policy, consider checking with the insurer or a tax adviser to clarify what the tax consequences may be.

Considering the purchase of cash-value life insurance

Don't expect to get objective information from anyone who sells cash-value life insurance. Beware of insurance salespeople masquerading under the guise of self-anointed titles, such as estate-planning specialists or financial planners.

As we discuss earlier in the chapter, purchasing cash-value life insurance may make sense if you expect to have an estate tax "problem." However, cash-value life insurance is just one of many ways to reduce your estate taxes (see the section on estate planning in Chapter 18).

If you want to obtain some cash-value life insurance, avoid local insurance agents while you're in the learning stage. Agents aren't as interested in educating as they are in selling (big surprise). Besides, the best cash-value policies can be obtained free of most (or all) sales commissions when you buy them from the sources provided in the preceding list, or from the companies with the lowest premiums listed after you've entered your information in an online insurance quotation service. The money saved on commissions (which can easily be thousands of dollars) is reflected in a much higher cash value for you.

Preparing for the Unpredictable: Disability Insurance

As with life insurance, the purpose of disability insurance is to protect your income. The only difference is that with disability insurance, you're protecting the income for yourself (and perhaps also your dependants). If you're completely disabled, you still have living expenses, but you probably can't earn employment income.

We're referring to long-term disabilities. If you throw out your back while reliving your athletic glory days and you wind up in bed for a couple weeks, it won't be as much of a financial disaster as if you were disabled in such a way that you couldn't work for several years. This section helps you figure out whether you need disability insurance, how much to get, and where to find it.

Deciding whether you need coverage

Most large employers offer disability insurance to their employees. Many small-company employees and all self-employed people are left to fend for themselves without disability coverage. Being without disability insurance is a risky proposition, especially if, like most working people, you need your employment income to live on.

If you're married and your spouse earns a large enough income that you can make do without yours, you may want to consider skipping disability coverage. The same is true if you've already accumulated enough money for your future years (in other words, you're financially independent). Keep in mind, though, that your expenses may go up if you become disabled and require specialized care.

For most people, dismissing the need for disability coverage is easy. The odds of suffering a long-term disability seem so remote — and they are. But if you meet up with bad luck, disability coverage can relieve you (and possibly your family) of a major financial burden.

Most disabilities are caused by medical problems, such as arthritis, heart conditions, hypertension, and back/spine or hip/leg impairments. Some of these ailments occur with advancing age, but more than one-third of all disabilities are suffered by people under the age of 45. The vast majority of these medical problems cannot be predicted, particularly those caused by random accidents.

If you think you have good disability coverage through government programs, you'd better think again:

- **Government benefits.** In order to receive CPP/QPP disability benefits, you generally must have paid into the Canada Pension Plan or Quebec Pension Plan for at least four of the six years leading up to the point at which you became disabled. Your disability must be severe, which means it prevents you from doing not only your former job but also any job on a regular basis, in order to qualify. The disability must also be prolonged, meaning it is expected to last at least a year or be likely to result in death. CPP/QPP disability payments are quite low because they are intended to provide only for basic, subsistence-level living expenses. The average late in 2009 was just $809, and the maximum for 2010 was about $1,126.

- **Workers' compensation.** Worker's compensation (if you have such coverage through your employer) pays you benefits when you're injured on the job, but it doesn't pay any benefits if you become disabled away from your job. You need coverage that pays regardless of where and how you are disabled.

Determining how much disability insurance you need

You need enough disability coverage to provide you with sufficient income to live on until other financial resources become available. If you don't have much saved in the way of financial assets and you want to continue with the lifestyle supported by your current income if you suffer a disability, get enough disability coverage to replace your entire monthly take-home (after-tax) pay.

The benefits you purchase on a disability policy are quoted as the dollars per month you receive if disabled. So if your job provides you with a $3,000-per-month income after payment of taxes, seek a policy that provides a $3,000-per-month benefit.

If you pay for your disability insurance, the benefits are tax-free (but hopefully you won't ever have to collect them). If your employer picks up the tab, your benefits are taxable, so you need a greater amount of benefits.

In addition to the monthly coverage amount, you also need to select the duration for which you want a policy to pay you benefits. You need a policy that pays benefits until you reach an age at which you become financially self-sufficient. For most people, that's around age 65. If you anticipate needing your employment income past your mid-60s, you may want to obtain disability coverage that pays you until a later age.

On the other hand, if you crunched some numbers (see Chapter 3) and you expect to be financially independent by age 55, shop for a policy that pays benefits up to that age — it'll cost you less than one that pays benefits to you until age 65. If you're within five years of being financially independent or able to retire, five-year disability policies are available, too. You may also consider such short-term policies when you're sure that someone (for example, a family member) can support you financially over the long term.

Identifying other features you need in disability insurance

Disability insurance policies have many confusing features. Here's what to look for — and look out for — when purchasing disability insurance:

- **Definition of disability:** An *own-occupation* disability policy provides benefit payments if you can't perform the work you normally do. Some policies pay you only if you're unable to perform a job for which you are *reasonably trained.* Other policies revert to this definition after a few years of being own-occupation.

  Own-occupation policies are the most expensive because a greater chance exists that the insurer will have to pay you. The extra cost may not be worth it unless you're in a high-income or specialized occupation and you'd have to take a significant pay cut to do something else (and you wouldn't be happy about a reduced income and the required lifestyle changes).

- **Non-cancellable and guaranteed renewable:** These features ensure that your policy can't be cancelled because of your falling into poor health. With policies that require periodic physical exams, you can lose your coverage just when you're most likely to need it.

- **Waiting period:** This is the "deductible" on disability insurance — the lag time between the onset of your disability and the time you begin collecting benefits. As with other types of insurance, you should take the highest deductible (longest waiting period) that your financial circumstances allow. The waiting period significantly reduces the cost of the insurance and eliminates the hassle of filing a claim for a short-term disability. The minimum waiting period on most policies is 30 days. The maximum waiting period can be up to one to two years. If you have sufficient emergency reserves, a waiting period of three to six months is a good choice.

- **Residual benefits:** This option pays you a partial benefit if you have a disability that prevents you from working full-time.

✓ **Cost-of-living adjustments (COLAs):** This feature automatically increases your benefit payment by a set percentage annually or in accordance with changes in inflation. The advantage of a COLA is that it retains the purchasing power of your benefits. A modest COLA, such as 4 percent, is worth having.

✓ **Future insurability:** A clause that many agents encourage you to buy, future insurability allows you, regardless of health, to buy additional coverage. For most people, paying for the privilege of buying more coverage later is not worth it if the income you earn today fairly reflects your likely long-term earnings (except for cost-of-living increases). Disability insurance is sold only as a proportion of your income. You may benefit from the future insurability option if your income is artificially low now and you're confident that it will rise significantly in the future. (For example, you just got out of medical school and you're earning a low salary while being enslaved as a resident.)

✓ **Insurer's financial stability:** As we discuss in Chapter 16, you should choose insurers that'll be here tomorrow to pay your claim. But don't get too hung up on the stability of the company; benefits are paid even if the insurer fails, because the province or another insurer will almost always bail out the unstable insurer.

Deciding where to buy disability insurance

The place to buy disability insurance with the best value is through your employer or professional association. Unless these groups have done a lousy job shopping for coverage, group plans offer a better value than disability insurance you can purchase on your own. Just make sure that the group plan meets the specifications discussed in the preceding section.

Don't trust an insurance agent to be enthusiastic about the quality of a disability policy your employer or other group is offering. Agents have a conflict of interest when they criticize these options, because they won't make a commission if you buy through a group.

If you don't have access to a group policy, check with your agent or a company you already do business with.

Tread carefully when purchasing disability insurance through an agent. Some agents try to load down your policy with all sorts of extra bells and whistles to pump up the premium along with their commission.

If you buy disability insurance through an agent, use a process called list billing. With *list billing,* you sign up with several other people for coverage at the same time and are invoiced together for your coverage. It can knock up to 15 percent off an insurer's standard prices. Ask your insurance agent how list billing works.

Other types of "insurance" for protecting your income

Life insurance and disability insurance replace your income if you die or suffer a disability. But you may also see your income reduced or completely eliminated if you lose your job. Although no formal insurance exists to protect you against the forces that can cause you to lose your job, you can do some things to reduce your exposure to such risk:

✔ Make sure that you have an emergency reserve of money that you can tap in to if you lose your job. (Chapter 4 offers specific guidelines for deciding how much money is right for you.)

✔ Attend to your skills and professional development on a continual basis. Not only does upgrading your education and skills ensure that you'll be employable if you have to look for a new job, but it may also help you keep your old job and earn a higher income.

Getting Care for the Road: Travel Medical Insurance

If you head out of Canada on vacation, for business, or even just for a day-shopping trip across the border, you need to ensure you are properly insured against unexpected medical expenses. An emergency ward or doctor's waiting room likely isn't on your list of must-sees when you head out of the country. But you simply can't predict whether a visit to a medical facility will end up being part of your itinerary when you leave our home and native land.

Without sufficient *travel medical coverage,* an accident or illness that strikes while you are out of Canada could severely damage your financial health.

Determining what coverage you already have

As long as you belong to your province's health care plan, you already have some coverage outside of Canada. However, each provincial plan covers you only up to certain levels, with maximums established for various procedures and other medical costs. The amounts that provincial plans will pay have been shrinking, though, and what your provincial health plan pays might be only a fraction of the final bill.

Don't assume that because you have a premium credit card that trumpets medical coverage you're adequately covered. The eligibility requirements can be highly confusing, and the rules are regularly changed. Some premium cards, for instance, cover you for only a certain number of days for each trip you make. You may be covered for trips up to 21 days in length, for instance, so if you're injured on the 22nd day, your card company won't pay any of the medical expenses.

Always check with your benefits department before you leave on a business trip. While most corporations provide medical insurance for employees who are travelling on business, the policies can be complicated and can leave you exposed. For instance, you may be covered during the week while you're on company business, but not if you choose to stay over for the weekend to enjoy a little skiing at a nearby resort. Should you break your leg on the slopes, you may find you're responsible for any bills because company policy doesn't cover injuries sustained on personal time.

Buying travel medical insurance

Be sure to take a look at your family's overall need. Many providers now offer plans that will cover your family. If you travel a lot, check into annual plans, which cover you up to a maximum number of days outside the country over 12 months.

Some sources for low-cost travel medical insurance include:

- ✔ **Canadian Automobile Association** (Call toll-free directory assistance at 800-555-1212 for the toll-free number for your province, or visit `www.caa.ca`)
- ✔ **Group Medical Services** (800-667-3699; `www.gms.ca`)
- ✔ **Ingle Health** (800-360-3234; `www.ingle-health.com`)
- ✔ **Tour+Med** (800-268-9633; `www.tourmed.ca`)
- ✔ **Travel Cuts** (866-246-9762; `www.travelcuts.ca`)

Long-Term Care Insurance

Insurance agents who are eager to earn a hefty commission will often tell you that long-term care (LTC) insurance is the solution to your concerns about an extended stay in a nursing home. Don't get your hopes up. Policies are complicated and filled with all sorts of exclusions and limitations. On top of all that, they're expensive, too.

The decision to purchase LTC insurance is a trade-off. Do you want to pay thousands of dollars annually, beginning at age 60, to guard against the possibility of a long-term stay in a nursing home? If you live into or past your mid-80s, you can end up paying $100,000 or more on an LTC policy (not to mention the lost investment earnings on these insurance premiums).

People who end up in a nursing home for years on end may come out ahead financially when buying LTC insurance. Many people who stay in a nursing home are there for less than a year, though, because they either pass away or move out.

Provincial health plans will cover only a portion of long-term care costs, generally requiring you to pay a fixed amount that can range from around $12,000 to $25,000 or more a year.

If you have relatives or a spouse who will likely care for you in the event of a major illness, you should definitely *not* waste your money on nursing-home insurance. You can also bypass this coverage if you have and don't mind using retirement assets to help pay nursing-home costs.

Even if you do deplete your assets, remember that you have a backup: government assistance programs. However, this will usually cover only basic accommodation. To find out what may be available to you, contact your province's ministry of health.

Consider buying nursing-home insurance if you want to retain and protect your assets and if it gives you peace of mind to know that a long-term nursing-home stay is covered. But do your homework. Do some comparison shopping, and make sure you buy a policy that pays benefits for the long term. A year's worth (or even a few years' worth) of benefits won't protect your assets if your stay lasts longer. Also be sure to get a policy that adjusts the daily benefit amount for increases in the cost of living. Watch out for policies that restrict benefits to limited types of facilities and settings. Get a policy that covers care in your home or other settings if you don't need to be in a high-cost nursing home, and make sure that it doesn't require prior hospitalization for benefits to kick in. To keep premiums down, also consider a longer exclusion or waiting period — three to six months or a year before coverage starts.

You may also want to consider retirement communities if you're willing to live as a younger retiree in such a setting. After paying an entrance fee, you pay a monthly fee, which usually covers your rent, care, and meals. Make sure that any such facility you're considering guarantees care for life.

Chapter 18

Covering Your Assets

· ·

In This Chapter

▶ Checking out homeowner's/renter's insurance

▶ Considering automobile insurance

▶ Looking at umbrella insurance

▶ Planning your estate

· ·

*I*n Chapter 17, we discuss the importance of protecting your future income from disability, death, or large, unexpected medical expenses. But you also have to insure major assets that you've acquired in the past: your home, your car, and your personal property. You need to protect these assets for two reasons:

✔ **Your assets are valuable.** If you were to suffer a loss, replacing the assets with money out of your own pocket could be a financial catastrophe.

✔ **A lawsuit could drain your finances.** Should someone be injured or killed in your home or because of your car, a lawsuit could be financially devastating.

In this chapter, we explain why, how, and for how much to insure your home, personal property, and vehicle. We also discuss excess liability insurance and how to determine where your money will go in the event of your death.

Insuring Where You Live

When you buy a home with a mortgage, most lenders require you to purchase homeowner's insurance. But even if they don't, you're wise to do so, because your home and the personal property within it are worth a great deal and would cost a bundle to replace.

As a renter, damage to the building in which you live is not your immediate financial concern, but you still have personal property you may want to insure. You also have the possibility (albeit remote) that you'll be sued by someone who's injured in your rental.

When shopping for a homeowner's or renter's policy, consider the important features that we cover in the following sections.

Dwelling coverage: The cost to rebuild

How much would you have to spend to rebuild your home if it were completely destroyed, for example, in a fire? The cost to rebuild should be based on the size (square footage) of your home. Neither the purchase price nor the size of your mortgage should determine how much *dwelling coverage* you need.

If you're a renter, rejoice that you don't need dwelling coverage. If you're a condominium owner, find out whether the insurance the condo association bought for the entire building is sufficient.

Be sure that your homeowner's policy includes a *guaranteed replacement cost* provision. This useful feature ensures that the insurance company will rebuild the home even if the cost of construction is more than the policy coverage. If the insurance company underestimates your dwelling coverage, it has to make up the difference.

Unfortunately, each insurer defines guaranteed replacement cost differently. Some companies pay for the full replacement cost of the home, no matter how much it ends up costing. Other insurers set limits. For example, some insurers may pay up to only 25 percent more than the dwelling coverage on your policy. Ask your insurer how it defines guaranteed replacement cost.

If you have an older property that doesn't meet current building standards, consider buying a *rider* (supplemental coverage to your main insurance policy) that pays for code upgrades. This rider covers the cost of rebuilding your home, in the event of a loss, to comply with current building codes that may be more stringent than the ones in place when your home was built. Ask your insurance company what your basic policy does and doesn't cover. Some companies include a certain amount (for example, 10 percent of your dwelling coverage) for code upgrades in the base policy.

Personal property coverage: For your things

On your homeowner's policy, the amount of personal property coverage is typically derived from the amount of dwelling coverage you carry. Generally, you get personal property coverage that's equal to 50 to 75 percent of the dwelling coverage. This amount is usually more than enough.

Regarding riders to cover jewellery, computers, furs, and other somewhat costly items that may not be fully covered by typical homeowner's policies, ask yourself whether the out-of-pocket expense from the loss of such items would constitute a financial catastrophe. Unless you have more than several thousands of dollars worth of jewellery or computer equipment, skip such riders.

Some policies come with *replacement cost guarantees* that pay you the cost to replace an item. This payment can be considerably more than what the used item was worth before it was damaged or stolen. When this feature is not part of the standard policy sold by your insurer, you may want to purchase it as a rider, if available.

As a renter or condominium owner, you need to choose a dollar amount for the personal property you want covered. Tally it up instead of guessing — the total cost of replacing all your personal property may surprise you.

Make a list of your belongings — or even better, take pictures or make a video — with an estimate of what each item is worth. Keep this list updated; you'll need it if you have to file a claim. Retaining receipts for major purchases may also help your case. No matter how you document your belongings, don't forget to keep the documentation somewhere besides your home — otherwise, it could be destroyed along with the rest of your house in a fire or other disaster.

Liability insurance: Coverage for when others are harmed

Liability insurance protects you financially against lawsuits that may arise if someone gets injured on your property, including wounds inflicted by the family pit bull or terrible tabby. (Of course, you should keep Bruno restrained when guests visit — even your cranky in-laws.) At a minimum, get enough liability insurance to cover your financial assets — covering two times your assets is better. Buying extra coverage is inexpensive and well worth the cost.

The probability of being sued is low, but if you are sued and you lose, you could end up owing big bucks. If you have substantial assets to protect, you may want to consider an umbrella, or excess liability, policy. (See "Protecting against Mega-Liability: Umbrella Insurance," later in this chapter.)

Liability protection is one of the side benefits of purchasing a renter's policy — you protect your personal property as well as insure against lawsuits. (But don't be reckless with your banana peels if you get liability insurance!)

Flood and earthquake insurance: Protection from Mother Nature

Purchase the broadest possible coverage when buying any type of insurance (see Chapter 16). The problem with homeowner's insurance is that it's not comprehensive enough — it doesn't typically cover losses due to earthquakes and floods. You must buy such disaster coverage separately.

If an earthquake or flood were to strike your area and destroy your home, you'd be out tens (if not hundreds) of thousands of dollars without proper coverage. Yet many people don't carry these important coverages, often as a result of some common misconceptions:

- ✔ **"Not in my neighbourhood."** Many people mistakenly believe that earthquakes occur only in California and Japan. We wish this were true for those of us who live in the True North, but it's not. Vancouver is built on a major fault line, and known (though not very active) fault lines lie in eastern Canada, including the Ottawa–Hull region. The cost of earthquake coverage is based on insurance companies' assessment of the risk of your area and property type, so you shouldn't decide whether to buy insurance based on how small you think the risk is. The risk is already built in to the price.

  Many communities across the country face potential damage from floods. And as those living in southern Alberta when the Red Deer River overflowed its banks in 2005 found out, floods are a very real and often financially devastating catastrophe. Communities in Quebec, Ontario, and Manitoba have also suffered extensive and costly damage from floods. But, like earthquakes, floods are not a covered risk in standard homeowner's policies, so you need to purchase a flood insurance rider. Check with your current insurer or with the insurers we recommend in this chapter.

- ✔ **"The government will bail me out."** The vast majority of government financial assistance is obtained through low-interest loans. Loans, unfortunately, need to be repaid, and that money comes out of your pocket. Even if you do receive government money with no strings attached, it may be a long time in coming and likely won't come anywhere near to covering all of your losses.

✔ **"In a major disaster, insurers would go bankrupt anyway."** This is highly unlikely given the reserves insurers are required to keep and the fact that the insurance companies reinsure — that is, they buy insurance to back up the policies they write. Also, regulatory agencies facilitate the merging of faltering insurers into strong entities.

People who have little equity in their property and are willing to walk away from their property and mortgage in the event of a major quake or flood may consider not buying earthquake or flood coverage. Keep in mind that walking away damages your credit report, because you're essentially defaulting on your loan.

You may be able to pay for much of the cost of earthquake or flood insurance by raising the deductibles (discussed in the next section) on the main part of your homeowner's/renter's insurance and other insurance policies (such as auto insurance). You can more easily afford the smaller claims, not the big ones. If you think flood or earthquake insurance is expensive, compare those costs with the expenditures you would incur to completely replace your home and personal property. Buy this insurance if you live in an area that has a chance of being affected by these catastrophes. To help keep the cost of earthquake insurance down, consider taking a 10 percent deductible. Most insurers offer deductibles of 5 or 10 percent of the cost to rebuild your home. Ten percent of the rebuilding cost is a good chunk of money. But losing the other 90 percent is what you want to insure against.

Deductibles: Your cost with a claim

As we discuss in Chapter 16, the point of insurance is to protect against catastrophic losses, not the little losses. By taking the highest deductibles you're comfortable with, you save on insurance premiums year after year, and you don't have to go through the hassle of filing small claims.

Special discounts

You may qualify for special discounts. Companies and agents that sell homeowner's and renter's insurance don't always check to see whether you're eligible for discounts. After all, the more you spend on policy premiums, the more money they make! If your property has a security system, you're older, or you have other policies with the same insurer, you may qualify for a lower rate. Remember to ask.

Also, be aware that insurers use your credit score as a factor in setting some of your insurance rates. They do this because their studies have shown that folks who have higher credit scores tend to have fewer accidents and insurance claims. See Chapter 2 for how to assess and improve your credit reports and scores.

Buying homeowner's or renter's insurance

Each insurance company prices its homeowner's and renter's policies based on its own criteria. So the lowest-cost company for your friend's property may not be the lowest-cost company for you. You have to shop around at several companies to find the best rates. The following list features companies that historically offer lower-cost policies for most people and have decent track records regarding customer satisfaction and the payment of claims:

- ✔ BelairDirect (888-280-8549; www.belairdirect.com)
- ✔ Coseco Insurance Company (formerly DirectProtect) (800-810-4990; www.coseco.ca)
- ✔ Desjardins General Insurance (formerly Certas Direct) (877-699-9923; www.desjardinsgeneralinsurance.com)
- ✔ e-Insurers (800-563-7283800; www.e-insurers.com)
- ✔ President's Choice Financial (877-251-8652; www.pcinsurance.ca)
- ✔ RBC Insurance (877-749-7224; www.rbcinsurance.com)

Don't worry that some of these companies require you to fill out a form online or call a toll-free number for a price quote. This process saves you money, because these insurers generally don't have to pay commissions to local agents hawking their policies. These companies have local claims representatives to help you if and when you have a claim.

A number of the companies mentioned in the preceding list sell other types of insurance (for example, life insurance) that may not be as competitively priced. Be sure to check out the relevant sections in this part of the book for the best places to buy these other types of coverage if you need them.

Some provincial insurance departments conduct surveys to determine the insurers' prices and tabulate complaints received. Look under "Insurance" in the blue pages (the government section) of your local phone directory, or visit the Web site of the Financial Services Commission of Ontario (www.fsco.gov.on.ca) for a list of provincial and federal regulators that oversee each province's insurance companies.

Auto Insurance 101

Over the course of your life, you may spend tens of thousands of dollars on auto insurance. Much of the money people spend on auto insurance is not spent where it's needed most. In other cases, the money is simply wasted. Look for the following important features when searching for an auto insurance policy.

Bodily injury/property damage liability

As with homeowner's liability insurance, auto liability insurance provides insurance against lawsuits. Accidents happen, especially with a car. To protect yourself, you need *third-party liability coverage,* which has two components.

The first part gives you coverage to pay for harm done to others — called *bodily injury liability insurance.* The second part — *property damage liability insurance* — covers you against damage caused by your vehicle to someone else's property. This coverage is a provincial requirement, but the amounts are quite low — $50,000 to $200,000, depending on your province. (Typically your premiums for the two coverage components are broken out, but with one single combined figure for your total liability coverage.)

If you're just beginning to accumulate assets, don't mistakenly assume that you don't need any more than the required minimum amount of coverage. Your future earnings, which are an asset, can be garnished in a lawsuit. Make sure that you have at least enough to cover your assets. Preferably, your coverage should be two to five times your assets.

Uninsured or underinsured motorist liability

When you're in an accident with another motorist and she doesn't carry her own liability protection (or doesn't carry enough), *uninsured or underinsured motorist liability coverage* allows you to collect for lost wages, medical expenses, and pain and suffering incurred in the accident.

If you already have comprehensive health and long-term disability insurance, uninsured or underinsured motorist liability coverage is largely redundant, but it is still generally required.

To provide a death benefit to those financially dependent on you in the event of a fatal auto accident, buy term life insurance (see Chapter 17).

Coping with teen drivers

If you have a teenage driver in your household, you're going to be spending a lot more on auto insurance (in addition to worrying a lot more). As soon as you decide to allow your teenager to drive, you can take a number of steps to avoid spending all your take-home pay on auto insurance bills:

✔ Make sure that your teen does well in school. Some insurers offer discounts if your child is a strong academic achiever and has successfully completed a driver's education class (which is not required).

✔ Get price quotes from several insurers to see how adding your teen driver to your policy affects the cost.

✔ Have your teenager share in the costs of using the car. If you pay all the insurance, gas, and maintenance bills, your teenager won't value the privilege of using your "free" car.

Of course, teen driving involves more than just keeping your insurance bills to a minimum. Auto accidents are the number-one cause of death for teens.

Deductibles

To minimize your auto insurance premiums and eliminate the need to file small claims, take the highest deductibles you're comfortable with. (Most people should consider a $500 to $1,000 deductible.) On an auto policy, two deductibles exist: collision and comprehensive. *Collision* applies to — no surprise here — claims arising from collisions. (Note that if you have collision coverage on your own policy, you can generally bypass collision coverage when you rent a car. However, be sure to first check with your insurer as to whether this applies to your particular policy.) *Comprehensive* applies to other claims for damages not caused by collision (for example, a window broken by vandals).

As your car ages and loses its value, you can eventually eliminate your comprehensive and collision coverages altogether. The point at which you do this is up to you. Insurers won't pay more than the book value of your car, regardless of what it costs to repair or replace it. Remember that the purpose of insurance is to compensate you for losses that are financially catastrophic to you. For some people, this amount may be as high as $5,000 or more — others may choose $1,000 as their threshold point.

Special discounts

You may be eligible for special discounts on auto insurance. Don't forget to tell your agent or insurer if your car has a security alarm, air bags, or anti-lock brakes. If you're older or you have other policies or cars insured with the same insurer, you may also qualify for discounts. And make sure that you're given appropriate "good driver" discounts if you've been accident- and ticket-free in recent years.

And here's another idea: *Before* you buy your next car, call insurers and ask for insurance quotes for the different models you're considering. The cost of insuring a car should factor into your decision of which car you buy, because the insurance costs represent a major portion of your car's ongoing operating expenses.

Little-stuff coverage to skip

Auto insurers have dreamed up all sorts of extras to sell you as part of your coverage — called *riders* — such as towing and rental car reimbursement. On the surface, these riders appear to be inexpensive. But they're expensive given the little amount you'd collect from a claim and the hassle of filing.

Riders that waive the deductible under certain circumstances make no sense, either. The point of the deductible is to reduce your policy cost and eliminate the hassle of filing small claims.

Accident benefits coverage replaces some of your income that is lost due to an accident, and pays for some other medical expenses. If you and your passengers are covered by a provincial health plan and you have disability insurance, this rider coverage isn't usually necessary. This is especially true when you are also covered by an extended health benefit plan. However, almost all provinces require you to carry a minimum level of this type of coverage.

Roadside assistance, towing, and rental car reimbursement coverage pay only small dollar amounts, and they aren't worth buying. In fact, you may already have some of these coverages through membership in an automobile club or as a feature of your credit card.

Buying auto insurance

You can use the homeowner's insurers list we present earlier in this chapter to obtain quotes for auto insurance, including university alumni associations, and organizations such as the Canadian Automobile Association, which often offer competitive rates for both automobile and property insurance.

Protecting against Mega-Liability: Umbrella Insurance

Umbrella insurance (which is also referred to as *excess liability insurance*) is additional liability insurance that's added on top of the liability protection on your home and car(s). If, for example, you have $700,000 in assets, you can buy a $1 million umbrella liability policy to add to the $300,000 liability insurance that you have on your home and car. Expect to pay a couple hundred dollars — a small cost for big protection. Each year, thousands of people suffer lawsuits of more than $1 million related to their cars and homes.

Umbrella insurance is generally sold in increments of $1 million. So how do you decide how much you need if you have a lot of assets? You should have at least enough liability insurance to protect your assets and preferably enough to cover twice the value of those assets.

To purchase umbrella insurance, start by contacting your existing homeowner's or auto insurance company.

Planning Your Estate

Estate planning is the process of determining what will happen to your assets after you die. Considering your mortality in the context of insurance may seem a bit odd. But the time and cost of various estate-planning manoeuvres is really nothing more than buying insurance: You're ensuring that, after you die, everything will be taken care of as you wish, and taxes will be minimized. Thinking about estate planning in this way can help you better evaluate whether certain options make sense at particular points in your life.

Depending upon your circumstances, you may eventually want to contact a lawyer who specializes in estate-planning matters. However, educating yourself first about the different options is worth your time. More than a few lawyers have their own agendas about what you should do, so be careful. And most of the estate-planning strategies that you're likely to benefit from don't require hiring a lawyer.

(For more in-depth information about estate planning, check out *Wills & Estate Planning For Canadians For Dummies,* by Margaret Kerr and JoAnn Kurtz, published by Wiley.)

Wills, living wills, and medical powers of attorney

When you have children who are minors (dependants), a will is a necessity. The will names the guardian to whom you entrust your children if both you and your spouse die. Should you and your spouse both die without a will (called *intestate*), your province (courts and social-service agencies) will decide who will raise your children. Therefore, even if you can't decide at this time who you want to raise your children, you should *at least* appoint a trusted guardian who can decide for you.

Having a will makes good sense even if you don't have kids, because it gives instructions on how to handle and distribute all your worldly possessions. If you die without a will, provincial rules determine how your money and other property will be distributed. Therefore, your friends, distant relatives, and favourite charities will probably receive nothing.

Without a will, your heirs are largely legally powerless, and the province may appoint a public executor to supervise the distribution of your assets at a fee of around 5 percent of your estate.

A living will and a medical power of attorney are useful additions to a standard will. A *living will* tells your doctor and your family what, if any, life-support measures you prefer. A *medical* (or *health care*) *power of attorney* grants authority to someone you trust to make decisions regarding your medical care options.

The simplest and least costly way to prepare a will, a living will, and a medical power of attorney is to use the high-quality, user-friendly software packages that we recommend in Chapter 20. You may then want to have a lawyer go over them for you to ensure you've covered all the bases and the documents are legally sound. Be sure to give copies of these documents to the guardians and executors named in the documents.

You don't need a lawyer to make a legal will. Most lawyers, in fact, prepare wills and living trusts using software packages! What makes a will valid is that two people witness your signing it.

If preparing the will all by yourself seems overwhelming, you can (instead of hiring a lawyer) use a paralegal service to help you prepare the documents. These services generally charge 50 percent or less of what a lawyer charges.

Avoiding probate through living trusts

Because of our quirky legal system, even if you have a will, some or all of your assets must go through a court process known as probate. *Probate* is the legal process for administering and implementing the directions in a will.

Property and assets that are owned in joint tenancy generally pass to heirs without having to go through probate. If you have designated a beneficiary, proceeds from an RRSP, RRIF, or insurance policy also do not require probate. Your family home, joint bank account, and other assets should also not be subject to probate if you register their ownership as "joint and survivor", sometimes also referred to as "joint with rights of survivorship". Most other assets pass through probate.

A *living trust* effectively transfers assets into a trust. As the trustee, you control those assets, and you can revoke the trust whenever you desire. The advantage of a living trust is that upon your death, assets can pass directly to your beneficiaries without going through probate. Probate can be a lengthy, expensive hassle for your heirs — with legal fees tallying as high as 1.5 percent of the value of the estate, depending on your province. In addition, your assets become a matter of public record as a result of probate.

Living trusts are likely to be of greatest value to people who meet one or more of the following criteria (the more that apply, the more value trusts have):

- Age 60 or older
- Single
- Assets worth more than $1 million that must pass through probate (including real estate, non-retirement accounts, and small businesses)

As with a will, you do *not* need a lawyer to establish a legal and valid living trust. (See our software recommendations in Chapter 20 and consider the paralegal services that we mention in the preceding section on wills.) Legal fees for establishing a living trust can range from hundreds to thousands of dollars. Hiring a lawyer is of greatest value to people with large estates (see the next section) who do not have the time, desire, and expertise to maximize the value derived from estate planning.

Note: Living trusts keep assets out of probate but have nothing to do with minimizing capital gains taxes triggered by your death.

Planning your estate to minimize taxes triggered by your death

Even though Canada doesn't have estate tax laws like those faced by Americans, your death will likely result in one final tax bill — a potentially large one! When you die, the government taxes your stocks, funds, real estate, and other assets as if you had sold them all at their fair market value at the time of your death. If those assets are worth more than their purchase price, the result will generally be a taxable capital gain.

The critical exception to this rule occurs when you leave your assets to your spouse, including a common-law spouse. If you do, the assets simply transfer tax-free to your spouse. When he or she in turn dies, the difference between the original purchase price and the market value at that time will be used to calculate any taxable gains. The rule also doesn't apply when you leave your assets to a spousal trust.

In addition, the assets in your registered plans such as an RRSP or RRIF are treated as regular income in the year that you die, and also taxed. However, you can avoid this tax bill by naming your spouse as the beneficiary of any RRSPs or RRIFs. Your spouse can then transfer the assets tax-free to his or her own RRSP or RRIF.

Whether you need to do some planning to reduce the tax bill that will arise when you die depends on several issues. How much of your assets you're going to use up during your life is the first and most important issue you need to consider. This amount depends on how much your assets grow over time, as well as how rapidly you spend money. During retirement, you'll (hopefully) be utilizing at least some of your money.

We've seen too many affluent individuals worry throughout their retirement about how taxes will impact their estate. If your intention is to leave your money to your children, grandchildren, or a charity, why not start giving while you're still alive so that you can enjoy the act? No limitations apply on the amount of money you can give away to adult family members other than your spouse.

If you give assets to your spouse while you are living, you'll be subject to the *attribution rules*. Whether you give cash, stocks, or bonds, you'll generally be taxed on any income or loss or any capital gains (or losses) on that money or investments. If you give your children or others assets beyond cold hard cash, there may also be a tax bill to pay. If you give away assets, Canada Revenue Agency deems that you have sold those assets at their market value. Any difference between what you paid and the value at the time you gave them away will be deemed a taxable capital gain.

In addition to gifting, establishing in your will that a trust will be set up when you die — called a *testamentary trust* — can also help reduce taxes. With a testamentary trust, you can choose to have some or all of your assets transferred to the trust when you die, with your intended heirs named as the beneficiaries.

Cash-value life insurance is another estate planning tool. Unfortunately, it's a tool that's overused — or, we should say, oversold. People who sell cash-value insurance — that is, insurance salespeople and others masquerading as financial planners — too often advocate life insurance as the one and only way to minimize taxes due upon your death. Other methods for reducing these taxes are usually superior, because they don't require wasting money on life insurance.

Small-business owners whose businesses are worth several million dollars or more may want to consider cash-value life insurance under specialized circumstances. If you lack the necessary additional assets to pay expected taxes and don't want your beneficiaries to be forced to sell the business, you can buy cash-value life insurance to pay expected estate taxes.

Part V
Where to Go for More Help

The 5th Wave   By Rich Tennant

"...and don't tell me I'm not being frugal enough. I hired a man last week to do nothing but clip coupons!"

In this part . . .

We help you sift through the morass of financial resources competing for your attention and dollars. Many people who call themselves financial planners claim to be able to make you rich, but we show you how you may end up poorer if you don't choose an adviser wisely. We also cover software and Internet resources and name the best of the bunch — and point out some pitfalls to watch for on financial Web sites. Finally, we discuss how to benefit from the financial coverage in print and on the air, as well as how to sidestep the sometimes problematic advice in these media.

Chapter 19

Working with Financial Planners

In This Chapter

▶ Checking out your financial management options

▶ Determining whether you need help from a financial planner

▶ Understanding why it's hard to find good financial help

▶ Searching for a stellar financial planner

▶ Interviewing financial planners before you hire them

*H*iring a competent and ethical financial planner or adviser to help you make and implement financial decisions can be money well spent. But if you pick a poor adviser or someone who really isn't a financial planner but a salesperson in disguise, your financial situation can get worse instead of better. So before we talk about the different types of help to hire, we discuss the options you have for directing the management of your personal finances.

Surveying Your Financial Management Options

Everyone has three basic choices for managing money: You can do nothing, you can do it yourself, or you can hire someone to help you. This section lays out these three options in more detail.

Doing nothing

The do-nothing approach has a large following (and you thought you were alone!). People who fall into this category may be leading exciting, interesting lives and are therefore too busy to attend to something as mundane as dealing with their personal finances. Or they may be leading mundane existences but are too busy fantasizing about more-appealing ways to spend their time.

But the dangers of doing nothing are many. Putting off saving for retirement or ignoring your buildup of debt eventually comes back to haunt you. If you don't carry adequate insurance, accidents can be devastating. Fires, earthquakes, flooding, and hurricanes show how precarious living in paradise actually is.

If you've been following the do-nothing approach all your life, you're now officially promoted out of it! You bought this book to find out more about personal finance and make changes in your money matters, right? So take control and keep reading!

Doing it yourself

The do-it-yourselfers learn enough about financial topics to make informed decisions on their own. Doing anything yourself, of course, requires you to invest some time in learning the basic concepts and keeping up with changes. For some, personal financial management becomes a challenging and absorbing interest. Others focus on what they need to do to get the job done efficiently.

The idea that you're going to spend endless hours on your finances if you direct them yourself is a myth. The hardest part of managing money for most people is catching up on things that they should have done previously. After you get things in order, which you can easily do with this book as your companion, you shouldn't have to spend more than an hour or two working on your personal finances every few months (unless a major issue, like a real estate purchase, comes up).

Some people in the financial advisory business like to make what they do seem so complicated that they compare it to brain surgery! Their argument goes, "You wouldn't perform brain surgery on yourself, so why would you manage your money yourself?" Well, to this we say, "Personal financial management ain't brain surgery — not even close." You can manage on your own. In fact, you can do a better job than most advisers. Why? Because you're not subject to their conflicts of interest, and you care the most about your money.

Hiring financial help

Realizing that you need to hire someone to help you make and implement financial decisions can be a valuable insight. Spending a few hours and several hundred dollars to hire a competent professional can be money well spent, even if you have a modest income or assets. But you need to know what your money is buying.

Financial planners or advisers make money in one of three ways:

- ✔ They earn commissions based on the sales of financial products.

- ✔ They charge a percentage of the assets they invest on your behalf.

- ✔ They charge by the hour (this can also be done through fixed-fee arrangements).

The following sections help you differentiate among the three main types of financial planners.

Commission-based "planners"

Commission-based planners aren't really planners, advisers, or counsellors at all — they're salespeople. Many stockbrokers and insurance brokers are now called *financial consultants* or *financial service representatives* in order to glamourize the profession and obscure how they're compensated. Ditto for insurance salespeople calling themselves *estate planning specialists.*

Salespeople and brokers masquerading as planners can have an enormous self-interest when they push certain products, particularly those products that pay generous commissions. Getting paid on commission tends to skew their recommendations toward certain strategies (such as buying investment or life-insurance products) and to cause them to ignore or downplay other aspects of your finances. For example, they'll gladly sell you an investment rather than persuade you to pay off your high-interest debts or save and invest through your employer's retirement plan, thereby reducing your taxes.

Table 19-1 gives you an idea of the commissions that a financial planner/ salesperson can earn by selling particular financial products.

Table 19-1	Financial Product Commissions
Product	*Commission*
Life Insurance ($250,000, age 45):	
Term life	$150 to $600
Universal/whole life	$1,000 to $2,500
Disability Insurance:	
$4,000/month benefit, age 35	$350 to $1,400
Investments ($20,000):	
Mutual funds	$200 to $1,200
Limited partnerships	$1,400 to $2,000
Annuities	$1,000 to $2,000

Percentage-of-assets-under-management advisers

A financial adviser who charges a percentage of the assets that are being managed or invested is generally a better choice than a commission-based planner. This compensation system removes the incentive to sell you products with high commissions and initiate lots of transactions (to generate more of those commissions).

The fee-based system is an improvement over product-pushers working on commission, but it has flaws, too. Suppose you're trying to decide whether to invest in stocks, bonds, or real estate. A planner who earns his living managing your money likely won't recommend real estate, because that will deplete your investment capital. The planner also won't recommend paying down your mortgage for the same reason — he'll claim that you can earn more investing your money (with his help, of course) than it'll cost you to borrow.

Fee-based planners are also only interested in managing the money of those who have already accumulated a fair amount of it — which rules out most people. Many have minimums of $250,000, $500,000, or more.

Hourly-based advisers

Your best bet for professional help with your personal finances is an adviser who charges for his time. Because he doesn't sell any financial products, his objectivity is maintained. He doesn't perform money management, so he can help you make comprehensive financial decisions with loans, retirement planning, and the selection of good investments, including real estate, mutual funds, and small business.

Hiring someone incompetent is the primary risk you face when selecting an hourly-based planner. So be sure to check references and find out enough about finances on your own to discern between good and bad financial advice. Another risk comes from not clearly defining the work to be done and the approximate total cost (consider getting this all in writing) of the planner's service before you begin. Also review some of the other key questions that we outline in "Interviewing Financial Advisers: Asking the Right Questions," later in this chapter.

An entirely different kind of drawback occurs when you don't follow through on your adviser's recommendations. You pay for his work but don't act on it, so you don't capture its value. If part of the reason you hired the planner in the first place was that you're too busy or not interested enough to make changes to your financial situation, look for this type of support in the services you buy from the planner.

Some planners charge a fixed fee to whip up a financial plan for you. Remember to ask how much of their time is involved in working with you so that you can assess the amount you're paying per hour.

If you just need someone to act as a sounding board for ideas or to recommend a specific strategy or product, you can hire an hourly-based planner for one or two sessions of advice. You save money doing the legwork and implementation on your own. Just make sure the planner is willing to give you specific advice, so you can properly implement the strategy.

Deciding Whether to Hire a Financial Planner

If you're like most people, you don't need to hire a financial planner, but you may benefit from hiring some help at certain times in your life. Good reasons for hiring a financial planner can be similar to the reasons you may have for hiring someone to clean your home or do your taxes. If you're too busy, you don't enjoy doing it, or you're terribly uncomfortable making decisions on your own, using a planner for a second opinion makes good sense. And if you shy away from numbers and bristle at the thought of long division, a good planner can help you.

How a good financial adviser can help

The following list gives you a rundown of some of the important ways a competent financial planner can assist you:

- **Identifying problems and goals:** Many otherwise intelligent people have a hard time being objective about their financial problems. They may ignore their debts or have unrealistic goals and expectations given their financial situations and behaviours. And many are so busy with other aspects of their lives that they never take the time to think about what their financial goals are. A good financial planner can give you the objective perspective you need.

  Surprisingly, some people are in a better financial position than they think they are in relation to their goals. Good counsellors really enjoy this aspect of their jobs — good news is easier and much more fun to deliver.

- **Identifying strategies for reaching your financial goals:** Your mind may be a jumble of various plans, ideas, and concerns, along with a cobweb or two. A good planner can help you sort out your thoughts and propose alternative strategies for you to consider as you work to accomplish your financial goals.

✔ **Setting priorities:** You may be considering doing dozens of things to improve your financial situation, but making just a few key changes is likely to have the greatest value. Identifying the changes that fit your overall situation and that won't keep you awake at night is equally important. Good planners help you prioritize.

✔ **Saving research time and hassle:** Even if you know which major financial decisions are most important to you, doing the research needed to make them can be time-consuming and frustrating when you don't know where to turn for good information and advice. A good planner does research to match your needs to the best available strategies and products. So much lousy information on various financial topics is out there that you can easily get lost, discouraged, sidetracked, or swindled. A good adviser can prevent you from making a bad decision based on poor or insufficient information.

✔ **Purchasing commission-free financial products:** When you hire a planner who charges for his time, you can easily save hundreds or thousands of dollars by avoiding the cost of commissions in the financial products you buy. Purchasing commission-free is especially valuable when you buy investments and insurance.

✔ **Providing an objective voice for major decisions:** When you're trying to figure out when to retire, how much to spend on a home purchase, and where to invest your money, you're faced with some big decisions. Getting swept up in the emotions of these issues can cloud your perspective. A competent and sensitive adviser can help you cut through the confusion and provide you with sound counsel.

✔ **Helping you to just do it:** Deciding what you need to do is not enough — you have to actually do it. And although you can use a planner for advice and then make all the changes on your own, a good counsellor can help you follow through with your plan. After all, part of the reason you hired the adviser in the first place may be that you're too busy or uninterested to manage your finances.

✔ **Mediating:** If you have a spouse or partner, financial decisions — particularly money decisions involving the extended family — can produce real fireworks. Although a counsellor can't be a therapist, a good one can be sensitive to the different needs and concerns of each party and can try to find middle ground on the financial issues you're grappling with.

✔ **Making you money and allowing you peace of mind:** The whole point of professional financial planning is to help you make the most of your money and plan for and attain your financial and personal goals. In the process, the financial planner should show you how to enhance your investment returns; reduce your spending, taxes, and insurance costs; increase your savings; improve your catastrophic-insurance coverage; and achieve your financial-independence goals. Putting your financial house in order should take some weight off your mind — like that clean, lightheaded feeling after a haircut.

Why advisers aren't for everyone

Finding a good financial planner isn't easy, so make sure you want to hire an adviser before you venture out in search of a competent one.

Also consider your personality type before you decide to hire help. Our experience has been that some people (believe it or not) enjoy the research and number-crunching. If this sounds like you, or if you're not really comfortable taking advice, you may be better off doing your own homework and creating your own plan.

If you have a specific tax or legal matter, you may be better off hiring a good professional who specializes in that specific field rather than hiring a financial planner.

Recognizing conflicts of interest

All professions have conflicts of interest. Some fields have more than others, and the financial-planning field is one of those fields. Knowing where some of the land mines are located can certainly help. Here, then, are the most common reasons why planners may not have 20/20 vision when giving financial directions.

Selling and pushing products that pay commissions

If a financial planner isn't charging you a fee for his time, you can rest assured that he's earning commissions on the products he tries to sell you. To sell financial products, this planner generally needs a broker's licence. A person who sells financial products and then earns commissions from those products is a salesperson, *not* a financial planner. Financial planning done well involves taking an objective, holistic look at your financial puzzle to determine which pieces fit it well — something most brokers are neither trained nor financially motivated to do.

To make discerning a planner's agenda even harder, you can't assume that planners who charge fees for their time don't also earn commissions selling products. This compensation double dipping is common.

Selling products that provide a commission tends to skew a planner's recommendations. Products that carry commissions result in fewer of your dollars going to the investments and insurance you buy. Because a commission is earned only when a product is sold, such a product or service is inevitably more attractive in the planner's eyes than other options. For example, consider the case of a planner who sells disability insurance that you can obtain at a lower cost through your employer or a group trade association (see Chapter 17). He may overlook or criticize your most attractive option (buying through your employer) and focus on *his* most attractive option — selling you a higher-cost disability policy on which he derives a commission.

"Financial planning" in banks

Over recent decades, banks have witnessed an erosion of the money in their coffers and vaults because increasing numbers of investors have realized that banks are generally lousy places to build wealth. The highest-yielding bank savings accounts and guaranteed investment certificates barely keep an investor ahead of inflation. If you factor in both inflation and taxes, these bank "investments" provide no real growth on your investment dollars.

Increasingly, banks have "financial representatives" and "investment specialists" sitting in their branches, waiting to pounce on bank customers with big balances. In many banks, these "financial planners" are simply brokers who are out to sell investments that pay them (and the bank) hefty sales commissions.

Although you may expect your bank account balances to be confidential and off-limits to the eager eyes of investment salespeople in banks, numerous studies have demonstrated that banks are betraying customer trust.

Customers often have no idea that these bank reps are earning commissions and that those commissions are being siphoned out of customers' investment dollars. Many customers are mistaken (partly due to the banks' and salespeople's poor disclosure) in believing that these investments, like bank savings accounts, are CDIC-insured and cannot lose value.

Another danger of trusting the recommendation of a commission-based planner is that he may steer you toward the products that have the biggest payback for him. These products are among the *worst* for you because they siphon off even more of your money upfront to pay the commission. They also tend to be among the costliest and riskiest financial products available.

Planners who are commission-greedy may also try to *churn* your investments. They encourage you to buy and sell at the drop of a hat, attributing the need to changes in the economy or the companies you invested in. More trading means more commissions for the broker.

Taking a narrow view

Because of the way they earn their money, many planners are biased in favour of certain strategies and products. As a result, they typically don't keep your overall financial needs in mind. For example, if you have a problem with accumulated consumer debts, some planners may never know (or care) because they're focused on selling you an investment product. Likewise, a planner who sells a lot of life insurance tends to develop recommendations that require you to purchase it.

Failing to recommend saving through your employer's retirement plan

Taking advantage of saving through your employer's retirement savings plan(s) is one of your best financial options. Although this method of saving may not be as exciting as risking your money in cattle futures, it's not as dull as watching paint dry — and most importantly, it's generally tax-deductible. Some planners are reluctant to recommend taking full advantage of this option: It doesn't leave much money for the purchase of their commission-laden investment products.

Ignoring debts

Sometimes paying off outstanding loans — such as credit card, auto, or even mortgage debts — is your best investment option. But most financial planners don't recommend this strategy because paying down debts depletes the capital with which you could otherwise buy investments — the investments that the broker may be trying to sell you to earn a commission or that the adviser would like to manage for an ongoing fee.

Failing to recommend real estate and small-business investments

Investing in real estate and small business, like paying off debts, takes money away from your investing elsewhere. Most planners won't help with these choices. They may even tell you tales of real estate and small-business investing disasters to try to give you cold feet.

The value of real estate can go down just like any other investment. But over the long haul, owning real estate makes good financial sense for most people. With small business, the risks are higher, but so are the potential returns. Don't let a financial planner convince you that these options are foolish — in fact, if you do your homework and know what you're doing, you can make higher rates of return investing in real estate and small business than you can in traditional securities such as stocks and bonds.

That said, certain real estate and small-business investments can be risky, inefficient, and illiquid — so caution by an adviser informed in these fields (and that's a key point) may be helpful. See Part III to read more about your real estate and small-business investment options.

Selling ongoing money-management services

The vast majority of financial planners who don't work on commission make their money by managing your money for an ongoing fee percentage (typically 1 to 2 percent of your investment annually). Although this fee removes the incentive to *churn* your account (frequently trade your investments) to run up more commissions, the service is something that you're unlikely to need. (As we explain in Part III, you can hire professional money managers for less.)

An ongoing fee percentage still creates a conflict of interest: The financial planner will tend to steer you away from beneficial financial strategies that reduce the asset pool from which he derives his percentage. Financial strategies such as maximizing contributions to your employer's retirement savings plan, paying off debts like your mortgage, investing in real estate or small business, and so on may make the most sense for you. Advisers who work on a percentage-of-assets-under-management basis may be biased against such strategies.

Selling legal services

Some planners are in the business of drawing up trusts and providing other estate-planning services for their clients. Although these and other legal documents may be right for you, legal matters are complex enough that the competence of someone who isn't a full-time legal specialist should be carefully scrutinized. And lower-cost options may be available if your situation is not complicated.

If you need help determining whether you need these legal documents, do a little investigating: Do some additional reading or consult an adviser who won't actually perform the work. If you do ultimately hire someone to perform estate-planning services for you, make sure you hire someone who specializes in estate planning and works at it full time. See Chapter 18 to find out more about estate planning.

Scaring you unnecessarily

Some planners put together nifty computer-generated projections that show you're going to need millions of dollars by the time you retire to maintain your standard of living, or that tuition will cost hundreds of thousands of dollars by the time your 2-year-old is ready for university.

Waking up a client to the realities of his financial situation is an important and difficult job for good financial planners. But some planners take this task to an extreme, deliberately scaring you into buying what they're selling. They paint a bleak picture and imply you can fix your problems only if you do what they say. Don't let them scare you; read this book and get your financial life in order.

Creating dependency

Many financial planners create dependency by making things seem so complicated that their clients feel as though they could never manage their finances on their own. If your adviser is reluctant to tell you how you can educate yourself about personal money management, you probably have a self-perpetuating consultant. Financial planning is hardly the only occupation guilty of this. As author George Bernard Shaw put it, "All professions are conspiracies against the laity."

Finding a Good Financial Planner

Locating a good financial planner who is willing to work with the not-yet-rich-and-famous and who doesn't have conflicts of interest can feel like trying to find a needle in a haystack. Personal referrals and associations are two methods that can serve as good starting points.

Soliciting personal referrals

Getting a personal referral from a satisfied customer you trust is one of the best ways to find a good financial planner. Obtaining a referral from an accountant or lawyer whose judgment you've tested can help as well. (Beware that such professionals in other fields may also do some financial planning and recommend themselves.)

Warning signs in planners' cultivation techniques

The channel through which you hear of a planner may provide clues to the planner's integrity and way of doing business. Beware of planners you find (or who find you) through these avenues:

✔ **Cold calling:** You've just come home after a hard day. No sooner has your posterior hit the recliner to settle in for the night when the phone rings. It's Joe the financial planner, and he wants to help you achieve all your financial dreams. *Cold calling* (whereby the salesperson calls you, without an appointment) is the most inefficient way for a planner to get new clients. Cold calling is intrusive, and it's typically used by aggressive salespeople who work on commission.

✔ **Adult education classes:** Here's what often happens at adult education classes offered at local universities: You pay a reasonable fee for the course. You go to class giddy at the prospect of learning how to manage your finances. And then the instructor ends up being a broker or financial planner hungry

for clients. He confuses more than he conveys. He's short on specifics. But he's more than happy to show you the way if you contact (and hire) him outside of class.

The instructors for these courses are paid to teach. They don't need to solicit clients in class, and, in fact, it's unethical for them to do so. We should note, however, that part of the problem is that some schools take advantage of the fact that such "teachers" want to solicit business, setting the pay at a low level. So *never* assume that someone who is teaching a financial-planning course at a local college is ethical, competent, or looking out for your best interests. Although we may sound cynical, assume that these people are none of the above until they clearly prove otherwise.

Ethical instructors who are there to teach do *not* solicit clients. In fact, they may actively discourage students from hiring them. Smart universities and colleges pay

(continued)

(continued)

their instructors well and weed out those who are more interested in building up their client base than they are in teaching.

✔ **"Free" seminars:** This is a case of "you get what you pay for." Because you don't pay a fee to attend "free seminars" and the "teachers" don't get paid either, these events tend to be clear-cut sales pitches. The "instructor" may share some information, but smart seminar leaders know that the goal of a successful seminar is to establish themselves as experts and to whet the prospects' appetites.

Note: Be wary of seminars targeted at select groups, such as special seminars for people who have received retirement-plan distributions or seminars touting "Financial Planning for Women." Financial planning is not specific to gender, ethnicity, or marital status.

Don't assume that the financial planner giving a presentation at your employer's office is the right planner for you, either. You may be surprised at how little some corporate benefits departments investigate the people they let in. In most cases, planners are accepted simply because they don't charge.

The best financial planners continue to build their practices through word of mouth. Satisfied customers are a professional's best and least costly marketers. However, *never* take a recommendation from anyone as gospel. We don't care *who* is making the referral — even if it's your mother or the pope. You must do your homework. Ask the planner the questions we list in the upcoming section "Interviewing Financial Advisers: Asking the Right Questions." We've seen people get into real trouble because of blindly accepting someone else's recommendation. Remember that the person making the recommendation is (probably) not a financial expert. He may be just as bewildered as you are.

You may get referred to a planner or broker who returns the favour by sending business to the tax, legal, or real estate person who referred you. Hire professionals who make referrals to others based on their competence and ethics.

Seeking advisers through associations

Associations of financial planners are more than happy to refer you to planners in your area. But as we discuss earlier in this chapter, the major trade associations are composed of planners who sell products and work on commission. Here are two solid places to start searching for good financial planners:

- ✔ **The Institute of Advanced Financial Planners (IAFP)** (888-298-3292; www.iafp.ca) was founded in 2002 by Registered Financial Planners after their existing association — the Canadian Association of Financial Planners — merged with the Canadian Association of Insurance and Financial Advisers to form Advocis. (In French, the designation is Planificateur financier certifié, or PFC.) In addition to letting you find RFPs in your area, the IAFP site lets you search for planners that meet a number of different criteria. In particular, you can narrow your search by specifying the type of compensation — commission only, fee only, fee and commission, or salary. Put another way, this lets you come up with a shortlist of advisers according to how you want to pay for their services.

- ✔ **Advocis** (800-563-5822; www.advocis.ca) is the Web site of the Financial Advisers Association of Canada. Like the IAFP site, the Advocis Web site has a feature that allows you to search for financial planners. Be sure to scroll down on the search page so you can specify the credentials.

Interviewing Financial Advisers: Asking the Right Questions

Don't consider hiring a financial adviser until you read the rest of this book. If you're not educated about personal finance, how can you possibly evaluate the competence of someone you may hire to help you make important financial decisions?

We firmly believe that you are your own best financial adviser. However, we know that some people don't want to make financial decisions without getting assistance. Perhaps you're busy or simply can't stand making money decisions.

You need to recognize that you have a lot at stake when you hire a financial adviser. Besides the cost of his services, which generally don't come cheap, you're placing a lot of trust in his recommendations. The more you know, the better the adviser you end up working with, and the fewer services you need to buy.

The following questions will help you get to the core of an adviser's competence and professional integrity. Get answers to these questions *before* you decide to hire a financial adviser.

What percentage of your income comes from clients' fees versus commissions?

Anything less than 100 percent means that the person you're speaking to is a salesperson with a vested interest in recommending certain strategies and products.

Sadly, more than a few financial advisers don't tell the truth. In an undercover investigation done by *Money* magazine, nearly one-third of self-proclaimed fee-only advisers turned out to be brokers who also sold investment and insurance products on a commission basis.

How can you ferret these people out? The simplest way is to have them put down in writing exactly how they are compensated.

What portion of fees paid by clients is for money management versus hourly planning?

The answer to how the adviser is paid provides clues to whether he has an agenda to convince you to hire him to manage your money. If you want objective and specific financial planning recommendations, give preference to advisers who derive their income from hourly fees. Many counsellors and advisers call themselves "fee-based," which usually means that they make their living managing money for a percentage.

If you want a money manager, you can hire the best quite inexpensively through a mutual fund. Or, if you have substantial assets, you can hire an established money manager (refer to Chapter 10).

What is your hourly fee?

The rates for financial advisers range from as low as $50 to $75 per hour all the way up to several hundred dollars per hour. If you shop around, you can find fine planners who charge around $125 to $225 per hour. As you compare planners, remember that what matters is the total cost you can expect to pay for the services you're seeking.

Do you also perform tax or legal services?

Be somewhat wary of someone who claims to be an expert beyond one area. The tax, legal, and financial fields are vast in and of themselves, and they're difficult for even the best and brightest adviser to cover simultaneously.

One exception is the accountant who also performs some basic financial planning by the hour. Likewise, a good financial adviser should have a solid grounding in the basic tax and legal issues that relate to your personal finances. Large firms may have specialists available in different areas.

What work and educational experience qualifies you to be a financial planner?

This question doesn't have one right answer. Ideally, a planner should have experience in the business or financial services field. Some say to look for planners with at least five or ten years of experience. We've always wondered how planners earn a living their first five or ten years if folks won't hire them until they reach these benchmarks! A good planner should also be good with numbers, speak using plain jargon-free language, and have good interpersonal skills.

Education is sort of like food. Too little leaves you hungry. Too much can leave you feeling stuffed and uncomfortable. And a small amount of high quality is better than a lot of low quality.

Because investment decisions are a critical part of financial planning, take note of the fact that the most common designations of educational training among professional money managers are MBA (master of business administration) and CFA (chartered financial analyst).

Have you ever sold limited partnerships? Options? Futures? Commodities?

The correct answers here are *no, no, no,* and *no.* If you don't know what these disasters are, refer to Chapter 9. Also be wary of any financial adviser who used to deal in these areas but now claims to have seen the light and reformed his ways. (Some sophisticated advisers may use some of these instruments to hedge or reduce risk, but be sure you understand what they're doing and that you and the adviser fully understand all costs and potential risks.)

Professionals with poor judgment may not repeat the same mistakes, but they're more likely to make some new ones at your expense. Our experience is that even advisers who have been "reformed" are unlikely to be working by the hour. Most of them either work on commission or want to manage your money for a hefty fee.

Do you carry liability (errors and omissions) insurance?

Some counsellors may be surprised by this question or think that you're a problem customer looking for a lawsuit. On the other hand, accidents happen; that's why insurance exists. So if the planner doesn't have liability insurance, he has missed one of the fundamental concepts of planning: Insure against risk. Don't make the mistake of hiring him.

You wouldn't (and shouldn't) let contractors into your home to do work without knowing that they have insurance to cover any mistakes they make. Likewise, you should insist on hiring a planner who carries protection in case he makes a major mistake for which he is liable. Make sure that he carries enough coverage given what he is helping you with.

Can you provide references from clients with needs similar to mine?

Take the time to talk to other people who have used the planner. Ask what the planner did for them, and find out what the adviser's greatest strengths and weaknesses are. You can find out a bit about the planner's track record and style. And because you want to have as productive a relationship as possible with your planner, the more you find out about him, the easier it'll be for you to hit the ground running if you hire him.

Some financial advisers offer a "complimentary" introductory consultation. If an adviser offers a free consultation to allow you to check him out and it makes you feel more comfortable about hiring him, fair enough. But be careful: Most free consultations end up being a big sales pitch for certain products or services the adviser offers.

The fact that a planner doesn't offer a free consultation may be a good sign. Counsellors who are busy and who work strictly by the hour can't afford to burn an hour of their time for an in-person free session. They also need to be careful of folks seeking free advice. Such advisers usually are willing to spend some time on the phone answering background questions. They should also be able to send background materials by mail and provide references.

Will you provide specific strategies and product recommendations that I can implement on my own if I choose?

This is an important question. Some advisers may indicate that you can hire them by the hour. But then they provide only generic advice without specifics. Some planners even *double dip* — they charge an hourly fee initially to make you feel like you're not working with a salesperson, and then they try selling commission-based products. Also be aware of advisers who say that you can choose to implement their recommendations on your own and then recommend financial products that carry commissions.

How is implementation handled?

Ideally, you should find an adviser who lets you choose whether you want to hire him to help with implementation after the recommendations have been presented to you. If you know that you're going to follow through on the advice and you can do so without further discussions and questions, don't hire the planner to help you implement his recommendations.

On the other hand, if you hire the counsellor because you lack the time, desire, and/or expertise to manage your financial life in the first place, building implementation into the planning work makes good sense.

Learning from Others' Mistakes

Over the many years that we've worked in the personal finance world, we hear too many problems that people encounter from hiring incompetent and unethical financial advisers. To avoid repeating others' mistakes, please remember the following:

- **You absolutely must do your homework before hiring any financial adviser.** Despite recommendations from others about a particular adviser, you can end up with bad advice from biased advisers.

- **Avoid conflicts of interest.** The financial planning and brokerage fields are minefields for consumers. The fundamental problem is the enormous conflict of interest that is created when "advisers" sell products that earn them sales commissions. Selling ongoing money management services creates a conflict of interest as well.

Imagine that you have flu symptoms. Would you be comfortable seeing a physician who didn't charge for office visits but instead made money only by selling you drugs? Maybe you don't need the drugs — or at least not so many expensive ones. Maybe what you really need is Mom's chicken soup and ten hours of sleep.

✔ **You are your own best advocate.** The more you know, and the more you understand that investing and other financial decisions needn't be complicated, the more you realize that you don't need to spend gobs of money (or any money at all) on financial planners and advisers. When you look in the mirror, you see the person who has your best interests at heart and is your best financial adviser.

Chapter 20

Using a Computer to Manage Your Money

In This Chapter

▶ Evaluating the different types of software and Web sites

▶ Performing financial tasks with your computer

*A*lthough a computer may be able to assist you with your personal finances, it simply represents one of many tools. Computers are best for performing routine tasks (such as processing lots of bills or performing many calculations) quickly and for aiding you with research.

This chapter gives you an overview of how to use software and cyberspace as you work with your finances. We tell you how to use this technology to pay your bills, prepare taxes, research investments, plan for retirement, trade securities, buy insurance, and plan your estate. We also direct you to the best software and Web sites.

Surveying Software and Web Sites

You can access two major repositories of personal finance information using your computer. Although the lines are blurring between these two categories, they're roughly defined as software and the Internet:

- ✔ *Software* refers to computer programs that are packaged in a box or DVD case or are available to be downloaded online. Most of the mass-marketed financial software packages sell for under $100.

- ✔ Most of the financial stuff on the Internet is supplied by companies marketing their wares and, hence, is available for free. Some sites sell their content for a fee.

Adding up financial software benefits

Although the number of personal finance software packages and Web sites is large and growing, quality has always had a hard time keeping up with quantity, especially among the free Internet sites. The best software can:

- ✔ Guide you to better organization and management of your personal finances
- ✔ Help you complete mundane tasks or complex calculations quickly and easily and provide basic advice in unfamiliar territory
- ✔ Make you feel in control of your financial life

Mediocre and bad software, on the other hand, can make you feel stupid or, at the very least, make you want to tear your hair out. Lousy products usually end up in the software graveyard.

Having reviewed many of the packages available, we can assure you that if you're having a hard time with some of the programs out there (and sometimes even with the more useful programs), you're not at fault. Too many software applications assume that you already know things such as your tax rate, your mortgage options, and the difference between stock and bond mutual funds. Much of what's out there is also too technically oriented, and most programs aren't user-friendly. Some are even flawed in their financial accuracy.

A good software package, like a good tax or financial adviser, should help you better manage your finances. It should simply and concisely explain financial terminology, and it should help you make decisions by offering choices and recommendations, allowing you to play with alternatives before following a particular course of action.

With increasing regularity, financial software packages are being designed to perform more than one task or to address more than one area of personal finances. But remember that no software package covers the whole range of issues in your financial life. Later in this chapter, we recommend some of our favourite financial software.

Surfing hazards online

Like the information you receive from any medium, you have to sift out the good from the bad when you surf the Internet. If you blindly navigate the Internet and naively think that what's out there is useful "information," "research," or "objective advice," you're in for a rude awakening.

Most personal-finance sites on the Internet are free, which — guess what — means that these sites are basically advertising or are dominated and driven by advertising. If you're looking for material written by unbiased experts or writers, well, finding it on the Web may seem like searching for the proverbial needle in the haystack because the vast majority of what's online is biased and uninformed.

Considering the source so you can recognize bias

A report on the Internet published by a leading investment-banking firm provides a list of the "coolest finance" sites. On the list is the Web site of a major bank. Because it has been a long time since we were in high school, we're not quite sure what "cool" means anymore. If cool can be used to describe a well-organized and graphically pleasing Web site, then we guess we can say that the bank's site is cool.

However, if you're looking for sound information and advice, then the bank's site is decidedly uncool. It steers you in a financial direction that benefits (not surprisingly) the bank and not you. For example, in the real-estate section, users are asked to plug in their gross monthly income and down payment. The information is then used to spit out the supposed amount that users can "afford" to spend on a home. No mention is given to the other financial goals and concerns — such as saving for retirement — that affect one's ability to spend a particular amount of money on a home.

Consider this advice in the lending area of the site: "When you don't have the cash on hand for important purchases, we can help you borrow what you need. From a new car, to that vacation you've been longing for, to new kitchen appliances, you can make these dreams real now." Click on a button at the bottom of this screen — and presto, you're on your way to racking up credit card and auto debt. Why bother practising delayed gratification, living within your means, or buying something used if getting a loan is "easy" and comes with "special privileges"?

Watching out for "sponsored" content

Sponsored content, a euphemism for advertising under the guise of editorial content (known in the print media as advertorials), is another big problem to watch out for on Web sites. You may find a disclaimer or note, which is often buried in small print in an obscure part of the Web site, saying that an article is sponsored by (in other words, paid advertising by) the "author."

A mutual fund site, for example, states that its "primary purpose is to provide viewers with an independent guide that contains information and articles they can't get anywhere else." The "content" of the site suggests otherwise. In the "Expert's Corner" section, material is reprinted from a newsletter that advocates frequent trading in and out of mutual funds to try to guess and time market moves. Turns out the article is "sponsored by the featured expert" — in other words, it's a paid advertisement. (The track record of the newsletter's past recommendations, which isn't discussed on the site, is poor.)

Even more troubling is the increasing number of Web sites that fail to disclose (even cryptically) that their "content" comes from advertisers. Print publications generally have a tradition for disclosing when an article is paid advertising, but in the Wild West atmosphere online, many sites fail to make this important disclosure. Mind you, we're not saying that disclosure makes paid-for content okay — we're simply stating that a lack of disclosure makes an already bad situation even worse.

Also, beware of Web sites, especially those that are "free," that make money in a clandestine way from two sources: companies whose products they praise, and affiliates to whom they direct mouse clicks/Web traffic. In perusing the Web, for example, we noticed that many "free" financial sites were singing the praises of the software You Need a Budget (YNAB). After test-driving the product (which is like a slimmed-down version of Quicken or Microsoft Money), it was clear that it's a decent but not exceptional product. However, we uncovered the fact that the makers of YNAB pay a whopping 35-percent commission to Web site affiliates who pitch and direct users to buy the product. At the time, YNAB Pro was their most popular product and was selling for $49.95, so a Web site flogging it for them was pocketing $17.48 for each copy it sold. Does that taint a site's recommendation of YNAB? Of course it does.

Increasingly, companies are paying Web sites outright to simply mention and praise their products; doing so is incredibly sleazy even when it's disclosed, but to do so without disclosure is unethical. Also, beware of links to recommended product and service providers to do business with — more often than not, the referring Web site gets paid an affiliate fee. Look for sites that post policies against receiving such referral fees from companies whose products and services they recommend.

Steering clear of biased financial planning advice

We also suggest skipping the financial planning advice offered by financial service companies that are out to sell you something. Such companies can't take the necessary objective, holistic view required to render useful advice.

For example, on one major mutual fund company's Web site, you'll find a good deal of material on the company's mutual funds. The site's financial planning advice is, unfortunately, off the mark: It urges readers to think of investing as putting money into financial instruments, and quickly moves on to — you guessed it — the benefits of mutual funds. It makes no mention of the fact that paying off high-cost consumer debt usually offers the best return, and that real estate and even small business are also worth considering. If you did that, though, you would put less money into mutual funds, which this area of the site prods you to do.

Shunning short-term thinking

Many financial Web sites provide real-time stock quotes as a hook to a site that is cluttered with advertising. Our experience working with individual investors is that the more short-term they think, the worse they do. And checking your portfolio during the trading day certainly promotes short-term thinking.

Another way that sites create an addictive environment to get you to return multiple times daily is to constantly provide news and other rapidly changing content. Do you really need "breaking news" updates that gasoline prices jumped 4 cents a litre over the past two weeks, or that *So You Think You Can Dance Canada* is having a contest with a Hollywood celebrity on Twitter to see who can sign up more followers in the next week?

Also, beware of tips offered around the electronic water cooler — message boards. As in the real world, chatting with strangers and exchanging ideas are sometimes fine. However, if you don't know the identity and competence of message-board posters or chat-room participants, why would you follow their financial advice or stock tips? Getting ideas from various sources is okay, but educate yourself and do your homework before making personal financial decisions.

If you want to best manage your personal finances and find out more, remember that the old expression "You get what you pay for" contains a grain of truth. Free information on the Internet, especially information provided by companies in the financial services industry, is largely self-serving. Stick with information providers who have proven themselves offline, or who don't have anything to sell except objective information and advice.

Accomplishing Money Tasks on Your Computer

In the remainder of this chapter, we detail important personal financial tasks that your computer can assist you with. We also provide our recommendations for the best software and Web sites to help you accomplish these chores.

Paying your bills and tracking your money

Plenty of folks have trouble saving money and reducing their spending. Thus, it's no surprise that in the increasingly crowded universe of free Web sites, plenty are devoted to supposedly helping you to reduce your spending.

More of these sites keep springing up, but among those you may have heard of and stumbled upon are Cake Financial, Geezeo, Mint, Wesabe, and Yodlee. As you can already see, attracting attention online starts with having a quirky name! We've kicked the tires and checked out these sites and frankly have mixed to negative feelings about them. Beyond their heavily American focus, the biggest problems we have with these sites are that they are loaded with advertising and/or have affiliate relationships with companies. What does this mean? The site gets paid when you click on a link to one of its recommended service providers and buy what it's selling.

We will give credit to Mint for at least admitting in black and white that it is soliciting and receiving affiliate payments when it states on its site:

> "How is Mint.com free? We make money when you save money with the Ways To Save feature on Mint.com. If you sign up for a checking, savings, credit card or brokerage account marked as sponsored, we earn a referral fee."

This, of course, creates an enormous conflict of interest and thoroughly taints any recommendation made by Mint and similar sites that profit from affiliate referrals. For starters, they have no incentive or reason to recommend companies that won't pay them an affiliate fee. And they provide little — if any — screening of companies for quality service levels that are important to you as a consumer.

Also, be forewarned that after registering you as a site user, the first thing most of these sites want you to do is connect directly to your financial institutions (banks, brokerages, investment companies) and download your investment account and spending data. If your instincts tell you this might not be a good idea, you should trust your instincts. Yes, security concerns do exist, but those pale in comparison to privacy concerns and concerns about the endless pitching to you of products and services.

Another problem that we have with these Web sites is the incredibly simplistic calculators they have. One that purported to help with retirement planning didn't allow users to choose a retirement age younger than 62 and had no provisions for part-time work. When it asked about your assets, it made no distinction between equity in your home and financial assets (stocks, bonds, mutual funds, and so on). Finally, if you encounter a problem using these sites, they generally offer no phone support, so you're relegated to ping-ponging e-mails in the hopes of getting your questions answered.

Quicken and Microsoft Money are good software programs that we've reviewed that help with expense tracking and bill paying. However, Microsoft Money has been discontinued, so Quicken is the best program we can recommend.

In addition to offering printed cheques and electronic bill payment, Quicken is a financial organizer. The program allows you to list your investments and other assets, along with your loans and other financial liabilities.

Quicken automates the process of paying your bills, and it can track your cheque-writing and prepare reports that detail your spending by category so you can get a handle on where the fat in your budget is. (For a complete discussion on how to track your spending, see Chapter 3.)

In addition to the significant investment of time necessary to figure out how to use Quicken, another drawback is the cost of computer cheques if you buy them from the software company. You can chop those costs by ordering from other companies.

You can avoid dealing with paper cheques — written or printed — by signing up for online bill payment. With such services, you save on cheques, stamps, and envelopes. Such services are available to anyone with a chequing account through an increasing number of banks and credit unions, as well as through Quicken. Another option is to use Canada Post's free epost service. To sign up, go to www.canadapost.ca, and click on the "Personal" link.

Planning for retirement

Good retirement planning software and online tools can help you plan for retirement by crunching the numbers for you. But they can also teach you how particular changes — such as your investment returns, the rate of inflation, or your savings rate — can affect when and in what style you can retire. The biggest time-saving aspect of retirement planning software and Web sites is that they let you more quickly play with and see the consequences of changing the assumptions.

You can find up-to-date links to other sources of software and online programs, including the following sites:

✔ **Service Canada's Web site** (www.servicecanada.gc.ca) has all the detailed information you need about Canada Pension Plan eligibility and payouts, as well as Old Age Security and the Guaranteed Income Supplement. The site also has a good retirement planning tool, and a useful list of questions to ask your employer about your pension plan.

✔ **Fiscal Agents Web site** (www.fiscalagents.com) offers a great number of planning tools, including a Registered Retirement Income Fund (RRIF) income calculator, and a tool to compare the income from different fixed-income investments. You'll find several useful worksheets, along with some helpful articles.

✔ **Retirementadvisor.ca's Web site** (www.retirementadvisor.ca) has some practical stories on health care costs, company pension plans, and estate planning. The online calculators are easy to use and up-to-date. The site has a tool that lets you compare returns from an RRSP versus a Tax-Free Savings Account, and calculators for everything from determining annuity income to a "life expectancy calculator" — which, if you can face it, will give you a sense of your longevity!

Preparing your taxes

Good, properly used tax-preparation software can save you time and money. The best programs "interview" you to gather the necessary information and select the appropriate forms based on your responses. Of course, you're still the one responsible for locating all the information needed to complete your return. More-experienced taxpayers can bypass the interview and jump directly to the forms they know they need to complete. These programs also help flag overlooked deductions and identify other tax-reducing strategies.

Studiotax (available at www.studiotax.com) is a terrific program that can easily handle everything but the most complicated returns. What's really surprising is that regardless of your income level, using the program is absolutely free. (The Ottawa-based developers do ask for a donation to help them maintain and improve the program.)

QuickTax and UFile are two other solid tax-preparation programs. QuickTax has the edge in terms of usability, but it's also more costly than UFile. Both of these programs offer free use of an online version for students and low-income households.

If you're mainly looking for tax forms, you can get them at no charge in tax-preparation books or through the CRA's Web site (www.cra-arc.gc.ca).

Researching investments

Instead of schlepping off to the library and fighting over the favourite investing reference manuals, ponying up hundreds of dollars to buy print versions for your own use, or slogging through voice-mail hell when you call government agencies, you can access a variety of materials on your computer. You can also often pay for just what you need:

✔ **Sedar.com:** The SEDAR (System for Electronic Document Analysis and Retrieval) site (www.sedar.com) is run for the Canadian Securities Administrators. It provides free access to the various documents publicly traded Canadian companies and mutual funds must file with the regulators. You'll find everything from annual reports and financial statements to news releases; this is a useful place to start when you already have particular stocks in mind and want to find out more about the companies' businesses and financials. The site is also loaded full of promotion-free material on mutual funds.

✔ **The SEC:** The U.S. Securities and Exchange Commission (SEC) allows unlimited, free access to its documents at www.sec.gov. All public corporations, as well as mutual funds, file their reports with the agency. Be aware, however, that navigating this site takes patience.

✔ **Globeinvestor.com:** The business and investing site run by *The Globe and Mail* — at www.theglobeandmail.com/globe-investor — lets you read many of the business stories published in the paper. You'll also find articles from the *Globe*'s helpful personal finance section, including Tony's "Me and My Money" column. Globe Investor offers excellent stock data, as well as information on the past performance, management, and top holdings of hundreds of different funds. You can also use the site's filters to get a list of funds that meet your criteria, such as low-cost, low-fee index funds that mirror the return of the major stock markets.

✔ **Morningstar.ca:** You can access Morningstar's mutual fund reports, as well as reports on U.S. stocks, at www.morningstar.ca. The reports are free, but they're watered-down versions of the company's comprehensive software and paper products. If you want to buy Morningstar's unabridged fund reports online, you can do so for a fee.

Trading online

If you do your investing homework, trading securities online may save you money and perhaps some time.

A number of the newer discount brokers have built their securities brokerage businesses around online trading. By eliminating the overhead of branch offices and accepting and processing trades only by computer, online brokers keep their costs and brokerage charges to a minimum. Cut-rate electronic brokerage firms are for people who want to direct their own financial affairs and don't want or need to work with a personal broker. However, some of these brokers have limited products and services. For example, some don't offer many of the best mutual funds.

Although online trading may save you on transaction costs, it can also encourage you to trade more than you should, resulting in higher total trading costs, lower investment returns, and higher income tax bills. Following investments on a daily basis encourages you to think short-term. Remember that the best investments are bought and held for the long haul (see Part III for more information).

Reading and searching periodicals

Many business and financial publications are online, offering investors news and financial market data. *The Globe and Mail*'s GlobePlus service offers an electronic version of the paper, access to articles and stories from the paper's archives, as well as a premium version of its investor's sites. The cost is $15.95 a month, or $159.95 per year.

The *Wall Street Journal* provides an online, personalized edition of the paper (http://online.wsj.com). You can tailor the content to meet your specific needs. The cost is US$103 per year (US$21 if you're already a *Journal* subscriber).

Leading business publications such as *Profit* magazine and *Canadian Business* (both found at www.canadianbusiness.com) and *BusinessWeek* (www.businessweek.com) put some or all of the content of their latest issues on the Internet. Some publications charge for archived articles and for some current content for nonsubscribers to their print magazine.

Be careful to take what you read and hear in the mass media with many grains of salt (see Chapter 21 for more on mass media). Much of the content revolves around tweaking people's anxieties and dwelling on the latest crises and fads.

Buying life insurance

If loved ones are financially dependent on you, you probably know that you need some life insurance. But add together the dread of life-insurance salespeople and a fear of death, and you have a recipe for procrastination. Although your computer can't stave off the Grim Reaper, it can help you find a quality, low-cost policy that can be more than 80 percent less costly than the most expensive options, all without having to deal with high-pressure sales tactics.

The best way to shop for term life insurance online is through a quotation service that we describe in Chapter 17.

The quotes are ranked by how cheap they are. Although cost is certainly an important factor, many of these services don't do as good of a job explaining other important factors to consider when doing your comparison shopping. For example, the services sometimes don't cover the projected and maximum rates after the initial term has expired. Be sure to ask about these other future rates before you agree to a specific policy.

If you decide to buy a policy from one of the online agencies, you can fill out an online application form. You'll then be mailed a detailed description of the policy and insurer, along with your completed application. In addition to having to deal with snail mail, you'll also have to deal with a medical technician, who will drop by your home to check on your health status . . . at least until some computer genius figures out a way for you to give blood and urine samples online!

Preparing legal documents

Just as you can prepare a tax return with the advice of a software program, you can also prepare common legal documents. This type of software may save you from the often difficult task of finding a competent and affordable lawyer.

Using legal software is generally preferable to using fill-in-the-blank documents. Software has the built-in virtues of directing and limiting your choices and preventing you from making common mistakes. Quality software also incorporates the knowledge and insights of the legal eagles who developed the software. And it can save you money.

If your situation isn't unusual, legal software may work well for you. As to the legality of documents that you create with legal software, remember that a will, for example, is made legal and valid by your witnesses; the fact that a lawyer does — or doesn't — prepare the document is not what makes it legal or invalid.

A good package for preparing your own will is the Complete Canadian Wills Kit on CD, by Alison Sawyer (Self-Counsel). The CD is loaded with all the worksheets and forms you'll need. In addition to allowing you to prepare wills, Complete Canadian Wills Kit can also help you prepare a living will and medical power of attorney document.

Although wills and powers of attorney are all fairly standard legal documents that you can properly create with the guidance of a top-notch software package, you should seek professional guidance for your situation if necessary.

Chapter 21

On Air and in Print

In This Chapter

▶ Recognizing the impact of the media and pundits on investors

▶ Deciding whether to tune in or tune out radio and television investing coverage

▶ Surfing safely on the Internet

▶ Evaluating newspapers and magazines

▶ Finding the best investing books

*Y*ou don't lack options when it comes to finding radio and television news, Web sites, newspapers and magazines, and books that talk about money and purport to help you get rich. Tuning out poor resources and focusing on the best ones are the real challenges.

Because you probably don't consider yourself a financial expert, more often than not you won't know whom to believe and listen to. We help you solve that problem in this chapter.

Observing the Mass Media

For better and for worse, the mass media has a profound influence on our culture. On the good side, news is widely disseminated these days. So if a product is recalled or a dangerous virus breaks out in your area, you'll probably hear about it, perhaps more than you want to, through the media — or perhaps from tuned-in family members!

The downsides of the mass media are plenty, though.

Alarming or informing us?

In case you didn't already know, you've recently lived through the second Great Depression. During the "financial crisis" of 2008–09, we were told over and over and over again how it was the worst economy and the worst economic crisis since the Great Depression. Endless parallels were drawn between the Great Depression of the 1930s and the recently slumping economy.

For sure, we suffered a significant recession (an *economic downturn*). But some in the news media (and pundit class) went overboard in suggesting we were in the midst of another depression. During the Great Depression of the 1930s, the unemployment rate hit 25 percent and remained in double digits for years on end. Half of all homes ended up in foreclosure during that period. Although job losses and home foreclosures mounted during the recent recession, they were nowhere near the Great Depression levels. The recessions of the late 1970s and early 1980s were actually worse because of the pain and hardship caused by the 10+ percent inflation rate and interest rates of that period. The unemployment rate was also above 10 percent in the early 1980s recession.

Stock markets suffered steep declines during the recent recession and, in fact, the percentage declines in the widely followed S&P/TSX Composite and the Dow Jones Industrial Average were the worst since the 1930s. Interestingly, the severity of the 2008–09 stock market decline was likely exacerbated by all the talk and fear of another Depression. Various research polls taken during late 2008 found that more than 6 in 10 believed we were about to enter another Great Depression. Those who panicked and bailed out when the markets sagged below 6,500 in early 2009 learned another hard lesson when the market surged back, as it inevitably does after a significant selloff.

Some news producers, in their quest for ratings and advertising dollars, try to be alarming to keep you tuned in and coming back for their "breaking news" updates. The more you watch, the more unnerved you get over short-term events, especially the negative ones.

Teaching questionable values

Daily doses of mass media, including all the advertising that comes with them, essentially communicate the following messages to us:

- ✔ Your worth as a person is directly related to your physical appearance (including the quality of clothing and jewellery you wear) and your material possessions — cars, homes, electronics, and other gadgets.
- ✔ The more money you make, the more "successful" you clearly are.
- ✔ The more famous you are (especially as a movie or sports star), the more you're worth listening to and admiring.

> ✔ Don't bother concerning yourself with the consequences before engaging in negative behaviour.
>
> ✔ Delaying gratification and making sacrifices are for boring losers.

Continually inundating yourself with poor messages can cause you to behave in a way that undermines your long-term happiness and financial success. Don't support (by watching, listening, or reading) forms of media that don't reflect your values and morals.

Worshipping prognosticating pundits

Quoting and interviewing experts are perhaps the only things that the media loves more than hyping short-term news events. What's the economy going to do next quarter? What's stock XYZ going to do next month? What's the stock market going to do in the next hour? No, we're not kidding about that last one — the stock market cable channel CNBC regularly interviews floor traders from the New York Stock Exchange late in the trading day to get their opinions about what the market will do in the last hour before closing!

Prognosticating pundits keep many people tuned in because their advice is constantly changing (and is therefore entertaining and anxiety-producing). They also lead investors to believe that investments can be manoeuvred in advance to outfox future financial market moves. Common sense suggests, though, that no one has a working crystal ball, and if he did, he certainly wouldn't share such insights with the mass media for free. (For more on experts who purport to predict the future, see Chapter 8.)

Rating Radio and Television Financial Programs

Over the years, money issues have received increased coverage through the major media of television and radio. Some topics gain more coverage in radio and television because they help draw more advertising dollars (which follow what people are watching). When you click on the radio or television, you don't pay a fee to tune in to a particular channel (with pay cable channels being an exception). Advertising doesn't necessarily prevent a medium from delivering coverage that is objective and in your best interests, but it sure doesn't help foster this type of coverage either.

For example, can you imagine a financial radio or television correspondent saying:

> *"We've decided to stop providing financial market updates every five min-utes because we've found it causes some investors to become addicted to tracking the short-term movements in the markets and to lose sight of the bigger picture. We don't want to encourage people to make knee-jerk reactions to short-term events."*

Soundbite-itis is another problem with both of these media. Producers and network executives believe that if you go into too much detail, viewers and listeners will change the channel.

Now, radio and television are hardly the only types of media that offer poor advice and cause investor myopia. The Internet can be even worse. And we've read plenty of lousy money books over the years.

Finding the Best Web Sites

Yes, the Internet is changing the world, but certainly not always for the better and not always in such a big way. Consider the way we shop. Okay, you can buy things online that you couldn't in the past. Big deal — what's the differ-ence between buying something by calling a toll-free number or doing mail order (which many of us did for years before the Internet) and buying some-thing by clicking your computer mouse? Purchasing things online simply broadens the avenues through which you can spend money. We see a big downside here: Overspending is easier to do when you surf the Internet a lot.

 Some of the best Web sites allow you to more efficiently access information that may help you make important investing decisions. However, this doesn't mean that your computer allows you to compete at the same level as profes-sional money managers. No, the playing field isn't level. The best pros work at their craft full-time and have far more expertise and experience than the rest of us. Some non-professionals have been fooled into believing that investing online makes them better investors. Our experience has been that people who spend time online every day dealing with investments tend to trade and react more to short-term events and have a harder time keeping the bigger picture and their long-term goals and needs in focus.

If you know where to look, you can more easily access some types of infor-mation. However, you often find a lot of garbage online — just as you do on other advertiser-dominated media like television and radio. In Chapter 20, we explain how to navigate safely online to find the best of what's out there.

Navigating Newspapers and Magazines

Compared with radio and television, print publications generally offer lengthier discussions of topics. And in the more financially focused publications, the editors who work on articles generally have more background in the topics they write about.

Even within the better publications, we find a wide variety of quality. So don't instantly believe what you read, even if you read a piece in a publication you like. Here's how to get the most from financial periodicals:

TIP

- ✔ **Read some back issues.** Go to your local library (or visit the publication's Web site) and read some issues that are at least one to two years old. Although reading old issues may seem silly and pointless, it can actually be enlightening. By reviewing a number of past issues in one sitting, you can begin to get a flavour for a publication's style, priorities, and philosophies.

- ✔ **Look for solid information and perspective.** Headlines reveal a lot about how a publication perceives its role. Publications with cover stories such as "10 hot stocks to buy now!" and "Funds that will double your money in the next three years!" are probably best avoided. Look for articles that seek to educate with accuracy, not make you a fortune overnight with predictions.

- ✔ **Note bylines.** As you read a given publication over time, you should begin to make note of the different writers. After you get to know who the better writers are, you can skip over the ones you don't care for and spend your limited free time reading the best.

- ✔ **Don't react without planning.** Here's a common example of how *not* to use information and advice you glean from publications: A would-be investor had some cash he wanted to invest. He would read an article about investing in real estate investment trusts and then go out the next week and buy several of them. Then he'd see a mention of technology stock funds and invest in some of those. Eventually his portfolio was a mess of investments that reflected the history of what he had read, rather than an orchestrated, well-thought-out investment portfolio.

Betting on Books

Reading a good book is one of our favourite ways to get a crash course on a given financial topic. Good books can go into depth on a topic in a way that simply isn't possible with other resources. Books also aren't cluttered with advertising and the conflicts inherent therein.

As with the other types of resources we discuss in this chapter, you definitely have to choose carefully — plenty of mediocrity and garbage exists out there.

Understanding the book publishing business

Book publishers are businesses first. And like most businesses, their business practices vary. Some have a reputation for care and quality; others just want to push a product out the door with maximum hype and minimum effort.

For example, you may think that book publishers check out an author before they sign him to write an entire book. Well, you may be surprised to find out that some publishers don't do their homework.

What most publishers care about first is how marketable a book and an author are. Some authors are marketable because of their well-earned reputation for sound advice. Others are marketable because of stellar promotional campaigns built on smoke and mirrors.

Even more troubling is that few publishers require advice guides to be technically reviewed for accuracy by an expert in the field other than the author, who sometimes is not an expert. You, the reader, are expected to be your own technical reviewer. But do you have the expertise to do that? (Don't worry; this book has been checked for accuracy.)

As financial authors, we know that financial ideas and strategies can differ considerably. Different is not necessarily wrong. When a technical reviewer looks at our text and tells us that a better way is out there, we take a second look. We may even see things in a new way. If we were the only experts to see our book before publication, we wouldn't get this second expert opinion. How do you know whether a book has been technically reviewed? Check the credits page or the author's acknowledgements.

Authors write books for many reasons other than to teach and educate. The most common reason financial book authors write books is to further their own business interests. Taking care of business interests may not always be a bad thing, but it's not the best thing for you when you're trying to educate yourself and better manage your own finances. For example, some investment newsletter sellers write investment books. Rather than teach you how to make good investments, the authors make the investment world sound complicated so that you feel the need to subscribe to their ongoing newsletters.

Books at the head of their class

In addition to books that we've recommended at various places throughout this book, here's a list of some of our other favourite financial titles:

- *Built to Last: Successful Habits of Visionary Companies* by Jim Collins and Jerry I. Porras (HarperCollins)

- *Good to Great: Why Some Companies Make the Leap . . . and Others Don't* by Jim Collins (HarperCollins)

- *A Random Walk Down Wall Street* by Burton G. Malkiel (Norton)

- *Starting a Successful Business in Canada Kit* by Jack D. James (Self-Counsel Press)

- Self-Counsel Press's Canadian legal titles

- *Tax Planning for You and Your Family* produced by KPMG (Thomson Carswell)

- And, not surprisingly, our very own *Investing For Canadians For Dummies,* published by John Wiley & Sons Canada

Part VI
The Part of Tens

The 5th Wave   By Rich Tennant

"I'd lend you advice on how to manage your money if you had a better credit score."

In this part . . .

You find some fun and useful chapters that can help you with financial strategies for ten life changes and guide you with ten tips for avoiding identity theft and fraud. Why "tens"? Why not!

Chapter 22

Survival Guide for Ten Life Changes

In This Chapter

▶ Handling the financial challenges that arise during life changes

▶ Minimizing financial worries so you can focus on what matters most

Some of life's changes come unexpectedly, like earthquakes. Others you can see coming when they're still far off, like a big storm moving in off the horizon. Whether a life change is predictable or not, your ability to navigate successfully through its challenges and adjust quickly to new circumstances depends largely on your degree of preparedness.

Perhaps you find our comparison of life changes to natural disasters to be a bit negative. After all, some of the changes we discuss in this chapter should be occasions for joy. But understand that what one defines as a "disaster" has everything to do with preparedness. To the person who has stored no emergency rations in her basement, the big snowstorm that traps her in her home can lead to problems. But to the prepared person with plenty of food and water, that same storm may mean a vacation from work and some relaxing days in the midst of a winter wonderland.

Here, then, are the major changes you may have to deal with at some point in your life. We wish you more of the good changes than the bad.

Starting Out: Your First Job

If you just graduated from university or some other program, or you're otherwise entering the workforce, your increased income and reduction in educational expenses are probably a welcome relief. You'd think, then, that more young adults would be able to avoid financial trouble and challenges. But they face these challenges largely because of poor financial habits picked up at home or from the world at large. Here's how to get on the path to financial success:

✔ **Don't use consumer credit.** The use and abuse of consumer credit can cause long-term financial pain and hardship. To get off on the right financial foot, young workers need to shun the habit of making purchases on credit cards that they can't pay for in full when the bill arrives in the mail. Here's the simple solution for running up outstanding credit card balances: Don't carry a credit card. If you need the convenience of making purchases with a piece of plastic, get a debit card (see Chapter 5).

✔ **Get in the habit of saving and investing.** Ideally, your savings should be directed into retirement plans that offer tax benefits unless you want to accumulate down payment money for a home or small-business purchase (see Chapter 4). Thinking about a home purchase or retirement is usually not in the active thought patterns of first-time job seekers. We're often asked, "At what age should a person start saving?" To us, that's similar to asking at what age you should start brushing your teeth. (When should you start brushing? Well, when you have teeth to brush!) We say you should start saving and investing money from your first paycheque. Try saving 5 percent of every paycheque and then eventually increase your saving to 10 percent. If you're having trouble saving money, track your spending and make cutbacks as needed (refer to Chapters 3 and 6).

✔ **Get insured.** When you're young and healthy, imagining yourself feeling otherwise is hard. But because accidents and unexpected illnesses can strike at any age, forgoing coverage can be financially devastating. When you're in your first full-time job with more limited benefits, buying disability coverage, which replaces income lost due to a long-term disability, is also wise. And as you begin to build your assets, consider making out a will so that your assets go where you want them to in the event of your untimely passing.

✔ **Continue your education.** After you get out in the workforce, you (like many other people) may realize how little you learned in formal schooling that can actually be used in the real world — and, conversely, how much you need to learn (like personal financial management) that school never taught you. Read, learn, and continue to grow. Continuing education can help you advance in your career and enjoy the world around you.

Changing Jobs or Careers

During your adult life, you'll almost surely change jobs — perhaps several times a decade. We hope that most of the time you'll be changing by your own choice. But let's face it: Job security is not what it used to be. Downsizing has impacted even the most talented workers.

Always be prepared for a job change. No matter how happy you are in your current job, knowing that your world won't fall apart if you're not working tomorrow can give you an added sense of security and encourage openness to possibility. Whether you're changing your job by choice or necessity, the following financial manoeuvres can help ease the transition:

✔ **Structure your finances to afford an income dip.** Spending less than you earn always makes good financial sense, but if you're approaching a possible job change, spending less is even more important, particularly if you're entering a new field or starting your own company and you expect a short-term income dip. Many people view a lifestyle of thriftiness as restrictive, but ultimately those thrifty habits can give you more freedom to do what you want to do. Be sure to keep an emergency reserve fund (see Chapter 8).

If you lose your job, batten down the hatches. You normally get little advance warning when you lose your job through no choice of your own. It doesn't mean, however, that you can't do anything financially. Evaluating and slashing your current level of spending may be necessary. Everything should be fair game, from how much you spend on housing to how often you eat out to where you do your grocery shopping. Avoid at all costs the temptation to maintain your level of spending by accumulating consumer debt.

✔ **Evaluate the total financial picture when relocating.** At some point in your career, you may have the option of relocating. But don't call the moving company until you understand the financial consequences of such a move. You can't simply compare salaries and benefits between the two jobs. You also need to compare the cost of living between the two areas: That includes housing, commuting, income and property taxes, food, utilities, and all the other major expenditure categories that we cover in Chapter 3.

Getting Married

Ready to tie the knot with the one you love? Congratulations — we hope that you'll have a long, healthy, and happy life together. In addition to the emotional and moral commitments that you and your spouse will make to one another, you're probably going to be merging many of your financial decisions and resources. Even when you're largely in agreement about your financial goals and strategies, managing as two is far different than managing as one. Here's how to prepare:

✔ **Take a compatibility test.** Many couples never talk about their goals and plans before marriage, and failing to do so breaks up way too many marriages. Finances are just one of the many issues you need to discuss. Ensuring that you know what you're getting yourself into is a good way to minimize your chances for heartache. Ministers, priests, and rabbis sometimes offer premarital counselling to help bring issues and differences to the surface.

✔ **Discuss and set joint goals.** After you're married, you and your spouse should set aside time once a year, or every few years, to discuss personal and financial goals for the years ahead. When you talk about where you want to go, you help ensure that you're both rowing your financial boat in unison, and in the same direction.

✔ **Decide whether to keep finances separate or manage them jointly.** Philosophically, we like the idea of pooling your finances better. After all, marriage is a partnership. In some marriages, however, spouses may choose to keep some money separate so they don't feel the scrutiny of a spouse with different spending preferences. Spouses who have been through divorce may choose to keep the assets they bring into the new marriage separate in order to protect their money in the event of another divorce. As long as you're jointly accomplishing what you need to financially, some separation of money is okay. But for the health of your marriage, don't hide money from one another, and if you're the higher-income spouse, don't assume power and control over your joint income.

✔ **Coordinate and maximize employer benefits.** If one or both of you have access to a package of employee benefits through an employer, understand how best to make use of those benefits. Coordinating and using the best that each package has to offer is like getting a pay raise. If you both have access to health insurance, compare which of you has better benefits. Likewise, one of you may have a better retirement savings plan — one that matches and offers superior investment options. Unless you can afford to save the maximum through both your plans, saving more in the better plan will increase your combined assets. (Note: Concerned about what will happen if you save more in one of your retirement plans and then you divorce? In most provinces the money is considered part of your joint assets to be divided equally.)

✔ **Discuss life and disability insurance needs.** If you and your spouse can make do without each other's income, you may not need any income-protecting insurance. However, if, like many husbands and wives, you both depend on each other's incomes, or if one of you depends fully or partly on the other's income, you may each need long-term disability and term life insurance policies (refer to Chapter 17).

✔ **Update your wills.** When you marry, you should make or update your wills. Having a will is potentially more valuable when you're married, especially if you want to leave money to others in addition to your spouse, or if you have children for whom you need to name a guardian. See Chapter 18 for more on wills.

✔ **Reconsider beneficiaries on investment and life insurance.** With RRSPs and life insurance policies, you name beneficiaries to whom the money or value in those accounts will go in the event of your passing. When you marry, you'll probably want to rethink your beneficiaries.

Buying a Home

Most Canadians eventually buy a home. You don't need to own a home to be a financial success, but home ownership certainly offers financial rewards. Over the course of your adult life, the real estate you own is likely going to appreciate in value. Additionally, you're going to pay off your mortgage some-day, which will greatly reduce your housing costs. If you're thinking about buying a home:

✔ **Get your overall finances in order.** Before buying, analyze your current budget, your ability to afford debt, and your future financial goals. Make sure your expected housing expenses allow you to save properly for retirement and other long- or short-term objectives. Don't buy a home based on what lenders are willing to lend.

✔ **Determine whether now's the time.** Buying a house when you don't see yourself staying put three to five years rarely makes financial sense, especially if you're a first-time home buyer. Buying and selling a home gobbles up a good deal of money in transaction costs — you'll be lucky to recoup all those costs even within a five-year period. Also, if your income is likely to drop or you have other pressing goals, such as start-ing a business, you may want to wait to buy.

For more about buying a home, be sure to read Chapter 15.

Having Children

If you think that being a responsible adult, holding down a job, paying your bills on time, and preparing for your financial future are tough, wait 'til you add kids to the equation. Most parents find that with kids in the family, the already precious commodities of free time and money become even scarcer.

The sooner you discover how to manage your time and money, the better able you'll be to have a sane, happy, and financially successful life as a parent. Here are some key things to do both before and after you begin your family:

- **Set your priorities.** As with many other financial decisions, starting or expanding a family requires that you plan ahead. Set your priorities and structure your finances and living situation accordingly. Is having a bigger home in a particular community important, or would you rather feel less pressure to work hard, giving you more time to spend with your family? Keep in mind that a less hectic work life not only gives you more free time but also often reduces your cost of living by decreasing meals out, dry-cleaning costs, daycare expenses, and so on.

- **Take a hard look at your budget.** Having children requires you to increase your spending. At a minimum, expenditures for food and clothing will increase. But you're also likely to spend more on housing, insurance, daycare, and education. On top of that, if you want to play an active role in raising your children, having both parents working at full-time jobs may not be possible. So while you consider the added expenses, you may also need to factor in a decrease in income.

  No simple rules exist for estimating how children will affect your household's income and expenses. On the income side, figure out how much you want to cut back on work. On the expense side, statistics show that the average household with school-age children spends about 20 percent more than those without children. Going through your budget category by category and estimating how kids will change your spending is a more scientific approach. (You can use the worksheets in Chapter 3.)

- **Boost insurance coverage before getting pregnant**. With disability insurance, pregnancy is considered a preexisting condition, so women should secure this coverage before getting pregnant. This means that if you don't already have coverage in place and get pregnant, a disability that is the result of your pregnancy will generally not enable you to receive benefits. And most families-to-be should buy life insurance. Buying life insurance after the bundle of joy comes home from the hospital is a risky proposition — if one of the parents develops a health problem, he or she may be denied coverage. You should also consider buying life insurance for a stay-at-home parent. Even though the stay-at-home parent is not bringing in income, if he or she were to pass away, hiring assistance could cripple the family budget.

- **Check maternity and paternity leave with your employers.** Many larger employers offer to top-up government Employment Insurance benefits, and may also allow for additional time off. Understand the options and the financial ramifications before you consider the leave and, ideally, before you get pregnant.

✔ **Update your will.** If you have a will, you'll need to update it; if you don't have a will, make one now. With children in the picture, you need to name a guardian who will be responsible for raising your children should you and your spouse both pass away.

✔ **Understand child-care tax benefits.** If you have children under the age of 18, you may be eligible for the Canada Child Tax Benefit (CCTB), a non-taxable benefit. In 2010, the annual basic benefit was set at $1,340 per child, plus an extra $93 for the third and subsequent children. These benefits are decreased on a sliding scale if your household income exceeds a certain amount, which in 2010 was $38,832. If you have one child, the basic benefit is reduced by 2 percent of the amount your net family income exceeds that level. If you have two or more children, it's reduced by 4 percent. (Note that Alberta has different payment schedules than the rest of the country.)

In addition, the CCTB also includes the National Child Benefit Supplement for low-income families. The amounts in 2010 were $2,076 for a one-child family, $1,837 for a two-child family, and $1,747 per child for families with three or more children. This benefit also gets gradually phased out when your family's net income exceeds a certain level, which in 2010 was $21,816.

Child-care expenses can also be deducted if they were incurred in order for you or your spouse to earn an income. In a two-parent family, the deduction must usually be claimed by the lower-earning spouse. Single parents who are students, as well as households where both spouses are studying at a postsecondary institution, can also claim this deduction. In 2010, you could claim up to $7,000 in expenses for each child under the age of 7, and $4,000 for children ages 7 to 16. The total you can claim is limited to two-thirds of your earned income. Some provinces also have an additional child-care tax credit for lower-income families.

Finally, to help pay for the cost of daycare for young children, families get the Universal Child Care Benefit. In 2010, the benefit was $100 per month for each child under the age of 6. This payment is taxed in the hands of the lower-earning spouse or common-law partner.

✔ **Don't indulge the children.** Toys, art classes, music lessons, travel, sports and associated lessons, field trips, and the like can rack up big bills, especially if you don't control your spending. Some parents fail to set guidelines or limits when spending on children's programs. Others mindlessly follow the examples set by the families of their children's peers. Introspective parents have told us that they feel some insecurity about providing the best for their children. The parents (and kids) who seem the happiest and most financially successful are the ones who clearly distinguish between material luxuries and family necessities.

As children get older and become indoctrinated into the world of shopping, all sorts of other purchases come into play. Consider giving your kids a weekly allowance and letting them discover how to spend and manage it. And when they're old enough, having your kids get a part-time job can help teach financial responsibility.

Starting a Small Business

Many people aspire to be their own bosses, but far fewer people actually leave their jobs in order to achieve that dream. Giving up the apparent security of a job with benefits and a built-in network of co-workers is difficult for most people, both psychologically and financially. Starting a small business is not for everyone, but don't let inertia stand in your way. Here are some tips to help get you started and increase your chances for long-term success:

- **Prepare to ditch your job.** To maximize your ability to save money, live as Spartan a lifestyle as you can while you're employed; you'll develop thrifty habits that'll help you weather the reduced income and increased expenditure period that come with most small-business start-ups. You may also want to consider easing into your small business by working at it part-time in the beginning, with or without cutting back on your normal job.

- **Develop a business plan.** If you research and think through your business idea, not only will you reduce the likelihood of your business failing and increase its success if it thrives, but you'll also feel more comfortable taking the entrepreneurial plunge. A good business plan should describe in detail the business idea, the marketplace you'll compete in, your marketing plans, and expected revenues and expenses.

- **Replace your insurance coverage.** Before you finally leave your job, get proper insurance. With disability insurance, secure coverage before you leave your job so you have income to qualify for coverage. If you have life insurance through your employer, obtain new individual coverage as soon as you know you're going to leave your job. (See Chapter 17 for details.)

- **Establish a retirement savings plan.** After your business starts making a profit, consider establishing a Registered Retirement Savings Plan, which allows you to shelter a good chunk of your income from tax. We explain all about RRSPs in Chapter 11.

Caring for Aging Parents

For many of us, there comes a time when we reverse roles with our parents and become the caregivers. As your parents age, they may need help with a variety of issues and living tasks. Although you probably won't have the time or ability to perform all these functions yourself, you may end up coordinating some service providers who will. Here are key issues to consider when caring for aging parents:

- ✔ **Get help where possible.** In most communities, a variety of non-profit organizations offer information and sometimes even counselling to families who are caring for elderly parents. You may be able to find your way to such resources through your province's ministry of health, as well as through recommendations from local hospitals and doctors. You'll especially want to get assistance and information if your parents need some sort of home care, nursing home care, or assisted living arrangement.

- ✔ **Get involved in their health care.** Your aging parents may already have a lot on their minds, or they simply may not be able to coordinate and manage all the healthcare providers that are giving them medications and advice. Try, as best as you can, to be their advocate. Speak with their doctors so you can understand their current medical condition, the need for various medications, and how to help coordinate caregivers. Visit home care providers and nursing homes, and speak with prospective care providers.

- ✔ **Understand tax breaks.** If you're financially supporting your parents, you may be eligible for a number of tax credits and deductions for elder care. You can generally claim most related medical expenses as a tax credit. If you are single, widowed, divorced, or separated and supporting a parent, you can also claim the eligible dependant credit (formerly the equivalent-to-married credit). If an elderly or infirm relative lives with you and you provide in-home care, you may also be eligible for the caregiver's credit. In 2010, this credit was worth up to $630. However, if you claim the eligible dependant or other dependant tax credits, you cannot also claim the caregiver's credit.

- ✔ **Discuss getting the estate in order.** Parents don't like thinking about their demise, and they may feel awkward discussing this issue with their children. But opening a dialogue between you and your folks about such issues can be healthy in many ways. Not only does discussing wills, living wills, living trusts, and estate planning strategies (see Chapter 18) make you aware of your folks' situation, but it can also improve their plans to both their benefit and yours.

- ✔ **Take some time off.** Caring for an aging parent, particularly one who is having health problems, can be time-consuming and emotionally draining. Do your parents and yourself a favour by using some vacation time to help get things in order. Although this time off may not be the kind of vacation you were envisioning, it should help you reduce your stress and get more on top of things.

Divorcing

In most marriages that are destined to split up, both parties usually recognize early warning signs. Sometimes, however, one spouse may surprise the other with an unexpected request for divorce. Whether the divorce is planned or unexpected, some important considerations come into play when getting a divorce:

- ✔ **Question the divorce.** Some say that divorcing is too easy to do. Although some couples are indeed better off parting ways, others give up too easily, thinking that the grass is greener elsewhere only to later discover that all lawns have weeds and crabgrass. Just as with lawns that aren't watered and fertilized, relationships can wither without nurturing.

  Money and disagreements over money are certainly contributing factors in marital unhappiness. Unfortunately, in many relationships, money is wielded as power by the spouse who earns more of it. Try talking things over, perhaps with a marital counsellor. If you invest in making your relationship stronger, you'll reap the dividends for years to come.

- ✔ **Separate your emotions from the financial issues.** Feelings of revenge may be common in some divorces, but they'll probably only help ensure that the lawyers get rich as you and your spouse butt heads. If you really want a divorce, work at doing it efficiently and harmoniously so that you can get on with your lives and have more of your money to work with.

- ✔ **Detail resources and priorities.** Draw up a list of all the assets and liabilities that you and your spouse have. Make sure you list all the financial facts, including investment account records and statements. After you know the whole picture, begin to think about what is and isn't important to you financially and otherwise.

- ✔ **Educate yourself about personal finance and legal issues.** Divorce sometimes forces non–financially oriented spouses to get a crash course in personal finance at a difficult emotional time. This book can help educate you financially. Visit a bookstore and pick up a good legal guide or two about divorce.

- ✔ **Choose advisers carefully.** Odds are that you'll retain the services of one or more specialists to assist you with the myriad issues, negotiations, and concerns of your divorce. Legal, tax, and financial advisers can help, but make sure you recognize their limitations and conflicts of interest. The more complicated things become and the more you haggle with your spouse, the more lawyers, unfortunately, benefit financially. Don't use your divorce lawyer for financial or tax advice — your lawyer may know no more than you do in these areas. Also, realize that you don't need a lawyer to get divorced. A variety of books and kits can help you. As for choosing tax and financial advisers, if you think you need that type of help, see Chapters 8 and 19 for advice on how to find good advisers.

✔ **Analyze your spending.** Some divorcees find themselves financially squeezed in the early years following a divorce because two people living together in the same property can generally do so less expensively than two people living separately. Analyzing your spending needs pre-divorce can help you adjust to a new budget and negotiate a fairer settlement with your spouse.

✔ **Review needed changes to your insurance.** If you're covered under your spouse's employer's insurance plan, make sure you get this coverage replaced (see Chapter 17). If you or your children will still be financially dependent upon your spouse post-divorce, make sure that the divorce agreement mandates life insurance coverage. You should also revise your will (see Chapter 18).

✔ **Revamp your retirement plan.** With changes to your income, expenses, assets, liabilities, and future needs, your retirement plan will surely need a post-divorce overhaul. Refer to Chapter 4 and Chapter 11 for a reorientation.

Receiving a Windfall

Whether through inheritance, stock options, small-business success, or lottery winnings, you may receive a financial windfall at some point in your life. Like many people who are totally unprepared psychologically and organizationally for their sudden good fortune, you may find that a flood of money can create more problems than it solves. Here are a few tips to help you make the most of your financial windfall:

✔ **Educate yourself.** If you've never had to deal with significant wealth, we don't expect you to know how to handle it. Don't pressure yourself to invest it as soon as possible. Leaving the money where it is or stashing it in a high-yield savings account or a money market fund, which we discuss in Chapters 9 and 12, is far better than jumping into investments that you don't understand and haven't researched.

✔ **Beware of the sharks.** You may begin to wonder whether someone has posted your net worth, address, and home telephone number in the local newspaper and on the Internet. Brokers and financial advisers may flood you with marketing materials, telephone solicitations, and lunch date requests. These folks pursue you for a reason: They want to convert your money into their income either by selling you investments and other financial products or by managing your money. Stay away from the sharks, educate yourself, and take charge of your own financial moves. Decide on your own terms whom to hire, and then seek them out. Most of the best advisers we know don't have the time or philosophical orientation to chase after prospective clients.

✔ **Recognize the emotional side of coming into a lot of money.** One of the side effects of accumulating wealth quickly is that you may have feelings of guilt or otherwise be unhappy, especially if you expected money to solve your problems. If you didn't invest in your relationship with your parents and after their passing you regret how you interacted with them, getting a big inheritance from your folks may make you feel badly. If you poured endless hours into a business venture that finally paid off, all that money in your investment accounts may leave you with a hollow feeling if you're divorced and you lost friends by neglecting your relationships.

✔ **Pay down debts.** People generally borrow money to buy things that they otherwise can't buy in one fell swoop. Paying off your debts is one of the simplest and best investments you can make when you come into wealth.

✔ **Diversify.** If you want to protect your wealth, don't keep it all in one pot. Mutual funds (see Chapter 10) are an ideally diversified, professionally managed investment vehicle to consider. And if you want your money to continue growing, consider the wealth-building investments — stocks, real estate, and small-business options — that we discuss in Part III of this book.

✔ **Use the opportunity.** Most people work for a paycheque their whole lives so they can pay a never-ending stream of monthly bills. Although we're not advocating a hedonistic lifestyle, why not take some extra time to travel, spend time with your family, and enjoy the hobbies you've long been putting off? How about trying a new career that you may find more fulfilling and that may make the world a better place? And what about donating some to your favourite charities?

Retiring

If you spent the bulk of your adult life working, retiring can be a challenging transition. Most Canadians have an idealized vision of how wonderful retirement will be — no more irritating bosses and pressure of work deadlines; unlimited time to travel, play, and lead the good life. Sounds nice, huh? Well, the reality for most Canadians is different, especially for those who don't plan ahead (financially and otherwise). Here are some tips to help you through retirement:

✔ **Plan both financially and personally.** Leaving behind a full-time career creates big challenges, such as what to do with all your free time. Planning your activities is even more important than planning financially. If the focus during your working years is solely on your career and saving money, you may lack interests, friends, and the ability to know how to spend money when you retire.

✔ **Take stock of your resources.** Many people worry and wonder whether they have sufficient assets for cutting back on work or retiring completely, yet they don't crunch any numbers to see where they stand. Ignorance may cause you to misunderstand how little or how much you really have for retirement when compared to what you need. See Chapters 4, 11, and 12 for help with retirement planning and investing.

✔ **Reevaluate your insurance needs.** When you have sufficient assets to retire, you don't need to retain insurance to protect your employment income any longer. On the other hand, as your assets grow over the years, you may be underinsured with regards to liability insurance (refer to Chapter 18).

✔ **Evaluate healthcare/living options.** Medical expenses in your retirement years (particularly the cost of nursing home care) can be daunting. Which course of action you take — supplemental insurance, buying into a retirement community, or not doing anything — depends on your financial and personal situation. Early preparation increases your options; if you wait until you have major health problems, it may be too late to choose specific paths. (See Chapter 17 for more details on healthcare options.)

✔ **Decide what to do with your RRSP.** When you're set to retire, you may have to elect what to do with your RRSP funds. Making the right choice is similar to choosing a good investment — different features carry different risks, benefits, and tax consequences. Read Chapter 11 for information on how to assess your different options for taking money out of your RRSP. Read Part III of this book to learn about investing.

✔ **Pick a pension option.** Selecting a *pension option* (a plan that pays a monthly benefit during retirement) is similar to choosing a good investment — each pension option carries different risks, benefits, and tax consequences. Pensions are structured by actuaries, who base pension options on reasonable life expectancies. The younger you are when you start collecting your company pension and Canada Pension Plan (or Quebec Pension Plan) benefits, the less you get per month. Check to see whether the amount of your monthly pension stops increasing past a certain age. You obviously don't want to delay access to your pension benefits past that age, because you won't receive a reward for waiting any longer and you'll collect the benefit for fewer months.

If you know that you have a health problem that shortens your life expectancy, you may benefit from drawing your company pension and CPP/QPP benefits sooner. If you plan to continue working in some capacity and earning a decent income after retiring, waiting for higher pension benefits when you're in a lower tax bracket is probably wise.

You'll also need to make a choice as to what amount your surviving spouse receives from your employer's pension plan should you die first. At one end of the spectrum, you have the risky single-life option, which pays benefits until you pass away and then provides no benefits for your spouse thereafter. This option maximizes your monthly take while you're alive. Consider this option only if your spouse can do without this income. The least risky option, and thus the least financially reward- ing while the pensioner is still living, is the *100-percent joint and survivor option,* which pays your survivor the same amount that you received while still alive. The other joint and survivor options fall somewhere between these two extremes and generally make sense for most couples who desire decent pensions early in retirement but want a reasonable amount to continue should the pensioner die first. The *75-percent joint and survivor option* is a popular choice, because it closely matches the lower expense needs of the lone surviving spouse at 75 percent of the expenses of the couple, while providing higher payments than the 100-percent joint and survivor option during the time when both spouses are alive.

✔ **Get your estate in order.** Confronting your mortality is never fun, but when you're considering retirement or you're already retired, getting your estate in order makes all the more sense. Find out about wills and trusts that may benefit you and your heirs. You may also want to con- sider giving monetary gifts now if you have more than you need.

Chapter 23

Ten Tactics to Thwart Identity Theft and Fraud

In This Chapter

▶ Protecting your personal information

▶ Paying attention to activity in your accounts and credit history

*H*ucksters and thieves are often several steps ahead of law enforcement officials. Eventually, some of the bad guys get caught, but many don't, and those who do get nabbed often go back to their unsavoury ways after penalties and some jail time. They may even be in your neighbourhood or on your local school board. (For an enlightening read, check out Dr. Martha Stout's book *The Sociopath Next Door* [Broadway Books].)

Years ago, when Eric lived on the West Coast, he got a call from his bank informing him that it had just discovered "concerning activity" on the joint chequing account he held with his wife. Specifically, a man with a bogus ID in Eric's name had gone into five different branches of his bank on the same day and withdrawn $80 from the joint chequing account at each one. After some detective work on Eric's part, he discovered that someone had pilfered his personal banking information at his wife's employer's payroll office. Fortunately, the bank made good on the money that it had allowed to be withdrawn by the Eric Tyson impostor.

Eric and his wife had been the victims of identity theft. In their situation, the crook had accessed one of their accounts; in other cases, the criminal activity may develop with a thief opening an account (such as a credit card) using someone's stolen personal information. Victims of identity theft can suffer trashed credit reports, reduced ability to qualify for loans and even jobs (with employers who check credit reports), out-of-pocket costs and losses, and dozens of hours of time to clean up the mess and clear their credit record and name.

Unfortunately, identity theft is hardly the only way to be taken to the cleaners by crooks. All sorts of scamsters hatch schemes to separate you from your money. Please follow the ten tips in this chapter to keep yourself from falling prey and unnecessarily losing money.

Save Phone Discussions for Friends Only

Never, ever give out personal information over the phone, *especially when you aren't the one who initiated the call*! Suppose you get a call and the person on the other end of the line claims to be with a company you conduct business with (such as your credit card company or bank). Ask for the caller's name and number and call back to be sure he is indeed with that company and has a legitimate business reason for contacting you.

But this approach alone doesn't offer much protection. Calling the number back may only reconnect you with the fraudster. Better to ask for a corporate number, then check that against the number for the company listed online or with directory assistance. You can then call that number and ask to be transferred to the person who initially called you. With caller ID on your phone line, you may be able to see what number a call is originating from, but more often than not calls from business-registered phone numbers come up as "unavailable." A major red flag: you call back the number that comes through on caller ID and discover the number is bogus (a nonworking number).

Never Respond to E-Mails Soliciting Information

If you're an e-mail user, you've likely heard about or even received yourself official looking e-mails sent from companies you know of and may even do business with asking you to promptly visit their Web site to correct some sort of billing or account problem. Tony regularly gets e-mails claiming to be from one or another of the big banks — including some he's never done business with — that look astoundingly official, right down to the colour of the logo.

Hackers have become very clever and can generate a return/sender e-mail address that looks like it comes from a known institution but really does not. This unscrupulous practice is known as phishing, and if you bite at the bait, visit the site, and provide the requested personal information, your reward is likely to be some sort of future identity theft problem.

To find out more about how to protect yourself from phishing scams, visit the Anti-Phishing Working Group's Web site at www.antiphishing.org.

Review Your Monthly Financial Statements

Although financial institutions such as banks may call you if they notice unusual activity on one of your accounts, some people discover problematic account activity by simply reviewing their monthly credit card, bank account, and other statements.

Do you need to balance bank account statements to the penny? No, you don't. We haven't for years (decades actually), and we don't have the time or patience for such minutiae. The key is to review the line items on your statement to be sure that all the transactions were yours.

Secure All Receipts

When you make a purchase, be sure to keep track of and secure receipts, especially those that contain your personal financial or account information. You could keep these in an envelope in your home and then cross-check them against your monthly statement.

If you don't need to retain your receipts, be sure to dispose of them in a way that would prevent a thief from being able to decipher the information on them should someone get into your garbage. Rip up the receipts. Better yet, buy a small paper shredder for your home and/or small business. Older models will just cut paper into long thin strips that, if someone could be bothered, could easily be pieced back together. Yes, as watching a bit of the TV show *C.S.I.* — Crime Scene Investigation — will show, even these little scraps can be reassembled, but it would take a would-be ID thief a lot more time and effort. Get a crosscut shredder that will slice and dice your documents — you can buy one at most office supply and electronic stores for less than $100.

Close Unnecessary Credit Accounts

Open your wallet and remove all the pieces of plastic within it that enable you to charge purchases. The more credit cards and credit lines you have, the more likely you are to have problems with identity theft and fraud (and the more likely you are to overspend and carry debt balances).

Also, reduce credit card offers by contacting the Canadian Marketing Association and signing up for the Do Not Contact Service. You can register online at www.the-cma.org. You can also reach them at:

Canadian Marketing Association
1 Concorde Gate, Suite 607
Don Mills, ON HIS 2Z2
416-391-2362

You can also call the number on the back of your credit card, speak to a customer service representative, and ask them to remove you from all direct mail and phone marketing programs.

Unless you maintain a card for small business transactions, you really "need" only one piece of plastic with a VISA or MasterCard logo. Give preference to a debit card if you have a history of accumulating credit card balances.

Regularly Review Your Credit Reports

You may also be tipped off to shenanigans going on in your name when you review your credit reports. Some identity theft victims have found out about credit accounts opened in their name by reviewing their credit reports.

Because you're entitled to a free credit report from each of the two major credit agencies every year, we recommend reviewing your reports at least that often. The reports generally contain the same information, so you could request and review one agency report every four months, which would enable you to keep a closer eye on your reports and still obtain them without cost. We don't recommend spending the $100 or so annually for a so-called credit monitoring service that will update you when something happens on your credit reports.

Keep Personal Info Off Your Cheques

Don't place personal information on cheques. Information that is useful to identity thieves and that you should not put on your cheques includes your credit card number, driver's licence number, social insurance number, and so on. We also encourage you to leave your home address off your pre-printed cheques when you order them. Otherwise, every Tom, Dick, and Jane whose hands your cheque passes through knows exactly where you live.

When writing a cheque to a merchant, question the need for adding personal information to the cheque. Use a debit card instead for such transactions and remember that your debit card doesn't advertise your home address and other financial account data — so, no need to publicize it to the world on your cheques.

Protect Your Computer and Files

Especially if you keep personal and financial data on your computer, consider the following safeguards to protect your computer and the confidential information on it:

- Install a firewall
- Use virus protection software
- Password-protect access to your programs and files

Protect Your Mail

Some identity thieves have collected personal information by simply helping themselves to mail in home mailboxes. Especially if your mail is delivered to a curbside box, stealing mail is pretty easy.

Consider using a locked mailbox or a post office box to protect your incoming mail from theft. And consider having your investment and other important statements sent to you via e-mail, or simply access them online and eliminate mail delivery of the paper copies.

Be careful with your outgoing mail as well, such as bills with cheques attached. Minimize your outgoing mail and save yourself hassles by signing up for automatic bill payment for as many bills as you are able. Drop the rest of your outgoing mail in a secure Canada Post box, such as those you find at the post office.

Clean Out Your Wallet

Minimize the number of items in your wallet that carry personal information. Take all the cards, licences, and memberships out of your wallet, and only put back those that you absolutely need to have on you on a regular basis. For example, for most of your daily life, you don't need your SIN card or your passport.

Take photocopies of both sides of all the cards, licences, and other pieces of identification that you do need to carry with you. If your wallet or purse is lost or stolen, this will provide you with a list of all the different accounts you need to cancel, along with the phone numbers to call.

Index

• Numerics •

78 Tax Tips For Canadians For Dummies (Wiley publications), 150
101 Tax Secrets For Canadians (Cestnick), 150

• A •

ABM outlets, 188
accountants, 152–153, 395
addictions, 47, 57, 126–127
adjusters, insurance, 345
adult education classes, 391
advertisers, pandering to, 17–18
Advocis (Web site), 393
age tax credit (age 65 or older), 143
aggressive retirement portfolio, 251–253
alcohol expenses, 127
alimony expenses, 137
allocation
  assets, 170–174, 270–271
  dollar-cost averaging (DCA), 173–174
  of RRSP funds, 250–254
alternative minimum tax (AMT), 134
American Arbitration Association, 180
amortizing mortgage payments, 292, 299–300
annual reports for mutual funds, 215
annuities. *See also* insurance
  fees, 255
  investing in, 204–205, 254–255, 275
  retirement accounts, 239, 242–244, 246, 247, 254–255
  RRIFs converted to, 240
  tax credits, 143, 242
arbitration consultants, 180
asset allocation funds, 212
assets
  allocating, 170–174, 270–271
  avoiding probate, 376
  calculating, 26
  insuring, 341
  in long-term investments, 270–271
  for retirement plans, 270
  signing over to financial adviser, 256
associations, financial planners', 392–393
attribution rules, 262, 377
audits, tax, 153–155
auto insurance, 128, 344, 371–373
automobile. *See* cars

• B •

bad debt danger ratio, 35
bad debt versus good debt, 34–37, 79
balanced funds, 212
balanced mutual funds, 249
balancing a chequebook, 52
bankruptcy, 89–94, 287
banks
  chequing account with, 187–188
  financial planning services, 388
  mortgages from, 308
  savings accounts, 165, 188–189, 388
basic personal tax credit, 140
Beacon scores (FICO scores), 30
Bear, John (*Send This Jerk the Bedbug Letter*), 103
bear market, 175
Better Business Bureau (BBB), 103
Beware icon, 6
bill paying, 52, 405
Bloomberg News, 17
Blue Cross (Web site), 355
bonds
  callable, 191
  described, 189
  guaranteed investment certificate (GIC) versus, 272–274
  inflation-indexed treasury bonds, 273
  interest and dividends, 221
  interest rates, 189–190
  junk, 190

bonds *(continued)*
  long-term, 272
  maturity, 189, 190, 210
  municipal, 190
  mutual funds, 210–211, 248
  ratings, 190
  return on investments, 164, 169–170
  short-term, 190, 272
  stocks versus, 166–167
  taxable distributions, 272
  treasury bonds, 273
book publishing business, 195, 416
books, financial, 417
brand names, 101
broad coverage insurance, 368
brokers. *See also* investment firms
  best firms, 176–177
  broker-dealer networks, 177
  commission-based, 196, 216, 310
  conflicts of interest, 383
  discount brokers, 177, 253–254, 407–408
  getting fleeced by, 180
  leaving your broker, 257
  mortgage, 310
  sales pitches, 184
Bruner, Robert (*Deals From Hell*), 15
budgeting, 105–106, 426
Built to Last: Successful Habits of Visionary Companies (Collins and Porras), 417
bulk buying, 105, 109
bullion, 204
business. *See also* small businesses
  business plan, 201, 428
  choosing, 102–103
  insurance, 331, 344
  losses, 137
  saving to buy, 59, 63
  starting a small business, 201–202, 428
BusinessWeek, 408
Buying & Selling a Home For Canadians For Dummies (Wiley publishing), 291

• C •

calculators, online, 406
callable bonds, 191
Canada Access Grants program, 287

Canada Child Tax Benefit (CCTB), 427
Canada Deposit Insurance Corporation (CDIC), 188, 274
Canada Disability Savings Bonds, 264
Canada Disability Savings Grant (CDSG), 147, 264
Canada Education Savings Grant (CESG), 280–282
Canada Mortgage and Housing Corporation (CMHC), 308
Canada Pension Plan (or Quebec Pension Plan), 68–70, 349–351
Canada Post, 405
Canada Revenue Agency (CRA), 135, 150, 406
Canada Student Loans Program (CSLP), 285
Canadian, U.S., international, and global funds, 212–213
Canadian Association of Credit Counselling Services, 85
Canadian Automobile Association, 355, 362, 373
Canadian Business, 15, 408
Canadian government securities, 189
Canadian Marketing Association, 438
Canadian Small Business Kit For Dummies (Kerr and Kurtz), 75
Canadian stock index fund, 213
Canadian stock market, 192
Canadian Tire Cash Advantage Mastercard, 118
Canadian Tire Financial Services, 268
Canadian Treasury bill money market funds, 270
cancer insurance, 335
career. *See* employment
caregivers tax credit, 144
cars
  auto insurance, 128, 344, 371–373
  buying, 100–101, 112–114
  cost of, 34, 113–114
  fuel-efficient, 116
  leasing, 113, 114
  loans, 34, 36, 45–46, 64
  reducing expenses, 114, 372
  researching, 112–113
  saving for, 64

selling, 114
teenage drivers, 372
car-sharing service, 115
CAs (chartered accountants), 152–153
cash purchases, tracking, 49
cash-value life insurance
   agents' commissions, 353–354
   borrowing against, 81, 353
   buying, 354, 356
   cost of, 351–352
   as estate planning tool, 378
   funding educational expenses with, 288
   quitting the policy, 354, 356
   tax breaks, 353, 378
   term life insurance versus, 351–353
cellphones, 121–122
certified general accountants (CGAs), 152
CESG (Canada Education Savings Grant),
   280–282
charitable donations credit, 141
chartered accountants (CAs), 152–153
chequing accounts, 52, 187–188, 266–267,
   438–439
children. *See also* educational expenses;
      family
   caring for, 425–428
   child support payments, 137
   child-care expenses, 136, 427
   CPP Children's Benefits, 350
   disability tax credits, 143–144
   spending on, 427–428
   teenage drivers, 372
churning investments, 177, 180, 388
clothing expenses, 117
CMHC (Canada Mortgage and Housing
   Corporation), 308
COLAs (cost-of-living adjustments), 360
collectibles, investing in, 205
college expenses. *See* educational
   expenses
Collins, Jim (author)
   *Built to Last: Successful Habits of Visionary
      Companies*, 417
   *Good to Great: Why Some Companies
      Make the Leap . . .and Others Don't*, 417
commissions
   bank representatives, 388
   brokers, 196, 216, 310
   financial planners, 177, 383, 387–388

insurance agents, 336–337, 339, 353–354
insurance without, 338–339, 356
limited partnerships (LPs), 199
mutual fund loads, 216–217
negotiating, 323
prospectus listings, 178
real estate agents, 314–317, 323–324
commodities, investing in, 163–164
common-law partners, 138, 262
commuter passes, 115
company stock, 249–250
Complete Canadian Wills Kit (Sawyer), 409
computers. *See also* Internet
   financial software, 400, 405
   identity theft and fraud prevention, 439
   legal documents software, 409
   organizing your tax information, 139
   retirement-planning software, 405–406
   software, described, 399
   tax-preparation software, 151, 406
   tracking your money, 53, 404–405
   trading online, 407–408
condominiums, 312
conflicts of interest
   advertisers', 17–18
   avoiding, 397–398
   brokers', 383
   common examples of, 179
   discount brokers and, 177
   financial planners', 179, 387–390, 397–398
   free financial Web sites and, 404
   insurance agents', 360
   investment salespeople's, 179
   medical care and, 125
   money management services, 397
   real estate agents', 314–315
conservative retirement portfolio, 251, 252
consumer help groups, 104
consumer loans. *See also* bad debt; credit
      cards
   avoiding, 24, 105, 422
   big purchases and, 64
   car loans, 34, 36, 45–46, 64
   paying off, 80–81, 117–118, 168
consumer proposal, 93–94
Consumer Reports, 113, 123
contact lens, 334
contractors, references for, 102
convertible mortgages, 304

Cook, Wade (financial guru), 16, 17
cooperatives, 312
cosmetics, 124
Costco, 109
Costco TrueEarnings American Express, 118
cost-of-living adjustments (COLAs), 360
CPP/QPP disability benefits, 358
CRA (Canada Revenue Agency), 135, 150, 406
credit cards
    annual fees, waived, 118–119
    buying with, 24
    canceling, 82
    cardholders "insurance," 45
    cash rebates/reward systems, 118
    cutting up, 83–84
    debit cards versus, 84–85
    disputing charges, 85, 103
    doubling manufacturer's warranty, 333
    grace period for, 82
    how many to have, 84
    identity theft and fraud prevention, 437–438
    low interest rate cards, 82, 83
    misusing, 44–45
    no-fee cards, 118
    overspending and, 44
    paying off, 45, 80, 117, 168
    playing the float, 37
    reducing card offers, 438
    terms and conditions, 83
    travel medical coverage, 362
credit counselling agencies, 85–89
Credit Counselling Canada, 85
credit delinquency, rate of, 30
credit life and disability policies, 334
credit monitoring service, 31, 438
"credit repair" firms, 33
credit report
    clearing up problems with, 311
    correcting errors, 32–33
    credit score, 29–30
    debt management programs (DMP), 87
    described, 29
    fees, 309
    identity theft and fraud prevention, 438
    improving, 31–32
    obtaining, 30–31
    understanding, 29–31
credit score, 29–31
credit union accounts, 266–267
credits. *See* tax credits
CSLP (Canada Student Loans Program), 285

• D •

DAP (lifetime disability assistance payments), 265
daytrading, 164
DCA (dollar-cost averaging), 173–174
Deals From Hell (Bruner), 15
debit cards, 84–85
debt. *See also* consumer loans; credit cards; mortgages
    avoiding bad debt, 79
    bad debt danger ratio, 35
    bad versus good, 34–37, 79
    credit card float and, 37
    filing bankruptcy, 89–93
    help from credit counselling agencies, 85–89
    paying down, 389
    paying off high-interest debt, 168, 260
    reducing, 80–85
    reducing spending and, 117–119
    stopping the spending/consumer debt cycle, 94–97
debt management programs (DMP), 88–89
deductibles
    auto insurance, 128, 372
    benefits of higher deductibles, 128, 332
    homeowner's/renter's insurance, 332
    insurance, 332, 369
deductions on taxes. *See also* tax breaks; tax credits
    alimony and maintenance payments, 137
    business losses, 137
    child support, 137
    child-care expenses, 136, 427
    interest on investment loans, 137
    married versus common-law partners, 138
    moving expenses, 138

retirement accounts, 60, 75
self-employment expenses, 144–145
tax credits versus, 139
union and professional fees, 137
deferred profit-sharing plan (DPSP), 232–234
defined-benefit pension plan, 71, 72, 234
defined-contribution plans, 72
defined-term annuity, 242
dental insurance, 334
depreciation, defined, 148
derivatives, 163–164
dining out, 107–108
direct trustee-to-trustee transfer, 255
disability
 assistance payments, 265
 CPP/QPP benefits, 358
 Registered Disability Savings Plans (RDSPs), 147, 263–265
 tax credit, 143–144
disability insurance
 credit life and disability policies, 334
 employer-sponsored, 357, 360
 features of, 359–360
 how much you need, 358–359
 pregnancy and, 426
 small business, 428
 where to buy, 360
disaster, natural, 335–336
discount brokers, 177, 253–254, 407–408
discounts, 250, 369–370, 373
diversification
 asset allocation, 170–173
 benefits of, 168–169
 defined, 168
 dollar-cost averaging, 173–174
 investing in individual stocks and, 194
 mutual funds for, 208
dividends, 148, 191, 211, 221
divorce, 430–431
DMP (debt management programs), 86–89
dollar-cost averaging (DCA), 173–174
Dow Jones Industrial Average (DJIA), 192
down payment on homes, 304–305
DPSP (deferred profit-sharing plan), 232–234

drug expenses, 126, 127
Dummies Approved icon, 5
dwelling coverage insurance, 366

• E •

earned income, 232
earthquake insurance, 368–369
eating out, 107–108
Edmonston, Phil (*Lemon-Aid*), 113
education
 adult education classes, 391
 continuing/upgrading, 361, 422
 financial planners', 395
 at home, 289
 in personal finance, 10–12
educational expenses
 borrowing to pay for, 34
 cash-value life insurance for, 288
 government student loans program, 285–287
 investing educational funds, 288–289
 loans, grants, and scholarships, 285, 287
 prepaid tuition plans, 289
 Registered Education Savings Plans (RESPs), 146, 280–283
 RRSP withdrawals for, 237–238, 278, 284
 saving for, 59, 64, 279–287
 strategies for paying for, 277–279
 strategies for saving for, 280–287
 tax credits, 141–142
 in-trust accounts, 280, 283–284
 university or college costs, estimating, 34, 278–279
e-mail, identity theft, 436
emergency reserves
 accessibility, 266
 in bank and credit union accounts, 266–267
 building, 29, 61–62
 in high-interest savings accounts, 267–268
 maintaining, 80, 166, 361
 in money market mutual funds, 268–270
 rate of returns, 266
 secondary cushion, 171
emotions, decisions based on, 24–25

employment. *See also* small businesses
disability insurance programs, 357, 360
employer-sponsored retirement plans, 172, 247–250, 258, 389
first job, 421–422
income shifting, 136
income taxes, 134–136
investing in your career, 203
job or career change, 422–423
maintaining professional development, 361
married partners and, 424
maternity and paternity leave, 426
relocating, 423
shares in company stock, 249–250
energy costs, reducing, 116
entertainment expenses, 119–121
equity (real estate)
borrowing against, 81, 306
described, 196
for education expenses, 278
as retirement savings, 71, 74
estate planning
described, 374
discussing, 429
estate taxes, 356, 377–378
legal services, 390
living trusts, 376
wills and medical powers of attorney, 375
estate planning specialists, 383
excess liability (umbrella) insurance, 374
exchange-traded funds (ETFs), 193, 213
expenses. *See also* educational expenses; medical expenses; spending
categories, 49–50
fund managers, 213
mutual funds, 208
extended warranty and repair insurance, 333

•F•

Fair Isaac and Company, 30
family. *See also* children; estate planning
borrowing from to pay consumer debt, 81
caring for aging parents, 429
divorce, 430–431
having children, 425–428
helping with family business, 145
investing in, 168
marriage, 423–425
mortgage down payment assistance from, 305
talking money at home, 10–12
fashion, 117
federal education tax credit, 142
fees. *See also* commissions
application and processing fees, 309
appraisal fees, 309
arbitration, 180
bank, 188
bankruptcy costs, 92
credit card, 118–119
credit report, 309
discount brokers, 177
financial planners, 384, 385, 389–390, 394
home inspectors, 318
lender fees on mortgages, 309
limited partnerships (LPs), 199
minimizing, 184
money managers, 193
on mutual funds, 208, 216–218, 235
stocks, 213
title insurance, 319
union and professional, 137
FICO scores (Beacon scores), 30
filing system for taxes, 138
financial administration, 52
Financial Advisers Association of Canada (Web site), 393
financial catastrophes insurance, 330–332
financial consultants, 383
financial crisis of 2008/2009, 182–183, 411–412
financial health
bad debt danger ratio, 35
bad debt versus good debt, 34–37
credit report and credit score, 29–33
developing good financial habits, 20–21
financial education at home and school, 10–12
insurance knowledge quiz, 40–41
investment knowledge quiz, 39–40
mistakes to avoid, 23–25
net worth, 25–29, 38

real and imaginary hurdles to success, 18–21

savings, analyzing, 37–39

taking care of yourself, 283

financial literacy, 9–12

financial planners

associations, 392–393

benefits of hiring, 385–386

choosing, 25

client cultivation techniques, 391–392

commission-based, 177, 383, 387–388

"complimentary" introductory consultations, 396

conflicts of interest, 179, 387–390, 397–398

dependency created by, 390

fees, 384, 385, 389–390, 394

finding, 25, 391–393

gurus, 12–17, 181–183, 195

hiring, 382–383

hourly-based, 384–385

interviewing, 393–397

legal services of, 390, 395

liability insurance, 396

mistakes to avoid, 397–398

money-management services, 389–390

narrow view taken by, 388

percentage-of-assets-under-management advisers, 384

qualifications, 395

reasons not to hire, 387

references/referrals, 391–392, 396

retirement plans and, 389

scare tactics, 390

signing assets over to, 256

small businesses and, 389

strategies for reaching financial goals, 385

tax services, 395

financial planning. *See also* goals

doing it yourself, 382

doing nothing, 381–382

hiring help, 382–383

importance of, 23–24

Financial Services Commission of Ontario (Web site), 370

financial software benefits, 400

financial statements, 436, 437

financial Web sites, 402, 403

financial-planning courses, 391–392

firms. *See* investment firms

Fiscal Agents (Web site), 406

fixed-rate mortgages, 303–304

flight insurance, 335

float on credit cards, 37

flood insurance, 368–369

food expenses, 107–109

foreign funds, 213

fraud and identity theft prevention, 435–440

friends, 81, 168

fund managers, 208, 213, 218–219

futures (investments), 163–164, 167, 203, 395

• G •

gambling expenses, 16, 127

gambling investments, 162–164

Gandel, Stephen (writer), 15

gasoline expenses, 114

General Insurance OmbudService (GIO), 344

GICs (guaranteed investment certificates), 190, 235, 248–249, 256, 272–274

gifts, 120–121, 128

global economy, 192

global funds, 212–213

The Globe and Mail, 407, 408

goals. *See also* financial planning

balancing financial and life goals, 57

for big purchases, 64

building emergency reserves, 61–62

buying a business, 59, 63

buying a home, 59, 62, 425

competing goals, dealing with, 61

creating your definition of wealth, 55–59

for educational expense savings, 59, 64, 279

financial planners' help with, 386

identifying problems and goals, 385

for investing, 159–160, 220

knowing what's important to you, 60

married partners sharing, 424

preparing for retirement, 65–75

prioritizing savings goals, 59–61

retirement planning, 59, 65–75

gold, investing in, 169, 170

good debt versus bad debt, 34–37, 79

Good to Great: Why Some Companies Make the Leap . . .and Others Don't (Collins), 417

Government of Canada securities, 210

government retirement benefits, 68–70

government student loans program, 285–287

Great Depression, 411–412

Group Medical Services (Web site), 362

group plans, 360

Growth Multiplier, 73–74

growth stocks, 211

growth-oriented investments, 167

guaranteed annuity, 242

guaranteed investment certificates (GICs), 190, 235, 248–249, 256, 272–274

guaranteed RRSPs, 235

gurus, 12–17, 181–183, 195

• H •

hair care, 124

Harmonized Sales Tax (HST), 129

health club expenses, 124

health insurance. *See also* medical expenses

  cancer insurance, 335

  dispute resolutions, 344–345

  for medical expenses, 125

  need for, 331

  travel medical insurance, 361–362

healthcare. *See also* medical expenses

  aging parents and, 429

  maintaining your health, 66

  medical information report, 340

  provincial plans, 361

hedge funds, 193

hedging, 163–164

high-interest savings accounts, 267–268

hobbies, as retirement income, 75

Home Buyers' Plan, 62, 237, 305–307

home ownership. *See also* mortgages; real estate

  affordability, 292–293

  buying a home, 59, 62, 425

  condominiums, town homes and cooperatives, 312

  converting to rental property, 324–325

  cost of owning versus renting, 294–297

  energy efficient, 116

  financing, 298–311

  finding the right property, 312–314

  home equity loans, 81, 306

  home inspectors, 315, 318

  homeowner's or renter's insurance, 365–370

  inspecting the property, 318

  monthly costs, 295, 297

  mortgage amount, calculating, 293–294

  negotiating the deal, 317

  opportunity cost of owning, 295

  prepayment penalties, 307

  property taxes, 111, 296

  real estate agents, 314–317, 323–324

  reducing expenses, 111–112, 116

  renting out a room, 111

  renting versus buying, 110, 291–298

  researching the neighborhood, 313–314

  sales prices, actual, 313

  saving for, 59, 62

  second homes, 200

  selling your house, 323–325

  title insurance, 319

home warranty plans, 333

homeowner's/renter's insurance, 331, 340–344, 365–370

hourly-based advisers, 384–385

HST (Harmonized Sales Tax), 129

Hulbert Financial Digest, 182

hybrid funds, 212

• I •

IAFP (The Institute of Advanced Financial Planners), 393

icons used in this book, 5–6

identity theft and fraud prevention, 435–440

IIROC (Investment Industry Regulatory Organization of Canada), 180

income
  deductions from, 133
  earned income, 232
  insuring future earnings, 331
  non-taxable, 133
  shifting to reduce taxes, 136
  tax brackets and rates, 133
index funds, 213–214
inflation, 164, 165, 204, 297
inflation-indexed treasury bonds, 273
ING Direct, 188–189, 268, 308
ING Investment Savings Account, 268
Ingle Health travel medical insurance, 362
inheritances, 75–76
insider trading, 163
inspectors, home, 315, 318
The Institute of Advanced Financial
    Planners (IAFP), 393
insurance. *See also* annuities; disability
    insurance; health insurance; life
    insurance
  adjusters, 345
  automobile, 128, 344, 371–373
  avoiding small-potatoes policies, 332–334
  broad coverage, 335–336, 368
  buying direct, 336–339
  buying online, 408–409
  cardholders "insurance," 45
  claims process, 340–343
  commission-free, 338–339
  commissions, 336–337, 339, 353–354
  on contact lens, 334
  credit life and disability policies, 334
  deductibles, 332, 369
  denial of coverage, 339–340
  dental insurance, 334
  discounts, 369–370
  dispute resolution, 343–345
  divorce and, 431
  dwelling coverage, 366
  employer plans, 337–338
  extended warranty and repair, 333
  for financial catastrophes, 330–332
  first full-time job and, 422
  flight, 335
  flood and earthquake, 368–369
  gifts, 128

group plans, 360
guaranteed replacement cost provision,
    366, 367
high-risk pools, 340
home warranty plans, 333
homeowner's/renter's, 331, 340–344,
    365–370
insurance knowledge quiz, 40–41
insurer ratings, 337
keeping low deductibles, 128
knowledge quiz, 40–41
liability insurance, 331, 367–368, 374, 396
list billing process, 360
long-term care (LTC), 362–363
married partners, 424
mortgage life insurance, 321–322
natural disaster, 335–336
need for, 25, 330
on packages in the mail, 334
personal property, 367
pregnancy and, 426
private mortgage insurance (PMI), 305
reducing spending on, 127–128
riders, 334, 366
salespeople, 383
shopping for, 336–340
small business, 331, 428
special mortgage insurance, 308
title insurance, 319
travel medical insurance, 361–362
umbrella (excess liability), 374
insurance agents, 336–337, 339, 353–354,
    360
insurance companies, choosing, 360
IntelliChoice (Web site), 113
interest rates
  bank savings accounts, 165, 188
  bonds, 189–190, 221
  consumer debt, 64
  credit cards, 82, 83
  government students loans, 286
  guaranteed investment certificate (GIC),
    190
  high-interest savings accounts, 267–268
  high-ratio mortgage, 308
  home equity loans, 306
  life insurance, 353

interest rates *(continued)*
  money market mutual funds, 268–270
  mortgages, 300–304, 308, 309
  for refinancing mortgages, 320–321
  renting-to-own and, 105
  special mortgage insurance, 308
interest-rate-differential (IRD) penalty for
    mortgages, 321
intermediate-term investments, 271
international funds, 212–213
international stocks, 192
Internet
  advertiser-driven investment sites, 18
  biased financial planning advice, 402
  buying insurance online, 408–409
  financial information on, 400
  finding the best Web sites, 414
  online bill payments, 405
  online hazards, 400–403
  periodicals, 408
  researching online, 406–407
  "sponsored" content, 401–402
  trading online, 407–408
in-trust accounts, 280, 283–284
Investigate icon, 6
investing. *See also* diversification;
        retirement accounts; risks of investing;
        specific types of investments
  in annuities, 204–205, 254–255, 275
  asset allocation, 170–174, 270–271
  broker's conflict of interest and, 383
  chequing accounts, 187–188
  churning investments, 177, 180, 388
  in collectibles, 205
  in commodities, 163–164
  daytrading, 164
  in derivatives, 163–164
  dollar-cost averaging (DCA), 173–174
  in education, 278–279
  educational funds, 288–289
  exchange-traded funds (ETFs), 193, 213
  final advice, 184–185
  in friends and family, 168
  in futures, 163–164, 167, 203, 395
  gambling, 162–164
  goals for, 159–160, 220
  gurus, 12–17, 181–183, 195
  investment newsletters, 13, 182, 195

knowledge quiz, 39–40
lending investments, 160–161
long-term, 171–172, 270–275
low-risk, high-return investments,
    167–168
making up for lost time, 74–75
online trading, 407–408
in options, 163–164
outside retirement plans, 259–275
ownership investments, 164–166, 191–203
paying off high-interest debt, 168, 260
in personal and career development, 168,
    203
in precious metals, 204
in real estate, 196–200, 389
reducing spending and, 106–107
reducing taxes, 75, 146–149
researching online, 406–407
return on investments, 164–165
risks, 165–168
safe investments, 187–191
sales pitches, 184
savings accounts, 188–189
selling investments to reduce debt, 81
in shares in the company you work for,
    249–250
in small business, 201–203, 389
in stocks, 191–195
tax-friendly, 147–148
time frame for, 271
uncertain times and, 175
unsuitable investments, 180
Investing For Canadians For Dummies, 255,
    417
investment firms
  best firms, 176–177
  discount broker, 253–254
  firms to avoid, 177–180
  research services, 181
  using more than one, 253
investment knowledge, 39–40

• J •

James, Jack (*Starting a Successful Business
    in Canada Kit*), 417
junk bonds, 190

• K •

Kerr, Margaret (author)
  Canadian Small Business Kit For Dummies, 75
  Wills & Estate Planning For Canadians For Dummies, 374
Kurtz, JoAnn (author)
  Canadian Small Business Kit For Dummies, 75
  Wills & Estate Planning For Canadians For Dummies, 374

• L •

large cap stock, 192
lawyers
  for broker misrepresentation, 180
  divorce, 430
  estate planning, 374, 390
  for insurance dispute resolution, 345
  for taxes, 153
The Learning Company, 14, 15
legal documents software, 409
Lemon-Aid (Edmonston), 113
lenders, mortgage, 308–310, 315
liability insurance, 331, 367–368, 374, 396
LIF (life income fund), 243
life changes
  caring for aging parents, 429
  divorce, 430–431
  financial decisions influenced by, 24–25
  first job, 421–422
  having children, 425–428
  home purchase, 425
  job or career change, 422–423
  marriage, 423–425
  receiving a windfall, 174, 431–432
  retirement, 432–434
  starting a small business, 201–202, 428
life income fund (LIF), 243
life insurance. *See also* cash-value life insurance
  agents' commissions, 336–337, 339, 353–354, 360
  amount needed, 348–349
  buying enough coverage, 354
  buying online, 408–409
  Canada Pension Plan survivor benefits, 349–351
  dispute resolutions, 344–345
  group plans, 338
  guaranteed renewal rates, 355
  interest rates, 353
  mortgage life insurance, 321–322
  "other," 350
  pregnancy and, 426
  quitting the policy, 353, 354
  retirement and, 352
  small business, 428
  term life insurance, 351, 353–356
  where to buy, 355
life-expectancy calculator, online, 406
lifetime disability assistance payments (DAP), 265
limited partnerships (LPs), 180, 199, 247
LIRA (locked-in retirement account), 243, 258
living for today mindset, 46
living trusts, 376
living wills, 375
living within your means, 100
loads (commissions), 178, 216–217
locked-in retirement account (LIRA), 243, 258
locked-in retirement income fund (LRIF), 243
locked-in RRSPs, 243, 258
long-term care (LTC) insurance, 362–363
long-term investments
  asset allocation, 171–172, 270–271
  bonds, 190
  real estate, 275
  savings, 165
LRIF (locked-in retirement income fund), 243

• M •

Madoff, Bernie (Ponzi-schemer), 15–16
mail fraud, 439
making up for lost time, 74–75
Malkiel, Burton (*A Random Walk Down Wall Street*), 417
managed accounts, 193
marginal tax rate, 132–133, 135, 231

market capitalization, 192

marriage, 423–425

married partners, 138, 262

maternity and paternity leave, 426

McQueen, Mark (president of Wellington Financial), 14

media, 183, 411–414

mediation, 386

medical expenses. *See also* health insurance

  reducing spending on, 125–126

  in retirement, 433

  tax credits, 142–143

  travel medical insurance, 361–362

medical information report, 340

medical power of attorney, 375

Microsoft Money software, 405

Mint.com (financial management service), 404

money

  balancing saving and spending, 57–59

  getting your money back, 102–104

  happiness not guaranteed with, 56

  long-term investments, 171–172

  mistakes to avoid, 23–25

  retirement needs, 66–68

  talking about at home, 10–12

Money magazine, 394

money managers, 193, 414

money market accounts

  emergency reserves in, 171

  employer-sponsored retirement plans, 247–248

  investing educational funds and, 288

  for short-term savings, 64

money market funds, 188–189, 210, 268–270

money-purchase pension plan, 234

Morningstar Web site, 407

mortgages

  affordability, 292–293

  amortization of payments, 292, 299–300

  amount to borrow, 293–294

  application and processing fees, 309

  appraisal fees, 309

  approval chances, 309–311, 315

  brokers, 310

  convertible, 304

  credit report fees, 309

  down payment, 304–305

  fees, 309

  fixed-rate versus variable-rate, 303–304

  high-ratio mortgage, 308

  Home Buyers' Plan, 305–307

  interest rates, 300–302, 309

  interest-rate-differential (IRD) penalty, 321

  lenders, 308–310, 315

  life insurance for, 321–322

  monthly payment on, 296

  open and closed, 302, 320

  paying off, 168

  preapproval or prequalification, 311

  prepayment penalties, 307

  private mortgage insurance (PMI), 305

  refinancing, 320–321

  reverse mortgage, 74, 322–323

  second mortgage, 308

  short-term versus long-term, 300–302

  special mortgage insurance, 308

  three months' interest penalty, 320–321

  variable-rate, 303–304

moving expenses, 138

municipal bonds, 190

mutual fund managers, 13

mutual funds

  annual reports, 215

  asset allocation, 209

  balanced mutual funds, 249

  benefits of, 168–169, 193, 207–209

  biased financial planning advice, 402

  bond funds, 210–211

  buying, 219

  Canadian, U.S., international, and global funds, 212–213

  costs, 208

  diversification, 208

  evaluating, 218–219, 222–223

  expenses, 208

  fees, 208, 216–218

  fund manager/fund family reputations, 218–219

  hybrid funds, 212

  index funds, 213–214

  interest and dividends, 221

  loads (commissions), 216–217

  management of, 208

money market mutual funds, 210, 268–270
monitoring and selling, 222–223
Morningstar's reports, 407
no-load (commission-free) funds, 176,
    185, 208, 217, 288
operating expenses, 217–218
outside a tax-sheltered plan, 221, 222
performance (historical rate of return),
    208, 218, 220–222
prospectus, 208, 215, 217
returns, 217, 220
risk level, 209, 218
in RRSP, 235
selecting, 215–220
share price changes, 222
socially responsible funds, 214
specialty (sector) funds, 214–215
stock mutual funds, 193, 211, 249
tax considerations, 219
total return, calculating, 220–222
types of, 209–215
underperforming, 223
Myers, David (psychology professor),
    56, 59

• N •

Nader, Ralph (consumer advocate), 103
NASDAQ (National Association of
    Securities Dealers Automated
    Quotations), 191
natural disaster, preparing for, 335–336
*Natural Resources Canada's Office of Energy
    Efficiency*, 116
net worth, 25–29, 38
networking, career, 201
New York Stock Exchange, 191
newsletters, investment, 13, 182, 195
newspapers and magazines, 415
Nortel stock, 250
nursing homes, 363

• O •

O'Leary, Kevin (financial guru), 14–15
OmbudService for Life & Health Insurance
    (OLHI), 344–345

101 Tax Secrets For Canadians (Cestnick),
    150
operating expenses, 217–218, 268–270
options, investing in, 163–164
ownership investments, 164–166, 191–203

• P •

packages in the mail, insuring, 334
paralegal services, 375, 376
parents, caring for, 429
pension plans. *See also* retirement
    planning
    asset allocation examples, 250
    Canada Pension Plan (or Quebec Pension
        Plan), 68–70, 349–351
    choosing, 433–434
    defined-benefit pension plan, 71, 72, 234
    defined-contribution plans, 72
    employer-sponsored, 172, 250
    making the most of, 71–72
    money-purchase pension plan, 234
    pension adjustment (PA factor), 233, 234
    pension adjustment reversal (PAR), 238
    pension income credit, 143, 242
    RRSP contributions and, 232, 233
    transferring to locked-in RRSP, 243, 258
percentage-of-assets-under-management
    advisers, 384
periodicals, online, 408
personal care expenses, 123–124
personal property insurance, 367
phishing, 436
planning. *See* financial planning; goals
PMI (private mortgage insurance), 305
Porras, Jerry (*Built to Last: Successful
    Habits of Visionary Companies*), 417
precious metals, 204
President's Choice Financial, 188–189,
    267–268, 308
President's Choice Financial Mastercard,
    118
private mortgage insurance (PMI), 305
probate, 376
professional associations, 360, 392–393
professional development, maintaining,
    361

professionals. *See also* financial planners; lawyers
  accountants, 152–153, 395
  arbitration consultants, 180
  divorce services, 430
  estate planning specialists, 383
  home inspectors, 315, 318
  for insurance dispute resolution, 343–345
  paralegal services, 375, 376
  reducing the cost of, 125
  tax-preparation, 151–153
Profit magazine, 408
property. *See* home ownership; real estate
property taxes, 111, 296
prospectus, 178, 208, 215, 217
provincial health plans, 363
provincial taxes, calculating, 139–140
public records, 29

• Q •

Quicken software, 405
QuickTax software, 151, 406

• R •

radio financial programs, 413–414
A Random Walk Down Wall Street (Malkiel), 417
RDSPs (Registered Disability Savings Plans), 147, 263–265
real estate. *See also* home ownership; mortgages
  agents, 314–317, 323–324
  best investment options, 198–199
  drawbacks, 197, 198
  financial planners, 389
  hidden values, 197
  investing in, 196–200
  leverage, 197
  limited partnerships (LPs), 199
  long-term investments, 275
  overview, 196
  rental property, 198
  return on investments, 164–165, 196
  second homes, 200
  stocks versus, 198
  timeshares, 200
  usability of, 196
  worst investment options, 199
  zoning, 197
Real Estate Investing For Canadians For Dummies (Wiley publishing), 291
real estate investment trusts (REITs), 199
recession (economic downturn), 175, 412
reducing spending. *See also* spending
  on addictions, 126–127
  avoiding brand names, 101
  avoiding consumer debt, 117–119
  budgeting, 105–106
  on clothing, 117
  eliminating the fat, 104–105
  on entertainment and recreation, 119–121
  on food, 107–109
  free Web sites, caution for using, 404–405
  on housing, 110–112
  on insurance, 127–128
  investing the money saved, 106–107
  living within your means, 100
  looking for best values, 100–104
  lowering energy costs, 116
  on medical expenses, 125–126
  on personal care, 123–124
  on phone bills, 121–122
  on professional services, 125
  returning items, 102–104
  on taxes, 128–129
  on technology, 123
  tracking on paper or computer, 48–53
  on transportation, 112–116
  on utility costs, 112
refinancing mortgages, 320–321
Registered Disability Savings Plans (RDSPs), 147, 263–265
Registered Education Savings Plans (RESPs), 146, 280–283
Registered Retirement Income Fund (RRIF), 239–241, 377, 406
Registered Retirement Savings Plan (RRSP)
  advantages of, 60–61, 149, 225–226
  allocating money in, 250–254
  allowable (maximum) contribution, 233–234
  automatic deduction plan, 230
  borrowing from for educational expenses, 238

borrowing from to buy a house, 62, 237, 305–308

buying annuities, 239, 242–244

closing down (maturing), 238–244

common-law partners and, 138

conservative and aggressive portfolios, 251–253

contribution rules, 230–234

contributions, 135–136, 228–234, 238, 278

deadline for contributions, 234

early contributions, 228–231

earned income, 232

educational expenses paid with, 237–238, 278, 284

interest and earnings, 227–228

investments held inside, 246

limits on contributions, 231–233

locked-in RRSPs, 243

maximizing the growth of, 228–230

payoff from tax-deferred compound growth, 227–228

penalties on withdrawals, 63

pension adjustment (PA factor), 233, 234

pension adjustment reversal (PAR), 238

retirement withdrawals, 433

returns, increasing, 229–230

savings/investment strategy, 71

spousal RRSP, 236

spouse as beneficiary of, 377

tax benefits, 226–228

tax credits, 143

tax on withdrawals, 237

tax rate, 61

types of, 235–236

unlocking locked-in RRSP and retirement accounts, 243

unused contributions, 231, 278

when not to fund, 149

withdrawals before retirement, 237–238

REITs (real estate investment trusts), 199

Remember icon, 5

rental property, 110, 198, 324–325

renting, 110, 111, 291–298

renting-to-own, dangers of, 105

replacement cost guarantees, 366, 367

reserves. *See* emergency reserves

RESPs (Registered Education Savings Plans), 146, 280–283

retirement accounts. *See also* pension plans; Registered Retirement Savings Plan (RRSP)

advantages of, 60–61

aggressive portfolios, 251–253

allocating money in, 245–254

annuities, 239, 242–244, 246, 247, 254–255

balanced mutual funds, 249

conservative portfolios, 251, 252

contributions, 135–136

employer-sponsored, 135, 172, 246, 258

inappropriate investments, 247

moving money from employer's plan, 258

prioritizing contributions, 246

reducing taxes, 135–136

risks of investing in, 246

small businesses/self-employment, 145

tax breaks, 60–61, 245

tax deductions, 60, 75

tax savings of, 128–129, 146

taxable withdrawals, 256

transferring, 255–257

retirement communities, 363

retirement planning

divorce and, 431

early retirement dreams, 65

financial needs, calculating, 66–68

government benefits, 68–70

Growth Multiplier, 73–74

inheritances and, 75–76

making up for lost time, 74–75

non-financial aspects, 66

pension plans, 71–72

preparing for, 59, 432–434

savings/investment strategy, 71

software and online tools, 405–406

worksheet, 72–73

Retirementadvisor (Web site), 406

return on investments

bonds, 164, 169–170

investing outside registered retirement plans, 260

lack of guarantee on, 169

overview, 164–165

real estate, 164–165, 196

retirement accounts, 60–61

stocks, 164–165, 169–170

reverse mortgage, 74, 322–323

Riedl, Mark (portfolio manager), 13
risks of investing
  diversification reducing, 169
  establishing goals and, 159–160
  low-risk, high-return investments,
    167–168
  mutual funds, 209
  overview, 165–166
  stocks versus bonds, 166–167
Roubini, Nouriel (investment guru),
  182–183
RRIF (Registered Retirement Income Fund),
  239–241, 377, 406
RRSP. *See* Registered Retirement Savings
  Plan (RRSP)

• *S* •

sales tax, 129
savings. *See also* retirement accounts
  analyzing, 37–39, 105
  balanced approach to, 57–59
  for big purchases, 64
  budgeting for, 105–106
  to buy a business, 63
  to buy a home, 59, 62
  cash-value life insurance as, 353
  debts paid with, 80–81
  for educational expenses, 59, 64, 279–287
  emergency reserves, 61–62
  prioritizing goals for, 59–61
  retirement planning, 60–61, 65–75
savings accounts
  banks, 165, 188–189, 388
  emergency reserves in, 171, 266–267
  employer-sponsored, 247–248
  high-interest, 267–268
  interest rates, 165
  investing educational funds and, 288
  investing in, 188–189
  money market funds versus, 268
  returns, 164, 247
  savings/investment strategy, 71
  Tax-Free Savings Accounts (TFSAs), 64,
    147, 261–263
Sawyer, Alison (Complete Canadian Wills
  Kit), 409
SEC (U.S. Securities and Exchange
  Commission) (Web site), 407

second homes, 200
sector (specialty) funds, 213
securities lawyers, 180
SEDAR (System for Electronic Document
  Analysis and Retrieval), 407
self-directed and brokerage-house RRSPs,
  236
self-directed RRSPs, 236, 253
self-employment. *See* small businesses
selling your house, 323–325
Send This Jerk the Bedbug Letter (Bear), 103
Service Canada, 350–351, 405–406
ShareOwner Web site, 196
shopping, for best values, 100–104
short-term bonds, 190, 272
short-term investments, 271
short-term savings, 64
silver, investing in, 169, 170
single-family homes, 312
skills, upgrading, 361
small businesses. *See also* employment
  buying an existing business, 202
  disability insurance, 428
  expense deductions, 144–145
  financial planners and, 389
  investing in someone else's, 202–203
  liability insurance, 331
  long-term investments, 275
  mistakes to avoid, 144–145
  quarterly estimated tax payments, 144
  retirement accounts, 145
  saving to buy, 59, 63
  starting your own, 201–202, 428
small cap stocks, 192
small claims court, 104
smoking, kicking the habit, 126
socially responsible funds, 214
The Sociopath Next Door (Stout), 435
software. *See* computers
specialty (sector) funds, 214–215
spending. *See also* reducing spending
  addiction to, 47, 57
  analyzing, 47–51
  balanced approach to, 57–59
  on children, 427–428
  overspending, 24, 44–47, 111
  renting-to-own, dangers of, 105
spousal tax credit, 140
Standard & Poor's 500 index, 213, 218

Starting a Successful Business in Canada Kit (James), 417
stock exchanges, 191
stock mutual funds, 193, 211, 249
stocks
  growth stocks, 211
  individual, 193–196
  international, 192
  investing in, 191–195
  in non-retirement accounts, 274–275
  overview, 191–192
  prices and dividends, 191
  real estate versus, 198
  research reports, 196
  returns, 164–165, 169–170
  risks of, 166
  tax-friendly, 148, 274–275
  total market value (capitalization), 211
  value stocks, 211
  volatility of, 167
Stout, Martha (*The Sociopath Next Door*), 435
Studiotax (software), 151, 406
superstores, 109
System for Electronic Document Analysis and Retrieval (SEDAR), 407

● *T* ●

target-maturity funds, 212
tax audits, 153–155
tax breaks. *See also* deductions on taxes
  cash-value life insurance, 353, 378
  child-care expenses, 427
  tax-friendly investments, 147–148
  tax-sheltered accounts, 146–147
tax credits
  age 65 or older, 143
  annuities, 143, 242
  basic personal tax credit, 140
  calculating, 140
  caregivers tax credit, 144
  charitable donations credit, 141
  commuter passes, 115
  disability credit, 143–144
  education tax credits, 141–142
  medical expenses, 142–143
  non-refundable, 139
  overview, 139–140
  pension income credit, 143, 242
  spousal credit, 140
  tax deductions versus, 139
  wholly dependent person credit, 140–141
Tax Planning For You and Your Family (Carswell), 150, 417
tax preparers, 151–152
taxes. *See also* deductions on taxes; tax breaks; tax credits
  alternative minimum tax (AMT), 134
  daytrading and, 164
  on dividend income, 221
  employment income, 134–136
  estate taxes, 356, 377–378
  income brackets and rates, 133
  income shifting to reduce, 136
  individual stocks and, 194
  investment consequences, 184
  on investment distributions, 146–148, 265–266
  on investments outside retirement plans, 265–266
  marginal tax rate, 132–133, 135, 231
  married versus common-law partners, 138
  obtaining forms, 406
  preparation and advice guides, 150
  professional help for, 151–153
  property taxes, 111, 296
  reducing, 128–129, 136
  on regular RRSP withdrawals, 237
  RRSP tax advantages, 135
  tax return resources, 149–153
  taxable income, 133
  total taxes paid, 131–132
Tax-Free Savings Accounts (TFSAs), 64, 147, 261–263
tax-on-income (TONI) method, 139, 140
tax-preparation software, 151, 406
Technical Stuff icon, 5
technology expenses, 123
technology stock investments, 173
telephone, 121–122, 436
television financial programs, 413–414
term life insurance, 351, 354–355

TFSAs (Tax-Free Savings Accounts), 64, 147, 261–263
therapy, 125
timeshares, 200
Tip icon, 5
title insurance, 319
Toronto Stock Exchange, 191, 213, 218
total debt-service ratio, 294
town homes, 312
transportation, 112–116. *See also* cars
travel agents, 120
travel expenses, 119–120
travel medical insurance, 361–362
Treasury bills, 190
treasury bonds, 273
treasury money market mutual funds, 270
tuition tax credit, 141
Tyson, Eric (author), 16, 182, 435

• U •

UFile (tax software), 151, 406
umbrella (excess liability) insurance, 374
uncertain times, investing during, 175
union and professional fees, 137
Universal Child Care Benefit, 427
university or college, 34, 278–279
U.S. Securities and Exchange Commission (SEC), 407
U.S. stock market, 192
utility costs, 112

• V •

vacations, 34, 119
value investments, 176
Value Line Web site, 196
value stocks, 211
VantageScore (credit score), 30
variable-rate mortgages, 303–304

• W •

Wall Street Journal, 408
wallet, stolen, 439–440
Warning! icon, 6
warranty and repair insurance, 333
wealth, 56–59
Wellington Financial, 14
wholesale superstores, 109
wholly dependent person credit, 140–141
wills, 375, 425, 427
Wills & Estate Planning For Canadians For Dummies (Kerr and Kurtz), 374
Wilshire 5000 index, 218
windfall, receiving, 174, 431–432
workers' compensation, 358
worksheet, retirement planning, 72–73
worldwide or global funds, 213
wrap (managed accounts), 185

• Z •

zoning, real estate, 197

BUSINESS & PERSONAL FINANCE

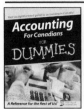

978-0-470-83878-5   978-0-470-73684-5

Also available:
- 76 Tips For Investing in an Uncertain Economy For Canadians For Dummies 978-0-470-16099-2
- Bookkeeping For Canadians For Dummies 978-0-470-73762-0
- Business Plans For Canadians For Dummies 978-0-470-15420-5

- Canadian Small Business Kit For Dummies 978-0-470-93652-8
- Investing For Canadians For Dummies 978-0-470-16029-9
- Trading For Canadians For Dummies 978-0-470-67744-5
- Wills & Estate Planning For Canadians For Dummies 978-0-470-67657-8

EDUCATION, HISTORY & REFERENCE

978-0-7645-2498-1   978-0-470-46244-7

Also available:
- Algebra For Dummies 978-0-7645-5325-7
- Art History For Dummies 978-0-470-09910-0
- Chemistry For Dummies 978-0-7645-5430-8

- English Grammar For Dummies 978-0-470-54664-2
- French For Dummies 978-0-7645-5193-2
- Statistics For Dummies 978-0-7645-5423-0
- World History For Dummies 978-0-470-44654-6

FOOD, HOME, & MUSIC

978-0-7645-9904-0   978-0-470-43111-5

Also available:
- 30-Minute Meals For Dummies 978-0-7645-2589-6
- Bartending For Dummies 978-0-470-05056-9
- Brain Games For Dummies 978-0-470-37378-1
- Gluten-Free Cooking For Dummies 978-0-470-17810-2

- Home Improvement All-in-One Desk Reference For Dummies 978-0-7645-5680-7
- Violin For Dummies 978-0-470-83838-9
- Wine For Dummies 978-0-470-04579-4

HEALTH & SELF-HELP

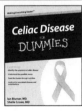

978-0-471-77383-2   978-0-470-16036-7

Also available:
- Borderline Personality Disorder For Dummies 978-0-470-46653-7
- Breast Cancer For Dummies 978-0-7645-2482-0
- Cognitive Behavioural Therapy For Dummies 978-0-470-01838-5
- Diabetes For Canadians For Dummies 978-0-470-15677-3

- Emotional Intelligence For Dummies 978-0-470-15732-9
- Healthy Aging For Dummies 978-0-470-14975-1
- Neuro-linguistic Programming For Dummies 978-0-7645-7028-5
- Understanding Autism For Dummies 978-0-7645-2547-6

HOBBIES & CRAFTS

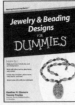

978-0-470-28747-7   978-0-470-29112-2

Also available:

- ✔ Crochet Patterns For Dummies
  97-0-470-04555-8
- ✔ Digital Scrapbooking For Dummies
  978-0-7645-8419-0
- ✔ Knitting Patterns For Dummies
  978-0-470-04556-5

- ✔ Oil Painting For Dummies
  978-0-470-18230-7
- ✔ Quilting For Dummies
  978-0-7645-9799-2
- ✔ Sewing For Dummies
  978-0-7645-6847-3
- ✔ Word Searches For Dummies
  978-0-470-45366-7

HOME & BUSINESS COMPUTER BASICS

978-0-470-49743-2   978-0-470-48953-6

Also available:

- ✔ Office 2010 All-in-One Desk
  Reference For Dummies
  978-0-470-49748-7
- ✔ Pay Per Click Search Engine
  Marketing For Dummies
  978-0-471-75494-7

- ✔ Search Engine Marketing For
  Dummies 978-0-471-97998-2
- ✔ Web Analytics For Dummies
  978-0-470-09824-0
- ✔ Word 2010 For Dummies
  978-0-470-48772-3

INTERNET & DIGITAL MEDIA

978-0-470-44417-7   978-0-470-39062-7

Also available:

- ✔ Blogging For Dummies
  978-0-471-77084-8
- ✔ MySpace For Dummies
  978-0-470-09529-4

- ✔ The Internet For Dummies
  978-0-470-12174-0
- ✔ Twitter For Dummies
  978-0-470-47991-9
- ✔ YouTube For Dummies
  978-0-470-14925-6

MACINTOSH

978-0-470-27817-8   978-0-470-58027-1

Also available:

- ✔ iMac For Dummies
  978-0-470-13386-6
- ✔ iPod Touch For Dummies
  978-0-470-50530-4
- ✔ iPod & iTunes For Dummies
  978-0-470-39062-7

- ✔ MacBook For Dummies
  978-0-470-27816-1
- ✔ Macs For Seniors For Dummies
  978-0-470-43779-7
- ✔ Mac OS X Snow Leopard All-in-One
  Desk Reference For Dummies
  978-0-470-43541-0

SPORTS & FITNESS

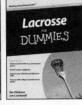

978-0-471-76871-5   978-0-470-73855-9

Also available:

- ✔ Exercise Balls For Dummies
  978-0-7645-5623-4
- ✔ Coaching Volleyball For Dummies
  978-0-470-46469-4
- ✔ Curling For Dummies
  978-0-470-83828-0
- ✔ Fitness For Dummies
  978-0-7645-7851-9

- ✔ Mixed Martial Arts For Dummies
  978-0-470-39071-9
- ✔ Ten Minute Tone-Ups For Dummies
  978-0-7645-7207-4
- ✔ Wilderness Survival For Dummies
  978-0-470-45306-3
- ✔ Yoga with Weights For Dummies
  978-0-471-74937-0